Computer Engineering

Computer Engineering

CIRCUITS, PROGRAMS, AND DATA

P. P. Silvester and D. A. Lowther

McGill University

New York   Oxford
OXFORD UNIVERSITY PRESS
1989

Oxford University Press

Oxford   New York   Toronto
Delhi   Bombay   Calcutta   Madras   Karachi
Petaling Jaya   Singapore   Hong Kong   Tokyo
Nairobi   Dar es Salaam   Cape Town
Melbourne   Auckland

and associated companies in
Berlin   Ibadan

Library of Congress Cataloging-in-Publication Data
Silvester, Peter P.
Computer engineering: circuits, programs, and data / P.P.
Silvester and D. A. Lowther.
p. cm.   Includes index.
ISBN 0-19-505943-3
1. Computer engineering.   2. Electronic digital computers.
I. Lowther, D. A.   II. Title.
TK7885.S555   1989
004—dc19   88-31783   CIP

9 8 7 6 5 4 3 2 1

Printed in the United States of America
on acid-free paper

Preface

This book introduces the art of computer engineering and deals briefly with those aspects of computing science that computer engineering relies upon. It is designed to serve as the basic textbook for the first course in a sequence satisfying the IEEE model curriculum specification in Computer Engineering. This should be, and usually will be, the beginning student's first course in *computers;* but it must not be a first course in *computing,* for it presupposes a little programming experience and some familiarity with a high-level language such as Pascal, Fortran, or C.

The content of this book is highly conventional in topic outline. Its principal ingredients comprise a chapter on binary number and character representation, two chapters on logic circuits, one chapter on architecture and organization as seen from the hardware engineer's perspective, and finally, two chapters on machine architecture and assembler language programming, mostly from the software engineer's viewpoint. The mixture of viewpoints is vital: devices and structures are introduced in response to the programmer's needs, while data processing techniques are shaped to accommodate the unbending realities imposed by the physical world. Computer engineering, in brief, is viewed as the art of getting computing tasks done effectively, by shaping the combination of hardware and software to suit the task.

Although its table of contents may harbor few surprises, most readers will find this book unusual in its presentation. It strives to develop, as rapidly as possible, an overall grasp of the field emphasizing the indivisibility of software and hardware. To this end, it relies heavily on simulation tools. In the authors' view, professional computer engineering is invariably also computer-aided engineering, so computer-aided simulation and analysis tools cannot be introduced at too early a date. Purely analytic techniques should play a key role in subsequent specialist courses as listed in the IEEE Model Curriculum; but in the first course or two, experimentation and simulation should take precedence. Accordingly, most of the material in this book is developed through the use of simulation packages and the reader would be ill advised to attempt serious study of this material without following the development—with a computer in one hand and the book in the other, as it were.

Three principal software packages accompany this book: Apodix, Simian, and Simile. Apodix is a simple logic simulator that permits virtually any circuit of interest to the student to be simulated in a matter of minutes. Circuit behavior, including timing problems and instabilities, can be quickly explored experimentally with Apodix. Although simple, Apodix includes a substantial range of circuit elements in its standard library. Simian is an interactive computer simulator, Simile is its accompanying assembler. Simian and Simile adhere closely to the IEEE-694 assembler language standard, so Simian could, without too much exaggeration, be described as an IEEE-694 machine—though admittedly it is a subset machine, a full implementation would be considerably beyond the level of a first course! The IEEE standard is aimed at industrially useful architectures, so 68000 programmers will feel quite at home with the structure of Simian. The assembler language of Simile will appear familiar too, for it conforms to the standard in all but a few minor points.

The authors wish to express their appreciation and gratitude to the many people who have helped shape the content as well as presentation of this text.

P.P.S.
D.A.L.

Contents

Computer Engineering

1
Data representation in digital computers

Digital computers are devices for storing and manipulating data. Any inquiry into what computers are and how they work should therefore begin by asking how data can be stored and processed. This chapter reviews the main forms of data representation, numeric as well as textual, and outlines the principal operations used in data processing.

Symbols and characters

Much of the information handled by digital computers is of a descriptive or quantitative nature, and its encoding very naturally takes the shape of words or numbers. The words or numbers themselves are symbols that represent things, ideas, or amounts. These symbols, words or numbers, are ordinarily encoded in turn as strings of characters, for example, the letters of the Roman alphabet or the Arabic numerals.

Information and data

In the world of digital computing, *information* and *data* are distinct terms with differing meanings. Information and data often go together as different aspects of the same message, as for example in the following text:

Wolfgang Amadeus Mozart was born on the 27th of January 1756.

This message certainly contains information—it communicates an item of historical knowledge about Mozart. *Information* in this sense is essentially synonymous with *knowledge,* an entity computing machines cannot easily deal with. On the other hand, the little message printed above also represents *data,* a physical representation of information, since the message is made up of a string of inked characters of a particular form. The string of characters is the communication medium that conveys the information contained in the message. Digital computers are not very good at handling information, but they are very well suited to the processing of data.

The information content of a message is related to the data that make up the message through some conventionally agreed upon encoding scheme. For example, the message about Mozart is written in the English language, using characters of the Roman alphabet. Exactly the same information is contained in

Wolfgang Amadeus Mozart wurde am 27. Januar 1756 geboren.

Here the encoding technique is different (a different language is used), so the data do not appear similar even though the information may be the same.

Digital computers generally process and manipulate data rather than information. People, on the other hand, are usually more interested in the information than the data. Computer processing of information is therefore achieved by first encoding the information of interest, then processing the data into some new form, and finally decoding the resulting data to yield the desired information.

Alphabets, character sets, and symbols

Data items are usually encoded for computation by using *symbols* or *characters*. If the set of characters used to represent information is finite, it is called an *alphabet*. The Roman, Greek and Cyrillic alphabets are obvious examples. Any one item of information may take many different symbolic shapes because a variety of different alphabets can be invented. The words

mozart

and

MOZART

differ in alphabet, but represent the same information. Other, often quite specialized, alphabets are used for certain kinds of information. For example, the 17-symbol alphabet

A K Q J 10 9 8 7 6 5 4 3 2
♠ ♥ ♦ ♣

is used to describe bridge or poker hands. Another common special alphabet is the set of characters employed in writing music.

Alphabets of various sizes are used in data processing. Internally, most computers work best with the simplest character set possible, containing just two symbols. These are conventionally represented by symbols **1** and **0**. Of course any two distinct symbols, say the words *on* and *off*, could serve equally well. One character of this minimal alphabet is referred to as a *bit* (supposedly a contraction of *b*inary dig*it*.) A bit is sometimes said to be *set*, meaning that the character is 1, or *cleared*, meaning that the character is 0. In other words, the three symbol pairs

0	*and*	1
off	*and*	on
cleared	*and*	set

are distinct (they look different in print) but convey the same information. What really matters for digital computation is that they are also equivalent to a fourth symbol pair, expressed as voltages at semiconductor device terminals. That fourth symbol pair is a pair of conventionally agreed voltage levels, e.g., 0 V and 5 V.

Were communication restricted to symbols containing only a single character at a time, a binary alphabet would not allow a wide range of expression. It is therefore common to form symbols by grouping bits together in strings of some fixed size, called *words*. Each word is taken to signify a single unit of information, and most computers are constructed so that they handle whole words (rather than bits) at a time.Formally, a word is defined as a string of n bits, and one often speaks of a computer as having n-bit word length, meaning that it ordinarily handles data in single entities of n bits. Common values of n are 8, 16, 32, 36, 48, 60, and 96 bits; other values occasionally encountered in general-purpose computers are 4, 12, 15, 18, 24, and 64 bits. Almost any word length may occur in specialized computers intended for particular tasks.

With a 2-character alphabet (each bit can be set or cleared), a 2-bit word can contain any of four distinct bit configurations,

$$00 \quad 01 \quad 10 \quad 11$$

A 3-bit word can contain one of just twice as many distinct words, since the newly added bit could be either 0 or 1 for each of the four possible settings of the existing two bits:

$$000 \quad 001 \quad 010 \quad 011 \quad 100 \quad 101 \quad 110 \quad 111$$

By a similar argument, a 4-bit word could contain any of 16 distinct bit configurations, a 5-bit word any one of 32, . . . , and an n-bit word any one of 2^n.

Computers with word lengths of 16 bits or longer are often built so that they are also able to deal with partial words. In such cases, the partial word is usually 8 bits long, and the word length is almost always a multiple of 8 bits. Common sizes are 16, 32, and 64 bits. The 8-bit entities are referred to as *bytes*.

The individual bits that make up a byte or word are normally referred to by their position numbers. The rightmost bit is called *bit 0* and the leftmost one *bit 7*:

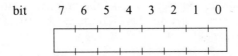

Similar numbering schemes are used for numbering the bits in a word, whether or not the word length is a multiple of 8. In both bytes and words, bit 0 is frequently also referred to as the *least significant bit* or the *low-order bit*, the leftmost bit being correspondingly called the *most significant bit*.

Numeric symbols

Numeric information was undoubtedly the earliest type of information encoded and processed by computers—indeed, that is probably why these machines are

"Here are

nine men."

Fig. 1.1.   Quantity may be represented by a character string such as *nine* or *9*.

called *computers*. Such information arises quite naturally in the process of counting things. For example, the picture of nine little hieroglyphic figures shown in Fig. 1.1 may be read to mean "Here are nine men." The number of men is represented by the character 9 and it should be noted immediately that the *quantity* implied by "nine" is the information content of the character 9. In and of itself, the *character* 9 is an ink-blob of a specific form, without any inherent quantitative value; it is merely a symbol.

The symbol 9 is conventionally associated with a quantity, but the quantity may be represented by other symbols as well. In fact there are many numeric *notations*, ways of associating symbols with quantitative information. The quantity "nine," for example, may be represented in at least the following ways:

nine	is represented by the symbol	9	in decimal notation
	or the symbol	1001	in binary notation
	or the symbol	14	in quinary notation
	or the symbol	11	in octal notation
	or the symbol	IX	in Roman notation.

Decimal notation uses a 10-character alphabet for the universe of all numbers. It is therefore possible to represent at most the first ten numbers (zero through nine) by single characters; other numbers require symbols made up of more than one character.

Conventional numeric notations

The number notations accepted in digital computing use a fixed *radix* or *base b* and assign place-value to individual characters within a symbol. That is to say, a number is represented by a character string in which the information conveyed by each character varies with its placement in the string. Characters at the head of the string represent large magnitudes, whereas characters at the tail of the string represent smaller ones, according to the following rule: If *x, y,* and *z* are three symbols which have been assigned numeric meanings, then the string

xyz means: x times b^2,   plus
                y times b^1,   plus
                z times b^0.

Thus the character string 1756 (to the base 10) means

1 times 10^3 or 1000,   plus
7 times 10^2 or   700,   plus
5 times 10^1 or   50,   plus
6 times 10^0 or   6.

Human languages generally use $b = 10$, with a distinct spoken word denoting each number up to (and often even beyond) nine, but with larger numbers made up by verbal compounding (e.g., *three hundred twenty-six*.) The choice of a decimal radix may be related to having ten fingers, although it is far from obvious why the choice should not be five (the number of fingers on one hand) or perhaps 20 (fingers and toes.) Machines generally work best with base 2, for which the "on" and "off" states are clearcut representations. Other commonly used bases are octal ($b = 8$) and hexadecimal ($b = 16$.)

When numeric data must be represented in bases other than decimal, it is usual to form number symbols out of the first b decimal numeric characters if the radix b is less than 10. For example, the characters 0 1 2 3 4 5 6 7 are used in octal notation. If the radix b exceeds 10, but is below 37, the ten decimal numeric characters are employed, followed by as many upper-case Roman alphabetic characters as may be required to make up b. For example, in hexadecimal notation ($b = 16$) the usual character set is 0 1 2 3 4 5 6 7 8 9 A B C D F, where A denotes "ten," B denotes "eleven," and so on. The hexadecimal number 2B thus represents

2   times 16^1 or 32_{10},   plus
B   times 16^0 or 11_{10},

i.e., it is equivalent to the decimal number 43.

Using the same symbols regardless of base makes numbers fairly easy to read, for the same character symbols always denote the same magnitudes, no matter which radix is used for numeric representation. However, numeric values are not unique. It is obvious on inspection that the character string *312* is intended to represent a number, but there is no way to tell its base. In most cases, the intended base is obvious from context. Where it is not, as where several bases are used in a discussion, the base may be indicated by a subscript. Thus 312_4 quite unambiguously means that the number is to be understood as referred to base 4 (i.e., $312_4 = 54_{10}$), 312_7 as base 7 ($312_7 = 156_{10}$), and so on.

Binary numbers

Numbers represented in a base 2 notation are referred to as *binary numbers*. They are by far the most common ones in computing machines. Only the two symbols 0 and 1 are required, so the alphabet is as small as it possibly could be.

One important result of this choice of base is that the electronic devices required for data processing are simple.

Binary numbers are translatable into other bases in accordance with the general rules regarding place-value. For example,

$$110 \quad 101 \quad 111 \quad 001 = \quad 1 * 2^{11} + 1 * 2^{10} + 0 * 2^9$$
$$+ 1 * 2^8 + 0 * 2^7 + 1 * 2^6$$
$$+ 1 * 2^5 + 1 * 2^4 + 1 * 2^3$$
$$+ 0 * 2^2 + 0 * 2^1 + 1 * 2^0$$

an expression which is easily evaluated in decimal notation as

$$2048 + 1024 + 256 + 64 + 32 + 16 + 8 + 1 = 3449_{10}.$$

The main difficulty with binary numbers, and it really is a nasty difficulty, is that they are very hard for people to read. Using a very small alphabet means that symbols involve many bits, so that even numbers of modest size are represented by long, confusing strings of digits. One way around this difficulty is to allow the machine to work in binary notation, but to convert the binary numbers to octal or hexadecimal for human use. Conversion of binary numbers to octal is very easy; it is only necessary to factor out as many eights as possible in the individual digit values. To illustrate by continuing the previous example, let the highest possible power of 8 be factored out in each term, and terms collected. The last three terms involve powers of 2 lower than the cube, so nothing can be factored out. The next to last three terms involve powers of 2 from 3 to 5, so 8 can be factored out of each. Continuing in this fashion, there results

$$110 \quad 101 \quad 111 \quad 001 = \quad (1 * 2^2 + 1 * 2^1 + 0 * 2^0) * 8^3$$
$$+ (1 * 2^2 + 0 * 2^1 + 1 * 2^0) * 8^2$$
$$+ (1 * 2^2 + 1 * 2^1 + 1 * 2^0) * 8^1$$
$$+ (0 * 2^2 + 0 * 2^1 + 1 * 2^0) * 8^0.$$

Now if each of the numbers in parentheses is replaced by a single octal number, there is obtained (in octal notation)

$$110 \quad 101 \quad 111 \quad 001 = \quad 6 * 8^3$$
$$+ 5 * 8^2$$
$$+ 7 * 8^1$$
$$+ 1 * 8^0 = 6571_8.$$

The conversion is in fact very easily done by inspection. It should be evident from the example that the last octal digit is determined entirely by the last three binary digits, the next to last octal digit by the next to last three binary digits, and so on. Hence the conversion can be done without even writing down intermediate steps, by simply taking the binary number three digits at a time and translating each three-digit group into octal notation on the spot:

$$110_2 = 6_8$$
$$101_2 = 5_8$$
$$111_2 = 7_8$$
$$001_2 = 1_8.$$

Conversion to hexadecimal notation is equally easy. The procedure is similar, except that the highest possible powers of 16 rather than 8 are factored out:

$$1101 \quad 0111 \quad 1001 =$$
$$(1 * 2^3 + 1 * 2^2 + 0 * 2^1 + 1 * 2^0) * 16^2$$
$$+ (0 * 2^3 + 1 * 2^2 + 1 * 2^1 + 1 * 2^0) * 16^1$$
$$+ (1 * 2^3 + 0 * 2^2 + 0 * 2^1 + 1 * 2^0) * 16^0.$$

The corresponding hexadecimal number is D79, obtained by converting each of the quantities in parentheses into hexadecimal notation. The first parenthesis yields

$$1 * 2^3 + 1 * 2^2 + 0 * 2^1 + 1 * 2^0 = 8 + 4 + 1 = D_{16}$$

and similarly for the others. The same result can be obtained by inspection if the binary number is taken in groups of four digits at a time, as suggested by the manner in which it is written.

Number base conversion

Conversion from one number base to another can be done by following a systematic procedure based on the general rules already outlined. It is perhaps most easily appreciated by examining the specific case of conversion from decimal to binary notation.

Let N_{10} be the decimal representation of some number N, and let N_2 be its binary counterpart. According to the general principles of numeric notations, the least significant digit of N_2 is the coefficient that multiplies 2^0, i.e., it counts the number of units. If the number N is exactly divisible by 2, then there is no odd units digit, and the least significant bit of N_2 is zero. The last digit of N_2 is therefore easily found, dividing N_{10} by 2 and noting the remainder; if the remainder is 1, so is the last digit of N_2. In other words, dividing N_{10} by 2 splits it into a remainder $R^{(1)}$ and a quotient $Q^{(1)}$, equal in value to the largest integer in $N/2$. That is, N may be written in the form

$$N = Q^{(1)} * 2 + R^{(1)}$$

where

$$Q^{(1)} = [N/2],$$

the square brackets denoting the largest integer contained in the bracketed quantity. To take a concrete example, suppose $N_{10} = 5_{10}$. Then the division gives $Q^{(1)} = 2$, with $R^{(1)} = 1$. Therefore, $N_2 = xxxxx1$, where the digits denoted by x are not yet known.

The next-to-last digit of N_2 can in its turn be derived from $Q^{(1)}$. Dividing by 2, $Q^{(1)}$ is given a representation as a quotient and a remainder:

$$Q^{(1)} = Q^{(2)} * 2 + R^{(2)}$$

where

$$Q^{(2)} = [Q^{(1)}/2].$$

The representation of N thereby becomes

$$N = (Q^{(2)} * 2 + R^{(2)}) * 2 + R^{(1)}$$

For the particular numerical example of $N = 5$, that corresponds to

$$5 = (1 * 2 + 0) * 2 + 1,$$

so the last two digits in the binary representation of 5_{10} must be 01, the leading ones remain to be determined. Repeating the process yet again,

$$N = ((Q^{(3)} * 2 + R^{(3)}) * 2 + R^{(2)}) * 2 + R^{(1)}$$

or

$$N = Q^{(3)} * 8 + R^{(3)} * 2^2 + R^{(2)} * 2^1 + R^{(1)} * 2^0$$

results. If $Q^{(3)}$ happens to vanish, as it does in the case of $N = 5$, the process terminates. Otherwise, the division operation is repeated until some quotient, say $Q^{(k)}$, does vanish. N then takes the form

$$N = R^{(k)} * 2^{k-1} + \ldots + R^{(3)} * 2^2 + R^{(2)} * 2^1 + R^{(1)} * 2^0,$$

which is exactly the factorization required to do number base conversion.

The process sketched out for decimal-to-binary conversion is equally applicable for conversions between other number bases. Its rules may be summarized briefly as

1. Set $Q^{(0)} = N$.
2. Form the sequence of quotients and remainders $Q^{(j)}$ and $R^{(j)}$,

$$Q^{(j)} = [Q^{(j-1)}/b], \quad R^{(j)} = Q^{(j-1)} - b * Q^{(j)},$$

   for $j = 1, \ldots, k$, until $Q^{(k)} = 0$.
3. Obtain the base-b representation N_b by writing down all the remainders in order; digit i of N_b is remainder $R^{(i+1)}$.

Such a prescription for carrying out a data manipulation process is known as an *algorithm*. Algorithms are important in computing because they consist of finite sequences of exactly defined steps, each of which can be carried out by a digital computer. The design of computers, and the design of algorithms, are strongly interdependent, for it is impossible to construct hardware that is equally fast and equally good at carrying out *all* algorithms; every machine is good at some class of algorithms, and perhaps not so good at some others.

Integer numbers in finite machines

The fundamental arithmetic process carried out on numeric data is addition. Addition of binary numbers is carried out by computers in a fashion not unlike the corresponding process done by pencil and paper. However, there is one important difference. As numbers grow large, the pencil and paper worker can write longer and longer strings of digits, but the machine cannot do so because it is restricted to working with a fixed number of characters. In this section the basic process of addition is therefore reviewed, with special attention to the notational implications and possibilities that arise from finite word length.

Addition of binary numbers

Working with pencil and paper, the rules for binary addition are exactly the same as for addition of decimal numbers (or indeed numbers to any other conventional base.) The rules are easiest to follow with familiar decimal addition: to add two numbers, say 4562 and 1719, the numbers are first written one beneath the other. Their last digits are added, ignoring all others. If there is a carry out of the last place, it is recorded. Then the next-to-last digits, plus any carry that may have occurred, are added in their turn, ignoring the other digits. Continuing, the process thus runs as illustrated below. In each step, only two digits and a carry are dealt with. To emphasize this point, only the digits actually being added, and the result in each step, are shown in this example. The digits temporarily ignored are replaced by dots, to clarify exactly which digits actually enter into the operation at each step.

```
                     ..1.  .0..  1...
4562   ...2  ..6.  .5..  4...  4562
1719   ...9  ..1.  .7..  1...  1719
????   ??11  ??81  1281  6281  6281
```

Exactly the same process applies to the binary addition problem 0101 + 0110 = ???? as seen below.

```
                     ..0.  .0..  1...
0101   ...1  ..0.  .1..  0...  0101
0110   ...0  ..1.  .1..  0...  0110
????   ???1  ??11  1011  1011  1011
```

One great simplification may be so obvious as to escape notice at first glance. To perform decimal addition with paper and pencil, it is necessary first to memorize an *addition table*: 1 + 1 = 2, 1 + 2 = 3, and so on. Because there are ten possible digits, 55 different number combinations must be remembered (addition is commutative, so it is not necessary to remember both 2 + 3 and 3 + 2.) In contrast, the binary addition table only contains three entries:

$$0 + 0 = 0$$
$$0 + 1 = 1$$
$$1 + 1 = 10$$

Just as the human arithmetician must memorize the addition table, so must any digital computer to be used for performing addition. In building computers, the "memorizing" is done by embedding the rules permanently in the electronic circuits. Binary arithmetic is clearly undemanding in this respect, at any rate when compared to decimal work. It leads to circuits simple to design and easy to manufacture.

Addition with fixed word length

Unlike the human working with pencil and paper, a digital computer always deals with numbers represented by symbols each having a fixed number of digits. This difference places some restrictions on the way operations can be carried out. With a computer word length of 8 bits, for example, it is simply impossible to attempt the addition problem $011101001 + 110 = ?$ because the first number is too long to fit into an 8-bit word, and the second number is too short to fill a word. However, the problem $11101001 + 00000110 = ?$ is perfectly sensible:

$$\begin{array}{r} 11101001 \\ 00000110 \\ \hline 11101111 \end{array}$$

The binary number range available in an 8-bit machine is from 00000000 to 11111111, equivalent to 000 to 377 octal or 000 to 255 decimal.

Finite-length arithmetic poses some curious and interesting problems. To see how they arise, consider the addition problem $10111001 + 11000100 = ?$. Following the usual rules, one has

$$\begin{array}{rcr} 10111001_2 & \text{or} & 271_8 \\ 11000100_2 & & 304_8 \\ \hline 01111101_2 & & 175_8 \end{array}$$

With pencil and paper, the answer would have been 101111101, a number nine bits long, not 01111101 (octal 575_8, not 175_8); but in the computer this answer is not possible to obtain because only eight bits are available for doing arithmetic and writing down the answer. The high-order bit (bit 8) of the answer simply is not there. In other words, the high-order digit is neither computed nor recorded, for there is no place to put it. This way of treating excessively large numbers is conventional in digital computers. It may seem brutal; but there is no sensible way to preserve the answer in this example, other than to use a computer with a greater word length.

Fixed-word-length addition with an 8-bit word length is generally called *addition modulo 256*. Counting (which really is only a repeated addition of ones) with a fixed 8-bit word length is similarly called *counting modulo 256*, for the count always runs from 000 to 255 (decimal) and then starts over.

When addition is carried out with a finite word length, the result may appear incorrect because the sum may be out of range for the word length. A particularly interesting situation arises in problems such as $01001000 + 10111000 = ?$ since

$$\begin{array}{r} 01001000 \\ 10111000 \\ \hline 00000000 \end{array}$$

modulo 256. (The answer would of course be 100000000 in a 9-bit computer.) In other words, the sum of these two numbers, modulo 256, is zero.

Twos complement notation

In ordinary arithmetic, a fundamental axiom is that *if two numbers sum to zero, then each one is the negative of the other*. This axiom may be generalized to cover arithmetic with finite word length, to read *if two numbers sum to zero, modulo K, then each one is the negative of the other, modulo* K. For example, saying "10111000 is the negative of 01001000, modulo 256," means just precisely that if these two numbers are added using modulo 256 arithmetic rules, the answer will be zero. Arithmetic is commonly carried out in digital computers using this axiom.

The negative of any number, under the rules of arithmetic modulo K, is the number that yields zero on addition. For example, in 8-bit arithmetic the number 00000001 has 11111111 as its negative because the sum of these two, evaluated modulo 256, is 00000000:

$$\begin{array}{r} 00000001 \\ \underline{11111111} \\ 00000000 \end{array}$$

The negative of any number may be constructed by a simple rule, which can be deduced as follows. First, each digit in the number symbol is complemented (inverted), i.e., every 0 is replaced by 1 and vice versa. (The result is called the *logical complement* of the symbol.) If its logical complement is added to a number, the addition will necessarily result in the digit 1 in every position, and no carries will ever take place. For example,

$$\begin{array}{r} A = 01001000 \\ \text{complement of } A = \underline{10110111} \\ 11111111 \end{array}$$

But 11111111 is the negative of 00000001. Adding 00000001 must therefore produce 00000000, the desired result. Thus, to find the negative of A, it is necessary to add 00000001 to its complement:

$$\begin{array}{r} \text{complement of } A = 10110111 \\ \underline{00000001} \\ \text{negative of } A = 10111000 \end{array}$$

The negative of A is often also called the *twos complement* of A, and arithmetic using this representation for negative numbers is called *twos complement arithmetic*. Twos complement notation is merely a way of associating values (information) with symbols (data), so every binary symbol S_2 may be interpreted in two ways, as either of

> an unsigned integer *int(S)*,
> a twos complement integer *int2(S)*.

There is no way of distinguishing between these two interpretations by looking at the symbols themselves; the symbol 10110111 is just a symbol, without any meaning other than that which an observer chooses to attach to it. Whether it is taken to mean $int(10110111) = 267_8 = 183_{10}$, or $int2(10110111) = -111_8 = -73_{10}$, is a matter of intention, a question of how the symbol is used, and not a matter of what the symbol itself looks like.

If negative as well as positive numbers are to be represented by a finite set of symbols, the largest possible number L cannot exceed half the number of symbols in the set, because a number and its negative require two distinct symbols for their representation. Thus, an 8-bit word can be used for counting from 0 to 255 in natural (unsigned) numbers; but 127 is the largest possible number for which a representation is feasible for both the number and its negative. In twos complement notation, the largest and smallest numbers will be $+127_{10}$ and -128_{10}. The negative of 00000000 is easily shown to be itself, i.e., there is only one zero, which accounts for the slight asymmetry in the range of numbers.

The twos complement binary numbers 00000000, 00000001, 00000010, ..., through 01111111 (decimal $+127_{10}$) are indistinguishable from the natural binary numbers in the same range, i.e.,

$$int(S) = int2(S) \quad \text{for all } S \text{ such that}$$
$$int(00000000) = 0 \le int(S) \le 127_{10} = int(01111111).$$

The corresponding range of negative twos complement numbers, from -1 to -128_{10}, begins at the symbol 11111111, and continues through 11111110, 11111101, ..., to 10000001, as may be easily verified by adding. It will be noted that all the negative numbers have the most significant bit set, whereas all non-negative numbers have this bit cleared. This fact permits digital computers (or people!) to tell positive from negative numbers at a glance, without having to perform a number conversion in full detail. The natural binary number symbols, their unsigned numeric interpretations, and the twos complement numbers they represent, are given in the following table. For convenience in reading, the numerical values are shown in decimal notation:

Binary symbol S	Decimal value of unsigned binary $int(S)$	Decimal value of twos complement binary $int2(S)$
00000000	000	000
00000001	001	001
00000010	002	002
00000011	003	003
00000100	004	004
. . . .	. . .	. . . .
01111101	125	125
01111110	126	126
01111111	127	127
10000000	128	-128

10000001	129	-127
10000010	130	-126
. . . .	. . . .	. . . . .
11111110	254	-002
11111111	255	-001

Twos complement notations are intimately related to the word length in use. If the word length is n bits, then any signed number N that can be represented at all must satisfy $-2^{n-1} \le N \le 2^{n-1} - 1$. For example, the twos complement number range available in a 12-bit word is $-2048 \le N \le 2047$.

Twos complement subtraction

Subtraction rules can be established in a manner analogous to addition rules. They involve writing down the subtrahend and minuend one below the other, then working digit by digit as in addition. The operations resemble addition, but require knowledge of a *subtraction table* of numbers: $1 - 1 = 0, 1 - 0 = 1$, etc. This table is, of course, closely related to the addition table and can be derived from it easily.

In digital computers, the subtraction operation is often considered unnecessary, indeed many computers get along quite well without it. Instead of providing the electronic circuits necessary to do subtraction, the negative of the subtrahend is formed and added to the minuend, so that the addition circuits serve for subtraction as well. To do so, the following algorithm is used:

1. Form the logical complement C of the subtrahend S.
2. Increment the complement C by 1 to obtain $-S$, the negative of the subtrahend.
3. Add $-S$ to the minuend D.

The first two steps form the negative of the subtrahend, permitting replacement of subtraction by addition in the third. Actually carrying out the first step requires digital circuitry to effect logical complementation (bit inversion); the second and third steps make use of addition circuits. As an example, the subtraction $010110 - 001011 = ?$ is carried out (in 6-bit arithmetic) as follows:

Subtrahend	S =	001011
Its logical complement	C =	110100 (step 1)
Increment (add 1)		000001
Negative of subtrahend $-S$ =		110101 (step 2)
Minuend	D =	010110
Negative of subtrahend $-S$ =		110101
Difference	=	001011 (step 3)

In the third step, a carry propagates out of the most significant bit and is lost. This event is neither unexpected nor bad; in fact it is the essence of twos complement subtraction. After all, subtraction by addition of the negative can only work by relying on the properties of twos complement notation, which in turn rely on finite word length.

The subtraction may be verified for correctness, if desired, by adding the difference and the subtrahend:

$$\begin{aligned}
\text{Difference} &= 001011 \\
\text{Subtrahend} &= \underline{001011} \\
\text{Minuend} &= 010110
\end{aligned}$$

which is clearly the correct answer.

Twos complement multiplication

Multiplication of binary numbers is carried out in exactly the same fashion as multiplication of decimal numbers. The task is simpler, however, because the multiplication table to be remembered is almost trivially small. It contains only three entries:

$$\begin{aligned}
0 * 0 &= 0 \\
0 * 1 &= 0 \\
1 * 1 &= 1
\end{aligned}$$

To illustrate the procedure followed in binary multiplication, suppose the problem is to find the product of 000000010111 and 000000011001 in 12-bit arithmetic. The numbers are written down (separating the digits into groups of three for ease in legibility), and the entire multiplicand is multiplied by each digit of the multiplier in turn. The partial results are written down as they are computed, and are summed afterward:

000	000	010	111	*	000	000	011	001
					000	000	011	001
			0		000	000	110	01
		00			000	001	100	1
	0	000			000	110	01	
				1	000	111	111	

When working with a computing machine, every digit position within its word length must be occupied by either a 1 or a 0. Leaving blanks, as is conventionally done in multiplication with pencil and paper, is not possible. Hence the above has a conventional appearance, but cannot really be carried out by computers. A small amount of reorganization, however, gives the process a shape better suited to computer use:

000	000	010	111	*	000	000	011	001
					000	000	011	001
					000	000	110	0<u>1</u>0
					000	001	100	<u>100</u>
					000	110	0<u>1</u>0	000
					001	000	111	111

Here leading zeros have been discarded if they would extend beyond the most significant bit in the 12-bit word, and trailing zeros have been written in where necessary to fill digit positions. The added trailing zeros are shown underlined, to clarify the matter. However, all vanishing partial results (i.e., those multiplied by zero digits in the multiplier) are not shown, for the sake of clarity.

Because every digit in a binary number must be either 1 or 0, the partial multiplications are by either 1 or 0. Multiplication by 1 actually consists of nothing more than copying the multiplicand; multiplication by 0 amounts to doing nothing at all. Every individual partial multiplication is thus very simple and easy to carry out. The whole process of multiplying two n-bit numbers M and N to find their product P may therefore be stated in an algorithm as follows:

1. Set $I_0 = M$.
2. For $j = 0, 1, \ldots, n-1$, do the following:
    3. If digit j of N is 1, set $R_j = I_j$, otherwise set $R_j = 0$;
    4. set $I_{j+1} = shl(I_j)$.
5. Set $P = R_0 + R_1 + R_2 + \ldots + R_{n-1}$.

Here the function $shl(X)$ denotes a process called the *left shift*. In performing it, the bit string X is shifted left one digit and a zero is placed in the least significant bit position when it is vacated. Whether the bit string represents a number or something else is not relevant; the bits are simply shifted one place. For example,

$$shl(11011) = 110110.$$

When a left shift operation is actually performed in a machine of finite word length, the high-order bit is lost because there is no place for it to be shifted to. This loss is similar to overflow in addition.

To perform multiplication in a digital computer by means of the technique detailed above, an additional type of electronic circuit is thus required, beyond those needed to carry out addition. This new kind of circuit must be capable of *shifting* a word leftward one bit, filling in a zero at the least significant bit position, and discarding the digit previously in the most significant bit.

Division is carried out in computers, as it is manually, by repeatedly subtracting and shifting, whereas multiplication is essentially a process of repeated adding and shifting. Both right and left shifts are needed. Consequently, the same arguments can be repeated, in slightly modified form, to the effect that no division operation is really required. It suffices to know how to subtract, and how to shift. However, both a left shift operation $shl(X)$ and a right shift $shr(X)$ must be provided.

Arithmetic with negative numbers

When twos complement multiplication is carried out, negative as well as positive factors may be encountered. Twos complement notation was introduced in the first place to make addition and subtraction processes identical; considering that multiplication is really a process of repeated shifting and addition, it would be surprising indeed if multiplication of negative numbers did not work satisfactorily. The multiplication process and its properties may again best be shown by example: Find 00011 * 11011 in 5-bit arithmetic. The first factor here represents a positive twos complement number, the second is negative. Ignoring for the moment how to make the process suited to machines, pencil-and-paper multiplication has the following appearance:

$$
\begin{array}{r}
00011 \quad * \quad 11011 \\
\hline
11011 \\
1 \quad 1011 \\
\hline
10 \quad 10001
\end{array}
\qquad \text{or} \qquad
\begin{array}{r}
3_{10} * -5_{10} \\
\hline
-15_{10}
\end{array}
$$

Here the binary digits have been separated in groups of five, to improve legibility. The result, to five bits, is 10001, or decimal -15, which is obviously the correct answer.

When two negative factors are encountered, as in the problem 1101 * 1110 = ?, the results still turn out correct:

$$
\begin{array}{r}
1101 \quad * \quad 1110 \\
\hline
1110 \\
11 \quad 10 \\
111 \quad 0 \\
\hline
1011 \quad 0110
\end{array}
\qquad \text{or} \qquad
\begin{array}{r}
-3_{10} * -2_{10} \\
\hline
+6_{10}
\end{array}
$$

The four result bits now yield 0110, the positive twos complement number equivalent to 6_{10}, as would indeed be expected from the multiplication of two negative numbers.

It should be noted that although addition of two n-bit numbers can produce a result $n+1$ bits long, the multiplication of two n-bit numbers can yield up to $2n$ nonzero bits. Out-of-range numbers can therefore be produced quite easily!

Shifting a bit string left is arithmetically equivalent to multiplication by 2. For example, let the 5-bit strings $a = 00101$ and $b = 11010$ denote the twos complement binary numbers $+5_{10}$ and -6_{10}, respectively. Shifting left results in

$$c = shl(a) = 01010$$

and

$$d = shl(b) = 10100$$

which are the twos complement representations of $+10_{10}$ and -12_{10}. However, shifting right does not restore the previous results in all cases because the digits dropped from the left end of the bit string in shifting left are lost and cannot be recovered by a right shift. To continue the previous example,

$$e = shr(c) = 00101$$

and

$$f = shr(d) = 01010.$$

The positive number $+5_{10}$ is correctly recovered in the shifting back and forth,

$$a = shr(shl(a)) = 00101$$

but the negative number is not, for the reason already mentioned: the operation *shr(b)* fills in the most significant bit with a zero, but the digit lost in left shifting was 1.

Most computers contain provision for both a true right shift *shr(X)* and another operation called the *arithmetic right shift*, denoted by *shra(X)*. In the latter operation, the high-order bit position is filled not with a zero, but with a copy of the previous value. Thus,

$$shra(01010) = 00101$$

and

$$shra(10100) = 11010.$$

The arithmetic right shift *shra(X)* is useful in arithmetic operations, as its name implies; the simple right shift *shr(X)* finds application in various nonnumeric computations. To distinguish between the two kinds of shifting operations, the simple shifting operation is usually called the *logical right shift*.

Carries and overflows

When arithmetic operations are performed in finite-length registers, as must always be the case in digital computers, the results of a computation may well exceed the available register length. The results are not necessarily wrong if this event occurs; indeed the whole idea of twos complement arithmetic is based on making the results come out right *because* the register length is exceeded. It is therefore worthwhile inquiring whether correct results are always obtained, and under what circumstances they might possibly be wrong.

To proceed by example, let some computer have a 3-bit word length. It is capable of representing $2^3 = 8$ distinct numbers. In normal twos complement notation, these are as follows:

3-bit	Decimal
011	3
010	2
001	1
000	0
111	−1
110	−2
101	−3
100	−4

If two numbers are added, and the result of the addition falls within the allowable number range, the results are correct even though a carry out of the high-order digit is lost. For example, the two additions

$$
\begin{array}{cc}
001 & 1 \\
\underline{010} & \underline{2} \\
011 & 3
\end{array}
\qquad
\begin{array}{cc}
111 & -1 \\
\underline{110} & \underline{-2} \\
1101 & -3
\end{array}
$$

both yield the correct results to within 3-bit register length, even though in the right-hand example a *carry* out of the high-order digit (bit 2) is lost. On the other hand, the pair of additions

$$
\begin{array}{cc}
011 & 3 \\
\underline{010} & \underline{2} \\
101 & -3
\end{array}
\qquad
\begin{array}{cc}
101 & -3 \\
\underline{110} & \underline{-2} \\
1011 & 3
\end{array}
$$

both give the wrong answers, because the correct answers cannot be represented at all in 3-bit twos complement notation. Because numbers "wrap around" in twos complement notation, the answer obtained by simply following the rules of addition is not only wrong, but it even has its sign wrong. This state of affairs is described by saying that an *overflow* has occurred.

It should be noted that wrong results can result from an addition only if the addend and augend have the same sign. If their signs are opposite, the absolute value of the sum must be smaller than the absolute value of the larger term. But since neither could exceed the limits of the number system in use (or they would not have been expressible in the first place!), their sum cannot exceed the limits either. Hence, an overflow is possible only if both addend and augend have the same sign; and overflow is always easily recognized because *the sign of the sum differs from the signs of the addend and augend.*

Overflows can occur in a similar fashion in subtraction. The phenomenon is exactly the same as in addition, (as already discussed), because subtraction is equivalent to negation followed by addition.

General complement notations

It is interesting to observe that complement arithmetic as set out in the foregoing paragraphs is not restricted to twos complementation in binary number systems. In fact, a similar process is applicable to any other conventional system of numeric representation. If a b-character alphabet is used to create numeric symbols of n digits, the natural result is a base-b representation for unsigned numbers in the range $0 \leq N \leq b^n - 1$. For arithmetic involving signed numbers, a bs complement notation may then be used to cover a range of values and extending in both the negative and positive directions, centered on zero. The arithmetic rules set out for the twos complement case are easily generalized to cover bs complement notations.

To proceed by example once again, suppose decimal notation is used, with a word length of three digits. There then exist 1000 distinct number symbols altogether, 000, 001, . . . , 999. Addition, which produces overflow from the most significant digit, may of course occur; for example,

$$499$$
$$\underline{626}$$
$$125$$

because a the fourth digit (which results on addition) cannot exist in a three-digit word. This result suggests that the *symbol* 626 is in fact a natural representation of the *value* -374, for

$$499 + (-374) = 125.$$

The value range representable in this fashion is then -500_{10} to $+499_{10}$. To form the negative of any number, say 374, a procedure is used that closely resembles that of twos complement arithmetic. Every digit is replaced with its complement with respect to the highest possible digit value (9 in the case of decimal notation), and 1 is added to the result. Thus, to pursue the same example,

$$
\begin{aligned}
\text{Number} &= 374 \\
\text{Nines complement} &= 625 \\
\text{Add 1:} &\quad\underline{1} \\
\text{Negative number} &= 626
\end{aligned}
$$

Similar arguments apply to any other base, or any other number of digits. It must be kept in mind, however, that the entire system of complemented arithmetic rests on use of a fixed word length, so that there really exists not *a* twos complement notation, or a tens complement notation, but rather one such notation for every choice of word length.

The two main advantages of any complemented notation are (a) the ability to represent both positive and negative numbers without any need to introduce additional symbols such as $+$ and $-$ and (b) the existence of a consistent system of arithmetic which takes care of sign automatically. All digital computers in use today are built of binary electronic devices, so binary arithmetic comes naturally. Ternary electronic devices, which possess three stable states, exist now and may become common in the future. For such devices, base-3 number representations and threes complement arithmetic would be the appropriate choices.

Sign and magnitude notation

In addition to complement notations, there are several other ways to provide for representation of negative numbers. One which is widely used, although it is not the easiest to implement in machines, is equivalent to the technique used with pencil and paper: a sign is prefixed to the number. To do so, a special sign (or indeed pair of signs) must be created, say $+$ and $-$. In the very special case of binary numbers, however, the number of signs just happens to coincide with the number of distinct characters used for the representation of numeric magnitude. The same two characters (0 and 1, *on* and *off*, etc.) may be employed to denote sign and numeric magnitude, so that special sign symbols can be dispensed with. Normally, the sign bit is the most significant bit in the word. An 8-bit machine word would thus have the configuration

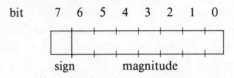

This way of representing numbers is known as *sign and magnitude representation*. It should be kept clearly in mind that exactly 2^8 distinct 8-bit words are possible, no more and no less. If one bit is reserved for storage of the sign, there are only 7 bits left for the magnitude, so that the smallest number that can be represented is then -1111111 (signed binary) and the largest is $+1111111$, equivalent to the decimal range -127_{10} to $+127_{10}$.

Twos complement notations always involve a slightly asymmetric number range. The total number of symbols in any base 2 system is even, but because there is only one number *zero*, there must be one extra number on either the negative or the positive side. With sign and magnitude notation, the available number range becomes perfectly symmetric. However, there is a price to be paid. Because the sign cannot ever be absent from a number in this notation, there must exist two distinct symbols for $+0$ and -0. Their existence, unfortunately, complicates the rules of arithmetic, by raising questions such as: should the sum of $+A$ and $-A$ be $+0$ or -0?

Sign and magnitude representation is not the best available for purposes of finite-length arithmetic. It is the normal notation used in manual work, where the signs are subject to a whole set of special rules. For example, in multiplication and division the rule is that magnitudes are treated independently first and the sign is determined separately from the signs of the two operands. School-children are expected to memorize a set of rules about signs, just as they are expected to memorize an addition table and a multiplication table. In digital computers, any such rules must be embedded in the machine circuitry. Considerable efforts are therefore made to minimize their number. Sign and magnitude notation requires more rules than binary notation, hence it is employed only in special applications where the burden of additional work imposed by the extra rules is not significant.

Machine operations for numeric data

The principal four arithmetic operations can be carried out in a computer equipped to perform the following operations on words of fixed length.

Moving: Almost redundant to mention because it is so obvious, the machine must possess some mechanism for moving data from one storage location or register to another.

Addition: Formation of the arithmetic sum of two fixed-length words, any resulting carry from the most significant bit of the result being discarded. If twos complement notation is used for numbers, no special arrangement is necessary for handling negative numbers.

Complementation: Replacement of a word by another, in which every bit has the opposite setting, i.e., replacement of every 0 by a 1 and vice versa. (Also called *logical negation* or *logical complementation*.)

Shifting: Moving all bits in a word to the right or the left, the digit shifted out of the endmost position being discarded. Two forms of shifting are found useful: the *arithmetic shift*, in which the most significant bit is left unaltered in a right shift, and the *logical shift*, in which the vacated digit position is filled with a zero.

Incrementation: The word is augmented by adding 00 ... 001. Incrementation as a separate entity is obviously not really necessary, for it is merely a special case of addition; but it is so often needed (e.g., in counting) that it is included as a separate operation in many computers.

Complicated numerical operations, such as trigonometric functions or square roots, are defined in terms of the four principal arithmetic operations. Consequently, these five elementary operations suffice to perform any numerical computations whatever.

Representation of nonnumeric data

Although a large proportion of the work done by digital computers consists of calculations carried out with numbers, a still larger part of their time is spent handling alphabetic text. How alphabetic characters are represented and manipulated is therefore a matter of considerable importance, and will be examined next.

Binary representation of characters

The characters of the Roman alphabet, Arabic numerals, and punctuation marks, form an alphabet often loosely termed *characters* by people in the computing profession. A minimal useful set of characters ought to contain, for convenience,

Upper and lower case alphabets	52 symbols
Arabic numerals	10 symbols
Punctuation, at least .,?!+-*/():=;"$	15 symbols
Blank, new line, skip line	3 symbols
Minimal alphabet	80 symbols

Because digital computers only know how to handle binary symbol strings, these 80 (or more) symbols are made to correspond to binary symbols through a conventionally accepted table of symbol equivalence. It is evident that binary strings of at least seven digits are required, for there can only exist $2^6 = 64$ distinct 6-bit symbols but the 7-bit symbols set numbers $2^7 = 128$. The 7-bit symbols are made to correspond to printed characters so that to every binary symbol S there corresponds a text character, here denoted by *ascii(S)*. The table of character equivalences has the following general form:

Binary symbol $S^{(2)}$			Octal symbol $S^{(8)}$	Hexadecimal $S^{(16)}$	Text symbol *ascii(S)*
0	110	000	060	30	0
0	110	001	061	31	1
. . .	. . .	. . .	. . .	. . .	. . .
1	000	001	101	41	A
1	000	010	102	42	B
. . .	. . .	. . .	. . .	. . .	. . .
1	011	001	131	59	Y
1	011	010	132	5A	Z
. . .	. . .	. . .	. . .	. . .	. . .

If the binary symbol set shows signs of being heavily used, it is! To every binary data symbol S there now correspond no fewer than three kinds of information entities,

a character *ascii(S)*,
an unsigned integer *int(S)*,
a twos complement integer *int2(S)*.

The symbols themselves give no hint as to which sort of information they are intended to convey. Their interpretation is entirely a matter for the information user to select.

Seven-bit character representations occur from time to time in data transmission, but an 8-bit internal representation within digital computers is more common because the great majority of computers are constructed to deal with 8-bit bytes, and words which are multiples of 8-bit bytes. The extra high-order bit is often used to simplify data processing tasks. For example, some tasks may require at least two distinct alphabets, as might be the case for a scholar constructing an English-Greek dictionary. The most significant bit in each byte can then be used to identify which of the two 128-character alphabets is meant. Some computer terminals also provide two character sets, the second one being purpose-built for specific applications. An example of this kind is furnished by terminals intended to be used with the APL programming language, which involves a substantial number of unusual special characters. Where the most significant bit is not needed for any coding purpose, it is usually left at 0.

Several 8-bit character sets are in widespread use. By far the most common of these is the ASCII (pronounced *ahs-key*) set of codes, which is described in detail below. It is an American national standard, and a *de facto* world standard as well. The second most common is probably the EBCDIC (often pronounced *ebbsy-dick*) code, which was introduced by one of the major computer manufacturers before there was a well-defined standard; it still survives.

There also exists a conventional, though somewhat restricted, 6-bit character set. It is similar to a 7-bit alphabet in principle, but it contains no lower case alphabetic characters. In other words, it saves on total symbol count by containing only capital letters. Such all-capitals usage is common in telephone bills, drivers' licenses, and other similarly brief records.

Historically, the term *character* early came to signify any thing or action that could be produced by a single keystroke on an electric typewriter. The term thus covers not only the alphabetics and numerals, which are ordinarily thought of as "characters," but also the blank (produced on a typewriter by striking the space bar) and such curious items as *carriage return, tab*, and *line feed*. The latter variety are known as *nonprinting* characters. They serve to control text placement on the printed page, but they neither make any marks, nor take up any character spaces on the printed page. The *blank*, on the other hand, is a *printable* character like any alphabetic character; it makes a mark (the blank space) that occupies exactly the width and height of one letter.

The ASCII character set

The usual binary symbol set used for character handling in computers is the ASCII (American Standard for Computer Information Interchange) code. An ASCII character is defined to be a 7-bit symbol, which may represent a printable or a nonprintable character. For ease in reading, the binary digits are often taken in groups of four, with each group given its natural number interpretation written in hexadecimal representation. Thus 110 0010 is normally written as 62, the groups 110 and 0010 having been interpreted as the hexadecimal numbers 6 and 2, respectively. Octal representations are also quite common. To convert, the same symbol would be written as 1 100 010 and transcribed into octal notation as 142.

Because an ASCII character is exactly seven bits long, 128 characters can be formed. These are given in Appendix 4 in tabular form. Every one of the possible characters is assigned a significance, there are no unused symbols. The left column (octal 000 to 032) and the last entry in the table (octal 177) are nonprinting characters, all the rest are printable. It is conventional to refer to the nonprinting characters in the left column as *control* characters, since they are formed on most keyboards by pressing a key while the CONTROL key is held down; for example, the *newline* character (octal 012) is generated by striking J while holding down the CONTROL key, and is ordinarily called *control-J*.

Perhaps surprisingly, there are some installation-dependent as well as national differences between the printed symbols that correspond to certain bit configurations. For example, 23 (010 0011) is rendered as the crosshatched "pounds" sign in American practice, but it produces the "pounds sterling" currency symbol on many printers in Britain. Similarly, 7B (111 1011) and 7D (111 1101) correspond to opening and closing braces ("curly brackets") in American practice, while they represent accented lower-case letters e in France. There is total agreement, however, about the upper case alphabetics and the numeric characters, as well as about the mathematical operators and common punctuation signs.

Fully one-quarter of the whole ASCII character set is composed of nonprinting characters. Some of these control printer or screen-display actions, e.g., 07 rings the terminal bell, 09 actuates horizontal tabulation, 0A begins a new line, 0B moves the paper up one line, 0C begins a new page. Other nonprinting characters control communication with other computers, as well as with printers and terminals. For example, 04 signals end of transmission, 06 acknowledges receipt, 7F deletes the immediately preceding character. The ASCII standard assigns to each nonprinting character a character name (e.g., *bel* = bell, *nl* = newline, *del* = delete), which indicates the nature and function of the character very clearly in most cases, poorly or not at all in others.

Character alteration

The ASCII character set is so constructed that the binary symbols for upper and lower case characters differ by exactly one bit. Comparing the first few characters, it is clear that the only difference lies in bit 5, which is set for lower case, cleared for upper case characters:

100	0001	41	A	110	0001	61	a
100	0010	42	B	110	0010	62	b
100	0011	43	C	110	0011	63	c
100	0100	44	D	110	0100	64	d

This fact is not accidental, but quite deliberately designed into the character set so as to make conversion of lower case to upper case characters easy. Such conversions are often necessary. For example, suppose it is desired to find all occurrences of the word *equation* in a text. Simply searching for the string of successive characters e-q-u-a-t-i-o-n is not good enough. Were it to occur at the beginning of a sentence, this word would normally be written *Equation*, with a capital *E*; indeed it might be written as *EQUATION* in a title. The only safe course is thus to convert all alphabetic characters in the text into their upper case equivalents, then search for *EQUATION*.

There are several ways character conversion can be accomplished. One rather simple way it might be tried would be to shift the character left twice, so that bit 5 is dropped (shifted out of the word), then to shift right twice:

fetch character *s*	111	0011
shift left twice	100	1100
shift right twice	001	0011

This scheme does not quite work; not only is bit 5 reset, but bit 6 as well! The problem is that bit 6 is shifted out and lost forever. The problem is cured by replacing the first shift by a different operation, called *rotation*, in which all bits are shifted, but the bit shifted out at the end is made to reappear as the replacement bit at the other end of the word. For example, in a left rotation all bits are shifted left, *and the leftmost bit is placed in the least significant bit position.* The character conversion then proceeds successfully:

fetch character *s*	**111**	0011
rotate left	110	011**1**
shift left	100	1110
shift right	010	0111
rotate right	**1**01	0011

Clearly both left and right shifts and rotations are needed. All four operations are provided in the majority of digital computers.

Text encoding and storage

Text processing operations largely consist of identifying, ordering, classifying, and altering words on a character-by-character basis, so the natural unit of data in text processing is an individual character. An ideal computer for text processing should therefore have a word length of 8 bits (or perhaps 7 bits.) However, most computers also need to do numeric calculations, for which word lengths of 32 or more bits are better suited. General-purpose computers are therefore usually built with rather longer word lengths, typically 32 bits. When handling character data, several 8-bit symbols are packed into a single word. For example, the name *Fred* contains four letters so it fits neatly into the four 8-bit bytes that comprise a single 32-bit word. It is encoded as

Printed	F		r		e		d	
Binary	0100	0110	0111	0010	0110	0101	0110	0100
Octal	106		162		145		144	
Hexadecimal	46		72		65		64	

Text units do not usually happen to be multiples of four characters long, so they do not fit the computer word length precisely except perhaps by sheer luck. Moreover, most text is much longer than the four, six, or eight characters that can be stored in conventional computer words. It is therefore usual to store text by using as many words as may be necessary to contain the text, and by placing an *end-of-text mark* after the last character. For example,

C	a	l	l		m	e		I	s
103	141	154	154	040	155	145	040	111	163
43	61	6C	6C	20	6D	65	20	49	73

					h	m	a	e	l	
					110	155	141	145	154	000
					68	6D	61	65	6C	00

contains 15 characters, including the blank characters between words, and therefore requires four 32-bit machine words. Only three characters of the fourth word are actually required; the last one contains an ASCII null character, which is a reasonably popular choice for an end-of-text mark. If any part of the final

word is left unused, it may contain anything at all, for any further bytes follow
the end-of-text mark and are not part of the text. In many systems, the null
character is used as a filler in such circumstances. In binary code, the complete
text is stored as

Call	43	61	6C	6C	01000011	01100001	01101100	01101100
me	20	6D	65	20	00100000	01101101	01100101	00100000
Ishm	49	73	68	6D	01001001	01110011	01001000	01101101
ael	61	65	6C	00	01100001	01100101	01101100	00000000

End-of-text, beginning-of-text, and the like markers are not well standardized.
In fact, they are sometimes not used at all. In some text processing applications,
the number of characters contained in the text is recorded and stored along with
the text, obviating the need for an end-of-text mark. In some other cases, texts
may be of a predefined and known length. For example, Canadian postal codes
always contain six characters, American short-form zip codes always have five.
Thus the employee records of a small company can be set up with postal codes
in home addresses having a fixed number of characters, for all the employees
presumably live in the same country. On the other hand, the company's register
of shareholders cannot be set up on the same assumption, for its shareholders
may well live anywhere at all.

Alphabetic ordering

In the ASCII character set table of Appendix 4, the natural order of the alphabetic characters corresponds precisely to the natural order of the numeric interpretations of the same symbols. In other words, if characters are encoded in
binary form and the binary codes are interpreted as natural numbers instead of
as characters, alphabetic sequence is preserved. Suppose $int(A)$ denotes the
unsigned integer value of the binary symbol A, and $ascii(A)$ represents the character value of the same string. For example, if $A = 01010010$, then $ascii(A) =$
R, $int(A) = 82_{10}$. By examining the ASCII character table, the following assertion
is easily proved: If two binary symbols S_1 and S_2 are such that $ascii(S_1)$ precedes
$ascii(S_2)$ alphabetically, then $int(S_1)$ precedes $int(S_2)$ in numeric order, and vice
versa:

$$\text{if} \quad ascii(S_1) \quad \text{precedes} \quad ascii(S_2)$$
$$\text{then} \quad int(S_1) \quad < \quad int(S_2).$$

As a result, alphabetic sorting of character data can be achieved simply by sorting their binary symbols as if they represented natural numbers, not characters.

To consider a very simple example, let the words JOHN, FRED, MARY,
BILL be sorted alphabetically. In a computer with 32-bit word length the words
would have the appearance

JOHN	= 01001010	01001111	01001000	01001110
FRED	= 01000110	01010010	01000101	01000100
MARY	= 01001101	01000001	01100101	01011001
BILL	= 01000010	01001001	01001100	01001100

with each character occupying exactly one of the four bytes that make up the 32-bit word. (The bytes have been separated for ease of reading, there would of course be no separating line or blank in a computer word.) To obtain the numeric interpretations *int(S)* for each symbol *S*, it is easiest to regroup all the digits four by four so as to allow immediate transcription into hexadecimal notation:

$$\begin{aligned}
\text{JOHN} &= 0100 \quad 1010 \quad 0100 \quad 1111 \quad 0100 \quad 1000 \quad 0100 \quad 1110 = 4A4F484E_{16} \\
\text{FRED} &= 0100 \quad 0110 \quad 0101 \quad 0010 \quad 0100 \quad 0101 \quad 0100 \quad 0100 = 46524544_{16} \\
\text{MARY} &= 0100 \quad 1101 \quad 0100 \quad 0001 \quad 0110 \quad 0101 \quad 0101 \quad 1001 = 4D416559_{16} \\
\text{BILL} &= 0100 \quad 0010 \quad 0100 \quad 1001 \quad 0100 \quad 1100 \quad 0100 \quad 1100 = 42494C4C_{16}
\end{aligned}$$

It then remains to resequence the words in order of increasing integer value:

$$\begin{aligned}
42494C4C_{16} &= 01000010 \quad 01001001 \quad 01001100 \quad 01001100 = \text{BILL} \\
46524544_{16} &= 01000110 \quad 01010010 \quad 01000101 \quad 01000100 = \text{FRED} \\
4A4F484E_{16} &= 01001010 \quad 01001111 \quad 01001000 \quad 01001110 = \text{JOHN} \\
4D416559_{16} &= 01001101 \quad 01000001 \quad 01100101 \quad 01011001 = \text{MARY}
\end{aligned}$$

For words containing more characters, the same process can be modified, sorting one four-character group at a time. An obvious way of doing this is to sort the leftmost (most significant) character group first, then the next group of four, and so on. For example, sorting the names

JONES
JOHN
JOHNSTON
JOHNSON

will initially result in

<u>JOHN</u>
<u>JOHN</u>SON
<u>JOHN</u>STON
<u>JONE</u>S

because only the first four characters will be considered in the sorting. Next, all those cases are considered whose first four characters were alike. Sorting all the JOHNs, the result is

JOHN<u>____</u>
JOHN<u>STO</u>N
JOHN<u>SON</u>
JONES

If it seems as if the first JOHN had been ignored, such is not the case. For a proper comparison to be made, the words have to be padded out so as to have equal lengths, otherwise a valid numeric comparison cannot be achieved. The padding is done with ASCII null characters whose 8-bit binary representation is

00000000. The numeric value of a null is lower than that of any other ASCII character, so that JOHN always precedes JOHNSON.

Sorting in the manner described is a complicated process, for each stage of work requires sorting only a subset of the original data (e.g., only the items whose leading four characters are JOHN). A better sorting scheme is actually to work from the least significant (rightmost) character group to the left, so the first stage of sorting would produce

JOHN____

JONES____

JOHNSTON

JOHNSON_

A second sorting of all the words, taking into account only the next most significant character group, will now produce the correct end result.

Numeric and quasi-numeric data

It is worth singling out the numerals 0, 1, 2, . . . and noting that they are included in the ASCII character set. Every printable numeric character symbol has a binary representation, *but that representation is in no way connected with the quantity represented by the numeral.* In other words, the table of equivalences between printed symbols and binary symbols defines only the equivalences between data encoding schemes, without regard to any information that the data may harbor. The ASCII representation of the printable character symbol 4, for example, is 00110100 (34 hexadecimal). If this binary symbol were to be interpreted as a signed integer, it would have a value of $+52$ (decimal), which bears no relationship to the decimal value $+4$. In an 8-bit word,

the ASCII character 4 reads   0011   0100
the unsigned integer 4 reads   0000   0100

and the two are obviously not the same.

Symbols can be manipulated in various ways, and a number may be treated most effectively either as a symbol string or as a numeric value, depending on the purposes in view. Quite frequently people use numeric characters for purposes far removed from counting or arithmetic. For example, the telephone book entry

Bloggs J Q   2751 95 Ave   286-5987

contains several symbol strings that look like numbers, and are indeed recorded in print by using numeric characters, but convey no quantitative information. The two numbers that make up Mr. Bloggs' address contain information of a nonquantitative kind; if there is any doubt about that, it should be cleared up by examining the next entry in the same phone book,

Bloggs, K K   Granger House   Elm Ave   945-3321

from which it is evident that *95* and *Elm* are both names of streets, *2751* and *Granger House* the names of buildings. Despite their numeric appearance, *95* and *2751* are not measures of quantity. In a similar fashion, the telephone numbers are not measures of quantity, but only the identifying labels of individual telephone lines. Many such numeric-looking but nonquantitative names are in common use: driver's license numbers, bank account numbers and insurance policy numbers. If there is any doubt whether some numerical-looking data item really represents quantitative information, a good test is to ask: Will its average value, taken over the population of this city, tell me anything I may want to know? The average age or average macaroni consumption of all New Yorkers may interest an insurance agent or a restaurateur. But who would want to know their average telephone number?

Encoding choices

Nonnumeric information most usually arises in verbal form, but is frequently given numeric expression. For example, health insurance records (or driver's permits) often use the numeric encodings 1 and 0 to differentiate male from female policyholders. Clearly the numeric characters used have no quantitative significance at all; the alphabetic characters M and F could not only serve equally well, they would in fact be far superior because there would be much less doubt about which represents which.

Birth dates, employment dates, and other times and dates may or may not have quantitative importance, depending on their use. Tax authorities and clerks of court habitually use birth dates merely to discriminate between the many taxpayers named John Smith. Employers and insurance firms, on the other hand, may wish to determine age, length of employment, and other quantitative information from dates, in which case the dates themselves really are of significance as measures of time. If quantitative use is to be made of dates, the dates should be encoded in a form in which numeric manipulation is most easily carried out. At the very least, they should be encoded with the most significant figures (the year) in the most significant character positions, e.g., 1756 01 27 to signify Mozart's birthdate (27th January 1756.) If true numeric manipulation is required, the best technique is probably to reduce all data to days, beginning at some datum. Where to choose the datum depends on the nature of the data file. For employment records, for example, setting the time origin fifty or more years in the past should suffice; for a file of composers' birth dates, on the other hand, the beginning of the Christian era might not be too distant a time. The resulting numbers are not particularly huge, about 700000 days having passed since the birth of Christ.

The choice of data representation is a major issue in designing computer systems for use by people, for the frequency of operator error is a significant cost factor in using computers. It can be very strongly affected by selection of alphabet and form of encoding. The basic principle to be observed is to *shift routine work from man to machine wherever possible, never the other way around.* This principle is violated, for example, by the encoding *male = 0, female = 1*, which forces people, not computers, to remember (or to look up) which way around the digits were made to correspond to sexes. A similar problem arises with date encodings; 27 01 1756 is definitely not a better choice than 27 JA 1756. The all-numerals encoding scheme for dates is open not only to ambiguity, but down-right conflict; for example, 03 07 1848 signifies *March 7th* in American practice, but means *3rd of July* to an Englishman. On the other hand, both are likely to understand 03 JY 1848, which requires exactly as many characters!

Text masking

In processing nonnumeric data, specific characters or character strings are often searched for or examined, without contextual reference to the characters that precede or follow them. For example, suppose a file of birth dates is stored in a machine with 64-bit word length, and that it is desired to find out in what month Mozart was born. The date might be encoded as characters, in the form

00110010 00110111 01001010 01000001 00110001 00110111 00110101 00110110
  2   7   J   A   1   7   5   6

In other words, the 64 bits of each data word are used to store the day d, month m, and year y in 2, 2, and 4 bytes, respectively:

```
****************_____*******************************
     day            month              year
```

An inquiry about Mozart's month of birth should be answered by placing the identifying characters of the month in the least significant positions of a 64-bit word, preceded by null characters:

00000000 00000000 00000000 00000000 00000000 00000000 01001010 010000010
 NUL   NUL   NUL   NUL   NUL   NUL   J   A

To achieve this goal, two operations are needed: (a) to mask out all the unwanted data (day and year) and (b) to shift right so as to place the desired data item in the proper position. In other words, it is required to convert all unwanted data into null characters, while preserving all wanted data. This objective can be achieved by means of an operation called the *logical conjunction, bitwise AND* or *logical product*, of two words.

Formally, the logical product of two binary numbers is computed by taking the arithmetic product, but ignoring all carries. Another way of saying the same thing is that the logical product of two binary symbols A and B is a bit string such that each bit in it is set to 1 if (and only if) both A and B have 1 in the corresponding position. For example, the logical product of 001010110 and 010111010 is formed as

first operand	001010110
second operand	<u>010111010</u>
logical product	000010010

The birth–month masking required is easily achieved by means of a mask having zeros in all the unwanted positions, 1's in the positions occupied by the month:

000000000000000011111111111111110000000000000000000000000000000000

Because the logical product operation can yield a set bit (1) only if *both* operands have 1 in corresponding positions, the product of this masking word with any date whatever must produce zeros in the day and year positions. Correspondingly, it must produce an exact replica of the original data in the month position. For example, the logical product of this mask and the full date representation, in the particular case above, yields

00000000	00000000	11111111	11111111	00000000	00000000	00000000	00000000
00110010	00110111	01001010	01000001	00110001	00110111	00110101	00110110
2	7	J	A	1	7	5	6
00000000	00000000	01001010	01000001	00000000	00000000	00000000	00000000
NUL	NUL	J	A	NUL	NUL	NUL	NUL

which is precisely the desired result, except for repositioning the characters.

An alternative technique may be used, which produces a different but equally useful result. It employs the *bitwise OR*, otherwise known as the *logical sum* or *logical disjunction*. The logical sum of two words is a word obtained by the following rule: bit K in the result is reset to 0 if bit K is reset (0) in *both* operands, otherwise bit K of the result is set to 1. For example, the logical sum of 001 010 110 and 010 111 010 is

first operand	001010110
second operand	010111010
logical sum	011111110

For eliminating unwanted characters in the birth date record, it suffices to create the mask

111111111111111100000000000000000011111111111111111111111111111111111111

Because the logical sum operation can yield a reset bit (0) only if *both* operands have 0 in the corresponding position, the product of this masking word with any date whatever must produce ones everywhere in the day and year positions. Correspondingly, it must produce an exact replica of the original data in the month position. In the particular case already treated, the logical sum of this mask and the full date representation yields

11111111	11111111	00000000	00000000	11111111	11111111	11111111	11111111
00110010	00110111	01001010	01000001	00110001	00110111	00110101	00110110
2	7	J	A	1	7	5	6
11111111	11111111	01001010	01000001	11111111	11111111	11111111	11111111
NUL	NUL	J	A	NUL	NUL	NUL	NUL

which is precisely the desired result, except that the unwanted fields are set to all ones, instead of all zeros as was the case above; and except that the characters still need to be repositioned by shifting.

Operations for text manipulation

The primitive machine operations needed for successful manipulation of textual data do not differ markedly from those required to effect arithmetic processing of numerical data, because the internal representation of a character is indistinguishable from the internal machine representation of a small integer. Because an 8-bit representation permits 256 distinct symbols to be defined, there is room for the numerals, punctuation marks, one or more sets of Roman alphabetics, and other (including nonprintable) symbols besides, so 8-bit encoding is the most usual form.

Comparison and sequencing of characters can be accomplished using the same machine operations as are used for numeric work. However, text manipulation often requires rotation and masking, operations not always encountered in arithmetic processing. The operations of logical product and logical sum are essential for easy creation of masks, and are therefore included in the processing functions of most general-purpose computers.

It should be noted that the data symbols which represent numeric characters (numerals) are encoded as characters, and their encoding is unrelated to the numeric values they usually represent.

Representation of fractional numbers

Numbers are generally used for two different and quite distinct purposes: counting and measuring. Counting is always done by means of integers: one dog, two dogs, three dogs, . . . for there is no meaning in any but whole units of a countable entity. Measuring, on the other hand, is just as likely to deal with whole or fractional amounts. For scientific as well as commercial computing, the ability to deal with fractional numbers is therefore essential.

Fractional numbers

Fractions in the ordinary sense (three fifths, four thirds) are rarely convenient to represent in a digital computer, so they are only found in a few highly specialized machines. The common way of dealing with fractions in computers is the same as when working with pencil and paper: number representations are generalized to allow negative as well as positive powers of the radix. For example, when working by hand the decimal number 428 is understood to mean

$$428 = 4 * 10^2 + 2 * 10^1 + 8 * 10^0$$

and in an analogous fashion, the number 428.75 is taken to signify

$$428.75 = 4 * 10^2 + 2 * 10^1 + 8 * 10^0 + 7 * 10^{-1} + 5 * 10^{-2'}$$

The well-known convention here is that the coefficient string is written for the fractional number in exactly the same fashion as for the integer; but a decimal point is placed after the units digit to signify that all following digits are associated with negative powers of the base. In other words, the point serves to establish the dividing line between negative and nonnegative powers. Integers, of course, need no such mark. The absence of a point is always understood to mean that the rightmost digit is the coefficient of 10^0.

Fractional numbers are represented in other number systems in a precisely analogous fashion. For example, the binary number 1101.01 means

$$1101.01_2 = 1 * 2^3 + 1 * 2^2 + 0 * 2^1 + 1 * 2^0 + 0 * 2^{-1} + 1 * 2^{-2}$$

and the quinary number 42.31_5 means

$$42.31_5 = 4 * 5^1 + 2 * 5^0 + 3 * 5^{-1} + 1 * 5^{-2} .$$

The character that separates nonnegative from negative exponents is known as the *decimal point, binary point, quinary point*, etc., according to the number system in use.

Radix conversion

An essential operation required whenever numbers occur in computing is radix conversion, the rewriting of a number initially known in one number system so as to have it represented in another with a different base. The essence of radix conversion with fractional numbers is just the same as it is with integers: radix conversion recasts the number so that the powers of its new base b are clearly associated with multiplying coefficients.

Specific techniques for actually performing the conversion are perhaps most easily introduced by example. Suppose the decimal number 0.8125 is to be represented in binary form. Clearly its binary representation contains no units (units are units in any number system!) and therefore has the form 0.*xxx*. . . where *x* denotes an as yet unknown digit. The first significant digit can be ascertained by writing

$$0.8125_{10} = [2 * 0.8125] * 2^{-1} + fract(2 * 0.8125) * 2^{-1}$$

Here the square brackets denote the largest integer contained in the bracketed quantity, while *fract( )* denotes the fractional part of a number. Writing out in detail,

$$0.8125_{10} = 1 * 2^{-1} + 0.6250_{10} * 2^{-1}.$$

Thus the first fractional digit is 1. Continuing, the remaining portion of the fraction may be rewritten analogously, multiplying by 2 and then subdividing into an integer and a fractional part:

$$0.8125_{10} = 1 * 2^{-1} + [2 * 0.6250] * 2^{-2} + fract(2 * 0.6250) * 2^{-2}$$

or

$$0.8125_{10} = 1 * 2^{-1} + 1 * 2^{-2} + 0.25_{10} * 2^{-2}.$$

The next step is to multiply the remaining decimal quantity by 2 again, then split it into integer and fractional parts:

$$0.8125_{10} = 1 * 2^{-1} + 1 * 2^{-2} + 0 * 2^{-3} + 0.5_{10} * 2^{-3}.$$

Continuing with another similar step,

$$0.8125_{10} = 1 * 2^{-1} + 1 * 2^{-2} + 0 * 2^3 + 1 * 2^{-4}$$

and the process terminates. The result is

$$0.8125_{10} = 0.1101_2.$$

The procedure used here is not specific to decimal–binary conversion, but could be used for conversion to any number system. To represent the fractional number N in a number system with base b, the following algorithm, of which the above process is an illustrative case, may be used:

1. Set $F^{(0)} = N$.
2. Form the sequence of fractions and integers $F^{(j)}$ and $I^{(j)}$, $F^{(j)} = fract(b * F^{(j-1)})$, $I^{(j)} = [b * F^{(j-1)}]$, for $j = 1, \ldots, k$.
3. Obtain the base-b representation N_b by writing down all the integer parts in order.

This procedure differs from the analogous algorithm for integer conversion, in that it generates digits $I^{(j)}$ in left-to-right order, beginning with the most significant one.

The above discussion has ignored throughout the possibility that the number N to be converted might be an improper fraction, i.e., that it might have both an integer and a fractional part. Indeed, the technique shown cannot work for such numbers; neither can the method given for integers. Both start at the digit associated with zero exponent, i.e., both start at the decimal point, and work outward from there, the one toward larger exponents, the other toward smaller ones. The best way of handling improper fractions is in fact to write them as sums of integers and proper fractions, then to convert these two parts separately. For example, the number 5.125_{10} is written in two parts,

$$5.125 = 5 + 0.125$$

of which the first part is a pure integer, the other a proper fraction. These are then converted to binary notation in two separate steps:

$$5_{10} = 101_2,$$
$$0.125_{10} = 0.001_2,$$

so that on rejoining the individual parts, the correct answer is obtained as $5.125_{10} = 101.001_2$.

Rounding

When fractional numbers are converted from one number system to another, as between decimal and binary notations, it is quite impossible to forecast exactly how many binary digits will correspond to a certain number of decimal places, or vice versa. The conversion algorithm shown here generates one additional significant digit at each step; but just how many steps are needed is never known in advance. Because working registers are invariably limited to a certain length, say k digits, the usual procedure is to carry out k steps of the conversion process, then stop. The conversion does not necessarily yield an exact representation of N, for the number of digits required may be larger than that. Indeed, many fractions are exactly expressible with a finite number of digits in one number system but not in another. For example, the fraction *one third* has the following representations in notations with various different bases b:

0.0101010101 ...	recurring	for $b =$	2
0.1	terminating	$b =$	3
0.1111111111 ...	recurring	$b =$	4
0.1313131313 ...	recurring	$b =$	5
0.2	terminating	$b =$	6
0.2222222222 ...	recurring	$b =$	7
0.2525252525 ...	recurring	$b =$	8
0.3	terminating	$b =$	9
0.3333333333 ...	recurring	$b =$	10

It cannot be known ahead of time whether a particular fractional number N has a finite (terminating) representation in a particular number system. In this respect, fractions contrast sharply with integers, for every integer has a finite representation in every number system.

When the number of digits required for exact representation is larger than the number k of digits available, two possibilities exist: to *truncate*, by simply leaving off any further digits, no matter what their values, or to *round*, by adjusting the last digit so as to minimize the error that arises from not continuing. To round, the remainder after the first k digits is examined to see whether to round up or down. Rounding is always carried out according to a well-known rule: *if the remainder is less than one-half unit in the least significant place, round down; otherwise, round up.* To four digits, then, one-third is approximated by

0.0101	for $b =$	2
0.1000	$b =$	3
0.1111	$b =$	4
0.1313	$b =$	5
. . . . .	. . . . .	
0.3333	$b =$	10

If the remainder happens to be just exactly half a unit in the kth place, the rounding error is equal whichever way rounding is done. The rule of rounding up in this case is really quite arbitrary.

Working in binary notation, the rounding process is particularly easy. In binary notation, any fraction smaller than one-half must begin with a zero digit, and any fraction larger than one-half must begin with a 1:

$$0.4999999999\ldots_{10} = 0.0111111111\ldots_{2}$$
$$0.5_{10} \qquad\qquad\quad = 0.1_{2}$$

To determine the correct way to round, it suffices to calculate one extra digit beyond the k digits to be retained. If the extra digit is 1, rounding up is indicated; 1 is therefore added to the kth digit previously calculated. If the extra digit is 0, rounding down is indicated; that is accomplished by adding 0 to the kth digit. The amount to be added to the kth digit to achieve correct rounding is precisely equal to the value of the extra $(k + 1^{st})$ digit in every case. Consequently, there is no need to examine numbers and to base decisions on the outcome of the examination; it suffices to compute the extra digit and to add its value to the kth digit, thereby achieving correct rounding in every case.

To illustrate the simplicity of this process, consider the number $0.84375_{10} = 0.11011_{2}$. If a three-digit representation is all that is permitted, $k = 3$, then the conversion is carried out to three digits,

$$0.84375_{10} = 0.110_{2} + remainder$$

Continuing the computation one more step, the fourth digit in the remainder (the first omitted digit) is found to be 1,

$$remainder = 0.0001xxxx_{2}.$$

The remainder is truncated at that digit,

$$truncated\ remainder = 0.0001_{2}.$$

It is doubled, so as to shift the $k + 1^{st}$ digit value into the kth digit. The doubled value is added to the k-digit result:

$$
\begin{aligned}
k\text{-digit result} &= 0.110 \\
\text{double truncated remainder} &= \underline{\quad 1} \\
\text{Rounded value of } 0.84375_{10} &= 0.111_{2}
\end{aligned}
$$

It should be evident that a similar process, with zero added, will apply to rounding at two figures, with 0.11_{2} the rounded result.

Representation in finite machines

Fractional numbers encountered in scientific computing range over a very wide spectrum of magnitudes. Distances, for example, vary from the subatomic to the intergalactic, covering more than fifty (decimal) orders of magnitude. As a convenience, written scientific communication often uses *scientific notation* for decimal numbers, with the *mantissa* separated from the *exponent* of 10. Thus, Avogadro's number is normally written as $6.02 * 10^{23}$, Planck's constant as $6.624 * 10^{-27}$ erg-seconds. In scientific computation, where subscripts and superscripts are only rarely available, the letter E (for *exponent*) is used, so Avogadro's number is rendered as 6.02E+23 and Planck's constant as 6.624E−27.

To represent fractional numbers on a digital computer, it is obviously desirable to make the best possible use of the finite number of digits available. The methods commonly used are similar in principle to the scientific notation employed with pencil and paper: the exponent and mantissa are given separate representations and stored in separate portions of the same computer word. The exponents are chosen to ensure that the binary point always falls at the same place; for once it is known where it is located, no space needs to be allotted for storing it. Probably the most common technique is to normalize numbers so that the first nonzero digit falls immediately to the right of the binary (or decimal) point. In this way Avogadro's number would be rendered as $0.602 * 10^{24}$ in a computer using decimal notation internally, and Planck's constant would appear as $0.6624 * 10^{-26}$. Of course, most computers work in binary rather than decimal notation internally. The number representation therefore uses a similar principle, but applied to binary rather than to decimal digit strings.

The internal representation of fractional numbers requires representation of a fraction (the mantissa of the number) and an exponent. Numbers so represented in registers of finite length are said to be in *floating-point* notation. In most computers the fraction is stored in sign and magnitude form, despite the inconvenience of a duplicated zero. The exponent is stored as a twos complement integer in some machines, and in a different form, called *excess-N* notation, in others. The principle of such notations is extremely simple: the number N, chosen to be conveniently large, is added to all exponents prior to storage, and subtracted before every processing step, so that only positive numbers are ever stored. These can then be stored as unsigned integers. Many small- and medium-sized computers use excess-128 notation, in which the exponents −128 to +127 (corresponding to the powers 2^{-128} to 2^{127}) are stored as the unsigned integers 000 to 255. Because 2^{-128} and 2^{127} correspond to $2.939 * 10^{-39}$ and $1.7014 * 10^{38}$ respectively, the resulting number range is quite sufficient for most scientific or technical calculations.

There are many floating-point representations of numbers, all differing slightly in details. In computers using 32-bit registers, for example, one acceptable floating-point number representation takes the form

bit 31:   sign, 0 for positive
bits 30–23:   exponent, in excess–128 form,
bits 22–0:   mantissa, with binary point at extreme left.

A simple example may serve to illustrate the technique. The number 4.3671875_{10} reads, in binary notation,

$$4.3671875_{10} = 100.0101111_2$$

or

$$4.3671875_{10} = 0.1000101111 * 2^3.$$

The sign is positive, so the high-order bit in the floating-point representation of this number is 0. The positive exponent 3 is augmented by 128 to bring it into the excess–128 notation, and bits 30–23 of the floating-point representation are set to the unsigned binary equivalent of 131_{10}, or 10000011. The balance of the 32 bits is occupied by the mantissa:

It should be noted that neither the mantissa nor the exponent is represented in twos complement notation.

To simplify discussion, the floating-point value of a binary symbol S in this representation will be referred to as *float(S)*. This notation parallels *int(S)*, *ascii(S)*, and the like. As with integers and characters, the binary symbol S itself is merely a collection of 32 bits; whether to interpret it as a floating-point number, an integer, or a character string is for the user to decide.

Relationship to integers

Fractional number representations in finite-length registers are frequently referred to as *real number* representations. This term is descriptive, but not entirely accurate. Mathematically speaking, real numbers are *dense*—there are infinitely many real numbers in the interval between any two real numbers—whereas the floating-point numbers representable in a computer are not, for they have only a finite number of digits.

The floating-point interpretation *float(S)* of a 32-bit binary symbol S establishes a one-to-one correspondence between the set of all 2^{32} possible symbols S, and a certain finite set of real numbers. Similarly, the twos complement integer interpretation *int2(S)* establishes a unique correspondence between the set of all symbols S, and the integers from -2^{31} to $+2^{31} - 1$, that is, from -2147483654 to $+2147483653$. Since there exist exactly 2^{32} such symbols, at most 2^{32} floating-point numbers can be represented, or the same number of integers. (Whether a particular binary symbol is intended to represent one or the other quantity cannot be discovered by examining the symbol itself.) The interesting point is that every symbol S corresponds uniquely to both an integer *int2(S)* and a floating-point number *float(S)*, so a correspondence must also exist between the floating-point numbers and the integers. To put the matter in a nutshell: every twos complement integer corresponds to exactly one floating-point number. The converse is not true, for *float(S)* is a sign-and-magnitude notation. Hence, there will be duplication at least to the extent of having two symbols for zero, one positive and one negative.

The correspondence of integers and real numbers, and the impossibility of covering all real numbers, is readily illustrated by examining a set of examples. A selection of binary symbols (expressed in hexadecimal notation for the sake

Symbol S	Value int2(S)	Mantissa (decimal)	Power of 2	Real number float(S)
7FFFFFFF	2147483647	+8388607	+104	1.7014116E+38
7FFFFFFE	2147483646	+8388606	+104	1.7014114E+38
7FFFFFFD	2147483645	+8388605	+104	1.7014112E+38
7FC00000	2143289344	+4194304	+104	8.5070592E+37
41C00000	1103101952	+4194304	-20	4.0000000E+00
41400000	1094713344	+4194304	-21	2.0000000E+00
40C00003	1086324739	+4194307	-22	1.0000007E+00
40C00002	1086324738	+4194306	-22	1.0000005E+00
40C00001	1086324737	+4194305	-22	1.0000002E+00
40C00000	1086324736	+4194304	-22	1.0000000E+00
40400000	1077936128	+4194304	-23	5.0000000E-01
3FC00000	1069547520	+4194304	-24	2.5000000E-01
3F400000	1061158912	+4194304	-25	1.2500000E-01
00400002	4194306	+4194306	-151	1.4693686E-39
00400001	4194305	+4194305	-151	1.4693683E-39
00400000	4194304	+4194304	-151	1.4693679E-39
00000000	0	+0	-151	0.0000000E+00
80000000	-2147483648	-0	-151	0.0000000E+00
BF400000	-1086324736	-4194304	-25	-1.2500000E-01
BFC00000	-1077936128	-4194304	-24	-2.5000000E-01
C0400000	-1069547520	-4194304	-23	-5.0000000E-01
C0C00000	-1061158912	-4194304	-22	-1.0000000E+00
C1400000	-1052770304	-4194304	-21	-2.0000000E+00
FFFFFFFD	-3	-8388605	+104	-1.7014112E+38
FFFFFFFE	-2	-8388606	+104	-1.7014114E+38
FFFFFFFF	-1	-8388607	+104	-1.7014116E+38

Fig. 1.2. Integer and floating-point interpretations of 32-bit symbols, expressed in hexadecimal notation.

of brevity) appears in Fig. 1.2, along with their integer (unsigned as well as twos complement) and floating-point interpretations. The largest number representable, as well as the smallest, are clearly finite. Unlike the real numbers of mathematics, *float(S)* numbers are not dense; the nearest numbers to 1.7014114E+ 38 are located 2.E+31 above and below, no intervening values can be given a representation because no binary symbols can exist between 7FFFFFFE$_{16}$ and 7FFFFFFD$_{16}$. Of course, exactly the same is true for negative floating-point numbers. Numerical analysts often describe how dense the floating-point numbers are by referring to the *machine epsilon*, the smallest number that can be added to 1 while still making the result distinguishable from unity. For a 32-bit machine using the *float(S)* notation, the machine epsilon is 2.E-07. This can be seen by examining the numerical values in Fig. 1.2: altering the symbol 40C00000, which represents 1.0000000E+00, by 1 in the least significant binary digit yields 1.0000002E+00.

It will be evident from Fig. 1.2 that there is no unique representation of the value *zero* in the *float(S)* notation; 00000000$_{16}$ and 80000000$_{16}$ differ in the sign

Symbol S	Value int2(S)	Mantissa (decimal)	Power of 2	Real number float(S)
3B000000	989855744	+0	-33	0.0000000E+00
00000000	0	+0	-151	0.0000000E+00
80000000	-2147483648	-0	-151	0.0000000E+00
8F800000	-1887436800	-0	-120	0.0000000E+00
A7000000	-1493172224	-0	-73	0.0000000E+00

Fig. 1.3.   The value *zero* does not have a unique floating point representation in the *float(S)* notation.

bit but are otherwise alike, so there is a distinction in symbols (though not in value) between $+0$ and -0. In fact, there are many more ways of representing zero, for *any* setting of the sign and exponent bits can represent zero, provided the mantissa bits are all zero. Thus there are no less than $2^9 = 8192$ ways of writing *zero*! A few of these appear, by way of illustration, in Fig. 1.3.

The particular choice of bit values in the floating-point representation described here may seem a little peculiar, but it has an interesting property that makes it advantageous in practical computing. With this choice of representation, positive floating-point numbers are in one-to-one correspondence with the positive integers. In fact, for all positive real numbers the correspondence is an *isomorphism*: the larger of two positive integers always corresponds to the larger of the corresponding floating-point numbers, and vice versa. Thus

$$\text{if} \quad int2(S_1) < int2(S_2) \quad (\text{provided } int2(S_1) > 0)$$
$$\text{then} \quad float(S_1) < float(S_2)$$

This assertion may be verified by examining Fig. 1.4. Furthermore, it is not difficult to prove in a general case. Leaving aside the sign bits and taking the most significant bits first,

1. If the exponents of *float(S₁)* and *float(S₂)* differ so that $float(S_1) > float(S_2)$, then bits 31–23 of S_1 make up a larger 9-bit twos complement integer than

Symbol S	Value int2(S)	Mantissa (decimal)	Power of 2	Real number float(S)
11400000	289406976	+4194304	-117	2.5243549E-29
10401000	272633856	+4198400	-119	6.3170502E-30
10400000	272629760	+4194304	-119	6.3108872E-30
91400000	-1858076672	-4194304	-117	-2.5243549E-29
90401000	-1874849792	-4198400	-119	-6.3170502E-30
90400000	-1874853888	-4194304	-119	-6.3108872E-30

Fig. 1.4.   Positive *float(S)* numbers are ordered like the positive integers, simplifying comparison.

the corresponding bits of S_2. In other words, if $float(S_1)$ and $float(S_2)$ differ because their exponents differ, then $float(S_2) > float(S_2)$ implies $int2(S_1) > int2(S_2)$.

2. If $float(S_1)$ and $float(S_2)$ have the same exponents, S_1 and S_2 only differ in bits 22–0. Since the mantissa bits of a floating-point number are stored in a natural binary fashion, $float(S_1) > float(S_2$ implies $int2(S_1) > int2(S_2)$.

These relationships are clearly illustrated by the first few lines in Fig. 1.4. The first and third numbers, $S = 11400000$ and $S = 10400000$, differ only in the exponent bits; clearly, the orderings of their integer and floating interpretations coincide. The second and third lines differ only in mantissa, their exponents are identical; again, the ordering is correct. It is worth noting that negative numbers are also ordered consistently, in descending order of absolute value.

Because the integer interpretations of the same bit patterns have precisely the same *ordering* as the floating-point numbers that their binary symbols represent, comparison of two floating-point numbers can be achieved without actually performing floating-point subtractions. Avoiding floating-point subtractions is advantageous in applications, because they require relatively large amounts of arithmetic. Instead, it suffices to sort the integers even though their *values* are only tenuously related to those of the fractional numbers. Only a small amount of additional work is required to take care of sign bits as well as of the multiple representations of *zero*.

Floating-point arithmetic

When fractional numbers are added their magnitudes must be adjusted so that digit positions coincide. To illustrate, suppose it is desired to add the numbers $A = 0.602501 * 10^{18}$ and $B = 0.310011 * 10^{16}$ using decimal arithmetic and carrying 6 mantissa digits. This task can be accomplished using only the basic tool of integer addition, as follows.

To begin, the two numbers are compared, to establish which has the larger magnitude; in the present case, of course, $A > B$. The larger number is then rewritten so that all its digits represent whole numbers:

$$A = 602501 * 10^{12}$$

Next, B is scaled so that its exponent is the same as that of A. Any remaining fractional part of B is discarded:

$$B = 3100 * 10^{12}.$$

The two numbers are then written beneath each other, and integer addition of the mantissas proceeds as usual:

$$
\begin{array}{rl}
A & = 602501 * 10^{12} \\
B & = \underline{3100 * 10^{12}} \\
A + B & = 605601 * 10^{12}
\end{array}
$$

Finally, the result is rescaled to fit the usual normalized form, with the decimal point in front of the most significant digit. The result is $A + B = 0.605601 * 10^{18}$.

Floating-point addition and subtraction operations are not subject to the same overflow problems as integers, because any tendency to an excess of digits can be handled by rescaling exponents and dropping some trailing digits from the mantissa. However, it is possible to overflow the exponent range. Similarly, attempts to compute very small numbers can lead to the exponent becoming too small to be representable, as must happen for any number smaller than 2^{-128} in the examples shown. A similar situation cannot occur with integers, because in the world of integers, the next smaller number after 1 is 0, both representable in twos complement arithmetic. In most computer systems, any attempt to compute such very small numbers is considered to lead to an error condition termed *floating-point underflow*. The opposite situation, in which the permissible exponent range is exceeded in the upward direction, is (reasonably enough!) called a *floating-point overflow* condition.

Floating-point multiplication and division, the remaining two elementary arithmetic operations, are comparatively easy operations to carry out. To multiply two floating-point numbers, it is necessary to multiply the mantissas, using the same multiplication rules as apply to integers, and to add their exponents. Division is handled analogously. Thus the four ordinary arithmetic operations on floating-point numbers require the computer only to be able to add, shift, and complement. There is no need for any data manipulation operations besides those required for integer arithmetic.

Standard floating-point formats

The subdivision of a bit string into exponent and mantissa fields, as well as the choice of twos complement or excess-128 notation for the exponent, are essentially arbitrary matters in which several different decisions could be taken. It should therefore not come as a surprise that computers made by various manufacturers have at times used different conventions for encoding floating-point numbers. To allow movement of data as well as processes from one computer to another, however, standardization of notation is desirable. Two standards are widely used: the IEEE floating-point format and the USASI Fortran format. Both prescribe the manner in which numbers are to be represented, and also the manner in which arithmetic is to be carried out. Hence, two more fractional numeric interpretations of a 32-bit word need to be considered: *ieee(X)* and *usasi(X)*. These are as set out in the following.

The floating-point representation adopted by the IEEE Computer Society is widely used, particularly in small computer applications. In its basic form, it assumes a 32-bit word organized in exactly the manner shown above: one sign bit and eight exponent bits are followed by 23 bits of mantissa. The difference between the *ieee(X)* and *float(X)* notations resides in a clever idea called *hidden bit normalization*. In *float(X)* notation, exponents are adjusted so that the first nonzero digit always falls immediately to the right of the binary point. In the IEEE notation, the binary point is placed just *after* the first nonzero digit. The only nonzero binary digit is 1, so this leading digit is always 1. But if that digit is known to be 1, there is no longer any point in storing it in a computer word. The mantissa actually stored is therefore the correct one, but with the leading 1 suppressed. It is known to be 1, so it can be omitted to save storage, restored easily whenever required for arithmetic or any other purpose.

Difficulties arise with hidden bit normalization in representing the number zero and numbers very close to it. If a number is zero or very small, it may not be possible to normalize it so as to have a nonzero digit following the binary point, because such normalization may require a smaller exponent than can be represented with the bits available for it. This difficulty is dealt with in the IEEE standard by interpreting numbers with a zero exponent differently from the rest: hidden bit normalization does *not* apply if the exponent bits are all zero. The exponent is written in excess-126 (not 128) notation to compensate for this exception.

A second key difference between the IEEE notation and the simpler *float(X)* form applies to large exponents. If all exponent bits are set to 1, the IEEE standard calls for the mantissa to have an exceptional interpretation: if all mantissa bits are cleared to 0, the number is taken as having *infinite* value, whereas a mantissa containing any nonzero bits signifies *not a number*. By adopting this special convention, it becomes possible to make mathematical computing routines signal impossibilities. For example, a program to compute the arc sine of a number may return the answer "not a number" to signify that there is no real angle whose sine is 2.

The USASI floating-point standard applies strictly only to the Fortran language, but is also employed elsewhere. It assumes a 32-bit word organized as follows:

bit 31	sign
bits 30–24	exponent (7 bits)
bits 23–00	mantissa (24 bits).

In *usasi(X)* notation the exponent bits do not represent the exponent of 2, but of 16. A larger range of exponent values is therefore available, even though the number of exponent bits is only 7, not 8 as in *ieee(X)*. Using a radix different from 2, however, precludes hidden bit normalization. The mantissa is therefore given in straightforward form, with all bits present. There is no hidden bit; but this shortcoming is exactly compensated by a mantissa one bit longer. The number 0.00 is taken care of in a manner similar to the IEEE standard, by clearing all 32 bits to zero.

Binary coded decimal representation

In financial data processing it is usual to carry accounts to the nearest minimal currency unit—cents, pence, kopecks, or gurushes. Binary scientific notation is sometimes not satisfactory for such purposes and an alternative notation, called *binary coded decimal* or *BCD* representation, is used instead.

Why the financial data processing community should have cause to be dissatisfied may be seen from a simple numerical example. Suppose some item to have a value of ten cents, or $0.10. In binary fractional representation,

$$0.1_{10} = 0.000110011001_2.$$

The binary fraction does not terminate, but continues forever with a recursion of the four-digit group 1100. However, in any real computer only a finite number of digits can be handled, and for illustrative purposes a mantissa length of 12 bits is assumed in this example.

If one item has a value of 10 cents, ten items have ten times as great a value. That is, the value V of ten items is calculated as

$$V = 10_{10} * 0.10_{10}$$
$$= 1010_2 * 0.000110011001_2.$$

The binary multiplication is readily carried out, yielding

$$V = 0.111111111010_2.$$

To find out just what this number represents in decimal notation, the base conversion algorithm described previously is applied: multiply by ten, separate integer and fractional parts, multiply the fractional part by ten again, and so on until done. The multiplication must be done in binary notation, of course, for that is the only notation in which the number V is known. The first step, multiplying by 1010 (the binary equivalent of decimal 10) runs

$$
\begin{array}{r}
1010 \quad * \quad 0.111111111010 \\
\hline
1.11111111010 \\
111.111111010 \\
\hline
1001.1111110001
\end{array}
$$

so that the first significant digit in the decimal representation is 9 (the decimal equivalent of 1001). Continuing until there are no more nonzero digits left in V,

$$V = 0.9985703125$$

or, to four decimal digits whose precision corresponds reasonably closely to that given by 12 bits,

$$V = 0.9986$$

Obviously, the error in computing 10 * 0.1 this way is 0.14%. Although this error may seem small, and would naturally be even smaller if more than 12 bits were carried in the binary fraction, it is considered unacceptable in many commercial applications because it is a *cumulative* error. The ten-cent items are all entered into the calculation slightly under their precise value, so that after extensive arithmetic has been performed the error may become quite significant.

To avoid the errors that may arise from truncation of recurring fractions, some commercial data processing is actually carried out in decimal arithmetic, using BCD encoding for the numbers. In this notation, each decimal digit is represented in four bits, in natural (unsigned) integer notation. The decimal number 827, for example, then appears in a 12-bit word as 1000 0010 0111, each grouping of four bits representing one digit.

It should be pointed out that the preference for BCD encoding has nothing to do with any inherent properties of binary notation, but rather with the habits of the world of commerce. The great majority of prices and quantities are specified as exact numbers in decimal notation, and some of them turn out not to have terminating binary fractional forms. Decimal arithmetic is neither better nor worse than binary when dealing with arbitrary numeric data. Financial computing, on the other hand, involves data exactly expressible in decimal notation, but only approximately representable in binary. For such data, decimal arithmetic and decimal representations will always be superior.

The existence of binary coded decimal notation adds yet another possible way of interpreting a binary symbol. In addition to the foregoing interpretations of a symbol S, there is now $bcd(S)$. The entire repertoire of interpretations thus amounts to

unsigned integer	$int(S)$
twos complement integer	$int2(S)$
character	$ascii(S)$
fractional number	$float(S)$
IEEE floating-point number	$ieee(S)$
USASI floating-point number	$usasi(S)$
BCD number	$bcd(S)$

Some binary symbols S do exist for which $bcd(S)$ is undefined. In fact, none of the 4-bit symbols $1010 - 1111$ have a BCD interpretation. In this respect, $bcd(S)$ differs from most other interpretations of binary symbols: not all the possible symbols in the available range are actually used.

Problems

1. Write the unsigned decimal numbers 3, 7, 10, 21, 127 in binary notation.
2. Write the unsigned binary numbers 00010, 00100, 01011, 11011 in decimal notation.
3. Write the unsigned binary numbers 00010, 00100, 01011, 11011 in octal notation.
4. Convert the numbers 113_{10}, 10110110_2, and $7E_{16}$ so as to express each number in binary, octal, decimal, and hexadecimal notations.
5. Express the binary number 1101 0111 1001 in base 4 notation by inspection. Verify correctness by writing out the numeric factors in detail.
6. Express the binary number 1101 0111 1001 in base 32 notation by inspection. Verify correctness by writing out the numeric factors in detail.

7. What is the largest number of digits that might be required for storage of the result when two n-bit binary numbers are added? Give a proof for the general case, and illustrate with numeric values for $n = 5$.

8. What is the largest number of digits that might be required for storage of the result when two n-bit binary numbers are multiplied? Give a proof for the general case, and illustrate with numeric values for $n = 5$.

9. Prove that $shra(shl(X)) = X$ provided that certain conditions are satisfied. What are these conditions?

10. Unsigned 8-digit binary coded decimal numbers are conveniently stored in a 32-bit computer register. Write the binary, octal, and hexadecimal representations of the 32-bit register contents corresponding to the decimal numbers 20117538 and 90091375.

11. Using the BCD coding scheme as described, do successive binary coded decimal numbers correspond to successive unsigned integers? to twos complement integers? Is the set of all values $bcd(S)$ ordered like the set of all integer values $int(S)$? like all twos complement integer values $int2(S)$?

12. A fractional number representation different from that discussed is obtained if binary numbers are written so that the mantissa is smaller than unity, while the exponent of 2 is always a multiple of 4. For example, the number $0.11001010 * 2^3$ may be written alternatively as $0.01100101 * 2^4$, which is equivalent to $0.01100101 * 16^1$. Fractional numbers could therefore be represented in 32-bit registers in the following form, which will be referred to as $float16(S)$:

> bit 31   sign, 0 denoting positive,
> bits 30–25   exponent of 16, in excess–32 notation,
> bits 24–0   mantissa.

Write the decimal number 5.34375 in both the $float16(S)$ and $float(S)$ forms. Under what conditions does $int2(S_1) > int2(S_2)$ imply $float16(S_1) > float16(S_2)$?

13. What is the *range of decimal numbers* representable in $float16(S)$ notation? If R is an arbitrary real number within the exponent range for both notations, is it likely to be approximated with greater precision using $float16(S)$ than when using $float(S)$? Why?

14. Write out the 32-bit binary symbol corresponding to the ASCII character string FRED. If S stands for this character string, calculate and express in decimal notation

> $int(S)$,
> $int2(S)$,
> $bcd(S)$,
> $float(S)$.

15. What is the range of available decimal numbers in $ieee(X)$ floating-point notation? Are the numbers ordered like the unsigned integers

16. What is the range of available decimal numbers in $usasi(X)$ floating-point notation? Are the numbers ordered like the unsigned integers?

17. For maintaining student records, a 16-bit date representation $date(S)$ may be used, in which

> bits 15–9   represent the year, less 1900,
> bits 8–5   represent the month,
> bits 4–0   represent the date.

Can dates be sorted chronologically by sorting the corresponding unsigned integers? i.e., is it true that that $date(S_1) > date(S_2)$ if and only if $int(S_1) > int(S_2)$?

18. Write the 16-bit string S corresponding to today's date according to the above scheme, i.e, so that

$$today = date(S).$$

Does this 16-bit string always represent a printable pair of ASCII characters?

19. A 16-bit number can always be printed as four ASCII characters by taking 4 bits at a time and adding 20_{16} to each 4-bit substring. What is the character string corresponding to the serial number of this month, reckoned from the beginning of the Christian era?

20. The *float(S)* representation as detailed in the foregoing text reserves 23 bits for the mantissa. How many decimal digits are needed to achieve comparable precision?

21. Show that one, and only one, floating-point number *float(S)* corresponds to any one binary symbol S. (Hint: suppose the contrary.)

22. One interesting scheme for encoding of decimally expressed numbers employs four bits per digit; the low-order three bits count from 0 to 4, and the most significant bit indicates the presence or absence of an additional 5. This scheme is called *biquinary* notation. Define procedures for converting BCD encoded numbers to biquinary form and back.

2
Digital logic circuits

Digital logic circuits are the fundamental working parts of computers. They are the devices able to manipulate data as required in digital computing—to add and shift, to complement and decrement. A study of computer engineering must involve at least a cursory study of these basic building blocks. This chapter examines the principles of simple logic circuits and briefly introduces the subject of digital circuit design, a fascinating area of study in its own right.

Digital circuit elements

The study of digital logic begins with the electronic circuits that actually make up computers, but it quickly departs from that electrical starting point to become a study of the logical functions, thus blending electronics and mathematics. In the world of digital logic, the term *logical function* denotes a function (in the mathematical sense of that word) whose value can can be either *true* or *false*, depending on its *arguments*, which also have logical (*true* or *false*) values. Logical functions are computed by means of *logic circuits*, which express logical function values as the presence (or absence) of an electrical signal. The principal logic circuit elements are outlined in the this and the following sections, both as to how they function physically and how they can fit together to constitute computing circuits.

Switches as circuit components

The simplest possible logic device known is an ordinary switch, which can make a signal appear or disappear and thereby signify the logical values *true* and *false*. Logic circuits constructed of simple switches are basic to the study of all logic circuits, because the fast electronic circuits employing transistors in fact operate in a switch-like fashion. Indeed the vast majority of electronic logic circuits are designed and built in exactly the same fashion as circuits using simple manual switches, the difference being that the switches themselves are made up of transistors. They are therefore both very fast and electronically controllable, characteristics fundamental to building computers.

To illustrate how switches may be used to construct logic circuits, consider the simple circuit of Fig. 2.1. This circuit contains two independent switches that may be either closed or open. If both switches are open, the output voltage y will

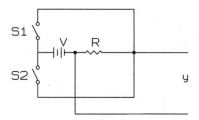

Fig. 2.1. A simple switch circuit.

clearly be zero; if either switch is closed, y must take on the value V. Closing both switches is equivalent to closing one, in that the output voltage remains at V when the second switch is closed. This circuit is of practical value in ringing a doorbell: if the load R represents a doorbell and the two switches are bellpushes at the front and back doors, then the bell will ring if either or both bellpushes are pressed.

The circuit of Fig. 2.1 clearly has four possible states: both switches closed, *S1* closed, *S2* closed, or both switches open. These possible states can be described in a table where one column corresponds to each switch, a closed switch being represented by writing 1 in the appropriate column while an open switch is denoted by 0. In a similar way, the output column contains 1 if a voltage appears at the output, 0 if it does not.

Switch $S1$	Switch $S2$	Output $f(S1,S2)$
0	0	0
0	1	1
1	0	1
1	1	1

A symbolic representation of the output can be given in algebraic form, as

$$y = f(S1,S2).$$

The function $f(S1,S2)$ is completely defined by giving all its possible values in a table, as shown. The particular function implemented by the circuit of Fig. 2.1 is easily recognized as logical summation (the OR operation): an output voltage appears when *either* switch *S1* is closed *or* switch *S2* is closed *or* when both switches are closed.

Another switch circuit is shown in Fig. 2.2. It will be evident that in this case, an output voltage appears if and only if *both* switches are closed,

Switch $S1$	Switch $S2$	Output $g(S1,S2)$
0	0	0
0	1	0
1	0	0
1	1	1

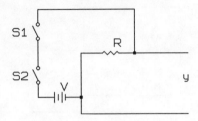

Fig. 2.2.   Series switch circuit.

This circuit is commonly used in domestic burglar alarms. Switches *S1* and *S2* are attached to the front and back doors, and the output voltage *y* is used to activate a relay that keeps the alarm bell or siren from sounding. If either door is opened, or if there is a power failure so that the alarm system ceases to function, the output voltage *y* falls to zero, the relay no longer restrains the bell, and the alarm sounds. Formally, the output voltage may be described by a functional representation such as

$$y = g(S1,S2)$$

where the function is defined by the table given. This function described is the *logical product*, obtained by the logical AND operation.

Tables that completely define a logical function, such as those shown above for the functions *f(S1,S2)* and *g(S1,S2)*, are known as *truth tables*. They are commonly used to describe logical functions. A truth table need not be limited to only two arguments, but may be extended to as many as required. For example, the circuit of Fig. 2.2 is often enlarged in burglar alarm applications to include many switches, one for every door and window of the house. The truth table then describes a logical function *y* with *n* arguments,

$$y = g(S1,S2,\ldots,Sn).$$

Correspondingly, the truth table that defines the function will have $n + 1$ columns (*n* inputs and one output) and 2^n rows.

Switch *S1*	Switch *S2*		Switch *Sn*	Output $g(S1, \ldots Sn)$
0	0	.....	0	0
0	1		0	0
. . .	. . .	.....	. . .	. . .
1	1		1	1

A logical function can only have one of two values, 0 or 1, and each of its *n* arguments can only take on the same two values. There will therefore exist exactly 2^n possible combinations of argument values, and exactly two possible function values. The number of possible combinations of argument values is finite, so a logical function can always be fully defined by enumeration, i.e., by means of a truth table that defines the function value for each and every possible set of argument values. Logical functions are quite different from ordinary continuous functions like cosines and square roots in this respect. For example, $\cos(x)$ is defined over an infinite number of values of its argument x so that all possible argument values can never be enumerated.

A third, very simple but useful and familiar, application of truth tables might be the design of a stairway light switching circuit. Stairway lights are frequently operated from two different switches, so that if the light is switched on by the downstairs switch it can be switched off either upstairs or downstairs. The usual arrangement is such that the light is on (denoted by 1) when the two switches are in opposite positions, one up and the other down; and off (denoted by 0) whenever the two switches are in similar positions. If a switch lever in the *up* position is represented by 1, *down* by 0, the truth table will be as follows:

Switch S1	Switch S2	Output g(S1,S2)
0	0	0
0	1	1
1	0	1
1	1	0

It should be noted that in this case the words *off* and *on* have no clear meaning as applied to the individual switches, only as applied to the light controlled by them.

The logical function which this table represents is almost, but not quite, the same as the OR function—it differs in the fourth row of the truth table. This function is usually known as the *exclusive OR*, sometimes abbreviated to XOR.

Transistors as switches

Although manual switches are useful for setting up burglar alarms and door bells, digital computers require switches capable of being opened and closed electrically rather than mechanically. This can be achieved by the use of simple transistor circuits, using one transistor (and sometimes two or more) for each switch. The switching action is achieved by using the base of the transistor to control it, so that its emitter–collector path conducts either very well or very poorly. The emitter and collector of the transistor then act just as a mechanical switch would, but under the control of an electrical signal applied to its base.

The principle of transistor switching is best illustrated by a simple example. In the electronic circuit of Fig. 2.3a, the output voltage is taken between collector and emitter, the input signal is applied between emitter and base, through a resistor R_B that limits the base current to a safe value in all circumstances. Similarly, the collector supply voltage V_{CC} is connected through a collector resistance R_C which ensures that the collector current remains within acceptable limits.

Suppose that at some particular moment the terminals marked IN are connected directly together, i.e., that there is no applied voltage at all in the base-

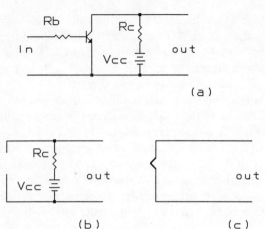

Fig. 2.3. (a) A single-transistor inverter circuit. (b) Important conductive paths in the single-transistor circuit with zero input voltage, and (c) with high input voltage.

emitter loop. The base current is then zero and the internal resistance between collector and emitter is very high, much larger than the collector resistance R_C. Very little current can then flow between emitter and collector; for practical purposes, the collector-emitter path appears as an open circuit. This situation is sketched in Fig. 2.3b, which repeats Fig. 2.3a but omits all parts of the circuit where little or no current flows. Clearly, the output voltage in this situation is equal to the collector voltage V_{CC}.

Suppose next that the input terminals IN are connected to a source of relatively high voltage, perhaps of a value similar to V_{CC}. The base current must then have a high value, and the emitter-collector path will appear to have a very low resistance, much lower than R_C. For practical purposes, the emitter and collector may be taken as having been short-circuited. This state of affairs is illustrated in Fig. 2.3c, which again repeats Fig. 2.3a but omits all paths where little or no current flows. The output voltage is now very nearly zero.

If high voltages (of magnitude similar to V_{CC}) are denoted by 1, low voltages by 0, then the circuit of Fig. 2.3a embodies a logical function with the following truth table:

IN	OUT
0	1
1	0

This function clearly represents negation, the so-called NOT operation: the function value OUT is always the logical inverse of the argument value IN. The corresponding circuit is often called an *inverter*.

Although the transistor can change its state much more rapidly than a mechanical switch, its operation is not instantaneous. All electronic circuits operate by transferring electrical charges, which move at some finite velocity

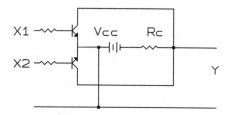

Fig. 2.4. Two-transistor NOR gate circuit.

considerably slower than the speed of light and thus take time to attain their final positions. During this transition period the output voltage changes gradually, reaching a steady state only when all the charges arrive in their rest positions. This delay between the application of an input signal and the appearance of a stable output signal limits the speed at which any logic device will operate. In one typical family of semiconductor devices, the migration time, and hence the delay between activating the switch and a complete response at the output side, is about 10 nanoseconds. If this time seems very short, it should be remembered that a digital computer may contain many millions of individual transistors. The cumulative delay of all the transistors in a complex circuit may be quite appreciable.

Transistor logic elements

To build up complicated switching circuits using transistors, it often suffices to draw a circuit incorporating mechanical switches and then to replace the mechanical switches by transistors. The logical sum (OR) function, for example, can be implemented in transistor logic by removing the mechanical switches in Fig. 2.1 and inserting transistors in their place. The result is illustrated in Fig. 2.4.

The truth table corresponding to the circuit of Fig. 2.4 is readily derived by tracing the four possible courses of events. If neither input is energized, both transistors are nonconducting, and the output voltage must be V_{CC}. If either one or the other input voltage is high, the corresponding transistor has substantially zero voltage between collector and emitter; V_{CC} appears across the collector resistance R_C and the output voltage falls to zero. If both transistors conduct, the situation remains similar to that of one or the other conducting. If zero voltage is denoted by 0, high voltage by 1, the behavior of the circuit is described by the following truth table:

Input X_1	Input X_2	Output $Y(X_1,X_2)$
0	0	1
0	1	0
1	0	0
1	1	0

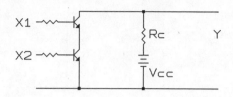

Fig. 2.5.   Two-transistor NAND gate circuit.

This table does not correspond exactly to any of those described earlier. How-ever, it somewhat resembles the OR (logical sum) function, differing only in the important detail that its value is always the inverse of the OR. This function is generally called the NOR (*not-OR*, or *negated OR*) function and the circuit that implements it is called a *NOR gate*. Similar terminology applies to other logical operations; circuits that implement the most basic logical functions are called *logic gates* and specific ones are identified by the names of the functions involved. For example, the circuit of Fig. 2.3a is a particular type of *NOT gate*, also called an *inverter*. Commonly encountered logic gates include the NAND (*not-AND*, or *negated AND*) gate, the AND gate, and the XNOR (exclusive negated OR) gate.

NAND gates are built up in a manner similar to the NOR gate already described. Fig. 2.5 shows a two-transistor circuit in which again the transistors act as switches. When both are conducting, the output voltage of this circuit is very low or zero. If either (or both) is not conducting, the output voltage is high.

If an OR gate is required for some purpose, the easiest procedure is to build a NOR gate and to feed its output into an inverter of the sort shown in Fig. 2.3a. Much the same applies to the AND function: a NAND gate is relatively easily built, but an AND gate is best made up by combining a NAND gate and an inverter. Logic gates built using the type of semiconductor technology described above invariably involve a signal inversion. Thus, the NAND and NOR gates are the more normal implementations. However, AND and OR gates may be found in practical circuits even though NAND and NOR tend to be more popular.

NOT gates are usually formed from simple inverting circuits, as in Fig. 2.3a. However, NAND and NOR gates may also be connected to create a NOT oper-ation. Consider a NOR gate whose two inputs have been tied together, so that $X_1 = X_2$ always. Because its two inputs now always have the same value, its truth table can no longer include any rows where the two differ, so there remain just two rows:

Input X_1	Input X_2	Output $Y(X_1,X_2)$
0	0	1
1	1	0

The two input columns are required to be identical so there really is only one distinct input:

Input X	Output Y(X)
0	1
1	0

Clearly, an inverter may be formed by connecting the two (or more) inputs of a NAND or a NOR gate together. It may appear that this way of proceeding is inefficient, for it uses more transistors than necessary. However, NAND and NOR gates are typically packaged in sets of four, eight, or more on a single semiconductor chip; if a circuit does not use all the available gates, some transistors would be wasted anyway.

Chip technology and device packaging

Logic gates are only rarely built individually; more commonly, they are packaged as sets of several similar gates arranged on a single semiconductor chip. Having several gates on one chip increases the circuit packing density, and thereby reduces the bulk of the computing device that incorporates the gates. At the same time, the lengths of all interconnections are shortened, delay times are reduced, and the speed of operation for the ensemble of circuits is increased. These advantages of large-scale packaging, with many gates on a single chip, have led to a trend for *large-scale integration*; thousands of transistors are commonly placed on a single chip, and chips with more than a million transistors do exist.

Semiconductor devices, often referred to as silicon chips, are made by taking a thin wafer of silicon crystal and altering its chemical and physical properties locally by a process of *doping*. In doping, another material, such as gallium, is introduced in small quantities. Individual transistors are thus formed as zones of varying properties within a single crystal, with the entire set of many transistors forming a mechanically rigid single block of solid material. Finally a metal layer is deposited over the doped areas to provide electrical contact. The chip is usually encased in a plastic or ceramic housing that also serves to anchor external electrical connections or *pins*. The deposited metal areas on the chip are connected to these pins by means of tiny wires. The reliability of such semiconductor devices is high, since the entire chip is a single piece of silicon perhaps a few millimeters square; there are no internal connections to shake loose or corrode. Usually the external connections are the least reliable part of such a device, spurring computer manufacturers to heighten reliability by *large-scale integration*, the inclusion of as many functions as possible into single chips with comparatively few external connections.

For reasons of speed, reliability, and manufacturing economy, it is rarely worthwhile to produce a single logic gate on a single chip. In fact, all gates need to be connected to external power sources so it is convenient to place several gates on the same chip with only one set of power supply leads. Given that each gate requires a minimum of three other leads (two input leads and one output lead for a two-input gate), the number of gates on a chip is limited by the number of contact pins that can be accommodated on a single plastic package which typically measures 20 mm long by 7.5 mm wide. Many general-purpose logic gates are mounted in 16-pin packages thus giving the possibility of four logic elements per chip, but much larger packages, with correspondingly increased numbers of gates, also exist.

One common family of commercially available logic circuit elements is based on *Transistor-Transistor Logic*, also known as TTL. This term refers to the way circuit elements are interconnected to create logic elements, as well as to the voltage levels required to operate the circuit. Under TTL conventions two voltage levels are recognized: logic 0 is considered to be represented by any value below 0.5 V, while logic 1 is represented by any voltage in excess of 2.7 V. The range between 0.5 V and 2.7 V is undefined in logic terms, and any signal voltage in this range is usually considered to indicate an erroneous or malfunctioning gate.

Many logic gates are built with more than two inputs. Three, four, or five inputs are quite commonly encountered. The truth table for a three-input NOR gate has three input columns and $2^3 = 8$ rows:

Input X_1	Input X_2	Input X_3	Output $Y(X_1,X_2,X_3)$
0	0	0	1
0	0	1	0
0	1	0	0
0	1	1	0
1	0	0	0
1	0	1	0
1	1	0	0
1	1	1	0

A circuit diagram for a three-input logic gate appears in Fig. 2.6. The basic scheme is very simple, consisting merely of the addition of another transistor.

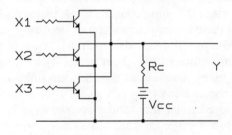

Fig. 2.6.   Three-input NOR gate.

Four-input and five-input gates are built in a similar way, by adding more transistors.

Common logic elements

Large-scale logic circuits commonly make heavy use of the elementary logical operations NAND, NOR, AND, OR, XOR, XNOR, and NOT. Where circuit diagrams need to be drawn, or interconnections shown, it is rarely convenient to show all of the many transistors and resistors individually. It is much more convenient to group together all the electronic components used to perform some particular logical operation and to denote them by a single symbol. In this way, clutter is reduced and clarity enhanced, for the components that can actually be purchased are in any case complete logic gates, not assemblages of individual transistors.

Table 2.1 gives the usual diagrammatic representations of the conventional logic elements, together with the applicable truth tables and the corresponding logical expressions. Except for the inverter (NOT gate), two inputs are shown in each case, although a larger number is permissible and gates with more than two inputs are used in practice. The following conventions are used for the logical (also called *Boolean*) expressions:

$'$ denotes negation, NOT
$\cdot$ denotes logical product, AND
$+$ denotes logical sum, OR

A and B are assumed to be the input variables and X to be the output.

TTL logic gates of the types shown in Table 2.1 are available from several manufacturers. Most chip makers adhere to a common type numbering code so that a chip made by one manufacturer is interchangeable with a chip from another source if its number code is the same, i.e., the pin connections, logical functions, and voltage levels are the same. One widely used family of chips is the so-called 74LS series. A few typical members of this set are listed in Table 2.2.

All the chip types listed in Table 2.2 are small, with only 14 external connecting pins. Vast numbers of different combinations can be created, differing in their numbers of inputs, gate types, and numbers of pins. Quite a few different combinations are actually useful, so that a broad range of chip types is available on the commercial market. The listing in Table 2.2 represents only the tip of a large iceberg, as it were.

One other point about TTL circuitry is worth noting. Because well-defined voltage levels denote the 0 and 1 logic values, the output from one gate may be directed to the input terminals of another without any need for further electronic devices. Indeed one gate may well feed the inputs of several other gates. From the point of view of mathematical logic, there is no problem; information is infinitely shareable, so there is no limit to the number of gates that may be driven from one output. However, any circuit implementation involves the laws

Table 2.1. Digital logic gates and their
representations

AND		A	B	X
		0	0	0
		0	1	0
		1	0	0
$X = A \cdot B$		1	1	1

OR		A	B	X
		0	0	0
		0	1	1
		1	0	1
$X = A + B$		1	1	1

NAND		A	B	X
		0	0	1
		0	1	1
		1	0	1
$X = (A \cdot B)'$		1	1	0

NOR		A	B	X
		0	0	1
		0	1	0
		1	0	0
$X = (A' + B)'$		1	1	0

XOR		A	B	X
		0	0	0
		0	1	1
		1	0	1
$X = (A' \cdot B) + (A \cdot B')$		1	1	0

XNOR		A	B	X
		0	0	1
		0	1	0
		1	0	0
$X = (A \cdot B) + (A' \cdot B')$		1	1	1

NOT		A	X
		0	1
$X = A'$		1	0

Table 2.2. Integrated circuit chips containing logic gates

Description	Type number	Pins
Four 2-input NAND gates	74LS00	14
Four 2-input NOR gates	74LS02	14
Four 2-input AND gates	74LS08	14
Four 2-input OR gates	74LS32	14
Six inverters	74LS04	14
Three 3-input NAND gates	74LS10	14
One 8-input NAND gate	74LS30	14
Four 2-input XOR gates	74LS86	14
Four 2-input XNOR gates	74LS266	14

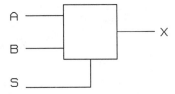

Fig. 2.7. A simple switch. X is identical to input A if $S = 1$, otherwise it is identical to B.

of physics as well as mathematics, so practical constraints are imposed on the designer. Because there is a limit to the amount of current a single physical device can furnish, there is a maximum number of logic gate inputs which the output of a single gate can drive. This number is known as the *fan-out* of the gate. Typical limits are of the order of 10, so that fan-out limitations are rarely a problem in the design of simple circuits, but may become worrisome in large ones.

Simulation of digital circuits

Digital computers are made up of large numbers of logic circuits. Although each logic gate may be very simple in itself, computer circuits are often staggeringly complicated because they contain thousands upon thousands of gates. Their design may at first sight appear overwhelmingly difficult because of the very large number of gates involved. Fortunately, it is not quite so bad as might seem, provided a systematic step-by-step approach is taken. One such approach is *simulation*, a process in which the individual circuit elements are described to a computer program which then combines their truth tables so as to predict the behavior of the combined circuit. In this section, a simple circuit simulation is described. The same technique will be applied to other, more complicated, circuits subsequently.

A routing switch

The principles involved in combinational circuits may best be introduced by the simple example of an electronic routing switch as shown in Fig. 2.7. This device connects its single output line X to either of its two inputs A and B, depending on the state of the switching control line S. In other words, the output X is a replica of A (input B being ignored totally) if S has the value 1, and a replica of B if its value is 0.

To state the matter a little more formally, the design requirement here is that X must be a logical function of A, B, and S. This function is fully defined by giving its description in a truth table:

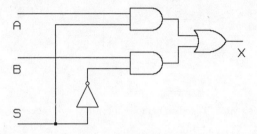

Fig. 2.8.   The routing switch circuit. X replicates A if $S = 1$, otherwise it replicates B.

S	A	B	X
0	0	0	0
0	0	1	1
0	1	0	0
0	1	1	1
1	0	0	0
1	0	1	0
1	1	0	1
1	1	1	1

It is asserted that the required truth table is satisfied by the circuit given in Fig. 2.8. The important question to be answered is then: Is it?

One way to tell whether the design in Fig. 2.8 meets specifications satisfactorily is to build and test it. Testing the design amounts to checking whether the circuit satisfies the prescribed truth table. Because the truth table constitutes the complete and only specification, any circuit that satisfies it represents a workable design. The design rarely, if ever, turns out to be unique, for many different circuits may lead to the same truth table. A selection must then be made from among the many possible designs, choosing one on the basis of economy, ease of fabrication, reliability, and other significant criteria. The first step, however, must always be to verify that the truth table is satisfied.

To test a proposed design on paper, the circuit is subdivided into less complicated pieces whose individual truth tables are known. For the circuit of Fig. 2.8, it is best to define a variable at every input and output of every gate, so that the uncomplicated pieces of circuit in fact comprise exactly one gate each. Taking T, Y, and Z to be the logical variables shown in Fig. 2.8, the circuit is then easily described by writing its Boolean describing equations, gate by gate:

$$T = S'$$
$$Y = A \cdot S$$
$$Z = B \cdot T$$
$$X = Y + Z$$

These four equations can be used to test, by embodying them into a program that defines X. The program can be written in any convenient language capable of dealing with logical-valued variables, for example, Pascal:

```
procedure Xvalue(var X, S, T, Y, Z, A, B: Boolean);
        begin
                T := not S;
                Y := A and S;
                Z := B and T;
                X := Y or Z;
        end;
```

By assigning every possible combination of values to the input variables A, B, and S and printing out the corresponding values of all variables, an extended truth table is obtained. It can be made to include the internal variables Y, Z, T as well as the externally accessible variables A, B, S, and X:

S	A	B	T	Y	Z	X
0	0	0	1	0	0	0
0	0	1	1	0	1	1
0	1	0	1	0	0	0
0	1	1	1	0	1	1
1	0	0	0	0	0	0
1	0	1	0	0	0	0
1	1	0	0	1	0	1
1	1	1	0	1	0	1

This truth table obviously satisfies the specification, since the S, A, B, and X columns in it are exactly the same as in the truth table that specifies the switch performance. The proposed design is therefore acceptable.

Although the routing switch can be built to contain only a few gates and its truth table is quite short, checking by hand is error-prone and unreliable. The same can obviously be said, with renewed emphasis, for more complicated circuits! Simulation by computer quickly becomes essential as complexity increases and logic circuit design in any realistic case invariably requires the techniques of computer-aided design to be used.

Digital circuit description

The design of logic circuits, like much other engineering design, proceeds in a cycle of alternately testing and modifying a proposed design, until the modified version meets specifications. Testing can be carried out on a hardware prototype and the final test of a design cannot be done in any other way; but preliminary tests are more easily carried out by simulating the hardware actions in a computer. This principle is illustrated by the electronic routing switch described immediately above, where the logical relationships between electronic gates are simulated by statements in a computer programming language.

Simulation of tests by writing programs in Pascal or Fortran is an acceptable procedure only for very simple circuits. Transcribing the circuit diagram into equations, then encoding the equations in a programming language, is a demanding process and easily leads to errors, so raising doubts whether the transcription has been done correctly. In other words, it is hard to be sure that the program accurately reflects the circuit, so if the program fails (or meets!) specifications one cannot be absolutely certain the circuit is wrong. To circumvent such problems, *digital logic simulators* are often used as design tools. They use special-purpose programming languages whose structure very closely parallels the structure of electronic circuits themselves, so that programming errors are minimized. Design and testing of the simulation can be substituted for design and testing of hardware in this way.

The logic circuits presented as examples in the remainder of this chapter are simulated using a logic simulator package called *Apodix*. (Its name derives from *apodeixis*, a term in Aristotelian logic denoting proof by syllogism.) Apodix is a small simulation system, suitable for checking circuits of modest complexity. The essentials of circuit simulation with Apodix are introduced here informally, with reference to specific examples; a full user manual for the Apodix simulator will be found in Appendix 1.

The circuit diagram of Fig. 2.8 may be said to constitute a description of the actual physical circuit. The formal describing equations of the circuit contain exactly the same information about the circuit elements and their interconnections, so they constitute an alternative description, equally complete and valid. In simulators such as Apodix, a third form of description is used, closely related to the circuit diagram but written in character form rather than as graphic pictures. In Apodix notation, the circuit of Fig. 2.8 is described as a set of gates, with specified inputs and output for each one:

```
circuit RtSwitch:
{    or:    Y, Z > X;
     and:   B, T > Z;
     and:   A, S > Y;
     not:   S > T;        }
```

This specification may be regarded as being written in a *circuit description language*. Such a language differs from programming languages like Pascal and Fortran in being essentially *descriptive* rather than prescriptive or algorithmic. In other words, it says that certain relationships are true, but it does not say how to carry out a particular computation. Like the circuit diagram but unlike the Pascal program, the Apodix description does not care in what order it is presented; shuffling the statements at random,

```
circuit RtSwitch:
{    and:   A, S > Y;
     not:   S > T;
     and:   B, T > Z;
     or:    Y, Z > X;        }
```

does not alter the information contained in the circuit description.

Apodix provides a selection of logic gates with various numbers of input lines. For the usual combinational logic elements, from two to eight inputs may be specified. To request a NAND gate with three inputs, for example, it is only

Table 2.3. Combinational logic gates recognized by Apodix

Name	Element description	Inputs	Outputs
not	Inverter (NOT gate)	1	1
and	*N*-input AND gate	2–8	1
nand	*N*-input NAND gate	2–8	1
or	*N*-input OR gate	2–8	1
nor	*N*-input NOR gate	2–8	1
xor	*N*-input exclusive-OR gate	2–8	1
xnor	*N*-input exclusive-NOR gate	2–8	1

necessary to write a list of three input signals and one output signal. The input line

```
nand: in1, Y, inp2 > signlout;
```

will cause Apodix to count the inputs (the signals listed before the right-arrow), and to match the number of input signals by selecting a three-input NAND gate. The elementary gates known to Apodix are listed in Table 2.3; some more complex circuit types will be described later.

In circuit descriptions, each gate is specified by a single statement. The name of the gate must be followed by a colon and the statement itself is terminated by a semicolon. Any number of blanks may appear between words in a statement. Statements may be written anywhere on a line; more than one statement may appear on a line and more than one line may be used for a statement. The list of input signals to a gate is written with commas separating the variable names; the input list is separated from the output by a right-pointing arrow. Both upper and lower case letters may be used, but it must be remembered that Apodix considers characters to be distinct; it regards *Fred*, *fred*, and *FRED* as totally unrelated. This rule extends to everything including gate names: Apodix recognizes *nand:* to be a logic gate but knows nothing about *NAND:*.

Signals as listed in Apodix statements represent logic circuit signals, hence they correspond to voltages at circuit nodes. At any particular moment, each variable (signal) may have one of three values,

unknown,	shown in screen displays as ˆ ,
1, or *logic high,* or *set,*	shown in screen displays as **1**,
0, or *logic low,* or *reset,*	shown in screen displays as __.

Signal names in Apodix begin with an alphabetic character, followed by up to seven numeral or alphabetic characters. Valid variable names thus include *A*, *latch3*, *PowrFail*. It should be noted, however, that there are certain *reserved words* in Apodix, which might be confused with the names of logic elements. These include element names such as *and, or, nand,* as well as descriptors such as *circuit*. Reserved words should not be used as variable names, lest confusion arise.

Circuit test specification

Circuit descriptions simply say what gates have been interconnected and how. Simulation is a dynamic process, however, that also requires specifying what external signals are to be impressed on the circuit and what measurements of circuit response are to be made. Apodix provides means for specifying both the inputs to be furnished and the outputs to be measured.

Externally impressed signals are described by stating how they vary with time and where in the circuit they are to be applied. In the simplest case, it suffices to name a circuit node and to state the signal value at that node. Thus

```
X = 1;
```

says that the signal *X* has the value 1 forever. Signals that change value at some time are described by stating when their values change from 1 to 0 or conversely. For example,

```
Y = 1 (5);
```

describes a signal that starts at value 1, then changes to 0 at $t = 5$. Similarly,

```
Y = 1 (5,8);
```

says that *Y* has the value 1 until $t = 5$, then the value 0 until $t = 8$, then the value 1 again forever.

Periodic signals are described in Apodix by describing the course of their values during one period, then stating the length of the period. Typically,

```
sigY = 0 (5,8) 10;
```

says that the signal *sigY* starts at value 0, switches to 1 at $t = 5$, switches to 0 at $t = 8$, then begins a new cycle so that its value at $t = 10$ is exactly the same as at $t = 0$. It then repeats its behavior cyclically, restarting at $t = 20$, $t = 30$, and so on.

To distinguish them from the circuit description, the external excitations to be applied are preceded by the word *input:* and enclosed in braces. For example,

```
input:
{    B = 0 (7) 14;
     A = 0 (14) 28;
     S = 0 (28) 56;    }
```

describes three periodic inputs with harmonically related periods.

In the earlier general discussion of transistor circuits it was noted that a delay time is always involved in changing the state of any logic circuit. When the input to any logic gate is altered, the output responds to the change only after a certain amount of time. This delay time is known as the *propagation delay* of the gate. To keep simulations realistic, Apodix inserts a propagation delay of one time unit into the activity of every gate. That is to say, the output of any logic gate appears one time unit later than its inputs are applied. The time unit is unspecified; indeed the delay time of a single gate is the fundamental time unit for

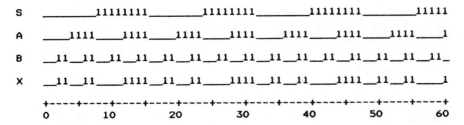

```
S          _____11111111_____11111111_____11111111_____11111

A       ___1111____1111____1111____1111____1111____1111____1111____1

B       _11_11_11_11_11_11_11_11_11_11_11_11_11_11_11_

X       _11_11____1111_11_11____1111_11_11____1111_11_11____1

        +----+----+----+----+----+----+----+----+----+----+----+----+
        0        10        20        30        40        50        60
```

Fig. 2.9. Output produced by Apodix. Each signal is monitored at preset sampling intervals and displayed with __ signifying logic low, 1 denoting logic high.

Apodix, the unit in which all other times are measured. This arrangement is convenient because all gates constructed using a given type of semiconductor technology have very nearly equal delay times. Actual figures for commercial circuits range from about 1 or 2 nanoseconds up to about 100 nanoseconds, with 10 nanoseconds a common value.

Circuit simulation is really experiment simulation: external stimuli are applied to a specified circuit and the circuit response at various nodes is measured, just as would be done in a laboratory experiment with prototype hardware. To specify what data should be gathered, it suffices to state (a) which variables are to be measured and (b) how long to continue measuring. The variables to be measured are given in a simple list terminated by a semicolon, as in

```
output:
{    S, A, B, X;
     time = 56;    }
```

The word *output:* and the braces are necessary, but the time specification is optional; if it is omitted, Apodix will choose a default value so as to just fill one display screen.

Apodix output has the form of a table with graphlike appearance. For example, monitoring the four variables S, A, B, X in a circuit might produce an output similar to that shown in Fig. 2.9. In this, as indeed in all Apodix output, the *logic high* state is denoted by 1, but the *logic low* state is shown as an underscore character _ instead of 0, to improve legibility. Each column represents one sampling time and each row corresponds to one output, as labeled at the left. The time intervals are shown along a time axis calibrated in propagation delay time units.

Testing the routing switch

The routing switch of Fig. 2.8 is now fully described and ready for testing. Adding an identifying title (which Apodix requires to be encased in the identifying marks /* and */) and collecting together the various parts of its description, the full simulation reads

```
      /* Routing switch test */
circuit RtSwitch:
      {
      and: A, S > Y;
      not: S > T;
      and: B, T > Z;
      or: Y, Z > X;
      }
input:
      {
      B = 0 (8) 16;
      A = 0 (16) 32;
      S = 0 (32) 64;
      }
output:
      {
      S, A, B, X;
      time = 64;
      }
```

This set of statements is prepared using a text editing program and is placed in a file. When Apodix is started, it reads this file and carries out the simulation.

In this specification, all three external stimuli are periodic, the switch S as well as the inputs A and B. Their periods are harmonically related, however; A varies half as fast as B, and S varies half as fast as A. The result is that one full cycle of the switching signal S covers all possibilities in both A and B for both possible settings of S. One full cycle of S therefore suffices to generate the entire truth table of the switch. This truth table is reproduced in Fig. 2.10, along with segments of Apodix output. In fact the two correspond directly, except for replacement of zeros in the truth table by underscore lines in the Apodix printout, and rotation of the table through 90 degrees.

It should be noted that every gate introduces a time delay of one time unit, so that the truth table will only be produced if the output is examined (sampled) at appropriate intervals. To simplify the examination of data, Apodix permits display at a specified sampling frequency. In the switch circuit of Fig. 2.8, the long-

```
S   A   B  ┊  X
-----------+----              Routing switch test
0   0   0  ┊  0
0   0   1  ┊  1              S        ____11111
0   1   0  ┊  0              A        _11___11
0   1   1  ┊  1              B        _1_1_11_1
1   0   0  ┊  0              X        _1_11__11
1   0   1  ┊  0
1   1   0  ┊  1                       +----+----+
1   1   1  ┊  1                       5        75
```

Fig. 2.10. Truth table of the routing switch (*left*) compared with a partial output display (*right*).

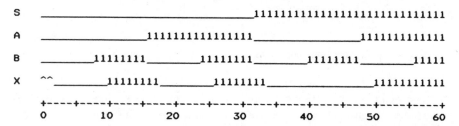

Fig. 2.11. Apodix output for the routing switch, with a sampling interval of one time unit. Sampling must be delayed until all logic levels have settled.

est path a signal ever needs to traverse passes through three gates—it is said that there are three *logic levels*—so that the maximum input-to-output delay is three time units. Choosing the fastest periodic external excitation to have a half-period of seven units (i.e., a period of 14 units, as *B* above) therefore permits all signals to settle. Sampling once per half-cycle, i.e., with a sample taken every 7 time units, will then secure the truth table for the switch, provided that sampling occurs late enough in each half-cycle for the outputs of all circuits to stabilize. In the present case, that means sampling at $t = 5, 12, 19, \ldots$ etc. These are the sampling times used to produce Fig. 2.11.

Any logic circuit takes time to react to an input signal. This point is illustrated by Fig. 2.11, which shows Apodix output sampled at intervals of one time unit. Clearly, changes in *B* precede those in *Y*, which precede those in *Z*. To ensure that logic levels have settled, i.e., that steady-state values are being measured, it is desirable but not always possible to calculate in advance what total delay times are likely to be encountered. The fastest-varying periodic stimulus should have a long enough period to ensure settling of all signals; but increasing its period considerably beyond that will ensure that true logic values are being recorded. For example, in the routing switch investigation it might be wise to take a period of 30 time units for variable *B*, 60 for *A*, and 120 for *S*. Whether the settling time is one, two, or four time units will then be quite unimportant, provided only that sampling is performed fairly late in the half-period, say at $t = 12$.

In many circuits it is not at all clear how long a settling time might be required. One way of attempting to determine it experimentally is to apply an aperiodic excitation (step function) at $t = 0$, and to measure all variables at intervals of one time unit. The resulting output may then be examined to see how long any transients might last. Unfortunately, this technique is not quite foolproof. It is possible for a gate to have a well-defined output even though the inputs are not completely defined, so some variables may become established more quickly in one state than the other. For example, the output of a two-input AND gate is 0 if only one of the inputs is known to be 0, so that the output of an AND gate

Fig. 2.12.   A simple closed-loop circuit in whose behavior delay time plays a critical role.

may be well defined at 0 long before both its inputs have settled. Thus, the set-tling time determined experimentally with one set of excitations need not nec-essarily be valid for some other set of impressed values.

It is tempting to guess that the propagation delay through the entire circuit cannot exceed the total number of gates in the circuit; but such a guess would be wrong, as illustrated by the next example.

An oscillating circuit

An interesting circuit, whose behavior depends strongly on the external stimulus applied, is shown in Fig. 2.12. It consists of two inverters and a two-input NAND gate. To analyze this circuit using Apodix, a circuit description must be made up along with a prescription of the stimuli to be applied. This task is car-ried out easily enough, in view of the simplicity of the circuit. The simulation reads

```
    /* Oscillating circuit example */
circuit oscillat:
    {
    nand: A, D > B;
    not: B > C;
    not: C > D;
    }
input:
    {
    A = 0;
    }
output:
    {
    A, B, C, D;
    time = 55;
    }
```

What external stimulus to employ for testing is a moot point. As a first try, a simple step function is applied: the input variable A is forced to a value of 0 at time zero. In due course other, more complicated, signals might also be tried.

The course of events that follows upon this stimulus is not hard to trace. Vari-ables B, C, and D are initially unknown. At $t = 0$ only A is therefore known. However, at $t = 1$ the value of B is well defined; the output of the NAND gate must be 1, no matter what the value of D, because A is zero. Thus at $t = 1$ only C and D are unknown. At $t = 2$, the value of C is well defined, for it is fixed by the inverter output as the negative of B; similarly, D assumes a known value at

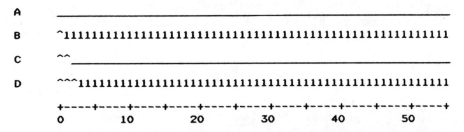

Fig. 2.13. The closed-loop circuit of Fig. 2.12 reaches a stable state in three delay times.

$t = 3$. At $t = 4$ all variables retain their values, and the circuit has reached steady state. Output from the simulator therefore will have the appearance shown in Fig. 2.13.

Consider next, however, the possibility of having A reverse its value at some time when the circuit is settled, say at $t = 20$. The circuit description and the output specifications will remain the same, except that the exciting signal will now be prescribed by

```
A = 0(20);
```

Because D has value 1 when the value of A is switched, the NAND gate output will alter, so that B switches value at $t = 21$. Variable C will therefore change value at $t = 22$, and D at $t = 23$. When D has switched value to 0, however, the NAND gate cannot maintain its output, and B must switch again at $t = 24$, followed by C and D at intervals of one time unit. Thus at $t = 26$, the input D to the NAND gate switches, and exactly the same cycle of events ensues as at $t = 20$. The output will then appear as in Fig. 2.14. Far from settling to a steady

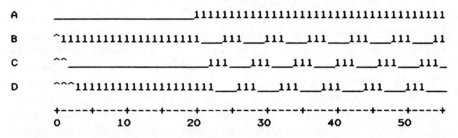

Fig. 2.14. For some excitations, the steady state behavior of the circuit of Fig. 2.12 is oscillatory.

state value in a few time units, this circuit will not settle down at all; it will keep oscillating forever, provided the input variable A is kept at value 1. In fact, this circuit can be used as an oscillator, to generate a train of pulses whenever A is set to 1 and to stop it when A is reset to 0.

Combinational logic circuits

Electronic logic gates are relatively easy to make so that logic circuits of considerable complexity are quite common. A few of the more common types of circuit are examined and simulations shown in this section. All these circuits are available in commercial integrated circuit chips, often in a variety of packages and combinations. More complex circuit types are examined later in this chapter and in the next.

The multiplexer

The simple electronic routing or selector switch discussed in the last section is a close relative of a widely employed circuit, the *multiplexer*. The two are very similar, except for one difference: the multiplexer contains provisions for more carefully controlled timing of events than the simple switch.

Time delays in the electronic selector switch are asymmetric: the time it takes to settle in one state is not necessarily the same as the time taken to settle in the other. One simple way of ensuring symmetry is to hold back the action of the circuit, so that the output is forcibly kept at zero until the circuit is enabled to act. If properly carried out, such an enabling process can ensure that the delay time after enabling is the same in all cases. The circuit operation is then closely controlled, with delay times known in advance.

When equipped with an enabling circuit to hold its output to 0 until enabled, the routing switch becomes a *multiplexer*, a well-known standard digital building block. Holding back is easily arranged, as illustrated in Fig. 2.15a. The output terminals of the simple switch are followed by a two-input AND gate, one of whose inputs is directly controlled from an external source E. When this line, usually called the *enable line*, is asserted (logic value 1), the AND gate replicates the output that would have existed without it; when it is reset to 0, the output from the AND gate is always zero. In circuits that include an AND or NAND gate near the output for other reasons, as is indeed the case for the switch circuit of Fig. 2.7, the enabling signal can be applied to one or more already existing gates, provided they are equipped with an additional input. In this way, the circuit of Fig. 2.15b results.

The two-input multiplexer of Fig. 2.15b actually has four inputs: the two inputs proper, A and B, the *select* line S which determines whether the output will replicate A or B, and the *enable* line E which holds the output at 0 until it is asserted. Precise control of output timing is achieved by appropriate use of

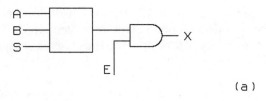

(a)

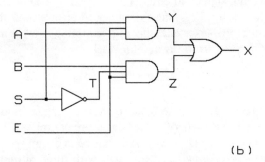

(b)

Fig. 2.15. Two-input multiplexer. (a) Principle of operation. (b) A circuit implementation.

the enable line. Its description in Apodix therefore requires one more line input to be provided at the two AND gates to allow the enabling signal E to be applied:

```
circuit mux2:
    {
    or:    Y, Z > X;
    and:   A, S, E > Y;
    and:   B, T, E > Z
    not:   S > T;
    }
```

One important application of multiplexers occurs in using a single wire to transmit two signals. To do so, the select line S is driven by a periodic signal whose period is considerably longer than the settling time of a typical gate. The multiplexer output line then alternately samples inputs A and B, thus serving to transmit both. Of course, a *demultiplexer* circuit is required at the receiving end to reconstitute the separate signals. In such an arrangement, timing is very important, because a signal sent too early or too late by the multiplexer may be misunderstood at the receiving end. Confusion is avoided by supplying the same enabling signal to both the multiplexer and the demultiplexer, so that they operate in perfect synchronism.

Delay times place limits on the speed of operation of logic circuits. For example, if the routing switch is driven by inputs that vary more rapidly than the slowest overall circuit response, the circuit output is unable to follow input vari-

ations faithfully and one can fairly say that the circuit does not work. No physical device can be built without time delays, so the designer can only choose their
duration, not whether they will be present. Thus the maximum speed at which
a computer built of logic circuits can process data depends on the delay times
inherent in its circuits.

The importance of timing in digital circuits is so great that all computing
machines, and practically all other devices that perform logical operations, have
their operating rates controlled by a *clock*. The clock is a pulse train generator
that provides enabling signals to circuits controlled by enable lines. It operates
at a frequency chosen by the system designer to ensure that all the logic will
function correctly. Multiplexer enabling and sampling control lines are usually
driven by signals derived from the system clock.

Comparators

Most computer circuits are not designed by assembling individual logic gates,
but by connecting together sets of somewhat more complicated circuits. In the
foregoing, one such circuit, the *multiplexer*, has been examined. Another useful
composite circuit is the *comparator*, a circuit with three outputs G, E, L, and
two inputs, A and B. The three output lines G, E, L assume the logic value 1
according to whether the value at A is greater than, equal to, or less than the
value at B. One, and only one, of these three carries the logic value 1 while the
remaining pair carry value 0. The truth table for such a circuit is clearly

A	B	G	E	L
0	0	0	1	0
0	1	0	0	1
1	0	1	0	0
1	1	0	1	0

Because there are three output variables, this table is really three truth tables in
one, for it defines three logical functions $G(A,B)$, $E(A,B)$, and $L(A,B)$.

To construct a comparator, it might first be noted that the function $G(A,B)$ has
only one nonzero entry in its column of the truth table, exactly as an AND function does. The nonzero value occurs for one of the cases in which $A = 1$, suggesting that G might in fact be made up as $G = A \cdot X$, where X depends on B
in some as yet undetermined way. A second look at the truth table makes it clear
that the desired function G is obtained if $X = B'$, so that $G = A \cdot B'$. This relationship can be realized by using one AND gate and an inverter. Following an
exactly similar argument, the function $L(A,B)$ may be written as $L = A' \cdot B$.
This function too is realized by using one AND gate and one inverter.

The E column of the comparator truth table may be recognized as describing
an XNOR gate. It is therefore realizable by using one such gate only. The resulting circuit diagram, combining all three functions, is then as shown in Fig. 2.16.

The purely verbal argument given above may be intuitively appealing, but it
cannot guarantee correctness. The right way to continue is to test the circuit,

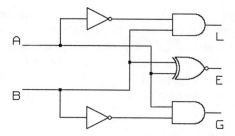

Fig. 2.16.   A comparator circuit, the result of combining three simple single-output circuits.

generating its triple truth table, and checking against the specification. Two-level logic is involved here (i.e., the largest number of cascaded gates in any path is 2), so an Apodix simulation can probably be relied upon if *A* and *B* are driven by periodic sources with half-periods much longer than two delay times. Hence, the Apodix experiment for this circuit reads as follows:

```
/* Comparator of AND, XNOR, NOT gates */
circuit comparat:
     {
     and:      B, U > L;
     and:      A, V > G;
     xnor:     A, B > E;
     not:      A > U;
     not:      B > V;
     }
input:
     {
     A = 0 (32, 64);
     B = 0 (16, 32);
     }
output:
     {
     A, B, G, E, L;
     time = 65;
     }
```

On carrying out this simulation, the circuit shown is found to satisfy the truth table. It should be observed, however, that the circuit is far from unique; many other combinations of logic gates will satisfy the requirement equally well. In practical cases, the choice will be made on other grounds. In some cases it may be desired to minimize the number of gates. In other circumstances, it may be preferable to restrict the range of gate types, because logic gates are often best fabricated by placing numerous gates of the same type on a single semiconductor chip.

Comparators are widely used in computers. They permit logical decisions to be based on whether or not two data items are equal, without actually performing a subtraction operation. For example, alphabetic sorting of data words involves many decisions of this kind. Because comparators are frequently encountered, they are available as ready-made components, several comparators to a semiconductor chip; it is rarely necessary or efficient to make up comparators out of individual gates. It is also possible to purchase ready-made comparators that compare multibit words interpreted as unsigned integers. Such a comparator still has only three output lines, but of course sufficient input lines must be available to handle both data words.

The half-adder

Another fundamental building block for computer circuits is the *half-adder*, a circuit able to add two 1-bit numbers a and b. Although adding 1-bit numbers is an operation rarely of direct interest to computer users, a circuit able to do so is very useful in building up more complex arithmetic functions.

Because the sum of two 1-bit numbers may be as large as 10_2, a half-adder circuit must have two output lines so as to be able to accommodate two output bits. The truth table for this circuit is thus

a	b	c	s
0	0	0	0
0	1	0	1
1	0	0	1
1	1	1	0

Here s is the 1-bit value of the sum, while c flags that a carry out of that bit was attempted. To put the matter another way, c and s are the two bits of the result of addition. It is conventional to call s the *sum*, and c the *carry*. This truth table really amounts to no more than an embodiment of the rules of binary arithmetic

$$0 + 0 = 0$$
$$0 + 1 = 1$$
$$1 + 0 = 1$$
$$1 + 1 = 10$$

In other words, the arithmetic knowledge required for addition is built into the truth table and subsequently embedded in the configuration of hardware logic gates.

Examination of the truth table shows that a half-adder can be built very easily out of just a few gates. In fact, the c column amounts to no more than the description of an AND gate, while the s column is precisely the set of outputs available from an XOR gate. The very simple circuit of Fig. 2.17 thus results.

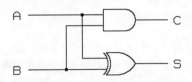

Fig. 2.17.   A half-adder circuit.

Half-adder simulation

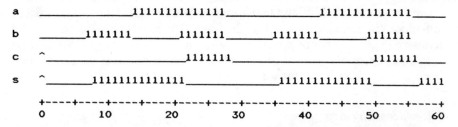

Fig. 2.18. The half-adder of Fig. 2.17, exercised by testing all four possible inputs.

An Apodix simulation of this circuit is easy to carry out; there are after all only two gates. The truth table is produced exactly as for the circuits already examined, by making inputs a and b cyclic, one at twice the rate of the other, and observing events for one full cycle:

```
/*    Half-adder simulation    */
circuit halfaddr:
    {
    and: a, b > c;
    xor: a, b > s;
    }
input:
    {
    a = 0 (14,28);
    b = 0 (7,14);
    }
output:
    {
    a, b, c, s;
    time = 64;
    }
```

Results for this simulation are shown in Fig. 2.18. Sampling the inputs and outputs at $t = 5, 12, 19, 26$, times when all signals have stabilized, the four rows of the truth table are seen to be satisfied. As might be expected from examining the circuit diagram of Fig. 2.17, the time taken to establish correct outputs is always just one gate delay time. It cannot be more, for there is only one gate between inputs and outputs along any possible path; it can never be less, for any change of input values always leads to a change in at least one of the output bits.

The half-adder is so common a circuit as to merit being included as a built-in element in Apodix, along with the elementary logic gates. Using the built-in half-adder, the performance of the circuit of Fig. 2.17 can be duplicated by

```
hfad: a, b > s, c;
```

This circuit element differs from all those introduced so far in having two output lines, not merely one.

It must not be assumed, of course, that the built-in half-adder of Apodix is composed of one AND gate and one XOR gate; all one can tell is that it satisfies the appropriate truth table and that it does so within a unit time delay. Various half-adder circuits other than Fig. 2.17 are possible, though most of them involve a larger number of gates. The choice made by the designer will depend on circumstances, for good design usually involves minimizing the expenditure of whichever resource is most scarce.

Full adder with carry

An unmodified half-adder of the sort described in Fig. 2.17 can correctly add 1-bit numbers. However, several half-adders cannot be combined to compute the sum of two multibit words; although they can generate carry bits on the output side, there is no provision for dealing with carries *in*. A *full adder* circuit provides the necessary three inputs: the two data bits a and b, and a carry bit ci that may be propagated from the next lower-order bit. It has two outputs, just as the half-adder does: the sum s and the carry out co.

One way to approach designing a full adder is to exploit the associativity of addition. If the arithmetic sum s of the three terms a, b, c is given by

$$s = a + b + c$$

then it may also be written as

$$s = (a + b) + c.$$

This suggests that the addition can be carried out in two steps. In the first step a partial sum p is formed,

$$p = a + b,$$

and in the second step this partial sum is augmented by the third term,

$$s = p + c.$$

The individual steps can be carried out using half-adders, for they only involve two inputs each. The arithmetic terms a, b, c may in fact be identified with the digital signals a, b, ci; however, their arithmetic sum s must correspond to the *pair* of signals (co,s) because three 1-bit numbers may combine to give a sum as high as 11_2. A circuit that satisfactorily performs this task is shown in Fig. 2.19. It may not be immediately clear whether the carry out is correctly handled by

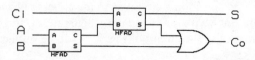

Fig. 2.19.   A full adder may be constructed by combining two half-adders and an OR gate to handle the carry out.

the circuit of Fig. 2.19. To see how *co* should be determined, the following rules can first be established:

1. If the addition of *a* and *b* generates a carry, the sum *s* must be either 2 or 3; therefore *co* must take on the value 1.
2. If the addition of *p* and *ci* generates a carry, the sum *s* must be either 2 or 3; therefore *co* must take on the value 1.
3. If neither addition generates a carry, the sum *s* must be either 0 or 1; therefore *co* must take on the value 0.

These rules are readily summarized by saying that *co* must equal 1 if either or both additions generate a carry. That, however, is exactly what the OR gate in Fig. 2.19 accomplishes.

To prove the circuit of Fig. 2.19 valid, its truth table must be constructed and verified. The truth table of the full adder, of course, includes that of the half-adder as a special case, since the full adder with no input carry must yield the same results as a half-adder. With three input lines, the truth table must have eight rows; they express the rules of addition, as follows:

ci	*a*	*b*	*co*	*s*
0	0	0	0	0
0	0	1	0	1
0	1	0	0	1
0	1	1	1	0
1	0	0	0	1
1	0	1	1	0
1	1	0	1	0
1	1	1	1	1

To prove the circuit of Fig. 2.19 valid it suffices to show that its behavior is exactly as prescribed by the table. This task is easily carried out by simulation:

```
/* Full adder simulation */
circuit fulladdr:
    {
    hfad: a, b > sum1, c1;
    hfad: ci, sum1 > sum, c2;
    or: c1, c2 > co;
    }
input:
    {
    ci = 0 (28) 56;
    a = 0 (14) 28;
    b = 0 (7) 14;
    }
output:
    {
    ci, a, b, c1, s1, c2, sum, co;
    time = 60;
    }
```

```
                        Full adder simulation

ci      _____1111111111111111111111111111__

a       _____11111111111111_____1111111111111__

b       _____1111111_____1111111_____1111111_____1111111__

c1      ^_____1111111_____1111111_

sum1    ^_____11111111111111_____11111111111111_____

c2      ^_____11111111111111_____

sum     ^^_____11111111111111_____11111111_____111111_

co      ^^_____1111111_____111111111111111111111111

        +----+----+----+----+----+----+----+----+----+----+----+--
        0        10       20       30       40       50
```

Fig. 2.20. The full adder of Fig. 2.19 tested for all eight possible inputs. This circuit is slower than the half-adder of Figs. 2.17 and 2.18.

When the simulation is run, the results shown in Fig. 2.20 are obtained. Clearly, the circuit works correctly. In every time interval of 7 units, the three input lines *a*, *b*, *ci* have a different combination of 1 and 0 values. In every time interval, the 2-bit number composed of *co* and *s* correctly shows the number of input lines at value 1, proving that the circuit satisfies the required truth table. Of course, the circuit takes a little time to stabilize, so the correct sum is not shown instantaneously. From the circuit diagram of Fig. 2.19, it would seem that three logic levels are involved, i.e., that the path from input to output can traverse at the most three logic gates. Indeed this maximum delay can and does occur, as may be seen in Fig. 2.20: when the input signals change at $t = 35$, the carry out signal *co* only rises at $t = 38$, three time units later.

It must be emphasized that the adder circuit of Fig. 2.19 is not unique. Many other full adder circuits can be devised, all with the same truth table but using different configurations of different gate types, requiring different numbers of gates, and with different operating speeds. The circuit shown here, for example, uses AND, OR, and XOR gates, but many designers actually prefer a mix of NAND, NOR, and XNOR gates. Some other possible designs are discussed in a later section.

Conventional combinational circuits

Practical large-scale circuits are designed using multiplexers, half and full adders, and various other combined circuits as well as the elementary logic gates

Table 2.4. Integrated circuit chips with combinational circuits

Description	Type number	Pins
4-bit magnitude comparator	74LS85	16
1-of-8 decoder/demultiplexer	74LS138	16
Eight-input multiplexer	74LS151	16
Two four-input multiplexers	74LS153	16
4-line to 16-line decoder	74154	24
8-bit magnitude comparator	74LS682	20
Three half-adders	4038	16

themselves. Semiconductor device manufacturers therefore furnish not only elementary gates, but sets of combinational circuits as well. These are generally packaged several to a chip. The circuits themselves are comparatively small, while their connecting wires are huge in relation to the transistors themselves; thus the major limitation in packaging is often not the complexity of the circuits, but the number of external connections required. A selection of common chips is shown in Table 2.4.

The various composite circuits find wide application as building blocks of digital systems. Word-width multiplexers are constructed of 1-bit multiplexers, arithmetic units are made up of full and half adders combined with overflow detectors. Apodix caters to this fact, as do most large-scale simulators, by including in its library of gate types a number of the combinational circuits most likely to occur, so that the user need not bother defining them as combinations of elementary gates. This approach to simulation closely parallels the reality of a laboratory, where half-adders and comparators would ordinarily be acquired as such, not constructed out of individual logic gates when required. The combinational circuits recognized by Apodix appear in Table 2.5. It is worth noting that nearly all of these have multiple outputs, unlike the elementary logic gates.

The combinational circuits provided in Apodix differ from equivalent gate combinations in one very important way: they are regarded as single devices for time-delay purposes. Thus the full adder implemented as a group of elementary gates would always have a characteristic speed of three time delay units. In contrast, the full adder provided by Apodix has exactly the same truth table, but stabilizes in one time delay unit.

The speed difference between built-in circuits and their equivalents assembled from elementary gates is easily demonstrated by comparing two full adders. Fig.

Table 2.5. Combinational circuits recognized by Apodix

Name	Element description	Inputs	Outputs
hfad	Half adder (no carry in)	2	2
flad	Full adder cell	3	2
mux	N-input enabled multiplexer	$2^N + N + 1$	1
dec	N to 2^N decoder	N	2^N
enc	2^N to N encoder	2^N	N

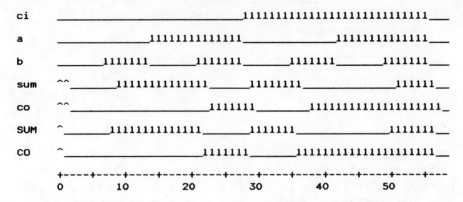

Fig. 2.21.   Comparison of a full adder built of logic gates (*sum, co*) with the built-in full adder (*SUM, CO*).

2.21 shows the results of driving two full adders with inputs ci, a, b, exactly as in Fig. 2.20; the outputs are SUM and CO for a full adder as provided by Apodix, sum and co for the full adder built up from elementary gates:

```
circuit fulladd2:
    {
    hfad: a, b > sum1, c1;
    hfad: ci, sum1 > sum, c2;
    or: c1, c2 > co;
    flad: a, b, ci > SUM, CO;
    }
```

exactly the same as given in Fig. 2.19, so the co and sum outputs are identical to Fig. 2.20. Examination of Fig. 2.21 shows that the truth tables produced by both circuits are identical.

Word-length addition

Elementary adder circuits, full and half, may be combined to yield digital circuits of considerable complexity. One frequent requirement that can be satisfied by combining adders is a *word-width adder*, a device to add two integers of n bits each. This circuit can be built out of one half-adder circuit and $n - 1$ full adders. Suppose $A_{n-1}, \ldots, A_0$ are the bits of the addend, $B_{n-1}, \ldots, B_0$ those of the augend. The addition of A_0 and B_0 is achieved by a half-adder, since there cannot be any carry in to the least significant digit. However, the addition of A_1 to B_1, of A_2 to B_2, ... requires full adders, with the carry out of the kth full adder becoming the carry in of the $k + 1^{st}$. The result, for $n = 4$, is shown in Fig. 2.22.

The working characteristics of a 4-bit adder are easily enough explored by simulation. A suitable circuit is given by

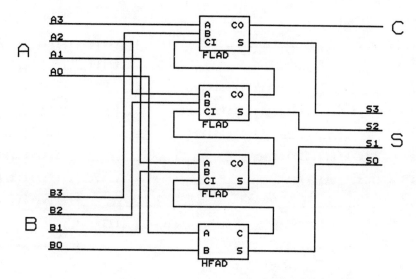

Fig. 2.22.   Four-bit adder, constructed of a half-adder and three full adders.

```
    /* Four-bit adder */
circuit wordaddr:
    {
    hfad: A0, B0 > S0, C0;
    flad: A1, B1, C0 > S1, C1;
    flad: A2, B2, C1 > S2, C2;
    flad: A3, B3, C2 > S3, C;
    }
```

to which suitable input specifications need to be added. Representative inputs, written as 4-bit words, might be

$$
\begin{array}{lll}
A = 0101 & B = 0001 & 0 < t < 15; \\
A = 0101 & B = 0011 & 15 < t < 30; \\
A = 0101 & B = 1101 & 30 < t < 45; \\
A = 0101 & B = 1010 & 45 < t.
\end{array}
$$

For simplicity, the input word A has been maintained at the same value 0101 throughout. Results for this simulation are given in Fig. 2.23.

Although every one of the individual circuit modules in Fig. 2.22 responds to its inputs within one delay time, the 4-bit adder as a whole cannot guarantee a correct result in less than four delay times. To yield a correct result, every one of the full adders must be provided a correct carry in as well as the values of its input bits A_k and B_k. However, the carry-in bit of one full adder is always the carry-out bit of another, so the input to any one full adder cannot be known with certainty until the previous adder has stabilized. With one time unit required to stabilize each adder in the chain, an n-bit adder may therefore take n time units to yield the correct result. This behavior is clearly visible in Fig. 2.23, where the result computed from inputs applied at $t = 15$ is not stable until $t = 18$, and

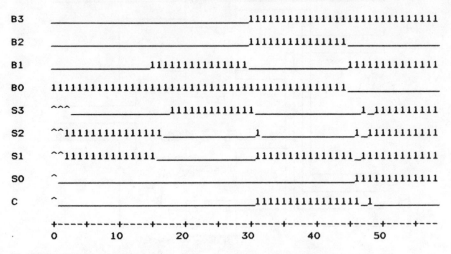

Fig. 2.23. The four-bit adder of Fig. 2.22 may take up to four delay times to produce a correct sum and carry. The input word is $A = 0101$ throughout and is not shown.

the result of new inputs at $t = 45$ only appears at $t = 49$. Even where no carries occur, correct results do not necessarily appear more quickly; the addition $0101 + 0111 = 1111$ which occurs at $t = 45$ generates no carries at all yet takes the maximum possible time to settle down.Correct results may appear sooner—the sum and carry at $t = 15$ are computed in three time units—but there is no way of knowing whether they are correct until four delay times have elapsed. At $t = 30$, for example, the S_2 bit responds to its inputs A_2, B_2 within one time unit; but it reverses subsequently because the carry C_1 arrives one time unit later to demand a different result.

The 4-bit adder of Fig. 2.22 may be extended to a greater arithmetic word length, i.e., to a larger number of bits, by including a larger number of full adder circuits. The carry in to each full adder, of course, remains the carry out of the previous one, just as in Fig. 2.22. Eight-bit, 32-bit, and other adders may be constructed in this way.

Status flags in additions

The adder of Fig. 2.22 is not entirely adequate for use in a practical computer, for simply computing the sum is rarely enough. For twos complement arithmetic to be successful, it is essential to show whether there was a carry out of the high-order digit, whether the twos complement numeric range was overflowed, and whether the result is positive or negative. These three questions can be handled if, in addition to the sum S, three 1-bit outputs are provided: the *carry bit* C, the *overflow bit* V, and the *negative bit* N.

The carry bit C is very simply handled: it is merely the carry out of the full adder that forms the most significant bit S_{n-1} of the sum. Since a full adder is used for forming the most significant bit S_{n-1}, this bit already exists and is shown in Fig. 2.19. Similarly, the negative bit N need be no more than a replica of the most significant bit S_{n-1} of the sum, for in twos complement notation all negative numbers have the most significant bit set to 1. Thus no additional circuitry is needed to provide C and N flag bits in a digital computer.

The overflow bit V conventionally serves to flag an arithmetic overflow, in which the true sum exceeds the range of numbers representable with n bits and therefore cannot be expressed in twos complement notation with the word length available. An overflow is considered to have occurred if the addend and augend have the same sign, but the result has a different sign. In other words, V is determined by the truth table

A_{n-1}	B_{n-1}	S_{n-1}	V
0	0	0	0
0	0	1	1
0	1	0	0
0	1	1	0
1	0	0	0
1	0	1	0
1	1	0	1
1	1	1	0

One direct realization of this truth table is implied in its verbal description. The phrase *if the addend and augend have the same sign* could be restated *if the exclusive OR function of the sign bits is false*, implying the use of an XNOR gate to compare A_{n-1} and B_{n-1}. Similarly, the phrase *but the result has a different sign* may be restated as *if the exclusive OR of the signs is true*, implying use of an XOR gate to compare S_{n-1} and A_{n-1}. These two conditions, as reflected in the outputs of the XNOR and XOR gates, are then compared in a two-input AND gate. The resulting circuit is shown in Fig. 2.24. A word-width adder suitable for use in the arithmetic unit of a computer can be constructed by combining the flag bit circuit given in Fig. 2.24 with the basic word-width adder circuit of Fig. 2.22.

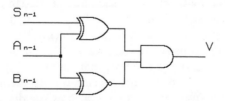

Fig. 2.24. Circuit for setting the overflow bit of a summing register (word-width adder).

Analysis of digital circuits

The design of digital circuits is the art of combining a few types of elementary building blocks in such a way as to make up a larger whole. The composite whole is constructed to be capable of performing some specified function that is often quite complicated, and one which the individual parts are unable to perform except by being cleverly combined. The task of the designer is to combine science, art, and experience to achieve the goals in view.

There is a great deal of similarity between circuit design and the writing of computer programs. Their resemblance should not be surprising, for logic circuits are structurally quite similar to programs. Both are required to fulfill prescribed functions, i.e., to establish a relationship between a specified domain of inputs and a specified range of outputs. Both combine large quantities of individually simple parts or functions into much more complex composites. Both are the products of careful analysis followed by verification through well-designed tests.

Logical variables and functions

Three distinct tools have been used to describe digital circuits so far: circuit diagrams, truth tables, and Apodix descriptions. There is a direct correspondence between an Apodix description and a circuit diagram, the two merely representing different notations for the same object. Truth tables are different, in that they specify what outputs correspond to what inputs, but they do not even hint at a circuit that might correspond to the table.There exists an algebraic notation often used to describe logic relationships, called *Boolean algebra*, which is related to truth tables in as intimate a way as Apodix descriptions are related to circuit diagrams. In other words, expressions written in Boolean algebraic notation correspond directly to truth tables, and conversely. Just as restating circuit diagrams in a formal notation permits simulation by means of Apodix, so the use of a formal algebraic notation allows truth tables to be manipulated and transformed by means of algebraic operations. So far as the circuit designer is concerned, Boolean algebra is a useful tool for dealing with truth tables, a tool which allows circuits to be deduced from tables and to be modified into convenient configurations.

The existence of Boolean algebra in no way obviates a need for computational tools such as Apodix. Digital circuit design, like the design of almost any engineering product, involves two main types of activity, analysis and simulation. Analysis employs Boolean algebra, and strives to establish possible circuit configurations through the construction and manipulation of truth relationships. Simulation amounts to carrying out tests that could equally well be performed in the laboratory—if one had infinitely accurate instruments and a very great deal of patience. Simulation employs tools such as Apodix; analysis is done in the first instance with pencil and paper, though computer programs do exist to help out in the routine aspects of analysis too.

Boolean algebra deals with *Boolean variables*, also known as *logical variables*. These are mathematical entities which may assume one of two values, *true* or *false*, and no others. The notation usually employed resembles the symbolism of ordinary real algebra: variables are given alphabetic names, possibly with subscripts or indices attached, and their two possible values are denoted by the words *true* and *false*, or occasionally *1* and *0*. Logical variables may be functions of each other, functional relationships being denoted in the customary algebraic fashion, as for example

$$Y = f(X_1, X_2).$$

Logical variables differ from ordinary real algebraic variables in their ability to assume only two values, in contrast to, say, the polynomial $x^2 + 2x + 1$, which can take on infinitely many different values. Truth tables are therefore a valid way of specifying logical functions, for it is actually possible to enumerate all combinations of argument values that can occur, and to give all the corresponding values of the function.

Boolean variables do not have arithmetic values, so that arithmetic operations do not make any sense in connection with them. Only two operations are defined for two Boolean variables, the *logical product*, also known as *logical conjunction* or *intersection*, and the *logical sum*, also called *disjunction* or *union*. Several notations are commonly used. Here the logical product will be denoted by the dot · as in

$$Y = A \cdot B,$$

which is usually pronounced "*A and B*". In a similar way, the plus sign + will denote the logical sum

$$Z = A + B,$$

which is read "*A or B*". The logical product is the function of a two-input AND gate, while the logical sum is the effect of a two-input OR gate. Their corresponding truth tables are given in connection with the gate symbols and definitions above.

Only one operation, negation, can be performed on a single logical variable. Here the apostrophe ′ is used to denote negation, so that A', pronounced "*not A*" stands for the value opposite to the value of A itself; if A is true, A' is false. Negation is exactly the logical function performed by a NOT gate.

There is no real need for algebraic symbols to denote the functions performed by other logic gates, such as NAND or XOR; none are required, since any desired truth value can be created using the logical product, sum, and negation symbols. For example, the operation of a two-input NAND gate is described by $(A \cdot B)'$, a three-input NOR gate by $(A + B + C)'$.

Rules and theorems of Boolean algebra

So far as the computer engineer is concerned, the point of studying Boolean algebra is that Boolean algebra permits formal manipulation of expressions which represent logic circuits. It thereby allows the engineer to determine whether two different circuits behave in an equivalent fashion, and furnishes a convenient formal tool for transforming circuits into others with equivalent characteristics. To perform such transformations, various rules of algebraic manipulation are needed. These rules and a few accompanying theorems are reviewed in this section, taking them in related groupings.

1. *Properties of 0 and 1*

$$0 + A = A$$
$$1 \cdot A = A$$
$$0 \cdot A = 0$$
$$1 + A = 1$$

Proof of these rules can be obtained by enumeration. For example, to prove the first rule, A can be assigned all the possible values (of which there are only two, 0 and 1) in turn. Thus, $0 + 1 = 1$, $0 + 0 = 0$, and the proof is complete. The other three cases can be dealt with similarly.

2. *Idempotence and complementarity*

$$A + A = A$$
$$A \cdot A = A$$
$$A + A' = 1$$
$$A \cdot A' = 0$$

Proof is carried out exactly as for the first four rules, by taking all the possible values of A in turn.

3. *Commutativity*

$$A + B = B + A$$
$$A \cdot B = B \cdot A$$

Proof can again be furnished by enumeration. Because there are now two variables, and each may take on either of two values, four possibilities exist in each case.

4. *Associativity*

$$(A + B) + C = A + (B + C)$$
$$(A \cdot B) \cdot C = A \cdot (B \cdot C)$$

Proof by enumeration is still the best approach. However, there are now eight possible combinations of values for the three variables A, B, and C; thus it may be better to write a short program in Pascal or Fortran than to attempt doing the enumeration by hand. In essence, these laws of associativity say that in a string of variables connected by similar operators, the parentheses may be moved about at will.

5. *Distributivity*

$$A + (B \cdot C) = (A + B) \cdot (A + C)$$
$$A \cdot (B + C) = (A \cdot B) + (A \cdot C)$$

These laws are sometimes interpreted informally as saying that A may be "moved into the parentheses, taking along its associated operator." Of course, they may also be viewed in the opposite sense, as rules for how A can be factored out of an expression.

6. *Absorption*

$$A + (A \cdot B) = A$$
$$A \cdot (A + B) = A$$
$$A + (A' \cdot B) = A + B$$
$$A \cdot (A' + B) = A \cdot B$$

Proof can be given by enumeration, as in the foregoing cases. But for the last two rules in particular, a more elegant approach is to work algebraically, applying the rules on associativity and distributivity.

7. *De Morgan's theorems*

$$(A \cdot B)' = A' + B'$$
$$(A + B)' = A' \cdot B'$$

Proof by enumeration is easy in this case, for there are only two variables and therefore four cases to consider. To take the second line, the same procedure can be followed; but it may be more elegant to employ the *principle of duality*, which follows.

8. *Duality*

Every law and theorem has a dual form, obtained by (a) interchanging all $+$ and $\cdot$ operators, (b) interchanging all 0 and 1 values explicitly given in expressions.

As it applies to the logical rules given here, the principle is obvious enough. However, it should be noted that *dual* does not mean *the same*; the word implies *distinct, though similar in form*. The two De Morgan theorems, for example, are related through the duality principle; so are the two rules on absorption, or those on distributivity. Nevertheless, every pair expresses two distinct truths, not the same one in two different forms of expression.

Circuit modification by Boolean algebra

The theorems of Boolean algebra and their associated rules of algebraic manipulation permit logical expressions to be converted between various forms. Simple examples may serve to illustrate this point.

Consider a logic circuit whose operation is represented by the following truth table:

A	B	f
0	0	1
0	1	0
1	0	0
1	1	0

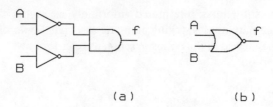

(a)   (b)

Fig. 2.25.   (a) A circuit using NOT and AND gates only. (b) A realization of the same function with a single NOR gate.

It is easy to verify that an algebraic expression which produces the output variable X correctly is

$$f = A' \cdot B'.$$

A circuit to produce this output variable is shown in Fig. 2.25a. The gates used here flow naturally from the algebraic expression: there are two inverters (NOT gates) to produce A' and B', and one AND gate which directly corresponds to the logical product operator.

In many applications NAND and NOR gates are preferred to their AND and OR equivalents. To obtain a circuit that employs such gates, the algebraic expression that describes the circuit may be recast, using the De Morgan theorems, as

$$f = (A + B)'.$$

The corresponding circuit consists of a single NOR gate, as shown in Fig. 2.25b.

It should be noted that both circuits shown in Fig. 2.25 satisfy the required truth table. However, the circuit of Fig. 2.25a not only requires both AND gates and NOT gates, but it represents a *two-level realization* of the function; in other words, it requires signals to pass through two gates on their way from input to output, and therefore involves two time delays. The circuit of Fig. 2.25b, on the other hand, requires only a single NOR gate; it is a *single level realization* of the function. Thus it saves space and in most cases will prove faster as well.

For a somewhat more ambitious example, consider the specification that led to the overflow bit circuit of Fig. 2.24: *if the addend and augend have the same sign, and the result has a different sign*, then (and only then) the overflow variable V has the value 1. This specification may be regarded as consisting of two parts: V has the value 1 if assertion T is true or if assertion U is false,

$$V = T \cdot U',$$

where T is the assertion *the addend and augend have the same sign*, while U represents *the sum and the addend have the same sign*.

The assertion T, regarding the signs of the addend and augend, may be rephrased as "if both sign bits are true or if both are not true". That is to say, T may be expressed as

$$T = C + D$$

where C is such as to have the value *true* if both the addend sign bit A and the augend sign bit B have the value *true*, while D is true only if both are *false*. Suitable expressions are

$$C = A \cdot B$$
$$D = A' \cdot B'$$

so that, on combining,

$$T = (A \cdot B) + (A' \cdot B').$$

The second part U of the specification can be formalized as

$$U = (A \cdot S) + (A' \cdot S')$$

which compares the sign bits of the addend and the sum, A and S. Substituting the expressions for T and U, V now becomes

$$V = [(A \cdot B) + (A' \cdot B')] \cdot [(A \cdot S) + (A' \cdot S')]'.$$

This expression is a formal statement of the specification, and can be implemented directly as a circuit. To do so, one gate is employed wherever the algebraic expression involves an operator, and the gates are connected so as to have the variables correctly interrelated. A circuit that directly realizes the above expression for V appears in Fig. 2.26a. In the algebraic expression, two logical

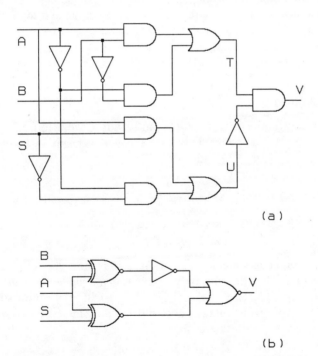

(a)

(b)

Fig. 2.26. (a) Direct realization of the overflow bit circuit in AND, OR, NOT gates. (b) An all-inverted-logic design for the same device.

sum symbols and five logical product symbols appear; accordingly, Fig. 2.26a contains two OR gates and five AND gates, as well as four inverters to produce the negated values A', B', S', and U' which are required.

The direct circuit realization procedure shown here always works, and will always lead to a circuit that satisfies the specification. It may not lead to the most desirable circuit forms, because the resulting circuits often contain many more gates than minimally necessary. The circuit of Fig. 2.26a is certainly a good deal more complicated than that shown in Fig. 2.24, which performs the same function.

To arrive at different circuits for the same task, the algebraic expressions may be rewritten in various ways. For the circuit under consideration, application of De Morgan's first theorem yields

$$V = (T' + U)'$$

which suggests combining T' and U with a NOR gate. T' is of course readily obtained from T by means of an inverter NOT gate. In their turn, T and U are directly realizable by XNOR gates, as in their defining equations immediately above. The result is shown in Fig. 2.26b: it involves negated-logic gates only. In fact, it can easily be modified to use only XNOR and NOR gates, since an inverter can be made by connecting together the two inputs of a NOR gate.

Algebraic manipulation of the circuit describing equations can rapidly produce a whole host of possible circuits, which are guaranteed to have the same behavior but different numbers of the various gate types. Devising the same circuits by verbal or graphical argument rather than symbolic manipulation is possible, but it is often more difficult and invariably more error-prone.

Another full adder

The process of algebraic manipulation can be put to work to produce an alternative circuit for the full adder. This time, the work is begun by taking the equations that describe Figs. 2.17 and 2.19:

$$C1 = A \cdot B$$
$$S1 = A \cdot B' + A' \cdot B$$
$$C2 = S1 \cdot Ci$$
$$S = Ci \cdot S1' + Ci' \cdot S1$$
$$Co = C1 + C2.$$

The weak spot in the full adder design of Fig. 2.19 is the carry out; it is computed by three-level logic but the sum only involves two logic levels. If the carry out can be implemented in two-level logic, the adder will perform one-third faster. The algebraic expression for the carry out Co is obtained by combining the above five equations, with the result

$$Co = A \cdot B + (A \cdot B' + A' \cdot B) \cdot Ci$$
$$Co = A \cdot B + A \cdot B' \cdot Ci + A' \cdot B \cdot Ci$$

By the principle of complementarity, the first term on the right may be rewritten in the form

$$A \cdot B = A \cdot B \cdot (Ci + Ci') = A \cdot B \cdot Ci + A \cdot B \cdot Ci'$$

so that

$$Co = A \cdot B \cdot Ci + A \cdot B \cdot Ci' + A \cdot B' \cdot Ci + A' \cdot B \cdot Ci$$

By the principle of idempotence, the right-hand side may be augmented by as many terms of the form $(A \cdot B \cdot Ci)$ as desired. Thus Co may be written as

$$\begin{aligned} Co = &\, A \cdot B \cdot Ci + A \cdot B \cdot Ci' \\ &+ A \cdot B \cdot Ci + A \cdot B' \cdot Ci \\ &+ A \cdot B \cdot Ci + A' \cdot B \cdot Ci \end{aligned}$$

Making use of the properties of commutativity and distributivity, Co next becomes

$$\begin{aligned} Co = &\, A \cdot B \cdot (Ci + Ci') \\ &+ A \cdot (B + B') \cdot Ci \\ &+ (A + A') \cdot B \cdot Ci \end{aligned}$$

The complementarity property of Boolean algebra, however, requires the quantities in parentheses to be true always. Hence

$$Co = A \cdot B + A \cdot Ci + B \cdot Ci$$

is obtained. This expression is easily realized in two-level logic, as shown in Fig. 2.27a: three AND gates followed by a three-input OR gate. A corresponding two-level realization of the sum function appears in Fig. 2.27b.

Should a negated-logic form of the carry circuit be desired, only a little algebraic manipulation is required. The final expression for the carry Co may be written

$$Co = (A \cdot B)'' + (A \cdot Ci)'' + (B \cdot Ci)''$$

since a double inversion leaves every term unaltered. Applying De Morgan's theorem, the outer negations may be collected,

$$Co = [(A \cdot B)' \cdot (A \cdot Ci)' \cdot (B \cdot Ci)']'$$

suggesting that the desired circuit consists of three two-input NAND gates and one three-input NAND, as in Fig. 2.27c.

An encoder circuit

Encoding problems are encountered in many signaling circuits. The circuitry to control an elevator furnishes a typical example. In a building comprising seven floors and a basement, the elevator control panel would ordinarily contain eight push buttons marked $B, 1, \ldots, 7$, or perhaps $0, \ldots, 7$. The eight possible floor

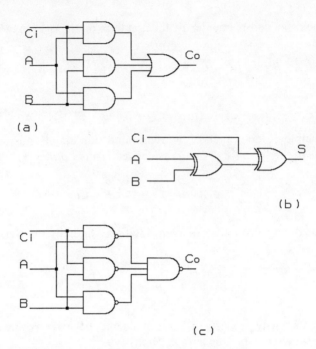

Fig. 2.27.   (a) Two-level carry bit circuit. (b) Sum bit circuit for full adder. (c) Carry bit circuit using NAND gates only.

selections certainly can be communicated and remembered as binary numbers in the range 000 to 111, requiring three signal lines. However, the push buttons would normally be simple 1-wire switches. To store and process the information gained from them, a conversion from single-wire signals to a 3-bit word must first take place. In other words, the eight possible logical signals must be *encoded* in a 3-bit word; the circuit to accomplish this task is termed an *encoder*. How such a circuit is used in practice is shown in Fig. 2.28; its truth table is given below.

P7	*P6*	*P5*	*P4*	*P3*	*P2*	*P1*	*P0*	*N2*	*N1*	*N0*
0	0	0	0	0	0	0	1	0	0	0
0	0	0	0	0	0	1	0	0	0	1
0	0	0	0	0	1	0	0	0	1	0
0	0	0	0	1	0	0	0	0	1	1
0	0	0	1	0	0	0	0	1	0	0
0	0	1	0	0	0	0	0	1	0	1
0	1	0	0	0	0	0	0	1	1	0
1	0	0	0	0	0	0	0	1	1	1

On examining the truth table, it is evident that the three outputs may be described by three Boolean algebraic expressions as

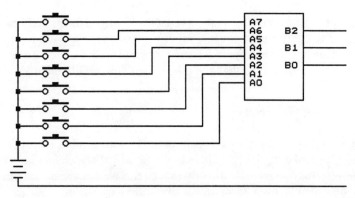

Fig. 2.28. An eight-line to three-line encoder for push button signals in an elevator.

$$N2 = P7 + P6 + P5 + P4$$
$$N1 = P7 + P6 + P3 + P2$$
$$N0 = P7 + P5 + P3 + P1$$

Each expression corresponds to one output column of the table. Their realization in digital logic circuits is easy, once it is recognized that each expression corresponds to a single four-input OR gate. A circuit that directly implements the algebraic expressions is shown in Fig. 2.29.

It should be noted that the circuit of Fig. 2.29 contains one flaw, which renders it less than totally satisfactory in some applications. In writing the algebraic descriptions to describe the truth table, it is assumed that only eight states of the input are possible, with one line asserted and the remainder not. In the elevator example, that would correspond to only a single button being pushed at a time. However, if two buttons are pushed simultaneously, wrong outputs can result. For example, asserting lines *P2* and *P4* simultaneously (i.e., requesting both the second and fourth floors) results in an output of $010 + 100 = 110$, the same as if only *P6* had been asserted, and the elevator presumably will go to the sixth floor. There is no way for the circuit of Fig. 2.29 to tell whether one or two buttons were pushed, so this particular circuit is only useful in applications where multiple inputs cannot appear.

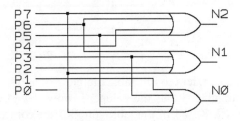

Fig. 2.29. An eight-line to three-line encoder circuit.

Encoder circuits are commercially available in various forms and line counts. They are quite common, so much so that the word *encoder*, used without any further qualifiers, is generally understood to mean a 2^M-line to M-line encoder with a truth table similar to that given here for 8-line to 3-line encoding.

Synthesis of digital circuits

The interest taken by computer engineers in Boolean algebra reflects that such expressions describe digital circuits in a precise way. Each elementary algebraic expression (term) corresponds directly to a circuit element and each circuit element is describable by a term in an algebraic expression. This fact can be exploited not only to recast existing circuits in different forms, but also to derive circuits in a systematic way, beginning with the algebraic expressions that describe their terminal behavior and associating a circuit realization to each term or group of Boolean terms. However, the first need is to set up the initial algebraic expressions and ensuring that they correctly represent the desired truth table. This section deals with the initial derivation of algebraic expressions and (to a lesser extent) with directing their manipulation.

Just as a single truth table can give rise to a host of different circuits, so can an algebraic expression yield several circuit configurations. There do exist some systematic methods for choosing circuits with particular properties from among the multitude. They, however, are beyond the scope of this chapter and will be mentioned only briefly.

Minterm realization of networks

One attractive systematic method for obtaining circuits from Boolean expressions is *minterm realization*. The method is best introduced by example. Consider once again the truth table which describes the logical function V of Fig. 2.24 (the overflow bit function). It reads

A	B	S	V
0	0	0	0
0	0	1	1
0	1	0	0
0	1	1	0
1	0	0	0
1	0	1	0
1	1	0	1
1	1	1	0

A logical expression equivalent to this table can be written in the following fashion. According to the table, V has the value 1 in rows 1 and 6, the value 0 in rows 0, 2, 3, 4, 5, and 7. Row 1 of the table contains the combination of values

$$A = 0, B = 0, S = 1$$

and row 6 contains

$$A = 1, B = 1, S = 0.$$

In other words, two logical variables, say m_1 and m_6, could be defined by

$$m_1 = A' \cdot B' \cdot S$$
$$m_6 = A \cdot B \cdot S'$$

so that m_1 is true in row 1 (but nowhere else) and m_6 is true in row 6 (but in no other). The statement that V has value 1 in these two rows may therefore be put in the form

$$V = m_1 + m_6.$$

Substituting the values of m_1 and m_6,

$$V = (A' \cdot B' \cdot S) + (A \cdot B \cdot S')$$

which is recognizable as two three-input AND gates and a single OR gate, along with three inverters, as shown in Fig. 2.30. Comparing with Fig. 2.24, this circuit is seen to be far from minimal in the number of gates; furthermore, it is a three-level circuit realization and therefore slower than that of Fig. 2.24, which only involves two logic levels. The superior circuit of Fig. 2.24 may, however, be obtained by suitable sequences of algebraic transformations of the minterm expression.

Minterm realizations of circuits are not always minimal—indeed they are not minimal very often! However, they are valid realizations and provide a systematic way of proceeding from truth table to algebraic expression.

To summarize, the minterm technique of transforming truth tables into algebraic expressions consists of the following steps:

1. For each row k in which the output column contains 1, define a variable m_k. Its value is the logical product of all the input variables, taken as negated or not according to whether the corresponding tabular column contains 0 or 1.
2. Set the output variable to equal the logical sum of all the row variables m_k.

If the words seem confusing, reference to the example may clarify the matter.

Minterms are also called *sum-of-products* canonic forms of the algebraic

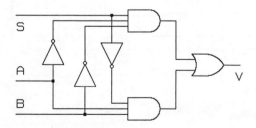

Fig. 2.30. Minterm realization of overflow circuit.

expressions, because the minterm expression always involves the logical sum of all truth table rows, with a logical product form for each row.

A decoder circuit

In doorbell, annunciator, and industrial control circuits, as well as in computers, the need for N-line to 2^N-line decoding often arises. A simple example of such a situation is shown in Fig. 2.31: a display panel contains eight lamps, which are used to indicate at a glance the source of an alarm signal. Only one lamp should be illuminated at a time, corresponding to the binary-encoded number presented at the 3-bit input.

This decoder clearly furnishes the inverse function of the encoder of Fig. 2.29, so the encoder and decoder can be used as a pair in some applications. The truth table to satisfy the requirements implied by Fig. 2.31 resembles that of the encoder, except for an exchange of inputs and outputs:

$N2$	$N1$	$N0$	$P7$	$P6$	$P5$	$P4$	$P3$	$P2$	$P1$	$P0$
0	0	0	0	0	0	0	0	0	0	1
0	0	1	0	0	0	0	0	0	1	0
0	1	0	0	0	0	0	0	1	0	0
0	1	1	0	0	0	0	1	0	0	0
1	0	0	0	0	0	1	0	0	0	0
1	0	1	0	0	1	0	0	0	0	0
1	1	0	0	1	0	0	0	0	0	0
1	1	1	1	0	0	0	0	0	0	0

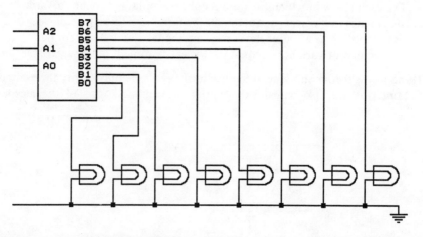

Fig. 2.31.   A conventional decoder circuit asserts only one of 2^N output lines in response to an N-bit input.

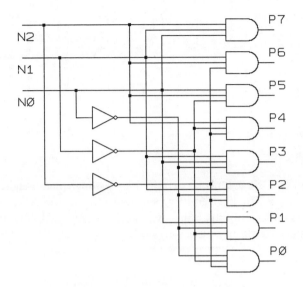

Fig. 2.32.   Three-line to eight-line decoder.

This design problem is readily solved by writing sum-of-products expressions for the output variables. Taking them one row at a time, they read

$$L0 = N2' \cdot N1' \cdot N0'$$
$$L1 = N2' \cdot N1' \cdot N0$$
$$L2 = N2' \cdot N1 \cdot N0'$$
$$L3 = N2' \cdot N1 \cdot N0$$
$$L4 = N2 \cdot N1' \cdot N0'$$
$$L5 = N2 \cdot N1' \cdot N0$$
$$L6 = N2 \cdot N1 \cdot N0'$$
$$L7 = N2 \cdot N1 \cdot N0$$

There is not much to minimize here. It is easily established that each input variable occurs four times, and its complement four times also; there is no great advantage in attempting to reduce one form to the other. The most straightforward and economical solution is the obvious one: to employ three inverters and eight AND gates, as shown in Fig. 2.32.

The decoder shown here happily does not lead to any ambiguities. Unlike the corresponding encoder, its inputs all lead to valid outputs.

A seven-segment display driver

Seven-segment displays are a familiar form of output device; they are used in electronic watches, digital counters, cash registers, and a host of other applications. A single-digit seven-segment display is a composite of seven light-emitting

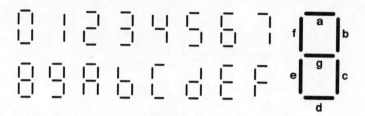

Fig. 2.33. *Left:* A seven-segment hexadecimal symbol set. *Right:* labeling of the seven segments.

diodes (or other visible objects) arranged in a rough figure-eight pattern, as shown in Fig. 2.33. The light-emitting segments are electrically separate, so the display unit is commonly made up as a single plastic package containing the seven illuminated portions and seven connecting pins to allow energizing them individually. An eighth (return or "ground") lead is usually common to all seven.

By lighting individual segments of the display, various different characters can be formed. Because there are seven segments, the total possible number of distinct symbols is $2^7 = 128$, but many of these are not useful because they do not resemble any normal written or printed characters. The octal and hexadecimal character subsets, however, are widely employed. The set of 16 characters shown in Fig. 2.33, and its octal subset, find application in counters and computer displays; its decimal subset is commonly used in calculators and watches.

Suppose it is desired to display an octal numeral, as for example in a counter or in an elevator floor display. The seven segments of the display unit cannot be driven directly from the count to be displayed because the octal numbers 0, . . . ,7 do not correspond directly to the segments to be illuminated. Instead, it is necessary to introduce a *code converter* circuit that will provide, for each binary-encoded number, the correct combination of seven signals to drive the lamps. These combinations, also called *seven-segment display codes*, are shown in Table 2.6. They are easily obtained by inspection of Fig. 2.33.

An easy way to construct a code converter for conversion from binary to seven-segment display codes is sketched in Fig. 2.34. The three input leads $B2$,

Table 2.6. Seven-segment display codes

Input code				Display code						
$B2$	$B1$	$B0$	Octal	a	b	c	d	e	f	g
0	0	0	0	1	1	1	1	1	1	0
0	0	1	1	0	1	1	0	0	0	0
0	1	0	2	1	1	0	1	1	0	1
0	1	1	3	1	1	1	1	0	0	1
1	0	0	4	0	1	1	0	0	1	1
1	0	1	5	1	0	1	1	0	1	1
1	1	0	6	1	0	1	1	1	1	1
1	1	1	7	1	1	1	0	0	0	0

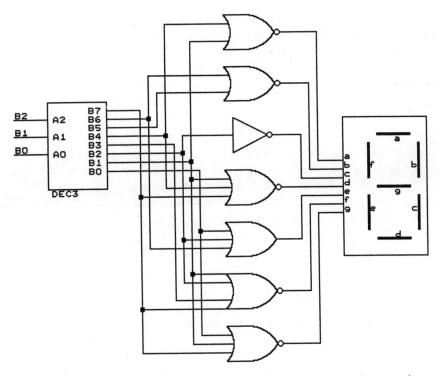

Fig. 2.34. The seven-segment display code is generated by two-stage code conversion.

$B1$, $B0$ carry the binary code corresponding to the desired number. A three-line to eight-line decoder driven by the input lines asserts one (and only one!) of its eight output lines. A small number of logic gates then suffices to produce the set of signals required for the seven segment leads a, b, c, d, e, f, and g.

The simplicity of the logic circuit in Fig. 2.34 derives from the fact that *only one decoder output line can be asserted at a time*. For example, the segment e is illuminated (the e signal is set) whenever decoder output line $d0$ or line $d2$ or line $d6$ is set; otherwise it is not illuminated. That is to say,

$$e = d0 + d2 + d6$$

and similarly for the other segment lines. In contrast to the elevator control problem discussed earlier, no protection is required against the possibility of two decoder output lines being asserted simultaneously.

Even a cursory glance at Table 2.6 will show that most columns of the table contain few zeros and many ones. This fact suggests that it will be more economic to work with negated logic. For example,

$$a = (a')'$$

or

$$a = (d1 + d4)'$$

since (according to Table 2.6) a' is false (hence a is true) when either $d1$ or $d4$ is set. Thus a NOR gate with two inputs may be used instead of an OR gate with six inputs.

Seven-segment displays are widely used and the corresponding code converters (binary to seven segment) are available as standard semiconductor chips.

Maxterm realizations

Truth tables may be turned into algebraic expressions, which lead to circuits, in two dual *canonic forms*. One, the minterm expression corresponding to a truth table, has already been discussed in detail; its dual is called the *maxterm* or *product-of-sums* form. The principle is simple, and its development parallels the argument given for minterms. It may be illustrated by considering the truth table of the overflow bit circuit once more:

A	B	S	V
0	0	0	0
0	0	1	1
0	1	0	0
0	1	1	0
1	0	0	0
1	0	1	0
1	1	0	1
1	1	1	0

The variable V is false in rows 0, 2, 3, 4, 5, and 7 of the table. Its value could therefore be written

$$V = M_0 \cdot M_2 \cdot M_3 \cdot M_4 \cdot M_5 \cdot M_7$$

where the M_k are variables such that M_i is false in row i, true in all the other rows. To see how an expression can be constructed to be true in all rows but one, consider, for example, row 3. This row is characterized by $A = 0$, $B = 1$, $S = 1$. The expression

$$M_3 = A + B' + S'$$

is false if and only if all three of its terms are individually false; and that can only happen in row 3. This algebraic expression is known as the *maxterm* corresponding to row 3. Analogous expressions can be set up for the remaining rows in which V is to have the value *false*. The complete expression

$$V = (A + B + S) \cdot (A + B' + S) \cdot$$
$$(A + B' + S') \cdot (A' + B + S) \cdot$$
$$(A' + B + S') \cdot (A' + B' + S')$$

finally results from substitution into V. This expression is quite obviously realizable as a circuit, in much the same way as the circuit derived from a minterm expression in Fig. 2.30. However, this circuit is quite complicated. It involves six three-input OR gates and a five-input AND gate in addition to several inverters. It certainly is not a minimal or even a reasonably economic way of implementing the truth table given.

It is interesting to note that construction of the maxterms themselves is a straightforward application of De Morgan's theorems, in the following fashion. Suppose a minterm expression is to be derived, but this time for the complemented value V' rather than for V itself. The truth table for the present example then takes the form

A	B	S	V'
0	0	0	1
1	0	0	1
0	0	1	0
1	0	1	1
1	1	0	0
1	1	0	1
1	1	1	0
0	1	1	1

The minterm expression for V' is a bit lengthy but otherwise straightforward. In terms of the minterms m_i of this truth table, it reads

$$V' = m_0 + m_2 + m_3 + m_4 + m_5 + m_7$$

If preferred, an expression for V is easily obtained, by negating both sides:

$$V = (m_0 + m_2 + m_3 + m_4 + m_5 + m_7)'$$

De Morgan's theorem permits removal of the global negation, provided that the individual minterms are negated:

$$V = m_0' \cdot m_2' \cdot m_3' \cdot m_4' \cdot m_5' \cdot m_7'$$

Let a typical term, say m_0', be examined:

$$m_0' = (A' \cdot B' \cdot S')'$$

Applying De Morgan's theorem again,

$$m_0' = A + B + S$$

is easily recognized as the maxterm M_0. Treating the remaining negated minterms in the same fashion, the result is exactly the product-of-sums expression for V already given.

From the example given here it appears that the sum-of-products form of algebraic expression is more compact than the product-of-sums form if only a few rows of the truth table contain the value 1 while the majority contain 0, because the sum-of-products expression contains one term corresponding to every 1 in the output column. Conversely, the product-of-sums expression is composed of terms that correspond to occurrences of the value 0 in the truth table, so it is the more compact form if the truth table exhibits only a few zeros and many rows contain 1. This observation furnishes both a criterion for which form to prefer, and at the same time a technique for making the other form almost equally attractive. The relative numbers of 0 and 1 values in a truth table column can be reversed by inverting the truth values, i.e., by constructing a table for the inverted variable. In the example given, that amounts to working with V' instead of V. For the truth table shown immediately above, the product-of-sums (maxterm) form is clearly the more compact one,

$$V' = (A + B + S') \cdot (A' + B' + S)$$

for it only contains two terms. Of course, this is the wrong function, V' and not V. That difficulty, however, is easily circumvented by inverting its value:

$$V = [(A + B + S') \cdot (A' + B' + S)]'.$$

In a circuit implementation, inversion of V' does not even require an inverter; it is only necessary to make the gate nearest the output a NAND instead of an AND. The circuit of Fig. 2.35 therefore represents another valid realization of the same logical function as Figs. 2.24, 2.26, and 2.30.

It should hardly be necessary to point out that a similar argument may be made for minterm expressions: if they are preferred but the truth table contains 1 in many rows, a compact sum-of-products can be built for the *inverse* function.

Circuit minimization

Many practical logic functions are extremely complicated and would require large amounts of hardware if they were to be implemented directly from their truth tables. Large numbers of logic gates obviously imply a high cost; but possibly more important is that logic circuits with large numbers of gates may respond slowly. To reduce the number of components, thus lowering cost and increasing speed, it is necessary to manipulate the original function to produce a minimal expression.

Simplifying or reducing a logical function such as those described here is done by applying the rules of Boolean algebra. To illustrate the systematic application of algebraic rules, consider the (arbitrarily chosen) function F described by the following truth table:

$X1$	$X2$	$X3$	F
0	0	0	1
0	0	1	1
0	1	0	0
0	1	1	0
1	0	0	0
0	1	1	1
1	1	0	0
1	1	1	0

The sum-of-products expression is the most compact algebraic way of stating this function, because only three rows of the table contain the value $F = 1$.

$$F = X1' \cdot X2' \cdot X3' + X1' \cdot X2' \cdot X3 + X1' \cdot X2 \cdot X3$$

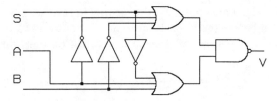

Fig. 2.35.   Negated-maxterm form of overflow circuit.

Implementation of this expression directly in circuit form requires at least a three-input OR gate and three three-input AND gates, as well as several inverters. If two-input gates are used, six AND and two OR gates will be necessary.

The number of gates needed can be reduced considerably by algebraic rearrangement. As a first step in simplification, the *idempotence* rule may be applied. To do so, the expression is first rewritten with the second term duplicated:

$$F = X1' \cdot X2' \cdot X3' + X1' \cdot X2' \cdot X3 +$$
$$X1' \cdot X2' \cdot X3 + X1' \cdot X2 \cdot X3$$

It should be noted that in a Boolean expression such a duplication does not alter the truth value of the function, in contrast to ordinary real algebra. Duplication permits simplification of both the first and last terms. The reason behind this strange first step is that only one variable changes state between the first two terms, i.e., $X3$ is negated in the first but not in the second. Similarly, only $X2$ changes state between the last two terms. Therefore the *distributive* property may be exploited to combine the first pair of terms, and then again the last two:

$$F = X1' \cdot X2' \cdot (X3' + X3) + (X1' + X1) \cdot X2' \cdot X3$$

Next, the *complementation* rule eliminates the bracketed quantities, since $A + A' = 1$ for any A:

$$F = X1' \cdot X2' + X2' \cdot X3$$

Although this expression is considerably simpler than the original, it is still not minimal. The *distributive* law may be used again to reduce it still further:

$$F = (X1' + X3) \cdot X2'$$

This form requires only two gates for its implementation, and possibly two inverters to furnish $X1'$ and $X2'$. This version of the function may be checked by reconstructing the truth table, either by writing a suitable small program in Fortran or Pascal, or (in view of its brevity) by hand.

It may sometimes be necessary to perform the reverse operations, taking a minimal form representation and reexpressing it. This may be desirable because of the availability of certain gate types rather than others. In this case it is useful to be able to regain the canonical form of the function. Obviously, one method is to draw the truth table corresponding to the function and then to write its minterm representation. However, if the table is complex it is often more convenient to use an algebraic approach. Proceeding in reverse, as it were, the minimal function can be expanded back into one of the two canonical form representations by using the rules of Boolean algebra. Consider, for example, the function

$$F = (X1' + X2) \cdot (X1 + X3').$$

If the *distributive* law is applied,

$$F = X1' \cdot X1 + X1' \cdot X3' + X2 \cdot X1 + X2' \cdot X3$$

results. Note that the term $(X1' \cdot X1)$ always has the value 0 and thus may be discarded from the logical sum. Each of the remaining terms may now be expressed as a function of all three variables by applying the *complementation* law:

$$F = X1' \cdot X3' \cdot (X2 + X2') + X1 \cdot X2 \cdot X3 + X3') + (X1 + X1') \cdot X2 \cdot X3'$$

Expanding, there is obtained

$$F = X1' \cdot X2 \cdot X3' + X1' \cdot X2' \cdot X3' + X1 \cdot X2 \cdot X3 + X1 \cdot X2 \cdot X3' + X1 \cdot X2 \cdot X3' + X1' \cdot X2 \cdot X3'$$

which, upon application of the *idempotence* rule, becomes

$$F = X1' \cdot X2' \cdot X3' + X1 \cdot X2 \cdot X3 + X1' \cdot X2 \cdot X3' + X1 \cdot X2 \cdot X3'$$

This expression is in true *sum-of-products* form, and is therefore the result sought.

The multiplexer revisited

The 1-bit multiplexer circuit was discussed earlier in some detail, but it is worth reconsidering as a relatively simple logic circuit which provides a good test of the algebraic minimization procedures. Omitting the *enable* signal, its truth table is as previously given,

S	A	B	X
0	0	0	0
0	0	1	1
0	1	0	0
0	1	1	1
1	0	0	0
1	0	1	0
1	1	0	1
1	1	1	1

Thus, if S has the value 0 then B is connected to the output X; if S has the value 1 then the output X echoes input A.

The output column X of this truth table contains the value 1 in exactly as many rows as the value 0. Hence, there is little to choose on grounds of complexity; the product-of-sums and sum-of-products forms both contain four terms. The minterm form is

$$X = m_1 + m_3 + m_6 + m_7$$

or, writing out the variable names in detail

$$X = S' \cdot A' \cdot B + S' \cdot A \cdot B + \\ S \cdot A \cdot B' + S \cdot A \cdot B$$

If S' is factored out of the first two terms and S out of the last two, there is obtained

$$X = S' \cdot B \cdot (A' + A) + S \cdot A \cdot (B' + B)$$

But $A + A' = 1$ always. This expression therefore reduces to

$$X = S' \cdot B + S \cdot A$$

which is the expression originally arrived at by purely verbal argument. The circuit that directly corresponds to the logical expression comprises one OR gate, two AND gates, and an inverter, as shown earlier in Fig. 2.8. The algebraic approach clearly has not caused any economies to be achieved, perhaps because the circuit intuitively and verbally arrived at was minimal in any case. However, a lack of great improvement is hardly a reason for rejecting algebraic analysis. The point is rather that a verbal argument can only be carried out by a human designer; the algebraic reduction is systematic and can be carried out, in principle and often in practice, by a computer. Algebraic representation of the requirements in the form of a truth table, and algebraic reduction to circuit form, are the essential first steps to *computer aided design* of digital circuits.

Because one type of gate or another is readily available, designers frequently wish to have alternative configurations for the same circuit function and in any case, they often prefer to use negated logic (NAND and NOR) gates. A realization of the multiplexer using such gates may be obtained by rewriting the above logical expression. Negating the right-hand side twice,

$$X = [(S' \cdot B + S \cdot A)']' .$$

Applying De Morgan's theorem, the logical sum operation is replaced by a logical product. Thus X assumes the form

$$X = [(S' \cdot B)' \cdot (S \cdot A)']'$$

which has a circuit implementation consisting of three NAND gates and one inverter; no other gate types are involved. The circuit diagram for this logical expression appears in Fig. 2.36.

Adding an enabling signal E to the multiplexer design shown is easy. The output X is to have the value shown for $E = 1$, and is to remain at 0 whenever

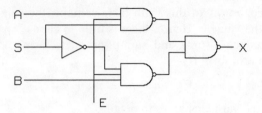

Fig. 2.36.   One-bit multiplexer using NAND gates.

$E = 0$. The final logical expression is easily amended to take care of this requirement,

$$X = E \cdot [(S' \cdot B)' \cdot (S \cdot A)']'.$$

This algebraic form is best rewritten so as to keep the number of logic levels low, hence the circuit operating speed high. Using De Morgan's theorem yet again,

$$X = [E' + (S' \cdot B)' \cdot (S \cdot A)']'$$

or

$$X = \{[E' + (S' \cdot B)]' \cdot [E' + (S \cdot A)']\}'$$

which may be rewritten in a form that suggests three-input NAND gates:

$$X = [(E \cdot S' \cdot B)' \cdot (E \cdot S \cdot A)']'$$

This is the form of circuit actually shown in Fig. 2.36. It merely requires the use of NAND gates with three inputs instead of two.

Problems

1. Show how a two-input NAND gate can be used to make a NOT gate (an inverter).
2. Show that an AND gate may be constructed out of a two-transistor NOR gate preceded by two one-transistor inverters.
3. Any two-input logic gate can be characterized by a truth table that contains two input columns and one output column. How many distinct two-input gates, and corresponding truth tables, can there be?
4. The conventional symbol for a NAND gate is that of an AND gate with a negation bubble attached to the output. Some designers prefer a symbol that resembles the OR gate, with negation bubbles attached to the inputs. Is there any logical justification for this practice? Can an alternative symbol for the NOR gate be devised?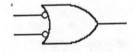

5. Prove that the XOR function, sometimes denoted by ⊕, is associative, i.e., that $(x \oplus y) \oplus z = x \oplus (y \oplus z)$.

6. If the property of associativity holds, then $(x \oplus y) \oplus z$ or $x \oplus (y \oplus z)$ may equally well be written $x \oplus y \oplus z$, the placement of parentheses being unimportant. The latter expression, however, describes a three-input XOR gate. Give its full truth table.

7. The XNOR gate of Fig. 2.16 can be eliminated, by noting that the *equality* signal can only have value 1 if neither the L nor the G signal has value 1. What is the resulting circuit? Verify by simulation that it is valid.

8. Show that a comparator circuit, whose truth table is identical to that given in the worked example in the text, can be made up by using NOR gates only. Test such a circuit, using Apodix.

9. Find the total time required for an addition by the full adder circuit given in Fig. 2.19. Verify this value using an Apodix simulation. Is the time taken the same for all possible input values?

10. Find the maximum time taken for adding two 4-bit words, using the 4-bit adder circuit of Fig. 2.22. How does this time compare with the time for adding two 8-bit words, using a similar circuit with extra full adders inserted?

11. Construct a full adder circuit corresponding to Fig. 2.19, using negated-logic gates (NAND, NOR, and NOT) only. Verify that it satisfies the truth table.

12. Construct a circuit made up of AND, OR, and NOT gates directly from the expression

$$V = [(A \cdot B) + (A' \cdot B')] \cdot [(A \cdot S) + (A' \cdot S')]'.$$

How many gates are required?

13. Construct an encoder to the same specifications as that of Fig. 2.29, but better behaved for ambiguous or multiple inputs. What specification problems are there? What design problems?

14. Determine how many distinct n-input circuits with one output can exist. How many are there for $n = 3$?

15. Prove the laws of commutativity of the logical product and logical sum operations, using a Fortran or Pascal program that generates truth tables by enumeration of all possible cases.

16. Prove De Morgan's theorems using a Fortran or Pascal program that generates truth tables by enumeration of all possible cases.

17. Is it true that the maxterm and minterm forms of a truth table may be regarded as *dual* forms? In other words, can one be derived from the other by interchanging 0 and 1 values, and also interchanging product and sum operators?

18. Write the maxterm expression corresponding to the truth table of the 1-bit multiplexer (ignoring the *enable* signal) and perform algebraic reduction to obtain a useful, nearly minimal circuit. Is it possible to build such a multiplexer using only NOR gates?

19. Prove that $(A + B + C)' = A' \cdot B' \cdot C'$. Show how this result can be generalized to apply to n variables: $(V_1 + \ldots + V_n)' = \ldots$

20. Construct the maxterm expression for the multiplexer of Fig. 2.36. Use it to derive an alternative circuit realization of the same truth table. Test your circuit using Apodix, to verify that it yields the correct performance.

21. A circuit is to have two inputs X and Y, and two output lines S and R. The outputs are to echo the inputs, so that $S = X$ and $R = Y$, except that in the case

$X = Y = 1$ the outputs are to be the complements of the inputs, i.e., $S = R = 0$. Write the truth table of this circuit, and write both maxterm and minterm expressions to describe it. Derive circuit realizations from both.

22. Test the circuits of Problem 21 with Apodix and determine which acts more quickly. By algebraic manipulation, minimize the time taken for these circuits to act (or, if your circuits are as fast as is possible, prove so by algebraic manipulation).

23. In data transmission, ASCII characters are often *parity encoded*: the seven bits of the ASCII characters are placed in bits 6 to 0 of an 8-bit byte, while bit 7 is given such a value that the total number of set bits in the byte is odd. Devise a combinational logic circuit to produce parity-encoded characters from 7-bit ASCII characters.

24. Parity encoding (as defined in Problem 23) is often used to spot data transmission errors: if a received message has lost a bit in transmission, the byte to which it belongs will not have the parity bit (bit 8) correctly set. Devise a combinational logic circuit to produce 7-bit ASCII characters from parity-encoded characters and to signal errors by setting a *parity error* line high.

25. A sequence of K bits is said to be *bitonic* if it contains zero or more 0s, followed by zero or more 1s, followed by zero or more 0s. (For example: 000110, 000000, 111111, 001111 are bitonic sequences, but 010111, 111001 are not.) Design a logic circuit with six input lines A_5-A_0 and one output line F, such that $F = 1$ if the sequence $A_5- A_0$ is bitonic, and $F = 0$ if it is not. Simulate the circuit using Apodix to prove that it works.

3

Logic circuits with memory

All the digital circuits discussed so far share an important property: their outputs are always determined by the current values of their input variables, except perhaps for time delays that represent a necessary (and sometimes serious) imperfection. Such structures are known as *combinational logic* circuits. There exists a second important class called *sequential logic* circuits, which differ from their combinational brothers in one major respect: their outputs depend not only on the presently existing inputs, but also on a past state. Because the past affects the present, the past state can be deduced from a knowledge of the present one, so circuits of this kind are able to remember past events; sequential logic circuits are said to possess *memory*. Circuits with memory and some of their applications are discussed in this chapter.

The simple latch

Perhaps the simplest widely used circuit possessing memory is generally called a *latch*, or a *simple latch*. One basic form of this device is made up of two NOR gates cross-connected in the manner shown in Fig. 3.1. Because this circuit is very common, it is known by a confusingly large number of different names: *latch*, *set-reset latch*, and *S–R latch*, are preferred by some authors, while others use names like *simple S–R flip-flop* or *unclocked S–R flip-flop*. Here the term *latch* will be used consistently, the term *flip-flop* being reserved for another class of circuit.

Latch performance

Despite its simplicity, the operation of a latch circuit is not immediately obvious, so it is best to study it initially by means of simulation. To do so, a

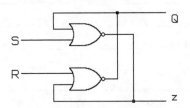

Fig. 3.1. A simple latch constructed of two NOR gates.

description of the circuit and of inputs S, R which exercise a wide range of circuit states is prepared:

```
    /*   Simple latch of 2 NOR gates */
circuit srl2nor:
    {
    nor:  S, Q  >  z;
    nor:  R, z  >  Q;
    }
input:
    {
    S = 0 (5,10,35,40);
    R = 0 (20,25,35,40);
    }
output:
    {
    S, R, Q, z;
    time = 60;
    }
```

The simulation is then run and its output is examined. The corresponding output display produced by Apodix appears in Fig. 3.2.

Initially the circuit of Fig. 3.1 is made to have both inputs zero, $S = R = 0$, but these values do not define an output state because one input of each NOR gate is unknown. The outputs are therefore also unknown, and remain so while the inputs S and R retain their values. However, at $t = 5$ input S is switched to 1. From this moment on, one input to its corresponding NOR gate is not zero, so the output of that gate must assume the value $z = 0$. As soon as z becomes known, the inputs to the other NOR gate are both well defined, as $R = 0, z = 0$. One gate delay time later, at $t = 7$, its output must therefore take the value $Q = 1$. At this time a stable state has been established, with all values known: $[S,R,Q,z] = [1,0,1,0]$. This state will persist until there is an input change.

At time $t = 10$ input S is switched back to value 0. But as may be seen from the simulation output, no change occurs in the output variables Q and z. The reason is easy to see: S is only connected to one NOR gate input, the other input

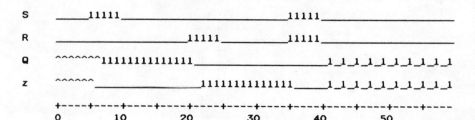

Fig. 3.2. Simulator output for the circuit of Fig. 3.1, with a variety of input signals.

being Q. But if $Q = 1$, this gate will have zero output no matter what the value of S. The output state therefore persists even after both inputs are returned to zero.

The next interesting event in the simulation occurs at $t = 20$ when input R is switched high. One delay time later output Q drops, because the NOR gate connected to R and z now has one of its inputs high and therefore must produce zero output. But once Q has switched, $S = Q = 0$, so z must rise to 1. Hence the circuit state $[S,R,Q,z] = [0,1,0;1]$ is established. The output values remain even after $t = 30$, when R is dropped to zero again. The reason for their persistence is as straightforward as before: if z is high, the NOR gate that it feeds must produce an output of 0.

The events from $t = 0$ to $t = 40$ take the input variables through a cycle of values: $[S,R]$ goes from $[0,0]$ to $[1,0]$ to $[0,0]$ again; then from $[0,0]$ to $[0,1]$ and back to $[0,0]$. These go-and-return cycles exhibit two important points:

1. So long as the input values are in one of the three states $[S,R] = [0,0]$ or $[1,0]$ or $[0,1]$, the two outputs must always be complementary, $Q = z'$.
2. If either S or R alone is temporarily raised to 1 from the state $[S,R] = [0,0]$, then either Q or z alone accompanies the corresponding input up, but remains high even after the input is returned to a low value.

The second point is usually described by saying the circuit *remembers* which of S or R was last raised to 1. The rise must have a duration of at least two gate delay times, so as to allow the output values to stabilize.

To summarize: the circuit of Fig. 3.1 can come to rest in either of two stable states with both inputs S and R at zero value. One state is characterized by $Q = 1, z = 0$, the other by $Q = 0, z = 1$. Which state it rests in depends on whether input S or input R was most recently raised to 1. It can be viewed as a *memory circuit*, for it remembers which of the two inputs, S or R, was most recently pulsed. The circuit is usually given the name *latch* because the last occurrence of either $S = 1$ or $R = 1$ is *latched* into the output, i.e., held even if the input signal that caused it disappears. It is called a *set-reset* latch because an input on S *sets* the output Q to logical 1, and an input on R *resets* it to logical 0. The alternative name *flip-flop* comes about because applying a temporary input at S will *flip* the circuit into one state while applying a temporary input to R will *flop* it back into the other. In modern usage, however, the term *flip-flop* denotes another class of circuits which also make clearcut transitions between two states, but in response to different stimuli. Flip-flops are treated in some detail later in this chapter.

Unstable states

In addition to the three input states discussed above, a latch may have a fourth input state imposed: $S = R = 1$. In the simulation of Fig. 3.2, the inputs are brought into this state at $t = 35$ and returned to $S = R = 0$ at $t = 45$. Both outputs stabilize at value 0 when both inputs rise; but when both inputs fall, an

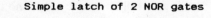

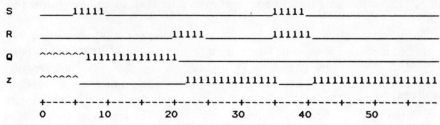

```
                  Simple latch of 2 NOR gates
S      _____11111_____11111_____

R      _____11111_____111111_____

Q      ^^^^^^^11111111111111_____

z      ^^^^^^_____11111111111111_____11111111111111111111111111

       +----+----+----+----+----+----+----+----+----+----+----+----
       0        10        20        30        40        50
```

Fig. 3.3.   Asymmetry in signal timing makes the circuit of Fig. 3.2 assume an asymmetric output state.

indefinitely prolonged oscillation results. Such an instability is undesirable in most applications, so the state $S = R = 1$ is ordinarily regarded as one to be avoided.

The instability seen in Fig. 3.2 is rarely observed in actual circuits, for its existence depends on precise symmetry of the two halves of the latch. So long as both NOR gates behave exactly alike, the circuit will oscillate; symmetry of both the circuit and the exciting signals requires a symmetric response. However, real devices differ from each other by at least some small amount, so the unstable state will be asymmetric. Fig. 3.3 shows another simulation, where the R signal lingers a little longer than S. As might be expected, the output now stabilizes in favor of R instead of oscillating.

If the latch circuit is slightly asymmetric, with one NOR gate a little slower than the other, a similar effect will be obtained. Asymmetric oscillations, with one half-period longer than the other, may also result. Correspondingly, if the signal S lasts a little longer than R, or if the difference in NOR gate time delays is in favor of the S side, the circuit will respond asymmetrically but with a bias to the S side. Because the response of a latch to the input $S = R = 1$ is sensitive to small differences in timing or component characteristics, this input state is sometimes said to lead to *indeterminate* or *undefined* outputs. Clearly, there is nothing undefined about a circuit voltage; *unpredictable* might perhaps be a better term. Whatever the name, this circuit state is usually avoided by designers.

Provided the state $S = R = 1$ is avoided, the outputs Q and z are inverses of one another, $Q = z'$. Data books frequently label them as Q and Q' for precisely this reason. So long as the two outputs are complementary, the state of Q can always be determined by examining the state of Q', and vice versa. The state of the latch is therefore usually described simply by stating the value of Q.

Switch debouncing

Digital signals for circuit testing can be generated, at least in principle, by the very simple means of connecting a small battery to a push button or other mechanical switch. In practice, this simple scheme is not entirely reliable. Even the best mechanical switches suffer from *contact bounce,* an intermittent on-off condition, for a short time when first actuated. In continuous-signal applications (e.g., music or speech), contact bounce is at worst a minor nuisance, a short-duration scratchy noise. In a digital circuit, however, the pulses created by contact bounce may become serious. Pressing the push button firmly and steadily for one second will not produce a single pulse one second long; instead, there will usually be a brief burst of short pulses of random length, followed by a steady signal a little less than a second long, then another brief burst of random pulses as the contacts gradually disengage from each other. The initial and final pulses are typically a few microseconds in length. They may activate digital circuits as separate pulses, so incorrect circuit behavior may result. For example, a mechanical switch in a turnstile may be connected to a counter circuit so as to determine the number of customers entering a supermarket. Contact bounce, however, will generate multiple pulses and cause each customer to be counted several times.

Correct pulse counts can be obtained from a mechanical switch if the switch is *debounced* by means of a latch. A suitable circuit is shown in Fig. 3.4. Here the switch arm is actuated so as to have one of S or R set true, the other false. However, while the switch is moving into position from, say, R to S, both R and S will become zero for a short time. As the switch closes on S, contact bounce will cause a sequence of input states alternating between $S = R = 0$ and $S = 1$, $R = 0$.

It is easy to see how the latch stabilizes the wobbly signal furnished by the mechanical switch. The first time the input to the latch actually achieves the values $S = 1$, $R = 0$, it will set the output to 1 so as to remember that S was the last signal to be set to 1. A subsequent return to $S = R = 0$ does not alter the output. Another occurrence of $S = 1$, $R = 0$ therefore finds the output at the correct values already, and changes nothing. The point is that the latch remembers *which input was last set to 1,* and does not care how many times that input was toggled. In this way, the first time S is set changes the output, and the output does not change again until the R input is activated. The consequence is

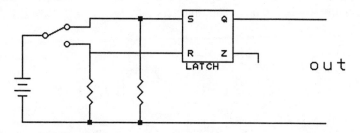

Fig. 3.4.   Debouncing a mechanical switch with a latch. The internal connections of the latch are not shown.

that a clean output pulse is obtained from the latch even if its input is somewhat unsteady.

An alternative latch circuit

A second and different circuit may be devised which exhibits memory behavior similar to the simple latch of Fig. 3.1. Because the two circuits are to behave similarly, their mathematical descriptions must be similar. The second form of latch may therefore be derived from the first by algebraic reformulation of the equations that describe it. These equations are

$$Q = (R + z)'$$
$$z = (Q + S)'$$

A straightforward application of De Morgan's theorem serves to convert both into product form:

$$Q = R' \cdot z'$$
$$z = Q' \cdot S'$$

Negating both sides,

$$Q' = (R' \cdot z')'$$
$$z' = (Q' \cdot S')'$$

results. Both right-hand sides are in the form $(A \cdot B)'$, suggesting circuit synthesis by means of NAND gates. It remains to note that in the conventional use of latches, Q and z are complementary. Hence

$$Q' = z$$

so that

$$Q' = (R' \cdot Q)'$$
$$Q = (Q' \cdot S')'$$

This pair of expressions leads directly to the circuit shown in Fig. 3.5, comprising two NAND gates cross-connected in a fashion resembling that of Fig. 3.1. Two inverters are needed, because the circuit behavior is described in terms of S' and R', not S and R. In some applications, however, the complemented signals arise naturally in circuits. The inverters may then be omitted. Indeed the

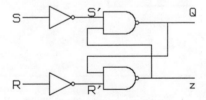

Fig. 3.5.   An alternative form of latch constructed using NAND gates.

choice of circuits depends largely on whether the input signals are available with one polarity or the other.

To verify that the latch built using NAND gates behaves in the expected fashion, a simulation may again be carried out. The circuit of Fig. 3.5, and excitation signals essentially similar to those applied to the earlier circuit, lead to the Apodix problem statement

```
/*   Latch of 2 NAND gates   */
circuit srl2nand:
    {
    nand:   notS, z  >  Q;
    nand:   notR, Q  >  z;
    }
input:
    {
    notS = 1 (5,10,35,40);
    notR = 1 (20,25,35,40);
    }
output:
    {
    notS, notR, Q, z;
    time = 60;
    }
```

To avoid any confusion that might arise from the inverters, the problem has here been cast in terms of the complementary variables $notS = S'$ and $notR = R'$. The simulations should therefore be strictly comparable, provided only that the excitation signals are also complements of those used earlier, as indeed they are. The results of this simulation are shown in Fig. 3.6.

Except for complementation of S and R, the results are precisely the same as obtained earlier. Again, the output effectively remembers which of the two inputs was last pulsed; again, confusion results when both input lines are asserted simultaneously. The circuit behavior is thus similar to that of the latch shown in Fig. 3.1.

There is a general lesson to be learned here: Many different circuit realizations

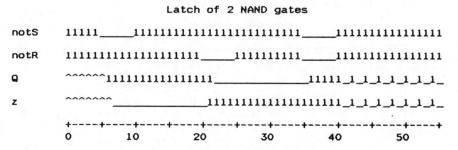

Fig. 3.6.   Simulator output for the circuit of Fig. 3.5. The results are the complements of those in Fig. 3.2.

can provide a given sequential circuit behavior, just as the terminal behavior of many possible combinational circuits is described by identical Boolean functions. Indeed, it is not quite correct to say that Fig. 3.1 shows the simple latch, or that Fig. 3.5 does so. Either diagram only shows one possible circuit that exhibits the particular form of set–reset memory behavior which digital engineers associate with the term *latch*. The proper definition of a latch is therefore not really a circuit, but a prescribed terminal behavior. To specify the behavior unambiguously, a formalism is required that passes beyond the vagueness of verbal description. A simple formal technique for describing and defining the latch as well as other sequential circuits will therefore be treated next.

Transition tables

The output of a latch depends not only on its current inputs but also on the prior state of the circuit. In this, it differs from a combinational logic circuit like a decoder or multiplexer whose outputs are entirely determined by its input values. To specify the prior state of a latch, it suffices to state the values of its output variables at the time the inputs are applied. Truth tables of the sort used to describe static circuits only give the outputs corresponding to given combination of inputs, so they are not sufficient to describe latches. However, they can be generalized to produce another type of table, called the *transition table*, which takes account of past history. How to construct and interpret transition tables is best seen by again examining the behavior of a simple latch, as presented in its NOR-gate form in Fig. 3.1.

The two NOR gates of Fig. 3.1 are explicitly described by the Boolean equations

$$Q(t+T_g) = [R(t) + z(t)]'$$

and

$$z(t+T_g) = [S(t) + Q(t)]'$$

where the symbol z has been used, rather than Q', so as not to assume from the outset that they are related. T_g represents the gate delay time. By De Morgan's theorem, the first equation of this pair may be rewritten as

$$Q(t+T_g) = R'(t) \cdot z'(t).$$

Because the circuit equations are valid for all times t, they may be written not only for time $t+T_g$ but also for time $t+2T_g$. Thus

$$Q(t+2T_g) = R'(t+T_g) \cdot z'(t+T_g).$$

But $z(t+T_g)$ is known; negating it, a value of $z'(t+T_g)$ may be substituted in the last equation:

$$Q(t+2T_g) = R'(t+T_g) \cdot [S(t) + Q(t)].$$

By symmetry, a corresponding expression for $z(t+2T_g)$ may be written down immediately:

$$z(t+2T_g) = S'(t+T_g) \cdot [R(t) + z(t)].$$

This equation may also be derived directly from the circuit describing equations.

The equation for $Q(t+2T_g)$ clearly restates the already known fact that the operational states of a latch are determined by its inputs S and R, and by its prior state as expressed by its prior output $Q(t)$. A table to describe the circuit behavior can be drawn up, somewhat like a truth table for a combinational circuit; but it must treat the variables $Q(t+2T_g)$ and $Q(t)$ as separate entities. It must therefore have three columns to describe independent variables, one each for S, R, and $Q(t)$, the output column being the *next state* as described by $Q(t+2T_g)$. Such a table resembles the conventional truth table; for the latch it appears as follows.

$S(t)$	$R(t)$	$Q(t)$	$Q(t+2T_g)$
0	0	0	0
0	0	1	1
0	1	0	0
0	1	1	0
1	0	0	1
1	0	1	1
1	1	0	*Undefined*
1	1	1	*Undefined*

To be strictly accurate, the second column of this table should be labeled $R(t+T_g)$, not $R(t)$. When tables of this type are used, it is tacitly assumed that the inputs S and R will be held at constant values for long enough to permit writing the input variables as simply $S(t)$ and $R(t)$, or even S and R, rather than $S(t)$ and $R(t+T_g)$. For clocked latches and flip-flops, which will be discussed at some length in the next section, this assumption is almost invariably valid.

Put in simple physical terms, the purpose of a latch is to serve as a memory element, to remember which of the two inputs was last raised to value 1. If both S and R are raised simultaneously, the circuit is faced with the impossible task of remembering that the correct answer is *both*. The abstract specification of the latch is therefore usually stated so as to forbid both inputs from being set to 1 at the same time. One way of doing so is to leave outputs for $S = R = 1$ undefined. The precise form of restriction necessary for the circuit of Fig. 3.1 is readily derived from the Boolean equations of the circuit by the following process. The equation for $Q(t+2T_g)$ is negated on both sides,

$$Q'(t+2T_g) = \{R'(t+T_g) \cdot [S(t) + Q(t)]\}'.$$

De Morgan's theorem is then applied to remove the negation on the right,

$$Q'(t+2T_g) = R(t+T_g) + [S(t) + Q(t)]',$$

and again, resulting in

$$Q'(t+2T_g) = R(t+T_g) + S'(t) \cdot Q'(t).$$

Next, the first term on the right is rewritten as

$$R(t+T_g) = R(t+T_g) \cdot [S(t) + S'(t)]$$

so that the equation for $Q'(t+2T_g)$ reads

$$Q'(t+2T_g) = R(t+T_g) \cdot [S(t) + S'(t)] + S'(t) \cdot Q'(t).$$

After some rearrangement of terms, it assumes the form

$$Q'(t+2T_g) = S'(t) \cdot [R(t+T_g) + Q'(t)] + S(t) \cdot R(t+T_g)$$

whose right-hand side is similar, but not exactly equal, to that given for $z'(t+2T_g)$ above,

$$z(t+2T_g) = S'(t+T_g) \cdot [R(t) + z(t)].$$

The two expressions become identical if two restrictions are imposed. First, the extra term $S(t) \cdot R(t+T_g)$ must vanish. In other words, $Q=z'$, $z = Q'$ requires that

$$S(t) \cdot R(t+T_g) = 0.$$

Secondly, the signals S and T must hold their values for longer than one gate delay time T_g, so that while the state transition takes place,

$$S'(t) = S'(t+T_g)$$

and

$$R(t+T_g) = R(t).$$

This statement of the condition to be placed on S and R is obviously more precise that the broad statement made earlier, to the effect that both must not be allowed to take on the value 1 concurrently; but it amounts to much the same thing in practice, since it is necessary to keep S and R at their values for longer than one gate delay time T_g in any case.

   The transition table may be regarded as the *definition* of a latch. In this view, circuits such as those shown in Figs. 3.1 and 3.5 merely represent particular realizations of the transition table, all equally valid. A circuit can at best be *a* latch, whereas the transition table defines an abstract entity which might be termed *the* latch. Saying that the general or abstract latch has an undefined output in certain circumstances really amounts to stating that *any* values of the output variables, quite possibly different ones in different latch circuits, are all acceptable so far as the abstract specification is concerned. To use a somewhat mathematical phrasing, the *domain* of inputs over which the operation of a latch is defined is smaller than the set of all possible inputs (in fact, it is a proper subset of all possible inputs). This situation is somewhat similar to what was encountered earlier with encoder circuits, where only one input at a time was allowed to have value 1. Responsibility for avoiding inputs outside the permitted domain rests entirely with the circuit designer.

Practical latches and flip-flops

The fundamental forms of latch discussed so far are not suitable for building large-scale computer memories. Although the memory elements actually employed in building computers and other digital circuits are closely related to latches, they differ in added details intended to avoid one or another of the shortcomings of the simple latch. Some of the more sophisticated forms of practical circuit elements are examined in this section.

Clocked latches

The time a latch takes to settle is dependent on the gate delay time T_g. It in turn depends on the circuit configuration used and also on the integrated circuit chip technology employed. Latch timings may therefore vary widely from one situation to another, even from one chip to another of the same type. These variations complicate the circuit designer's task enormously and quite frequently make circuit performance sensitive to such environmental parameters as temperature and supply voltage. Circuits of the kind shown in Figs. 3.1 and 3.5 are called *asynchronous*, implying that their timings are not synchronized with other events.

Practical digital systems involve large numbers of circuit chips. Their delay times may differ considerably, because of differences in design or manufacturing technologies. Asynchronously operated latches are therefore comparatively rare in computer internal circuits, even though they are commonly used in latching circuits such as the switch debouncer discussed earlier. Most digital circuits used in computers and other data processing devices are operated synchronously and are controlled by a master clock.

Clocked latches and other synchronous circuits are forced into synchronism by means of a *system clock*, a device for generating a train of pulses distributed to all the circuits that make up the digital system. The clock pulse is made to achieve synchronization of latches by connecting the inputs to each clocked latch through AND gates, and enabling the AND gates by means of the system clock as illustrated in Fig. 3.7. The enabling AND gates permit the latch to

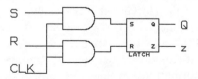

Fig. 3.7.   A clocked latch is composed of a simple latch and an input isolating circuit. *clk* is the clock line.

receive input signals only when the clock pulse appears (i.e., when the clock signal has value 1). The latch will therefore only begin operation when the clock input is present. If all clocked latches in a large circuit are controlled by the same clock, they will all operate in synchronism.

So long as the clock line *clk* in Fig. 3.7 is cleared to zero, the outputs A and B of both enabling AND gates are zero. Like any simple latch with both inputs cleared, the circuit of Fig. 3.7 then holds its state no matter what values S and R may have. While the clock line is asserted, on the other hand, the AND gates do not affect the S and R signals. The whole circuit then behaves very much like an ordinary unclocked latch. Thus the clocked latch is free to alter its state whenever the clock signal *clk* is set, but it holds its state unaltered while the clock signal is cleared. This behavior is clearly visible if the following simulation is carried out:

```
    /* Clocked latch, 2 NOR gates */
circuit clklatch:
    {
    nor: a, Q > z;
    nor: b, z > Q;
    and: S, clk > a;
    and: R, clk > b;
    }
input:
    {
    clk = 1 (4,20) 32;
    S = 0 (8,16,24,32);
    R = 0 (40,48,56);
    }
output:
    {
    clk, S, R, Q, z;
    time = 60;
    }
```

The results of this simulation appear in Fig. 3.8. Although the S input is toggled at time $t = 8$, the outputs remain undefined because the clock line is reset so the S and R signals do not reach the latch. When S is toggled again at $t = 24$, the outputs respond immediately because the clock line is high at this time. It should be noted, however, that simply raising the clock line, as at $t = 20$, has no effect until the input line is asserted. Similar reasoning, and similar results, are evident for the R input: asserting it at $t = 40$ has no effect, but asserting it at $t = 56$ does, again because the clock signal *clk* is high at this time.

The transition table of the clocked latch is usually written without including the clock line input *clk* explicitly. The reason is simple: the device does nothing at all until it is enabled to act by the clock pulse. Were the clock signal included in the transition table, it would merely double the number of rows in the table without adding any information, because every row with *clk* = 0 would show *no action*. Thus abbreviated, its transition table is

S(t)	R(t)	Q(t)	Q(t + T_d)
0	0	0	0
0	0	1	1
0	1	0	0
0	1	1	0
1	0	0	1
1	0	1	1
1	1	0	*Undefined*
1	1	1	*Undefined*

This table contains exactly the same entries as the transition table of the simple latch. However, there is a vital difference: no matter when the inputs are altered, the clocked latch only acts when the clock signal has risen to 1. The output column of the transition table therefore becomes valid not at a time dictated by the gate delay T_g, which is an intrinsic property of the semiconductor chip, but at a time determined by the clock cycle length T_d, which is specified for all the latches and flip-flops in a digital system by the choice of clock pulse rate. For circuits to operate satisfactorily, it is clearly necessary to choose the cycle time to be much longer than the gate delay time.

Clocked latches, also known as *level-sensitive flip-flops* for reasons which will become apparent in due course, are widely used. In medium-scale integrated circuits, several similar latch circuits are often placed on a single semiconductor chip. In such packages it is usual to bring out only a single common clock line to an external pin connection and to drive all the clocked circuits on the same chip with the same clock signal, thereby synchronizing their actions.

Presetting and preclearing

In Fig. 3.8, and in other simulations shown earlier, it is evident that time is taken for latches to establish their states unequivocally; the initial few time units

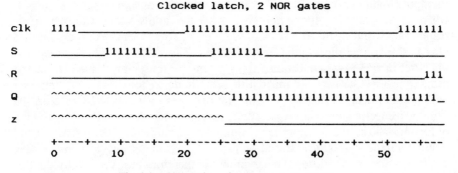

Fig. 3.8. Simulation of a simple clocked latch.

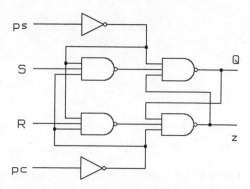

Fig. 3.9.   Preset/precleared latch. The inputs *S* and *R* can be overridden by control signals *pc* and *ps*.

invariably show the circuit output state as undefined. This unhappy situation occurs not only in simulation but also in real life. Real electronic circuits of course do not have undefined voltage values. What happens in real circuits is that one state or the other is reached—but which one, depends on chance. Practical digital circuits are often built to allow them to be placed in a known state initially—either set or cleared, as the user wishes. Such circuits are said to be *preset* or *precleared*, the prefix *pre-* indicating that the most common use of this mechanism is as a preliminary to beginning the circuit's intended task.

Presetting is easily accomplished in circuits such as the simple latch based on NAND gates shown in Fig. 3.5. It is only necessary to include an extra input to each NAND gate, and to replace the inverters at the *S* and *R* inputs by NAND gates, as shown in Fig. 3.9. The operation of this modified circuit is easily traced. When the *pc* signal is high and the *ps* signal low, the lower right NAND gate has at least one input at zero value, therefore produces an output $Z = 1$. Both left-hand NAND gates derive one input signal from the *pc* signal through an inverter; both therefore have one input at zero and produce equal outputs, $a = b = 1$. With the *ps* signal at zero, the lower right NAND gate must then have all its inputs high, hence produce $Q = 0$. Thus the pair of signals $pc = 1$, $ps = 0$ will always clear the outputs, no matter what the inputs *S* and *R* may be. Correspondingly, the signal pair $pc = 0$, $ps = 1$ will always set the outputs, so that $Q = 1$, $Z = 0$, regardless of the state of *S* and *R*. The latch is said to be *precleared* or *preset* in these two conditions. Both *ps* and *pc* must not be asserted at the same time—indeed it would make little sense to do so, for the circuit cannot be both precleared and preset at the same moment. On the other hand, resetting *pc* $= ps = 0$ effectively turns the presettable circuit of Fig. 3.9 into the simple latch of Fig. 3.5; the action of either is then indistinguishable from the other.

When circuit behavior is traced by physical arguments such as given above, errors can very easily occur. The argument is therefore best verified by the following simulation.

```
/* Preset latch of 2 NAND gates */
circuit pslatch:
    {
    nand:   a, z, nps  >  Q;
    nand:   b, Q, npc  >  z;
    nand:   S, npc, nps  >  a;
    nand:   R, npc, nps  >  b;
    not:    pc  >  npc;
    not:    ps  >  nps;
    }
input:
    {
    ps = 0;
    pc = 0 (8,10);
    S = 0 (15,20,45,50);
    R = 0 (30,35,45,50);
    }
output:
    {
    S, R, ps, pc, Q, z;
    time = 60;
    }
```

This simulation repeats that shown in Fig. 3.6, except that all events take place 10 time units later. As may be seen from Fig. 3.10, or from Fig. 3.6, the outputs Q and Z are initially indeterminate and remain so while no inputs are applied, because at least one input to each NAND gate is initially unknown.

In the simulation of Fig. 3.10, the preclear signal pc is pulsed at $t = 8$ but the preset signal ps is left permanently at zero. Pulsing the preclear line removes all ambiguity by furnishing the upper NAND gate one input certain to be zero; its output Z therefore rises to 1 and establishes itself there. This output is cross-

```
              Preset latch of 2 NAND gates

S   _____11111_____11111_____

R   _____11111_____11111_____

ps  _____

pc  _____11_____

Q   ^^^^^^^^^^^_____1111111111111111_____11111_1_1_1_1_

z   ^^^^^^^^^^11111111_____1111111111111111111111_1_1_1_1_

    +----+----+----+----+----+----+----+----+----+----+----+----+
    0        10       20       30       40       50       60
```

Fig. 3.10.   Simulator output for the circuit of Fig. 3.9. The results are similar to those in Fig. 3.6.

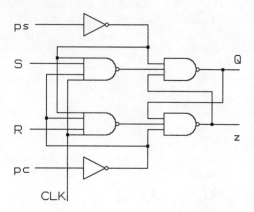

Fig. 3.11.   Clocked preset/precleared latch. The left-hand NAND gates serve for both clocking and presetting.

connected to the lower NAND gate, whose inputs then become known as well. The circuit is thus reset, as is clearly visible in the simulation output of Fig. 3.10. The subsequent circuit behavior is exactly like that in Fig. 3.6. After their initial use, the preset and preclear lines are left at $pc = ps = 0$ so the circuit behaves exactly like an ordinary simple latch.

Preset latches may of course be clocked, by attaching a pair of enabling gates to the S and R inputs in exactly the same way as was done in Fig. 3.7. However, clocking may be added to the preset latch of Fig. 3.9 even more simply, by merely employing four-input NAND gates instead of of the three-input gates at the left of Fig. 3.9. The resulting circuit is shown in Fig. 3.11.

Examination of the clocked preset latch of Fig. 3.11, sometimes also called a *level-sensitive preset S–R flip-flop*, shows that when the clock signal *clk* is high, the circuit functions in exactly the same way as its unclocked cousin in Fig. 3.9. On the other hand, when the clock is reset, both four-input NAND gates are disabled, so the S and R inputs are ignored. The clocking operation therefore works exactly as would be expected. Consequently, its simulation and detailed examination are omitted here.

Edge-triggered flip-flops

Clocking a latch ensures that the circuit only operates while the clock signal is high, thereby forcing all circuits controlled by the same clock to operate in synchronism. By ensuring that the latch only responds to input signals during a limited period of time, clocking also provides partial protection against unsteady input signals such as might result from a manual switch without proper debouncing circuitry, or from electrical noise in circuit connections.

In contrast to combinational circuits, all circuits with memory are sensitive not only to their input values, but also to the sequence of states traversed to arrive at these values. Unsteadiness of the input value while the clock signal is set could therefore produce wrong results—or it might not, depending on the internal delay times of the circuit gates. This situation is exactly what clocked circuits are intended to avoid, so it must be concluded that clocking by itself is not always enough. Ideally, it would be preferable to take a "snapshot" of the input values at a particular instant, for example at the very beginning of a clock pulse when the signal changes value from 0 to 1, then to isolate these values from the circuit input so that any further change in the inputs cannot affect flip-flop operation until the next "snapshot" is taken. This principle is sometimes described by saying that the circuit should have a narrow *sensitivity window*—that it should only be receptive to input values for a quite short time.

One method of achieving a narrow sensitivity window is simply to make the clock pulse short. Unfortunately, this technique has many drawbacks, chief among which is that a complex system often contains some parts that respond quite rapidly and others which are much slower. If the clock pulse is made very short, the slower circuits may quite easily not respond at all; but if the clock pulse is made long enough to trigger the slowest circuit reliably, fast-responding circuits may not be adequately protected against input ambiguity.

A better method for reducing the time during which circuits remain sensitive to input changes is to employ *edge-triggered* flip-flop circuits. These comprise a large family of which one representative, the S–R flip-flop composed of NAND gates, appears in Fig. 3.12. As its name implies, this circuit carries out all state transitions at the edges of clock pulses. Such circuits can be built to be either

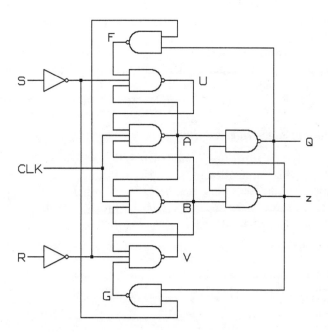

Fig. 3.12. An edge-triggered S–R flip-flop.

rising edge triggered, as in Fig. 3.12, or *falling edge triggered*; the two differ in making state transitions on either the rising (0 to 1) or falling (1 to 0) edge of the clock signal. Their physical difference may lie in the arrangement of gates that make up the flip-flop, or simply in inversion of the clock signal itself.

The flip-flop circuit of Fig. 3.12 is evidently a good deal more complicated than the latches encountered so far. It may be viewed as consisting of a simple latch (whose outputs are Q and Z) preceded by a clocked latch (outputs A and B) and some additional logic gates. The output of this circuit is independent of S and R so long as the clock signal CLK does not change. When $CLK = 0$, A and B both remain at 1 regardless of S and R; Q and Z therefore preserve whatever values they may have.

When the clock signal CLK of Fig. 3.12 is high, two cases of interest arise: (a) $A = 0$, $B = 1$; (b) $A = B = 1$. The combination $A = 1$, $B = 0$ is a symmetric image of case (a), hence need not be considered separately; the case $A = B = 1$ must be excluded because it would make the right-hand latch (hence Q and Z) unstable. Taking case (a) first: if $A = 0$, then $U = 1$ and $B = 1$ because signal A is applied to the two NAND gates from which B and U derive. The values of V, F, G, hence S and R, cannot influence A or B. In case (b), the same argument obviously applies to B as well as A. A steady clock signal $CLK = 1$ therefore leads Q and Z to ignore the inputs S and R.

While the clock signal CLK is either low or high, the right-hand latch remains effectively isolated from the inputs on the left. But the mechanisms of isolation are different and the time delays are different also. When the clock signal falls from 1 to 0, the clocked (left) latch acts immediately, i.e., within one gate delay time. When the clock signal rises from 0 to 1, an extra gate delay time is required for the new values of U and V to appear at the clocked latch inputs, and during this brief time A and B are free to change. In other words, the isolating properties of the clocked latch are repeated here, but with the difference that the latching circuit proper is isolated from the inputs S and R at all times except when the clock pulse makes the transition from low to high value.

Simulation of edge-triggered flip-flops

Detailed analysis of intricate circuits, such as Fig. 3.12, is relatively complex and a matter for digital circuit design specialists; it is not at all easy to carry out using the simple algebraic tools presented here. On the other hand, a simulation using Apodix is straightforward and will establish quickly enough whether the circuit in fact works. The circuit of Fig. 3.12 is described by

```
circuit etsrff:
    {
    nand:   A, z    >   Q;
    nand:   B, Q    >   z;
    nand:   U, B, CLK   >   A;
    nand:   V, A, CLK   >   B;
    nand:   F, A, nS    >   U;
    nand:   G, B, nR    >   V;
```

```
nand:   Q, nR  >  F;
nand:   z, nS  >  G;
not:    S  >  nS;
not:    R  >  nR;
}
```

The results of this simulation appear in Fig. 3.13. Several points worthy of discussion arise from it.

To begin, rising edge triggering obviously works. The rising edge at $t = 8$ produces $Q = 1$ from $S = 1$, as would be expected; but the input at S has no effect until the transition in the clock signal CLK actually takes place. Similarly, the rising edge at $t = 24$ resets the state of the flip-flop, in accordance with $R = 1$, which prevails at that time. The rising edges at $t = 40$ and $t = 56$ also yield the results that would be expected from the transition table of an ordinary S–R latch. On the other hand, the circuit is clearly insensitive to falling edges of the clock pulse.

A second point of importance is that while the clock signal CLK is either high or low, but no edge occurs, input changes are not propagated to the output. In fact even the coincident raising of both S and R lines at $t = 27$ has no effect; the flip-flop simply ignores both inputs.

The response time of this circuit is clearly somewhat longer than that of a simple clocked latch. The rising edge of the clock signal at $t = 24$, for example, leads to a new stable output state only at $t = 27$, three gate delays later. Similarly the initial stabilization of the circuit, in response to the rising edge at $t = 8$, takes till $t = 11$. Although brief, the time during which input changes have an effect (the *window of sensitivity* of the flip-flop) is still of finite breadth. Any input changes during this transition period are likely to produce unpredictable outputs, as old and new input values are combined through the feedback loops. Signals presented to the flip-flop inputs therefore need to remain constant for a short time, called the *setup time*, immediately preceding the rising edge, as well as during the *hold time* immediately following the clock pulse edge. Aside from

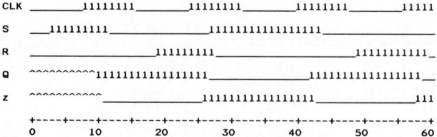

Fig. 3.13.   Simulation of the edge-triggered flip-flop of Fig. 3.12. Even $S = R = 1$ is permissible while the clock signal is constant.

those brief periods, however, the flip-flop is not sensitive to input signal alterations.

Flip-flops can be built to respond at either rising or falling edges of the clock signal. In consequence, it will be assumed from here on that *wherever flip-flops are mentioned, rising edge triggered flip-flops are meant* unless the contrary is explicitly stated.

Transition tables of edge-triggered devices

The output state transitions of an edge-triggered flip-flop always occur at clock pulse edges. The transition table of such a flip-flop must not only distinguish between old and new output states, but also between old and new clock states. Clock signal values both before and after any particular moment should therefore enter the transition table as variables. For example, if the clock signal value is the same at some time t as well as at a slightly later time, say $t + T_0$, no rising clock edge has occurred and no state transition can take place at any intervening time. A full transition table for the rising-edge-triggered S–R flip-flop must therefore regard five variables as independent: the inputs $S(t)$ and $R(t)$, the clock states $C(t)$ and $C(t+T_0)$, and the old output state $Q(t)$. For the S–R flip-flop, the full transition table is therefore as follows.

$CLK(t)$	$CLK(t+T_0)$	$S(t)$	$R(t)$	$Q(t)$	$Q(t+T_0)$
0	0	*don't care*		0	0
0	0	*don't care*		1	1
0	1	**0**	**0**	**0**	**0**
0	1	**0**	**0**	**1**	**1**
0	1	**0**	**1**	**0**	**0**
0	1	**0**	**1**	**1**	**0**
0	1	**1**	**0**	**0**	**1**
0	1	**1**	**0**	**1**	**1**
0	1	**1**	**1**	***undefined***	***undefined***
0	1	**1**	**1**	***undefined***	***undefined***
1	0	*don't care*		0	0
1	0	*don't care*		1	1
1	1	*don't care*		0	1
1	1	*don't care*		1	1

This table may be viewed as consisting of four segments. The first, comprising its first two rows, involves no clock signal transition and therefore no state transition. The second part of the table, the third through tenth rows, involves a rising clock pulse edge (a clock transition from 0 to 1) and state transitions certainly will take place here. This portion is shown in boldface print, for the sake of emphasis. This part of the table is formally identical to the transition table of a simple latch, but with the difference that state transitions occur *only* at clock pulse edges. The third section of the table (rows 11 and 12) involves a falling clock pulse edge; no transition can take place here. In the final, fourth segment of the table the clock signal remains unaltered at 1; there is no transition between

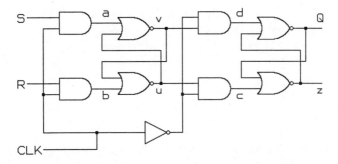

Fig. 3.14. Master–slave flip-flop built of two latches. The inverter ensures that only one is active at a time.

clock values and hence no change in the output. Transition tables of edge-triggered devices are conventionally abbreviated to include only the portion printed in boldface; it is assumed that no one would be interested in states that do not involve rising clock edges and therefore cannot produce changes in circuit output.

To summarize the matter briefly, the idea behind edge-triggered flip-flops is to ignore any irregularities that the input signals may exhibit, and to capture momentary snapshots of their states only at the edges of clock pulses. Any remaining circuitry then makes use of the controlled, momentarily captured, values. Compared to a simple clocked flip-flop, the timing is made more precise, but the transition table of the flip-flop is not changed.

Master–slave flip-flops

Another technique for increasing circuit reliability, widely used though with different performance from edge-triggered flip-flops, is the *master–slave* arrangement. Its principle is to isolate the circuit output totally from any events at the input, by a sort of "bucket brigade" approach. Two circuits with memory are connected in cascade and so arranged that the first or *master* circuit acquires and remembers data, then detaches itself from the input lines and passes on to the second or *slave* circuit whatever data it is holding. The slave circuit is never directly affected by events on the input lines.

One simple master–slave arrangement combines two clocked S–R latches, arranged as in Fig. 3.14. The master latch (on the left of Fig. 3.14) is similar to that shown in Fig. 3.7; the slave latch (on the right) is similar to it. The two latches differ only in their periods of sensitivity. The master latch is active and acquires data when the clock line *clk* is high; when the clock signal is low, the slave latch becomes active because its clock line is fed through an inverter.

Operation of the master–slave circuit of Fig. 3.14 is easily traced through a simulation. The circuit and suitable signals for testing it may be described as follows:

```
/*   Master-slave SR flip-flop */
circuit mastslav:
    {
    and:    S, clk  >  a;
    and:    R, clk  >  b;
    nor:    a, u    >  v;
    nor:    b, v    >  u;
    not:    clk     >  nCk;
    and:    u, nCk  >  c;
    and:    v, nCk  >  d;
    nor:    c, Q    >  z;
    nor:    d, z    >  Q;
    }
input:
    {
    clk = 0 (8,20) 24;
    S = 0 (4,16,28,32,36,40,44,48,52,56);
    R = 0 (24,28,32,36,40,44,48,52);
    }
output:
    {
    S, R, a, b, u, v, Q, z, clk;
    time = 60;
    }
```

Here the input R is held low for a considerable time, while S rises and falls once; thereafter, both inputs alternate for somewhat longer than a clock period. The simulation results are shown in Fig. 3.15.

During $0 < t < 4$, the master latch is unable to respond to $S = 1$ because the clock signal blocks its input AND gates. When the clock signal rises at $t = 8$, the master latch responds by securing the data: $u = 1$, $v = 0$, just as soon as a few gate delay times have passed. As would be expected, the latch holds these values even after S drops at $t = 16$. There is no effect at all on the slave latch during this period. When the clock signal *clk* drops at $t = 20$, the master latch is disabled and remains so until $t = 32$; the rise of R at $t = 24$ has no effect. One gate delay time after the master latch is disabled, a delay imposed by the inverter in the clock line of the slave latch, the slave latch uses its input values u, v to determine the values $Q = 1$, $z = 0$. These remain even after the clock signal rises again at $t = 32$, because the slave latch is effectively disconnected from the master at $t = 33$. Only at $t = 44$, when the clock signal falls again, is the slave latch able to acquire new data.

The main performance difference between edge-triggered and master–slave flip-flops becomes evident when the events during $32 < t < 44$ are examined. After the clock signal rises at $t = 32$, the master latch is able to follow its input signals S and R and follow them it does. The rise in R at $t = 32$ causes the master latch to switch state, as do the input reversals at $t = 36$ and $t = 40$. This behavior is quite different from the edge-triggered flip-flop, which would have acquired, then held, the input state prevailing at $t = 31$ (immediately preceding the rising clock edge).

Master-slave SR flip-flop

```
S       ____111111111111_____1111____1111____1111____1111_____

R       _____1111____1111____1111____1111_____

a       ^_____11111111_____1111_____

b       ^_____1111____1111_____

u       ^^^^^^^^^^^111111111111111111111111111_____111_____

v       ^^^^^^^^^^_____111_____111111111111111111111

Q       ^^^^^^^^^^^^^^^^^^^^^^^^^^^^^^111111111111111111111111111_____

z       ^^^^^^^^^^^^^^^^^^^^^^^^^^^^^_____111111111111111

clk     _____111111111111_____111111111111_____11111

        +----+----+----+----+----+----+----+----+----+----+----+----+
        0        10        20        30        40        50        60
```

Fig. 3.15. The master latch of Fig. 3.14 accepts inputs while *clk* = 1, moves them to the slave when *clk* = 0.

Flip-flops and counters

The edge-triggered S–R flip-flop is only one of an extensive family of flip-flop circuits used in applications. It is of great importance, however, because almost all other useful flip-flop types may be viewed as being modifications of the S–R flip-flop, which emerges in this way as the granddaddy of them all.

Flip-flops in themselves are useful enough where small quantities of data—a bit or a few bits—must be remembered. Truly intricate circuits, with very complex behavior, become possible when flip-flops are used as circuit building blocks of such devices as digital counters. A few such higher-complexity circuits are therefore examined in this section, in addition to discussing briefly some common flip-flop types.

The D flip-flop

An interesting special case of the S–R flip-flop is obtained by inserting an additional inverter in the circuit of Fig. 3.1 (or Fig. 3.5) so as to guarantee that *R* is always the complement of *S*, $R = S'$. Fig. 3.16 illustrates an appropriate circuit for achieving this goal. This arrangement is entirely proof against the possible indeterminacies encountered with the S–R flip-flop, for the only possible inputs to the S–R flip-flop in Fig. 3.16 are those in which values of *R* and *S* differ. In effect, the circuit really only has a single independent input.

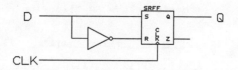

Fig. 3.16.   A delay flip-flop (D flip-flop) circuit.

It should be noted that the circuit of Fig. 3.16 includes a clock input, in accordance with the statement made in the last section: from here on, all flip-flops will be rising edge triggered flip-flops and will therefore require an externally provided clock signal. In other words, the S–R flip-flop in Fig. 3.16 is assumed to be of the edge-triggered type shown in Fig. 3.12. Other types of internal circuitry may, of course, lead to the same externally measurable performance, as expressed in the flip-flop transition table. For example, there exists a NOR gate equivalent of Fig. 3.12 that could be used as an alternative.

A flip-flop circuit arranged in the manner shown in Fig. 3.16 is called a *delay flip-flop* or a *D flip-flop*. Because it has only one independent input, conventionally labeled D, and a single output Q, the transition table for this device contains only four rows. These are obtained easily from the transition table of the S–R flip-flop, by eliminating all rows in which the restriction $R = S'$ does not hold. There results the table

$D(t)$	$Q(t)$	$Q(t+T_0)$
0	0	0
0	1	0
1	0	1
1	1	1

Because a rising edge triggered S–R flip-flop is assumed, the time interval T_0 now refers to a clock period, not to a single gate delay time. For present purposes, it is assumed that the gate delay time of the inverter is small compared to the clock period, so that it need not be considered separately.

Although the modification made to the S–R flip-flop to create a D flip-flop may appear simple, it results in two rather important effects. First, the transition table shows that, unlike the S–R flip-flop, the D flip-flop has no long-term memory. Second, its output exactly follows the input but *one clock cycle later*. In other words, the D flip-flop merely delays a signal by one clock time unit. Unlike its parent S–R flip-flop, this circuit has no undefined states; but the price of this unambiguous behavior is that the device has only a brief memory, forgetting its input after one clock pulse.

The J–K flip-flop

The most common single type of flip-flop employed in computers is probably the J–K flip-flop. It is similar to the S–R flip-flop, with one exception: the domain of acceptable inputs (inputs for which the transition table is defined)

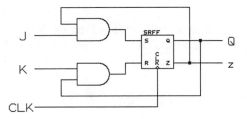

Fig. 3.17. The J–K flip-flop.

includes *all* inputs that can possibly be applied to two input lines. In other words, the J–K flip-flop has a transition table exactly like that of the S–R flip-flop, but with defined next states in the two rows which were left undefined for the latter:

$J(t)$	$K(t)$	$Q(t)$	$Q(t+T_0)$
0	0	0	0
0	0	1	1
0	1	0	0
0	1	1	0
1	0	0	1
1	0	1	1
1	1	0	1
1	1	1	0

A common way of actually realizing this transition table is to add a symmetric pair of AND gates to the S–R flip-flop circuit, thereby creating a pair of additional feedback paths. Such an implementation is shown in Fig. 3.17. Of course, this is only one circuit realization out of a whole range of possibilities; various others can be built to yield the same transition table.

The widespread use of J–K flip-flops in design should not be surprising. Because the transition table of the S–R flip-flop is contained within the transition table of the J–K flip-flop, it is obvious that the J–K flip-flop can do anything its simpler cousin is capable of; because the designer need not worry about the forbidden pair of input states, it can do quite a few other worthwhile things besides. It does involve a larger number of logic gates so its cost is a little higher, and in the early days of computer engineering this economic fact tended to discourage the use of J–K flip-flops where an S–R flip-flop would do. More recently, however, the cost of computer circuits has come to depend much more heavily on pin counts and numbers of external connections than on the number of gates in the circuit. As a result, the J–K flip-flop has gained in popularity and occupies an important position in digital circuit design.

From the circuit analyst's point of view, one interesting feature of the J–K flip-flop is that it has no prohibited or ill-defined states, so it can be precisely described by a logical expression,

$$Q(t + T_0) = Q'(t) \cdot J(t) + Q(t) \cdot K'(t).$$

This expression is easily constructed by applying either the maxterm or the minterm approach to the transition table of the J–K flip-flop.

Because the flip-flop circuit shown here is based on an S–R flip-flop assumed to be edge-triggered, the transition table for the J–K flip-flop should properly be given in edge-triggered form also. It reads as follows:

$CLK(t)$	$CLK(t+T_0)$	$J(t)$	$K(t)$	$Q(t)$	$Q(t+T_0)$
0	0	*don't care*		0	0
0	0	*don't care*		1	1
0	1	**0**	**0**	**0**	**0**
0	1	**0**	**0**	**1**	**1**
0	1	**0**	**1**	**0**	**0**
0	1	**0**	**1**	**1**	**0**
0	1	**1**	**0**	**0**	**1**
0	1	**1**	**0**	**1**	**1**
0	1	**1**	**1**	**0**	**1**
0	1	**1**	**1**	**1**	**0**
1	0	*don't care*		0	0
1	0	*don't care*		1	1
1	1	*don't care*		0	0
1	1	*don't care*		1	1

The time delay T_0 to reach the next state is one clock period, of course, not the gate delay time of the circuits themselves.

Simulation of the J–K flip-flop

Because the edge-triggered S–R flip-flop is the fundamental building block for both D and J–K flip-flops, both derivative flip-flops are built by adding a few logic gates to the S–R device. Although simple, this ask is still not quite so trivial as might appear at first glance. Why not, becomes clear when Fig. 3.17 is examined closely.

When the circuit of Fig. 3.17 is first assembled and energized, the gates included in the S–R flip-flop assume states dependent on manufacturing tolerances, environmental factors, and perhaps pure chance. Their initial state therefore cannot be predicted and must be considered unknown. The two AND gates included in the circuit of Fig. 3.17, however, take the unknown outputs as their inputs. Consequently, their outputs S and R cannot assume the known state 1; they can only remain indeterminate, or have the value 0. But $S = R = 0$ as input to an S–R flip-flop asks for preservation of the already existing output state. In other words, the output state will remain at its indeterminate value— or will be indeterminate by virtue of the indeterminacy of S and R. In a physically real circuit a known state will be reached eventually, but when and which state cannot be forecast. Building a practical J–K flip-flop therefore requires that its design be based on an edge-triggered S–R flip-flop that will permit presetting and preclearing.

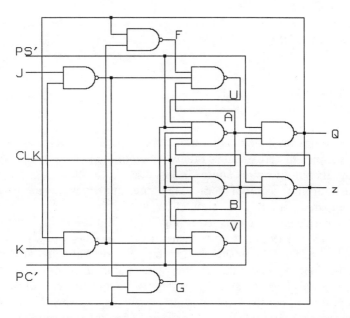

Fig. 3.18.   Rising-edge-triggered J–K flip-flop derived from the S–R flip-flop of Fig. 3.12.

To build an edge-triggered J–K flip-flop, the S–R flip-flop of Fig. 3.12 is first augmented with preset and preclear lines. A pair of AND gates is then added at the input, following the scheme of Fig. 3.17. These AND gates, however, are immediately followed by inverters in Fig. 3.17, suggesting that they may be combined to yield a pair of NAND gates. The result is a circuit entirely composed of NAND gates, as shown in Fig. 3.18. Simulation then follows the same lines as for earlier circuits:

```
/* Rising edge triggered JK flip-flop */
circuit etjkff:
    {
    nand: A, z, nps > Q;
    nand: B, Q, npc > z;
    nand: U, B, CLK > A;
    nand: V, A, CLK > B;
    nand: F, A, nS > U;
    nand: G, B, nR > V;
    nand: Q, nR > F;
    nand: z, nS > G;
    nand: J, z > nS;
    nand: K, Q > nR;
    }
input:
    {
    CLK = 0 (8) 16;
    J = 0 (4,12,52,60,68,76,84,92);
    K = 0 (36,44,68,76,84,92);
```

```
    nps = 1;
    npc = 0 (3);
    }
output:
    {
    CLK, J, K, Q, z;
    time = 150;
    }
```

The excitations employed in this simulation exercise a sufficient combination of *J* and *K* inputs to verify a substantial portion of the transition table of the J–K flip-flop. Its output results appear in Fig. 3.19. Gate delay times may appear somewhat short in this output, because the time scale shown is compressed two-fold as compared with previous simulations in this chapter.

The preclearing circuit employed in Fig. 3.18 is not clocked, so that clearing takes place in Fig. 3.19 even before the first rising clock pulse edge occurs. (This very simple preclearing provision avoids complication, but better arrangements are possible.) Subsequently, the flip-flop state is altered as appropriate at each rising edge of the clock signal. Perhaps the most interesting part of the simulation occurs for $t < 65$: the flip-flop is alternately toggled from $J = K = 1$ to $J = K = 0$ and back. Its state shifts as expected from the transition table and no instability appears.

To achieve satisfactory operation, the simple latch of Fig. 3.1 has now grown to the circuit of formidable complexity shown in Fig. 3.18. It is clearly quite difficult to perform detailed algebraic analysis on a gate-by-gate basis when numerous flip-flops are involved in computer circuits. From here on, circuits of the sort shown in Fig. 3.18, and others analogous to them, will be regarded as building blocks available routinely. In the rest of this chapter they will therefore appear simply as flip-flops, their internal structure will be taken for granted. This viewpoint closely parallels that of physical circuit design, in which it is normally

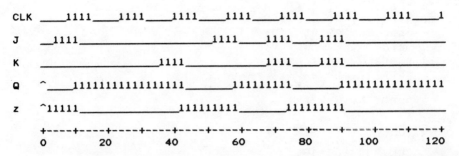

Fig. 3.19. Simulation of edge-triggered preset/preclear J–K flip-flop. Note the compressed time scale.

accepted that flip-flops are purchasable in chip form and will only very rarely be constructed by combining individual logic gates.

Simulation of sequential circuits

Analytic investigation of circuits containing flip-flops is more difficult than algebraic analysis of combinational logic circuits because the prior states of logic devices represent, in a certain sense, hidden additional input variables. Algebraic work is therefore limited to detailed investigation of relatively simple devices such as a single flip-flop. For larger circuits, analysis by simulation is frequently more attractive. In practice, design engineers use both algebraic and graphical tools to guide their thoughts and imaginations, but resort to computational simulation to check out the results of hard thinking.

In the foregoing, elementary logic gates were used to construct the necessary J–K or toggle flip-flops. This approach leads to circuits of great complexity when many flip-flops are needed. Simulations using such complex sets of gates run slowly; Apodix spends a good deal of time tracing the details of internal signal flow within circuits which the user is not interested in examining minutely. A second and probably more serious difficulty involves internal timing problems. A circuit including J–K flip-flops, for example, may show up instabilities that are the result of poor internal design of the flip-flop itself, not related to the main goal of analysis of a larger device such as a counter. Both these difficulties are in fact avoided in Apodix by including in the repertoire of available circuit elements a set of basic flip-flops. These appear in Table 3.1.

The predefined flip-flops are used in circuit descriptions precisely the same way as static logic elements. Circuits are still described by listing their elements and indicating the element interconnections by listing the input and output variables associated with each element. Like the multiplexer and the decoder, but unlike elementary gates, a flip-flop may have several outputs.

There is an important difference between flip-flops built up as collections of gates and the predefined flip-flops built into Apodix: the built-in flip-flops are fast. They are able to establish their new states within just one gate delay time unit, two or three times faster than flip-flops built out of individual gates.

In the following, both built-in Apodix flip-flops and combinational elements (e.g., multiplexers) will be used freely. Because Apodix simulates these circuits directly, not through substitution of large numbers of individual logic gates, very complicated circuits can be created quite readily without involving large numbers of gates, even though the circuits being simulated may in physical reality require them.

Table 3.1. Edge-triggered flip-flops recognized by Apodix

Name	Element description	Inputs	Outputs
srff	Set-reset flip-flop	3	2
dff	Delay flip-flop	2	1
jkff	J–K flip-flop with preset/preclear	5	1

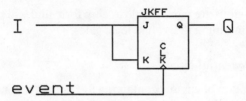

Fig. 3.20.   A toggle flip-flop may be obtained by tying together the two input lines of a J–K flip-flop.

The toggle flip-flop

Counting is a simple but important task which digital circuits are often called to do. Counting circuits or *counters* are usually built of special flip-flop circuits called *toggle flip-flops* or *T flip-flops*. These are in fact nothing more than J–K flip-flops whose two inputs have been tied together, as shown in Fig. 3.20. Their internal arrangement of logic gates may be similar to that of Fig. 3.18, or radically different; what matters is that their external behavior is the same as would be expected from such a J–K flip-flop.

The transition table for the T flip-flop is obtained by specializing the table applicable to the J–K flip-flop. Because $J = K$ for the toggle flip-flop, all rows are retained for which J and K are equal, all rows are discarded in which they differ. Only one independent input I actually exists in such a circuit, $I = J = K$, so its transition table contains only four rows:

$I(t)$	$Q(t)$	$Q(t + T_0)$
0	0	0
0	1	1
1	0	1
1	1	0

As is usual in describing edge-triggered circuits, all rows have been omitted in which rising clock edges do not occur.

The name *toggle flip-flop* may seem strange but it may be seen from the transition tables that it is actually quite descriptive of the circuit action. Whenever the input I is zero, the previous and next states are the same; leaving the input at zero value preserves the state of the flip-flop unaltered. Whenever I has the value 1, the next state is the inverse of the current state. In other words, if $I = 1$ at the time the clock pulse rises, the output is *toggled* from its current state into the complementary state; if $I = 0$ the previous state is maintained.

Toggle flip-flops are frequently used in a curiously reversed fashion, with the clock input driven by signals other than a real clock. For example, in counting circuits it is sometimes convenient to fix the input I permanently at 1 and to employ the clock input as the circuit driving point. One reason for doing so is that the circuits considered here are *rising edge triggered*; the counter will therefore count rising edges rather than pulses, so that somewhat round-topped or wobbly pulses do not give rise to a false count. It can, of course, be made to count falling rather than rising edges, by inverting the clock input signal.

Toggle flip-flops are widely used in counters. A single T flip-flop will toggle in response to an input pulse, and therefore can be thought to constitute a 1-bit counter. With a word length of one bit, it can only cover the span of numbers from 0 to 1. Building more ambitious counting circuits is clearly a matter of increasing the counting range. This task is considered in the next section.

Counting circuits

Counting circuits or *counters* are widely used in digital systems—indeed counting may well be the most fundamental operation of which computers are capable. Because they are important, a large variety of counting circuits is quite commonly employed. Most of these, however, are closely related to one of two types of basic counting circuit, the *asynchronous* or *ripple* counter and the *synchronous* counter. These two basic types are described and examined in this section.

The ripple counter

The ripple counter, or *ripple-through counter*, is based on the observation that when counting in any number base, each digit is augmented by 1 whenever the next lower digit has completed a full count. A single T flip-flop is capable of counting from 0 to 1, the full range available to every digit of a number in the binary number system. By using a second toggle flip-flop to count the number of full counts of the first, two T flip-flops can be made to count 0, 1, 2, 3. Three T flip-flops can, in the same way, count up to 7, four up to 15, and n up to 2^n-1.

Circuits to do the counting in this fashion are readily enough devised. Consider the natural manner of binary counting,

$$
\begin{array}{c}
0000 \\
0001 \\
0010 \\
0011 \\
0100 \\
0101 \\
0110 \\
0111 \\
1000 \\
1001 \\
\cdots
\end{array}
$$

The correct digits in this sequence may be deduced by repeatedly applying just one simple rule: *the kth digit changes value whenever the $(k-1)^{st}$ digit changes from 1 to 0*. A falling-edge-triggered toggle flip-flop changes state (i.e., its output

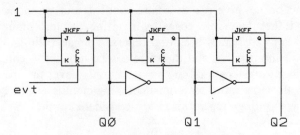

Fig. 3.21.   Three-bit ripple counter circuit using three T flip-flops.

changes value) whenever its input changes downward, from 1 to 0. To build a counter, it is therefore sufficient to arrange a set of T flip-flops, one for each digit position desired, and to interconnect them so that the output of one becomes the input of the next. A circuit to satisfy these requirements is shown in Fig. 3.21. It will be noted that an inverter is inserted between successive flip-flops. This extra gate is necessary only because the flip-flops shown are *rising* edge triggered (in accordance with the convention stated previously); the inverter serves to turn falling edges into rising ones.

The counter of Fig. 3.21 operates in the expected way, the flip-flops being driven by their clock lines. The first flip-flop in the cascade is driven by the events being counted, while each successive flip-flop is driven by the output of its immediate predecessor. In other words, the circuit of Fig. 3.21 counts events on the *count* or *event* line *evt*, which is connected to the clock input terminal of the first flip-flop but is not really a clock signal at all.

Simulation of the circuit of Fig. 3.21 is readily achieved. A rising edge triggered J–K flip-flop is available in Apodix; by connecting its *J* and *K* inputs together, as in Fig. 3.18, a toggle flip-flop is obtained. Its inputs are *J*, the clock, and the preset and preclear lines. Its output is the state *Q*. Three such devices are combined in the manner shown in Fig. 3.21:

```
/* Three-bit ripple up-counter */
circuit rippl3u:
    {
    jkff: one, one, evt, ps, pc > Q0;
    not: Q0 > nQ0;
    jkff: one, one, nQ0, ps, pc > Q1;
    not: Q1 > nQ1;
    jkff: one, one, nQ1, ps, pc > Q2;
    }
input:
    {
    one = 1;
    evt = 0 (6,16) 20;
    pc = 1 (4);
    ps = 0;
    }
```

```
output:
    {
    Q2, Q1, Q0, pc, evt;
    time = 120;
    }
```

Fig. 3.22 shows test results for this circuit, counting the events *evt* on an infinitely-running clock signal with a half-period of 20 time units (each equal to one gate delay time).

The event signal is applied after initially clearing the flip-flops. Its rising edge at $t = 6$ causes the first flip-flop to change state, in accordance with the behavior rules of rising edge triggered flip-flops. A subsequent falling edge at $t = 16$ has no effect, but the next rising event signal edge triggers another change of state of *Q0*. That change, however, carries *Q0* from 1 to 0; it represents a falling edge of signal *Q0*. It therefore evokes a change of state of *Q1*, and counting proceeds. The counting steps shown in Fig. 3.22 are the first six states of a binary counter,

$Q2$	$Q1$	$Q0$
0	0	0
0	0	1
0	1	0
0	1	1
1	0	0
1	0	1
1	1	0

What results is clearly a true binary count of the pulses—or more precisely, rising pulse edges—applied to the event terminal *evt* at the left of Fig. 3.21. The count "ripples through" the sequence of flip-flops, hence the name of the circuit.

A common application of ripple counters is as clock frequency dividers. If the input signal to a ripple counter really is derived from a clock, then successive

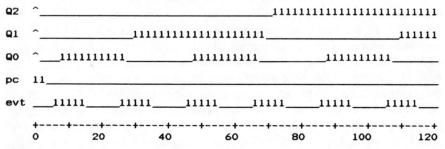

Fig. 3.22.   Simulation of three-bit ripple counter composed of three edge-triggered toggle flip-flops.

outputs $Q0, Q1, \ldots$, will exhibit regular pulse trains at half, one-quarter, one-eighth, $\ldots$, etc. of the original clock frequency.

It should be noted that there is no need for the event pulses to arrive at regular intervals, nor need they be of uniform length. The counting process is not tied to any system clock signals, only to events in the external world. Thus, randomly occurring events may be counted. For example, the counter of Fig. 3.21, if driven by a photocell, could be used to count customers passing through a supermarket checkout line.

Downward and bidirectional counters

In many applications it is natural to count down rather than up. For example, an airline reservations clerk is likely to be more interested in how many seats are left on a particular flight than in the total number of seats already booked. Down-counting from full capacity to keep a running score of seats available, rather than upward counting to determine seat sales to date, is likely to be needed. Down-counters are easily built in a manner analogous to up-counters. However, counting is done a little differently in this case. Consider again the sequence of binary numbers beginning at 1111 and proceeding downward,

$$1111$$
$$1110$$
$$1101$$
$$1100$$
$$1011$$
$$\ldots$$

The counting rule here is: *the kth digit changes value whenever the $(k-1)^{st}$ digit changes from 0 to 1*. This rule is exactly opposite to the rule for up-counters, corresponding to the behavior of rising (rather than falling) edge triggered T flip-flops. Consequently, the counters are identical except for use of falling edge triggering for up-counting, rising edge triggering for down-counting. To build a three-bit down-counter, in other words, it is only necessary to remove the inverters from Fig. 3.21.

Two-way or *bidirectional* counters are useful for keeping track of fluctuating quantities such as the number of people in a room or the number of parts in a stock bin—or, for that matter, the number of aircraft seats still available. They require two forms of input information: the stream of events to be counted, and whether each one is to be counted as incoming or outgoing. In other words, there must not only be an *event* signal but also an *up/down* signal to indicate whether the previous count is to be increased or decreased by one event. One very simple way to build a bidirectional counter is to employ the circuit of Fig. 3.21 again, but to replace the simple inverter by an inverter and a multiplexer, as in Fig. 3.23. Here the multiplexer select line is driven by the *up/down* signal; choosing whether or not to include the inverter effectively makes the flip-flops trigger either on falling or rising edges so the natural counting direction is either upward or downward. Other approaches to the same problem are also feasible in which

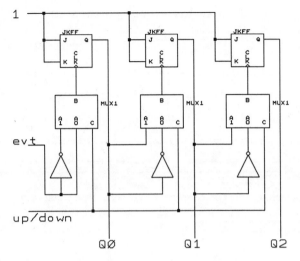

Fig. 3.23. Three-bit ripple up/down counter circuit, using three T flip-flops and up/down inverters.

the circuit function remains exactly the same but greater economy is achieved in parts count as well as total delay times.

Shortcomings of ripple counters

The ripple counter is a device attractive in its simplicity, but like most things in the universe, it is not perfect. Its major shortcoming can be appreciated by a closer examination of the timing diagram of Fig. 3.24, which shows part of an event sequence similar to that in Fig. 3.22, but with the difference that the clock has been speeded up so that its semi-period is eight gate delay time units.

At time $t = 50$ in Fig. 3.24, the count has reached 011: $Q2 = 0$, $Q1 = 1$, and $Q0 = 1$. The rising event signal edge at $t = 52$ causes all three counter digits to change state, and indeed they do so in Fig. 3.24, yielding a new count of 100.

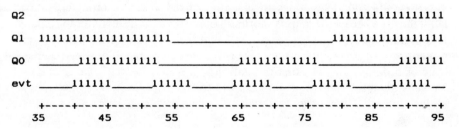

Fig. 3.24. Up-counting at higher speed: events *evt* occur at intervals of 16 time units.

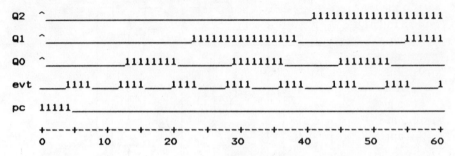

Fig. 3.25.   Up-counting at very high speed: events occur 8 time units apart while counts stabilize in 4.

Each change of state is subject to the time delay that would reasonably be expected of a logic gate and a flip-flop, some 2 gate delay times. In other words, the count does not change instantaneously, it takes time for changes to ripple through the circuit. As may be seen from Fig. 3.24, the transition from a count of 011 to 100 in fact proceeds in the sequence 011, 010, 000, 100 so that, for a temporary duration equal to a few gate delay times, false counts 010 and 000 appear: 010 for $52 < t < 55$ and 000 for $54 < t < 57$. For times after $t = 57$, the count is correct at 100. Nevertheless, incorrect counts are indicated for a period of 4 delay time units. Because the count of 100 is retained correctly for a duration of eight time units, the counter shows a wrong reading one-third of the time.

At higher counting speeds, the performance of ripple counters worsens because the gate delay times, hence the durations during which incorrect counts are held, are essentially fixed. Fig. 3.25 shows a simulation similar to that of Fig. 3.24, but with events occurring only 8 gate delay times apart. In this case, the transition from a count of 011 to 100 takes four delay times, exactly as long as in Fig. 3.24; but the correct count is subsequently held for only four delay times. In other words, the indicated count is wrong half the time!

It is hardly surprising that performance degrades as the counting speed is increased; after all, delay times are essentially fixed so any counting circuit will fail if the time between events is shorter than the time for the counter to respond. It appears from Figs. 3.22, 3.24 and 3.25 that the maximum time taken for one flip-flop in a ripple counter to stabilize is T_d, the delay time of one logic element (gate or flip-flop). In the worst case, all flip-flops may need to change state, as happens when the count changes from 011 to 100 in the examples shown. In an n-bit counter, the worst-case total delay T_D, during which a wrong count may be indicated, is

$$T_D = n\,T_d.$$

This duration is proportional to the number n of flip-flops because the flip-flop that counts the kth bit must wait for data to ripple through from all k lower-order bits. If the time separation T_C between events is greater than T_D, a correct count will be indicated for part of the time; if T_C is shorter, there will never be a time at which a correct count is indicated, because a new data ripple will begin to propagate from the least significant digit position before the most significant bit has stabilized. Indeed the case illustrated in Fig. 3.25 comes close to this situation, with a correct count shown only about 30 percent of the time.

For a given event separation time T_C there exists a maximum number of flip-flops that can be used in a ripple counter. In the limiting case, when the correct count appears for just one delay time,

$$T_C = T_D + 1,$$

the maximum number of counting stages is

$$n_{max} = \frac{T_C - 1}{T_d}.$$

Counters are rarely driven fast enough to yield so fleeting a result. Designers usually attempt to choose hardware components so that $T_C \gg T_d$ and the correct count is indicated most of the time. It should be clear, however, that the longer the counting chain, the faster the individual gates must be to fit within a given total event time, and the more difficult the designer's task becomes.

Synchronous counters

Synchronous counters are the most common type employed in high-speed counting. In principle, ripple counters may be employed in any counting application. However, high-order carries can take a long time to ripple through a long chain of flip-flops, causing concern if rapid events need to be counted. Synchronous counters do not suffer from this deficiency; a brief examination of their structure is therefore in order.

The synchronous counter is based on yet another critical examination of the conventional binary counting sequence

$$
\begin{array}{c}
0000 \\
0001 \\
0010 \\
0011 \\
0100 \\
0101 \\
0110 \\
0111 \\
1000 \\
1001 \\
\cdots
\end{array}
$$

If *all* digits are examined, not just adjacent ones, it is seen that the behavior of digits may be described by the following rule: *the kth digit changes value if and*

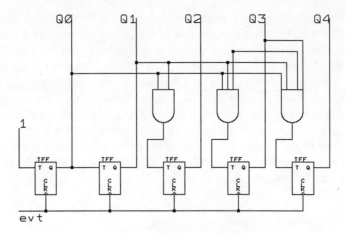

Fig. 3.26.   Five-bit synchronous counter.

only if all digits of lower significance have the value 1 and an additional event must be counted. For example, a carry from the third to the fourth digit only occurs if the count is at 0111. This principle leads to the circuit of Fig. 3.26, which differs from the ripple counter of Fig. 3.21 in two ways. First, the event signal is applied to all flip-flops simultaneously, so that the occurrence of a new event is known to all parts of the circuit at once; there is no waiting for information to propagate from lower-order digits. Second, the decision whether to alter state or not is made at each flip-flop separately, by examining *all* lower-order digits in a multi-input AND gate. This gate only enables the toggle input *T* if all preceding digits in the count are at 1. Unless this condition is satisfied, the *T* input is low so the event signal has no effect on a flip-flop.

All the flip-flops of Fig. 3.26 are triggered by the same *event* signal. All the flip-flops enabled to change state by the multi-input AND gates therefore change state at the same time. All state changes are synchronous, so this circuit is called a *synchronous counter.*

Synchronous counter operation may be examined by a simulation essentially similar to those already described. A 5-bit counter directly comparable with that of Fig. 3.21 is simulated by

```
    /* Five-bit synchronous counter */
circuit synch5:
    {
    jkff: one, one, evt, ps, pc > Q0;
    jkff: Q0, Q0, evt, ps, pc > Q1;
    jkff: T1, T1, evt, ps, pc > Q2;
    jkff: T2, T2, evt, ps, pc > Q3;
    jkff: T3, T3, evt, ps, pc > Q4;
    and: Q0, Q1 > T1;
    and: Q0, Q1, Q2 > T2;
    and: Q0, Q1, Q2, Q3 > T3;
    }
```

```
input:
    {
    one = 1;
    ps = 0;
    pc = 1 (3);
    evt = 0 (4) 8;
    }
output:
    {
    Q4, Q3, Q2, Q1, Q0, evt, pc;
    time = 300;
    }
```

The circuit is comparatively simple because the first and last flip-flops of a synchronous counter need no AND gates; in a 5-bit circuit only three enabling AND gates are therefore required. Results of such a simulation are shown in Fig. 3.27.

In Fig. 3.27, the rising event signal edge at $t = 124$ causes a change in all the flip-flops, taking the count from 01111 to 10000; only one gate delay time then elapses between the rising signal edge and the change in flip-flop outputs. Here, as in all other state transitions shown in Fig. 3.27, *all flip-flops alter state concurrently*. False counts therefore cannot arise; the change from 01111 to 10000 takes place directly, without any other values appearing. There is a delay in the appearance of the correct count, of course; the old count is shown for one time unit after the edge to be counted has arrived. The count shown is therefore correct at all times except for the first time unit after an event; in Fig. 3.27, that amounts to 94 percent of the time. This situation may be contrasted with Figs. 3.24 and 3.25, which show a ripple-through counter. In these, not only is the new counter output delayed, but false counts appear briefly during transitions from one counter output value to another.

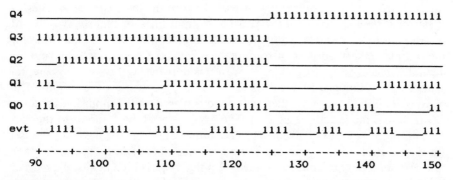

Fig. 3.27. Operation of a five-bit synchronous counter similar to Fig. 3.26. The time delay is identical for all output signals.

The performance superiority of the synchronous counter becomes all the more obvious when the number of digits to be counted is large. It should be evident from both the argument and the simulation shown that the delay inherent in the synchronous counter is T_d regardless of the number of bits counted. Similarly, the duration of false counts is limited to one time unit independently of the number of flip-flops. The price paid for superior performance is circuit complexity: every high-order digit is dependent on *all* the preceding digits, so the AND gates that control high-order digit flip-flops require many inputs indeed. Because many-input gates can cause difficulties for the designer, they are sometimes replaced by complexes of several AND gates with a smaller number of inputs each. Speed is only slightly degraded by the additional gate delays thus introduced, but false counts can appear. Difficulties of circuit layout and complexity of individual gates may be resolved in this way, even though complexity of the circuit is not reduced.

Registers

Flip-flop circuits are capable of storing single bits, but most digital data processing involves operations on words several bits long. Words are sets of bits, so they can be stored and manipulated in sets of flip-flops, one bit per flip-flop. Such collections of interrelated flip-flops are called *registers*. Because there are various ways of combining them, and because they have many applications, they form an extensive subject for study in their own right. A few register types, however, may be regarded as basic, most others being modifications or variations on these prototypes. Some such key types are discussed in this section.

Parallel registers

A parallel register may be regarded as a bank of N delay flip-flops. Its purpose is to accept an N-bit data word for storage and to permit retrieval of this word when required. It has N input lines so N bits of an N-bit data word can be moved into the flip-flops in parallel (concurrently), hence the term *parallel register*. It is said that the *register is loaded* over the N input lines, or that the N-bit word is *written into the register*. An N-bit parallel register also has N output lines for the complementary purpose of *reading* the contents. A simple circuit layout for a parallel register appears in Fig. 3.28. In this drawing, $x_{N-1}, x_{N-2}, \ldots, x_0$ represents the N-bit input word, the lines $y_{N-1}, y_{N-2}, \ldots, y_0$ constitute the output word.

To write into the register, the input word is placed on the input lines and the *LOAD* line is made active (set to 1). The AND gates at the D inputs of the various flip-flops are thus enabled to receive information. At the next clock pulse, the data word is moved into the D flip-flops; the state of each flip-flop is made to correspond to one input bit so the ith flip-flop reflects bit x_i. Once the register is loaded in this way, the *LOAD* signal is reset to 0 so subsequent input alterations will have no effect.

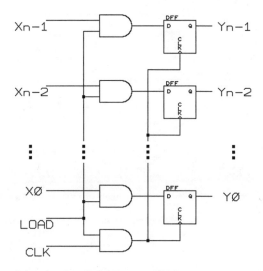

Fig. 3.28.   Parallel register comprising one edge-triggered delay flip-flop per data bit.

Delay flip-flops are so called because they are useful for storing data for the duration of precisely one clock period. When $LOAD = 0$, system clock pulses are disconnected from the flip-flops and data remain in the register until the next time $LOAD$ is activated and another data word is written into the register. In other words, the clock pulse as seen by the D flip-flops may last rather a long time, for the $LOAD$ signal also enables the connection of the CLK line to the various flip-flops.

No special arrangements need be made for reading data from the register of Fig. 3.28; the output bits y_i remain available at all times. Reading the register contents does not in any way affect the stored data, so the data may be read any number of times, provided of course the register has not been loaded with new data in the meantime. Reading takes no time at all, since the data actually reside on the output lines of the register at all times. Writing, on the other hand, requires a few gate delay times because it takes time both for the flip-flops to settle into their new states and for the AND gates to assume their new output values. Clearly, reading should never be attempted until some reasonable length of time after writing.

Shift registers

Loading the parallel register of Fig. 3.28 presupposes that the full N-bit data word is available on N lines. A rather different way of writing data to a register, which is slower but requires only one data bit to be available at a time, is *serial* loading. Serial loading is particularly valuable where data transmission takes place over a single wire pair, as for example over telephone lines. In essence, the bits $z_{N-1}, z_{N-2}, \ldots, z_0$ that make up the data word are sent out sequentially, one

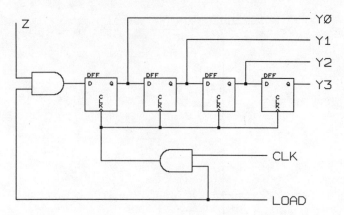

Fig. 3.29.   Shift register composed of delay flip-flops.

at a time, and are therefore received one at a time. The task at the receiving end
is to recompose them into words of *N* bits. One way of doing so is to employ a
shift register.

A shift register is a cascade of flip-flops so arranged that at each clock pulse
all bits are shifted one place to the right or left. One possible circuit configuration
for a 4-bit shift register appears in Fig. 3.29. A similar configuration can serve
for *N* bits; it is only necessary to extend the register by adding more flip-flops.

The operation of the 4-bit shift register shown in Fig. 3.29 is easily traced by
means of the following simulation. Longer register lengths may be constructed
simply by adding more D flip-flops:

```
/* 4-bit serial load shift register */
circuit sershift:
    {
    and: LD, CLK > C;
    and: LD, Z > D0;
    dff: D0, C > Y0;
    dff: Y0, C > Y1;
    dff: Y1, C > Y2;
    dff: Y2, C > Y3;
    }
input:
    {
    CLK = 0 (4) 8;
    Z = 1 (16,24,40,56);
    LD = 0 (17,49);
    }
output:
    {
    Y3, Y2, Y1, Y0, Z, CLK, LD;
    time = 60;
    }
```

In this simulation the loading signal LD is low for the first two clock cycles, so that the input value Z should be irrelevant to counter performance. Subsequently, loading is begun at $t = 17$ and continued until $t = 49$, or for exactly four clock cycles. During that time the input signal Z takes on values 0, 1, 1, 0 so that the eventual output should read 0110. After the LD signal is reset at $t = 49$, the input signal Z should again be irrelevant because the AND gate at the register serial input is deactivated by the zero value of LD. The details of this simulation appear in Fig. 3.30.

As is clearly visible in Fig. 3.30, the shift register actually does shift its entire contents one bit position at each rising clock edge. All four flip-flops are pre-cleared initially and show zero outputs throughout. However, once the LD signal is asserted, shifting begins and the value $z_3 = 0$ is carried through the register, one place per clock cycle. It is followed by $z_2 = 1$, $z_1 = 1$, and $z_0 = 0$ in their turn. The values taken on by the output word Y are thus successively

$$0000 \text{ at } t = 18,$$
$$0000 \text{ at } t = 26,$$
$$0001 \text{ at } t = 34,$$
$$0011 \text{ at } t = 42,$$
$$0110 \text{ at } t = 50.$$

The inspection times are chosen to fall well after shifts take place, and well before the next rising clock edge. They therefore represent stable values. After the events shown here, the data word 0110 will remain in the register until another loading sequence replaces it by another value.

It is worth noting that the shifts, loosely said to occur at each rising clock edge,

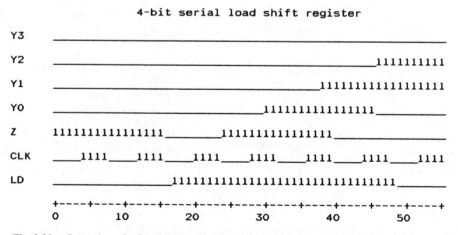

Fig. 3.30.   Operation of a four-bit serial-load shift register. Until the LOAD signal is asserted, all flip-flops remain in their initial, precleared, states.

actually occur two delay times later. This time delay should not be surprising in view of the two levels of logic gates involved in Fig. 3.29. It is important to note, however, that *all* flip-flops are only two logic levels removed from the clock signal, so that the time delays are not cumulative. Unlike the ripple counter, to which the shift register may perhaps bear some slight resemblance, the shift register retains its characteristic timings independently of the number of flip-flops it may contain.

Serial-parallel data conversion

The simple shift register shown in Fig. 3.29 may be used for serial to parallel conversion of data. For example, ASCII characters sent to a terminal over the telephone line arrive serially (one bit at a time) but are needed for display in parallel. ASCII characters comprise seven bits each, so a shift register at least seven bits wide is required. An 8-bit register is often used, to allow transmission and reception of an error check (parity check) bit as well as the character itself.

An outline sketch of the hardware needed to perform serial to parallel conversion of characters appears in Fig. 3.31. The heart of the device is the 8-bit shift register, which receives the individual bits at its input. It is loaded by the *DATA_READY* line, which must be toggled at the correct intervals for the transmission speed actually used. A 3-bit counter is employed to determine when eight bits have arrived. It counts from 0 to 7 (000 to 111 binary), so every time its output count reaches 111, the shift register must contain a whole new character. A three-input AND gate is employed to determine that the count has reached this level.

Whenever a new character is known to reside in the 8-bit shift register, this register is read in parallel, its content being copied to the parallel register. It is usually said that the character is *transferred* or *moved* to the parallel register, but these terms are in fact not quite correct. The shift register content is not removed, all the data originally resident in the shift register remain in the shift

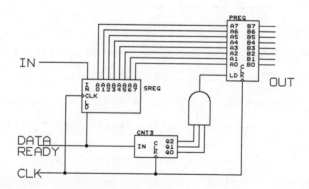

Fig. 3.31.   Outline sketch of arrangements for transfer of serially received ASCII characters to parallel storage.

register, even though a copy is made and written into the parallel register. Of course, the character must be moved from the parallel register to some other storage area, or processed, in the time it takes for the next character to arrive at the serial input.

It is worth noting that there is no arrangement of any sort for clearing the shift register so as to make it ready for the next character. None is required, for the shifting operations are destructive: once shifted out of the last flip-flop in the cascade, a data bit vanishes without trace. Eight successive shifts thus automatically destroy the old register content and replace it with the new.

The design shown in Fig. 3.31 is not complete, but only illustrative of principles. A complete design for a serial to parallel conversion unit requires taking care of further detail. The *DATA_READY* line must be activated in synchronism with the input bits, but separately from them, for otherwise the 3-bit counter will see no rising edges to count. On the output side, arrangements must also be made to unload (read) the parallel register within the time taken by transmission and storage of the next character, otherwise the register content will be overwritten and the character lost. How these and related problems are solved is part of the field of *computer communications*, a fascinating subject in its own right.

Parallel-load shift register

On comparing the parallel register of Fig. 3.28 with the shift register of Fig. 3.29, it is evident that both registers are composed of similar building blocks arranged in somewhat different ways. It is tempting to inquire whether a single cascade of flip-flops could be assembled to serve either purpose, perhaps by including sufficient extra gates to switch the circuit connections whenever required. Such a generalization of the circuits is in fact possible.

Each D flip-flop input in the shift register of Fig. 3.29 is connected to the output of the preceding flip-flop. In the parallel register, on the other hand, there is no connection between the various flip-flops; each is connected to its own input. The interstage connection shown in Fig. 3.32 is more complicated, but serves both purposes, as may be seen from the following two-way argument.

Suppose first that the *SHIFT/LOAD* signal has value 1. The inverter tied to this line ensures that the AND gate labeled *P* disconnects the input terminal *IN* from the rest of the circuit. At the same time, gate *S* has its lower input high and therefore effectively connects the output of the left flip-flop to the input of the right one, via the OR gate. That is to say, setting *SHIFT/LOAD* to 1 connects the output of one flip-flop to the input of the other, and thereby turns a sequence of flip-flops into a shift register.

Suppose next that *SHIFT/LOAD* is reset to 0. In this case, gate *S* isolates the output of the left flip-flop from the input of the right one. Gate *P*, however, now ensures that the signal applied to the *IN* terminal appears at the input of the right flip-flop (via the OR gate). Thus *SHIFT/LOAD*=0 establishes the same connections as appear in Fig. 3.28, thereby turning the collection of flip-flops into a parallel register.

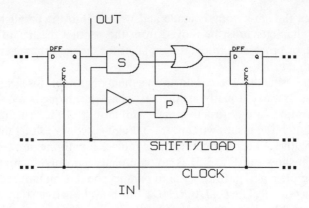

Fig. 3.32.   Connection between flip-flops to permit shifting or parallel loading in the same register.

A fully combined version of the *N*-bit register is shown in Fig. 3.33. The *LOAD* and *SHIFT* functions have not been combined here, but have been left separate; clearly only one at a time may be set to 1, although both may be reset to 0 simultaneously. When *LOAD* = 1, the register is loaded from the inputs $x_{N-1}, x_{N-2}, \ldots, x_0$ in the parallel fashion. When *SHIFT* = 1, the register contents are shifted, a new low-order bit being acquired from input line *L*. The high-order

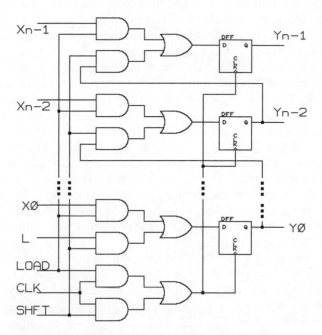

Fig. 3.33.   A parallel-load or serial-load shift register.

Table 3.2. Registers recognized by Apodix

Name	Element description	Inputs	Outputs
rcnt	Modulo 2^N counter, $N < 9$	3	N
cntr	Parallel-load N-bit counter	$4 + N$	N
sreg	N-bit shift register	$4 + N$	N
regs	Parallel-load register	$3 + N$	N
bsrr	Bidirectional shift/rotate	$5 + N$	N
plsr	Parallel-load N-bit shift register	$4 + N$	N

bit is shifted out and vanishes. Outputs are available from $y_{N-1}, y_{N-2}, \ldots, y_0$ in parallel, but serial output may also be obtained from y_{N-1}. In other words, this general register can be loaded either serially or in parallel, and can be unloaded either serially or in parallel. Of course, it is possible to build a still more general register that will allow shifts either to the right or to the left. Such more complex registers are based on the principles already discussed. These more complex registers will therefore not be discussed individually.

The Apodix simulator includes the register types shown in Table 3.2, so that fairly complicated circuits can be simulated without the need to build up registers out of individual flip-flops. The built-in registers are used in exactly the same way as other Apodix elements. There are actually 48 different registers, for each type is available in sizes from one bit to eight bits. Apodix automatically chooses the right size by counting the number of inputs, just as it does for multi-input logic gates such as OR and NAND.

Semiconductor memories

Data storage in computers is usually arranged in a manner termed *two-level memory*: there is a relatively small amount of fast-access but comparatively expensive storage accompanied by another, slower but much bigger, storage device. The large, slow memory devices are usually magnetic. Fast random-access memories, on the other hand, are generally made of semiconductor circuits, and are *volatile*; that is to say, their contents vanish when the circuits are deenergized. In this section, the principles of semiconductor memory units are outlined.

Memory cells

The set-reset latch is the fundamental building block for semiconductor memories, in much the same way as the delay flip-flop is the basic ingredient for the construction of registers. The atomic unit of memory is the *memory element*, also called the *memory cell*, a circuit able to store exactly one bit and capable of being located among many other similar cells. All the cells taken together make up the *memory* of a computer. The number of memory cells in a computing system may be quite large. Computer memories of several million cells would

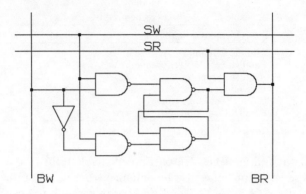

Fig. 3.34.   Memory element based on an S–R latch.

ordinarily be considered to be of moderate size, and a large computer may have as many as a billion.

A typical memory cell derived from an S–R latch is shown in Fig. 3.34. It comprises the latch, plus a few logic gates, all tied to a set of four external signal lines: *select write SW, select read SR, bit write BW, bit read BR.* The select signals are connected to only one memory cell, the other two are global to many (or all) the cells in a memory. A latch of NAND gates is shown in Fig. 3.34, although other forms of latch circuit would be equally acceptable.

The principle of operation of the memory cell is quite simple. The S–R latch holds data (it is, after all, the fundamental circuit possessing memory) until required. Data reading takes place when the *SR* line is asserted: the AND gate at the right of Fig. 3.34 is allowed to pass the state Q of the latch to the *BR* line, which serves as the output line of the memory cell. Writing is done by asserting the *SW* line, which permits the data value on the *BW* line to be deposited in the latch circuit. The inverter at the left of Fig. 3.34 ensures that either one side or the other of the latch input is high, never both; thus there is no danger of the forbidden input $S = R = 1$ occurring.

As with most other circuits shown in this chapter, a good way of studying the simple memory cell is by simulation. A first experiment can be performed by Apodix using the following simulation description:

```
    /* One-bit memory cell */
circuit memcell:
    {
    not:  BW > nBW;
    nand: BW, SW > nS;
    nand: nBW, SW > nR;
    nand: nS, z > Q;
    nand: nR, Q > z;
    and:  SR, Q > BR;
    }
```

```
input:
    {
    BW = 1 (30);
    SW = 0 (5,10,35,40);
    SR = 0 (20,25,50,55);
    }
output:
    {
    Q, BW, SW, SR, BR;
    time = 60;
    }
```

The state Q of the latch is initially indeterminate, as is evident in Fig. 3.35. At $t = 5$ the SW line is asserted, causing the bit value 1 resident on the BW line to be transferred to the latch. After two delay times the latch stabilizes in the state $Q = 1$; the memory cell has been written to and remembers the value written. In a similar way, asserting the SW line again at $t = 35$ causes the then current value of BW to be written into the latch, resulting in $Q = 0$.

Reading the data stored in the memory cell is done by asserting the SR line. When this is done at $t = 20$, BR assumes the value of Q as long as SR remains high (except for a small time delay). Similarly, BR echoes Q for $50 < t < 56$. At other times, BR remains reset because the AND gate at the right of Fig. 3.34 forces it to. Reading does not affect the state Q of the latch, so a single writing operation may be followed by as many reading operations as desired; reading is said to be *nondestructive* in this circuit.

From Fig. 3.34, it should be evident that writing to a particular memory cell is only possible if its SW line is asserted; the bit written is the value available on the BW line. Only one bit write line BW is required for a memory regardless of how many cells it contains; the write select lines, of which there must be many, choose the cell whose content is to be modified. If the select write line SW of a cell is not asserted, writing does not take place (not to that cell at any

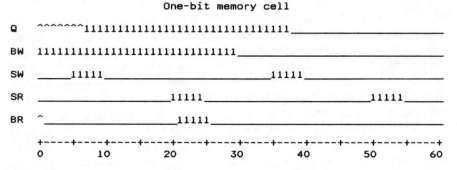

Fig. 3.35. The simple memory cell absorbs data from the BW (bit write) line while the SW (select write) line is high, reads it back on the BR line while SR is asserted.

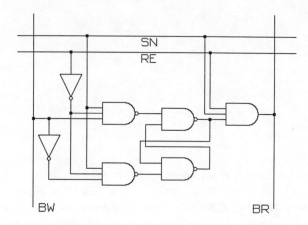

Fig. 3.36.   Alternative arrangement of a memory cell, with a single cell select line and a read enable line.

rate) and the setting of the input line *BW* is irrelevant. In very small memory structures, each memory cell may be connected to its own individual select lines *SW* and *SR*. For large memory structures, more complex schemes are worked out. It is clearly impractical to build systems involving millions of parallel select lines!

An alternative organization of a memory cell is shown in Fig. 3.36. The basic ingredients here are the same—a set–reset latch with enabling gates—but there is only a single *cell select* line *SN* instead of the two select lines *SW* and *SR*. This line merely selects a particular memory cell for reading or writing, it does not specify whether reading or writing is to be done; another control line, the *read enable* line *RE*, is set high to specify reading. The advantage of this scheme is that a single read enable line can serve many memory cells, whereas in Fig. 3.34 each cell must have two select lines *SW* and *SR*.

The memory cell described here is of a type known as *static memory*. There exists another type of semiconductor memory, called *dynamic memory*, which uses somewhat different circuits. Dynamic memory will not be discussed here; suffice it to say that although the individual cells operate on a different principle, the way in which cells are interconnected and controlled is the same regardless of their internal structure. In fact, even static memory structures are normally simpler than would be suggested by Fig. 3.34. When millions of identical bit cells are used for a computer memory, saving even a single transistor per cell represents a great economy, so designers take a great deal of trouble to combine gate functions and simplify circuits. With clever design, memory cells functionally equivalent to Fig. 3.34 can be built using as few as four transistors. Dynamic memory designs are even possible using only a single transistor per cell; they require complicated control circuitry but result in very large amounts of memory at a cheap price.

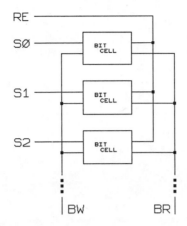

Fig. 3.37. A row of bit cells shares a common read enable line *RE* and common bit lines *BR*, *BW*; there is a separate select line *SN* for the *N*th cell.

Three-state gates for memory reading

The single memory cell of Fig. 3.34 obviously does not suffice by itself, it has to form part of a much larger memory collection of bit cells to be useful.Part of such an array is shown in Fig. 3.37. Here a row of bit cells is connected to two bit lines *BW* and *BR*. The bit value *BW* to be written is thus available to all cells; deciding which cell actually accepts the data is the job of the select lines. With an eye to economy, the cells in this array do not have two select lines each (*SW* and *SR*) as above; instead, they use a *select* line *SN* and a *read enable* line *RE*, as in Fig. 3.36. This relatively minor change in signals achieves a substantial economy: the *RE* line can be common to all cells, just like the bit lines *BR* and *BW*. Thus only one select line per cell is necessary, not two as in the above.

The arrangement of Fig. 3.37 permits efficient writing: the bit value to be written is placed on the bit line *BW*, the correct select line is asserted, and the read enable line is set. Unfortunately, the same arrangement does not work for reading. If multiple bit cells of the types shown in Figs. 3.34 or 3.36 are connected to the bit line *BR*, this line is driven by the outputs of numerous AND gates which very likely do not agree whether *BR* should be set or reset.

The main problem in any such scheme for sharing output lines is the difficulty of establishing connections from the many memory cell outputs to the single output line. In principle, K memory cells could be connected to the output by means of a K-to-1 multiplexer. In practice, however, the construction of multiplexers with thousands of inputs is not feasible. The upper limit for multiplexer design lies in a range from 10^1 to 10^2, more or less. Even if larger multiplexers were practical, the need to bring thousands of input signal lines to a single multiplexer would cause problems. A better scheme is clearly needed. The method most widely used relies on a class of logic gate not discussed so far, known as *three-state logic devices*.

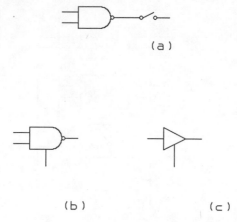

Fig. 3.38.   (a) NAND gate and mechanical disconnect switch. (b) NAND gate with open-collector output. (c) Three-state buffer.

Three-state logic devices differ from normal logic gates, as their name implies, in having *three* possible electrical output states: high, low, or not connected at all. The principle is simple and may be easiest to explain by means of an illustrative example. Fig. 3.38a shows a simple two-input NAND gate followed by a mechanical switch. The gate operates in the normal fashion, but may be disconnected from whatever follows it by opening the switch. The output of this gate therefore has *three* possible states: *set*, *reset*, and *disconnected*. When the switch is closed, the gate forces the circuits connected to its output line to follow its output logic signal; when the switch is open, the external circuits are free to assume any other voltage levels independently of the NAND gate.

Mechanical switches are, of course, not suitable for computer circuits. However, an equivalent electronic action may be arranged in several ways. All involve the use of an extra signal line, the *enable* line *EN*, which indicates whether a connection between gate and output terminal is to be made. When reset, this line causes the output to be isolated in much the same way as a mechanical switch would do. If the *EN* line is set, the output is enabled, i.e., connected to the gate. In this state, the circuit operates exactly like any normal logic gate would. Three-state logic devices can be made in any one of the usual logic configurations, by attaching an enabled (switched) output to an otherwise normal logic gate. The simplest and perhaps most widespread three-state device, however, may be thought of as just a switch, possessing one input line and one output line. The output of such a device exactly echoes its input if the enable line *EN* is set; if *EN* is reset, the output is disconnected. Such devices are often denoted by the symbol shown in Fig. 3.38c, similar to the symbol for a three-state NOT gate but lacking the inversion bubble on the output side. They are known as *three-state buffers*.

Using three-state buffers, memory control is easily accomplished. One single

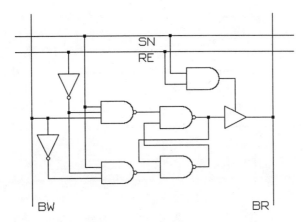

Fig. 3.39. When output is taken from a memory cell via a three-state device, the output (bit read) line may be shared with other cells.

output line is provided for the entire ensemble of memory cells. It is connected to each and every one of the cells through a three-state buffer, which in turn is controlled by the select line for that cell. Such an arrangement is shown in Fig. 3.39. Because the select line associated with any one memory cell controls the corresponding three-state buffer, a memory cell is actually connected to the output line only if its select line is asserted. Consequently, many select lines are still needed to address the many memory cells; but only one input line is required, and one output line.

Word and bit selection

Almost all computer memory is dealt with as bytes or words, only rarely are individual bits of primary interest. In other words, the large number of bit cells that make up a memory must be organized in such a fashion that they can be addressed, written, and read in word-length groups, not as individual bits.

Fig. 3.40 shows a memory of 6 bits, organized as three words of two bits each. A word is stored in the pair of horizontally adjacent cells that share a common select line. For example, select line $S2$ controls the two bit cells at the bottom of Fig. 3.40; when $S2$ is asserted, both bit cells are connected to bit read and bit write lines. There is one bit read line and one bit write line for each bit in a word; $BW1$ writes to the high bit in any word, $BW0$ to the low bit in any word. The cells themselves are taken to be functionally equivalent to Fig. 3.39. To write new data into, say, word 0 of the memory, the data bits are placed on bit write lines $BW1$ and $BW0$. The *read enable* line common to all cells is reset, enabling writing and disabling reading. Select line $S0$ is then asserted, thereby enabling the inputs to both bit cells in word 0. The act of writing itself then takes a few gate delay times, until all gates in each cell have stabilized.

The select lines $S0$–$S2$ in Fig. 3.40 actually do not select bit cells, they select

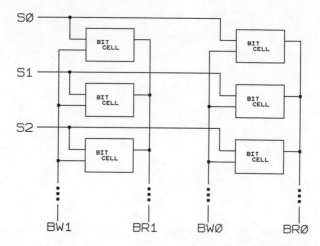

Fig. 3.40.   A 6-bit memory organized as three words of two bits each. The *read enable* signal, common to all cells, is not shown.

entire words. They are therefore called *word select* lines, or very frequently just *word* lines.

Reading memory contents is even simpler than writing. The read enable line is asserted and the appropriate word select line, say $S1$, is asserted at the same time. The bit read lines $BR1$ and $BR0$ then display the content of word 1. The reading is nondestructive, as discussed previously, so the state of the latch in each bit cell remains unchanged.

With the cell structure shown in Fig. 3.39, data to be written must remain present on the BRn lines for long enough to ensure that all gates stabilize. Conversely, data read back from memory remains available only as long as the word select and read enable lines remain asserted. It is common practice to connect the bit lines to a register, called the *memory data register* or *memory buffer*, which captures the word read and leaves it available until the register is needed for another read or write operation. This register need only be a simple set of delay flip-flops.

Memory chips

Random access memory is commercially manufactured as integrated circuit chips containing large numbers of individual memory cells. Memory chips are commonly available with storage for 16K, 64K or 256K (meaning $256 * 2^{10} = 262144$) bits on a single chip. Larger ones, up to about 4096K, are also made but less common. At the opposite end of the size range, memory chips containing as few as 64 cells exist, although they are rare; 1024 is a more common small size.

A simple organization of cell selection, with one select line per word, is adequate for very small chips but quickly becomes unwieldy as the number of cells

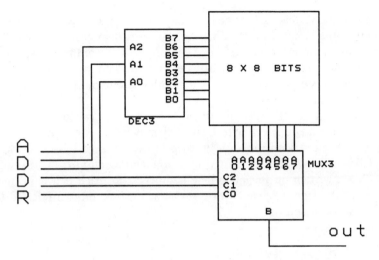

Fig. 3.41.   Bit addresses A5–A0 in a 64-bit memory chip are subdivided into row and column addresses of three bits each. An eight-way demultiplexer is required for writing.

is increased. A small number of lines, say 64, can be tolerated; but 262144 lines placed on the chip would consume an intolerable amount of space. Practical memory chips are therefore designed with the cells laid out in a square array, with one *row select* line for each row of cells. Such an arrangement is roughly illustrated in Fig. 3.41 for a 64-bit chip. (For simplicity, the chip is assumed to be organized as 64 words of 1 bit each.) There are eight rows of eight cells, and correspondingly eight row select lines. There are also eight output lines, one corresponding to each *column* in the array. When one of the select lines is asserted, all eight cells of the corresponding row are connected to the eight output lines. Because only the information stored in one cell is wanted, a further selection needs to be made. In Fig. 3.41, column selection is achieved by a multiplexer which chooses one of its eight inputs, each input being one column output line.

To identify each of 64 cells uniquely they must be numbered from 0 to 63. A 6-bit binary number suffices to cover this counting range. In Fig. 3.41 the 6-bit cell address is in fact subdivided into a 3-bit row address and a 3-bit column address, with the former serving to identify row select lines and the latter controlling the column selection multiplexer. This arrangement permits relatively small numbers of select lines to address quite large amounts of memory. For example, a 64K memory chip contains 65536 memory cells, hence requires a 16-bit address ($2^{16} = 65536$). Were 65536 select lines placed on the chip, they would consume most of the space available, leaving little for the memory cells themselves. An arrangement similar to that of Fig. 3.41, on the other hand, results in $2^8 = 256$ row select lines and 256 column output lines, a total of 512. This number is substantial but just possibly manageable.

The chip organization sketch shown in Fig. 3.41 does not show the *read enable* line common to all cells. It also omits any input arrangement for information to be written, so the sketch really relates to a *read-only* memory. Writing is handled in very much the same way as reading. An eight-way demultiplexer is employed to connect the input information to one column, and one of the row select lines is asserted concurrently so as to identify both the row and the column of the cell to which writing is to take place. These details have been omitted in Fig. 3.41 in the interest of clarity.

Memory devices of the type illustrated here are often called *random access memory*, because any one cell within an array may be accessed with equal ease; there are no preferred positions in the array to which access is easier than to others. Such memory is also referred to by the abbreviation *RAM*. By way of contrast, data written on magnetic tape is quickest to reach if it is nearer the beginning of the tape. Devices with this characteristic are often referred to as *sequential access* memories.

Word-width memory organization

Word selection is easily combined with row and column addressing schemes to permit large amounts of memory to be handled. In general, an array of memory cells organized as M words of N bits each requires N output and input lines, and must make provision for M distinct addresses. If M and N are relatively small numbers—for example, if 64 words of 12 bits each are required—so that all the memory will fit on one semiconductor chip, then a structure of word-width registers similar to Fig. 3.40 is frequently used. The addressing scheme will be similar to that of Fig. 3.41. This time, however, the memory cell array will comprise eight columns and eight rows of *words*, not bits. Correspondingly, the eight-way output multiplexer of Fig. 3.41 is replaced by 12 eight-way multiplexers, one for each bit position. Such an organization of memory may be thought of as three-dimensional, in the sense that the 12 bits of each word may be thought of as placed one above the other, the whole memory array thus forming a cube: eight rows high, eight columns wide, and each word 12 bits deep. The actual physical layout of the chip will of course still be planar, even though the circuits topologically form a cube.

An example drawn from industrial practice is the type 2114 static RAM chip. This chip contains 4K bit cells organized as 1024 words of 4 bits each. The internal organization of bit cells is thus a set of four bit cell arrays containing 32 rows and 32 columns of cells. (It could also be viewed as an array $32 \times 32 \times 4$.) The row decoder is of the 5-to–32 line type. Externally, the chip has four data pins, shared between input and output because at any given moment the chip is either being written or read, but never both at the same time. There are ten address pins to communicate the ten bits of address (5 row bits, 5 column bits). There is a read enable pin (called *not-write* in the specification sheets) and a *chip select* pin that allows the entire chip to be either enabled or disabled. When two pins are added to supply power to the chip, the total pin count is 18. This is a perfectly reasonable number, while 1024 pins (to handle select lines to the individual words) would not be practical.

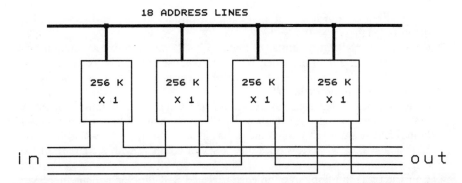

Fig. 3.42. Memory chips organized into a word-width array. The *write enable* line common to all chips is omitted from the diagram.

Where the total amount of memory is substantial, it is usual to employ chips whose internal organization assumes a word-width of one bit and to combine as many such chips as there are bits in the word. Such an organization is shown in Fig. 3.42, where each rectangular box represents a memory chip. The internal organization of each chip is taken to be similar to that of Fig. 3.41, but comprising a 512 × 512 cell array instead of 8 × 8. Correspondingly, the address size must be 18 bits (2^{18} = 262144). Any one N-bit word stored in this memory is spread out over the entire set of chips, one of the N bits being placed in each chip. Hence the set of N input lines to the entire memory is simply the collection of individual input lines to the individual chips. (An analogous statement naturally holds for the output lines.) The address lines are common for all chips, since the various bits that make up a single word are all located at similar addresses on their respective chips.

It will be noted that addresses, rather than row and column select signals, are supplied to the various chips. This arrangement may seem wasteful because every one of the 256K chips shown in Fig. 3.41 then must possess its own address decoder which duplicates the work done by decoders on all the other chips. A 512 × 512 cell array, however, requires 512 row select lines and 512 column lines. Were a single decoder employed for the entire array of chips, over 1024 external connections would need to be made to each chip. So high a number is quite unmanageable, while the 18 pins needed to communicate addresses can be accommodated fairly easily. In fact, very few connection pins are required beyond the address pins themselves because each chip only possesses one data line.

Problems

1. Construct an S–R latch, such as shown in Fig. 3.1, in an Apodix simulation. Show that the memory behavior described verbally above is valid. What output

results if both S and R are set to 1 when the initial state is $y = 1$, $z = 0$? when the initial state is $y = 0$, $z = 1$?

2. Construct an S–R latch similar to that in Fig. 3.1 but with one side requiring a longer delay time than the other. (For example, use OR and NOT gates instead of one of the NOR gates.) What are the differences in behavior as compared to the perfectly symmetric latch?

3. Construct an S–R latch such as shown in Fig. 3.4 in an Apodix simulation. Show that the memory behavior described verbally is valid. What output results if both S and R are set to 1 when the initial state is $y = 1$, $z = 0$? when the initial state is $y = 0$, $z = 1$? How does this behavior compare with the circuit of Fig. 3.1?

4. Construct a D flip-flop out of an edge-triggered S–R flip-flop and any necessary logic gates in an Apodix simulation. Verify the transition table given for it above. What is the delay time for such a device?

5. Write a Fortran, Pascal, or C program to generate all values of the expression

$$Q(t + T_0) = Q'(t) \cdot J(t) + Q(t) \cdot K'(t)$$

and thereby prove that this expression is a valid description of the J–K flip-flop.

6. Build a J–K flip-flop out of an edge-triggered S–R flip-flop and any other necessary logic gates, in an Apodix simulation. Verify its transition table and determine the maximum time required for a stable output to appear in each case. In other words, determine the time after which the output can be relied on to have its new value.

7. Show, by means of an Apodix simulation, that preclearing or presetting is effective in the circuit of Fig. 3.7 regardless of the values of S and R.

8. Devise a latch circuit analogous to Fig. 3.7 but based on NOR gates. Show that it works, by means of an Apodix simulation.

9. Show that a J–K flip-flop may be built out of an S–R flip-flop, analogously to Fig. 3.17, by adding NOR gates. Perform an Apodix simulation of both forms of flip-flop to show that their transition tables are identical.

10. Show that a delay flip-flop can be constructed by adding gates to a J–K flip-flop.

11. Write the full transition table of a clocked D flip-flop, including both D and the clock line C as inputs.

12. Write the transition table of an edge-triggered S–R flip-flop. Derive from it the transition table of an edge-triggered D flip-flop.

13. Write the rule or rules that describe synchronous *down*-counting. From these, devise a 4-bit synchronous down-counter circuit. Simulate suitable tests, to verify that your counter works properly.

14. Devise a modification of the counter of Fig. 3.26 that will permit setting the output to a count value specified by a set of data lines $P_{N-1}, \ldots, P_0$ whenever an additional control line *LOAD* is asserted. Such circuits are called *parallel-load counters*.

15. Build a 4-bit parallel load register similar to that in Fig. 3.28 using the appropriate number of D flip-flops and gates. What tests are necessary to verify that it works properly? Perform these tests and write an appropriate test report. What is the maximum time taken to load a word?

16. The circuit of Fig. 3.28 has no provision for clearing the register contents to all zeros. Devise an improved circuit that will have an additional control line CLR

such that asserting this line will clear the register at the next rising clock pulse edge, regardless of what the input word X may contain. Build and test your proposed design.

17. The shift register of Fig. 3.29 contains no provision for clearing the register contents. Improve this circuit, adding a few gates and an extra control line CLR so that all flip-flops are simultaneously cleared at the first rising clock edge after the CLR line is asserted. Test the resulting circuit in an Apodix simulation.

18. Devise a circuit analogous to Fig. 3.31 for converting parallel register contents to serial form for transmission.

19. Write algebraic (logical) expressions corresponding to the memory cell of Fig. 3.34. Derive its transition table by writing an appropriate program in Pascal or some other language, or by Apodix simulation.

20. Build a memory cell similar to that shown in Fig. 3.34, but using a J–K latch. If the *write*, *input*, and *output* lines are regarded as inputs, how many rows has its transition table? Construct an Apodix simulation of such a 1-bit memory cell, and generate the transition table.

21. Simulate a memory containing two 2-bit words, similar to Fig. 3.40, using S–R latches and any necessary additional gates. How long a time is required to guarantee that the output has its correct value?

22. Common memory chip sizes are 1K, 4K, 16K, 64K, 256K, and 1024K. Why are there no 32K or 128K chips? Could they be built if desired? Propose an addressing scheme suitable for a 512-bit chip.

23. A read-only memory chip, which has no input lines, is organized into N-bit words placed in $M_r = 2^r$ rows and $M_c = 2^c$ columns. How many row select lines and how many output lines will be required? Assume $N = 2^w$. What should the values of r and c be to minimize the number of lines on the chip, if the total number of bits is 1K? if it is 256K?

24. A sequence of K bits is said to be *bitonic* if it contains zero or more 0s, followed by zero or more 1s, followed by zero or more 0s. (For example: 000110, 000000, 111111, 001111 are bitonic sequences, but 010111, 111001 are not.) Show that a parallel-load shift register with six input lines A_5–A_0 can be used to construct a circuit with one output line F, such that $F = 1$ if the sequence A_5–A_0 is bitonic, and $F = 0$ if it is not. Simulate the circuit using Apodix to prove that it works.

4

Organization of the Simian computer

This chapter outlines the structure of Simian, a small general-purpose 32-bit computer, and shows how its internal organization is related to the operations it can perform. Although the structure of Simian is typical of present-day computers, no machine exactly like it has ever been built and probably never will; Simian is a *simulator*, a computer program that makes one computer act as if it were another. However, many practical computers do resemble Simian quite closely. They differ mainly in additional features not included in Simian.

Registers and instructions

The heart of any digital computer is its *central processing unit*, also referred to as its *CPU* in computer literature which sometimes seems inordinately fond of three-letter abbreviations. The central processor comprises three main parts: an arithmetic and logic unit (ALU), circuits for timing and control, and a set of working registers. In most computers, the central processing unit additionally includes a few registers dedicated to special purposes. Simian adheres to this broad pattern, as will be seen in the description to follow.

Register organization

Simian is a general-purpose 32-bit machine possessing eight general registers and three special registers, as indicated in Fig. 4.1. The *general registers* are general in the sense that none is dedicated to any particular task; all are equally capable of performing data manipulation, counting, and arithmetic. Which operations (if any) are to be performed on which register contents is determined by *instructions* given to the computer in the form of a *program*. All register instructions in the Simian instruction set may be applied to any one of the general registers equally well, so that the registers in this set are interchangeable as to function.

In addition to its general registers, Simian possesses three *special registers*. Of these, two are restricted to serve for address storage: the *program counter* and the *stack pointer*. The program counter normally serves to identify the memory location of the instruction to be decoded or executed next. The stack pointer keeps track of memory locations where data are stored on a temporary basis. The third special register is the *processor status register*. It keeps track of events

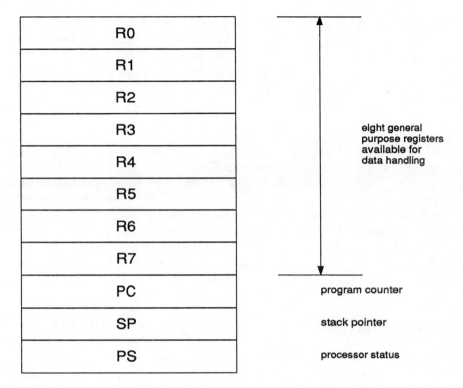

Fig. 4.1.   Simian has eight general registers labeled R0 through R7 for data or address manipulation, and three special registers: PC, SP, and PS.

that occur in the course of computation, including in particular any errors or other exceptional conditions. All three special registers are dealt with in detail in this chapter.

Each register in the Simian computer is 32 bits long. Bits in registers are numbered to allow easy identification when it is necessary to refer to them individually. Their numbering follows conventional usage: the most significant (leftmost) binary digit is called bit 31, the least significant (rightmost) is called bit 0. With this numbering scheme, bit n shows the coefficient that multiplies 2^n, if the word stored in the register is interpreted as an unsigned binary integer. The numbering scheme for bits is shown diagrammatically in Fig. 4.2.

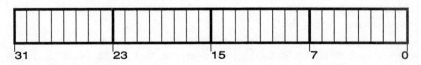

Fig. 4.2.   Bits in a 32-bit word are conventionally numbered with bit 0 in the least significant position.

Registers are often spoken of as if they were subdivided into four groups of eight bits, each group being referred to as a *byte*. Thus one may speak of the *most significant byte* of a register, meaning bits 31–24. When it is necessary to discuss the individual bytes within a register, they are numbered in a manner similar to bits, with the least significant byte called byte 0 and the most significant (leftmost) byte numbered 3.

Two-operand instructions

Simian allows arithmetic and logical operations to be carried out in registers and understands a set of instructions that specify what operation is to be performed at any given time. Simian is of a type called a *two-address machine*, meaning that two operands may be specified in a single operation. Instructions which request operations to be carried out are all stated in a register transfer notation which specifies an *operation*, the location of the *destination operand*, and the location of the *source operand*. Operations may change the destination operand, never the source. For example, the instruction

```
LD.L R3, R1
```

means "load register R3 with the content of R1": a copy of the content of register R1 is placed in R3. The previous content of R3 (the destination operand) is destroyed in the process but the content of R1 (the source) is not changed.

Simian recognizes six different two-operand instructions. These include both arithmetic and logical data manipulations:

Addition	destination := destination + source
Subtraction	destination := destination − source
Comparison	neither operand is changed
Loading	destination := source
Logical product	destination := destination · source
Logical sum	destination := destination + source

Operations are described by writing down the name of the operation, followed by the destination and source of the operands:

$$<operation> \; <destination>, \; <source>$$

the operands being separated from each other by a comma. The ordering of operands in all operations is reminiscent of the usual notation of algebra: $D - S$ means that in the subtraction operation, the destination operand D is diminished by the value of the source operand S. Detailed descriptions of these operations are given later in this chapter and all operations available in Simian are tabulated in Appendix 2.

In some applications the 32-bit word length of Simian is inconveniently large, a shorter word might be preferable. For example, most text processing and character manipulation operations would be easier to describe and to program if the register length were only 8 bits so that a register could always contain one (and only one) ASCII character. Simian provides for such applications by making it possible to disable the high-order 16 or 24 bits of the general registers, thereby effectively shortening the register length and temporarily turning the 32-bit computer into a 16-bit or 8-bit machine. Register shortening is made effective, and remains effective, for the duration of one instruction execution only, so the request to shorten registers is made part of the instruction itself. All the two-operand instructions therefore exist in three versions, capable of operating on the full register content, or on half the register content, or one byte only. The instructions are named accordingly, with a suffixing character to indicate how many bytes participate in the execution. The characters are B for single *bytes*, S for *short* words of 16 bytes, and L for *long* words of 32 bytes. The three addition instructions, for example, read

ADD.L R4, R1   adds to the entire content of R4 all four bytes contained in R1,

ADD.S R4, R1   adds to the low-order two bytes of R4 the low-order two bytes of R1, *without changing the high bytes,*

ADD.B R4, R1   adds the low-order byte of R1 to the low-order byte of R4, *without changing the high bytes.*

Shortened-register instructions like ADD.B and ADD.S, in which only the low-order part of a register participates, are commonly available in computers. Older books dealing with small machines often speak of *byte* instructions, *word* instructions, and *double-word* instructions, because a byte pair (16 bits) was long regarded as a *word* when discussing minicomputers. Unfortunately, exactly the same amounts of data are called *byte*, *half-word*, and *word* instructions in some other books, because the term *word* has traditionally denoted a 32-bit data unit in large business machines. The confusion arises because *word*, taken in a strict sense, merely refers to machine register length, not to any specific number of bits or bytes. To avoid misunderstanding, the terms *byte*, *short word*, and *long word* will be used consistently with reference to Simian. The term *word* will simply refer to a coherent unit of data regardless of its number of digits.

Byte and short word instructions *never affect the unused high-order bytes,* even though sometimes it might seem useful to do so. In effect, the high-order portions of the registers are electrically disconnected for the duration of the instruction. If the addition of short words, for example, results in a carry out of the high-order bit (bit 15), such a carry is *not* propagated to bit 16. To illustrate, suppose that the registers R1 and R4 contain

R1: 00000010   00010000   10000000   11000011
R4: 00011000   00000100   11000110   10010101

If the register contents were added using a full-length addition such as ADD.L R4, R1 then the result would be

R1: 00000010 00010000 10000000 11000011
R4: 00011010 00010101 01000111 01011000

Note that a carry has been propagated across the byte boundary from bit 15 to bit 16, and another from bit 7 to bit 8. On the other hand, the instruction ADD.S R4, R1 would only add the low-order 16 bits, ignoring the existence of the high-order bytes of both registers. Adding with the ADD.S R4, R1 instruction would therefore result in

R1: *00000010 00010000* 10000000 11000011
R4: *00011000 00000100* 01000111 01011000

Here the carry from bit 7 to bit 8 has taken place, but there is no carry from bit 15 to bit 16 because bit 16 simply does not exist during the execution of a short word instruction. Bits 16 to 31 of R4 thus remain unaffected. In a similar way, the instruction ADD.B R4, R1 applied to the original register contents results in

R1: *00000010 00010000 10000000* 11000011
R4: *00011000 00000100 11000110* 01011000

where no carry has taken place from bit 7 to bit 8 and the most significant 24 bits of R4 retain their original values.

Although it may initially seem that Simian is capable of executing six distinct two-operand instructions, the number is actually 18 because every one of the six exists in three versions. The conventional abbreviations used for these are

Addition	`ADD.B`	`ADD.S`	`ADD.L`
Subtraction	`SUB.B`	`SUB.S`	`SUB.L`
Comparison	`CMP.B`	`CMP.S`	`CMP.L`
Loading	`LD.B`	`LD.S`	`LD.L`
Logical product	`AND.B`	`AND.S`	`AND.L`
Logical sum	`OR.B`	`OR.S`	`OR.L`

The one- and two-byte instructions (*xxx*.B and *xxx*.S) all work in the same way: the high-order bytes are simply ignored for the duration of the instruction. Although instructions involving three bytes could also be devised, such instructions are very rarely encountered in practical machines. None exist in Simian.

Addition and subtraction are carried out in twos complement arithmetic. Subtraction is effected by combining logical complementation, incrementation, and addition, all involving the proper operand lengths. Simian makes no provision for any other kinds of arithmetic operations. However, twos complement arithmetic and logical operations suffice to construct any others that may be desired, such as floating-point additions or multiplications.

Comparisons

The Simian instruction set includes an operation for comparing two numbers to determine which is the larger. At first glance, such an operation may seem superfluous, because two numbers can in principle be compared by subtracting one from the other and examining the sign of their difference. In digital computers, however, comparing by subtraction is sometimes impossible. To start with the essential: a subtraction can only be performed on twos complement numbers. It cannot be carried out on *unsigned* numbers because a negative difference, should it arise, is not expressible in unsigned form. When working with twos complement numbers, subtraction may be impossible because the answer would overflow the available number range. Fortunately, the actual value of their difference is often not wanted anyway. Comparisons are therefore made in Simian without subtracting.

The easiest way of comparing two unsigned numbers without subtracting is to examine their most significant bits. If the most significant bit of one number is set, the other reset, then clearly the former number must be the larger; the values of the remaining bits do not matter. If the most significant bits of both numbers are the same, then the next bits may be examined, and so on until a difference is found. This method requires only the *examination* of single bits, never a modification of the numbers themselves. It does not create or store any new number and therefore cannot give rise to results that cannot be handled within the register length available. In other words, it establishes only whether a negative result *would* be obtained by a subtraction. However, the subtraction is never performed, so both the destination and source operands remain unchanged. A similar, though slightly more complicated, method may be applied to twos complement numbers.

Were a comparison operation to have no result, there would be little point in performing it. Although the *arithmetic* difference between operands is ignored in comparison, the *logical* result is both desired and retained. Like any other logical variable, the result of a comparison is binary: either the source operand is smaller than the destination, or it is not. A single bit therefore suffices to show the result. In Simian, this logical result is shown in bit 2 of the processor status register. As already indicated, the destination operand is left intact.

The comparison of two numeric operands can be dealt with using a logic circuit that performs comparisons; it is actually not even necessary to know how to perform subtractions. Because it is easy to build logic circuits to perform several operations at the same time, Simian logic is arranged to do three comparisons simultaneously:

1. A comparison to determine whether the difference between operands is *negative*, both operands being understood to be twos complement integers.
2. A comparison to determine whether the difference between operands is *less than zero*, both operands being understood to be unsigned integers.
3. A comparison to determine whether the difference between operands is *zero*, i.e., whether they are exactly equal.

The results are reported in the three low-order bits of the processor status register. Bit 2 is referred to as the N (*negative* difference) bit; it is set if the twos complement comparison reports that the first (destination) operand is smaller than the second (source) operand. Bit 1 is called the L (*less than zero* difference) bit; it is set if the unsigned integer comparison shows the first operand to be the smaller. Bit 0 of the processor status register is called the Z (*zero*) bit. It is set if the two operands are exactly equal, i.e., if the two bit patterns are identical. To illustrate, suppose the contents of registers R2 and R5 are

$$\text{R2: } 00000010 \quad 00010000 \quad 10000000 \quad 11000011$$
$$\text{R5: } 10011000 \quad 00000100 \quad 01000110 \quad 01011000$$

and the comparison CMP.L R5, R2 is made. The content of R5 represents a negative twos complement number, that of R2 a positive number. Subtraction of R5 from R2 must then produce a negative number, so $N = 1$. If the register contents are interpreted as unsigned numbers, however, R5 is the larger; hence $L = 0$. Because the two numbers are different, $Z = 0$.

When short word comparisons or byte comparisons are effected, the settings of the N, L, and Z bits of the processor status register reflect comparisons of the appropriate parts of register contents, the most significant bytes being ignored. When the instruction CMP.B R5, R2 is applied to the register contents described above, $N = 0$, $L = 1$, $Z = 0$ results. Comparing only the least significant bytes of the two registers, their roles are reversed: this time it is R2 that contains the negative number (if interpreted as a twos complement number) or the large positive number (unsigned interpretation).

Processor status register

The processor status register keeps track of recent events in the arithmetic and logic unit and reports them by setting five flagging bits usually called *status bits* or *status flags*. These are bits 4 through 0, the low-order end of the least significant byte of this register, as illustrated in Fig. 4.3. (This register could actually be much shorter, but it is made to contain 32 bits so as to retain consistency in the machine structure.) The status bits are set and reset by all comparisons, most arithmetic operations, and some logical operations.

The setting of the N, L, and Z bits by comparisons has already been discussed. They are affected in precisely the same way by ADD and SUB operations. The logical operations AND and OR also manipulate the Z bit. However, they leave the N and L bits unaltered, for the concepts of *greater* and *lesser* have no meaning in logical operations. Purely manipulative operations that do not change data, such as LD.S, leave the processor status register unchanged from its previous state.

The V and C bits in the processor status register, also known as the *overflow* and *carry* bits, flag events resulting from arithmetic operations (and some

Fig. 4.3.   Status bits in the least significant byte of the processor status register.

manipulative operations yet to be discussed). Arithmetic overflows in twos complement addition or subtraction are signaled by setting the V bit, while the C bit is set by attempts to propagate carries beyond the most significant bit. Carries and overflows, of course, refer to the most significant bit that actually can be affected by the operation. Thus the C and V bits flag overflows and carries beyond bit 31 in an ADD.L operation, beyond bit 15 in an ADD.S operation, and beyond bit 7 in an ADD.B operation.

All five flagging bits in the processor status register keep their values until such time as another operation sets or resets them. For example, suppose a CMP.S operation sets the C bit. This bit can be examined, and the correct result is certain to be still there, even after executing LD.S, because no LD operation ever affects the C bit. On the other hand, were a SUB.L operation to follow CMP.S before the C bit is examined, the result of the CMP.S would be lost because the SUB.L operation sets or resets the C bit in accordance with its own result.

To summarize, the five status (flag) bits of the processor status register are set by the following events:

V   Twos complement arithmetic *overflow* resulted from an addition or subtraction. The true arithmetic result lies outside the valid range of twos complement numbers.

C   An attempt was made to *carry* beyond the most significant bit in an arithmetic operation (bit 7, 15, or 31 depending onoperand length).

N   A *negative* value was obtained in arithmetic, or the destination operand is smaller than the source in a twoscomplement integer comparison.

L   The destination operand is *less than* the source in a comparison (both numbers taken to be unsigned integers).

Z   *Zero* was obtained in arithmetic or logic, or the two operands are identical in a comparison.

Not every processor operation manipulates all five flags, indeed some affect no flags at all. A full description of which operations set which flags and how may be found in Appendix 2.

The CMP and SUB operations manipulate the N and Z bits in a similar way. Thus if SUB.L R5, R1 yields N = 1, indicating that the number in R5 is the smaller, then so will CMP.L R5, R1. This arrangement is sometimes described by saying "the CMP instruction is the same as SUB but with the arithmetic result thrown away." Quite aside from the fact that CMP does not work by performing subtractions, this hasty statement is inaccurate in a vital point: CMP also manipulates the L bit but SUB does not.

Digital computers spend a great part of their productive lifetimes performing table searches and comparing bit strings (which may denote quantities or character information) to determine whether they are the same. Hence the processor status register flags and the arithmetic notations are largely chosen so as to make comparisons both easy and swift.

Single-operand instructions

Simian is a two-address machine, so up to two operands may enter into a single operation. In addition, Simian also performs a number of operations on single operands. These are

Rotation	Operand is rotated left n bits
Logical shift left	Operand is shifted left n bits
Arithmetic shift left	Operand is shifted left n bits
Incrementation	Operand is increased n
Complementation	Operand is logically complemented.

Each of these instructions affects only one operand, i.e., it replaces the original value of the operand by a new one. The old value is not preserved, so a copy must be made and stored somewhere for later reference if it is likely to be required for any future purpose.

All the single-operand instructions exist in byte, short and long forms. That is, there are not really five single-operand instructions, but fifteen:

Rotation	`ROL.B`	`ROL.S`	`ROL.L`
Logical shift left	`SHL.B`	`SHL.S`	`SHL.L`
Arithmetic shift left	`SHLA.B`	`SHLA.S`	`SHLA.L`
Incrementation	`INC.B`	`INC.S`	`INC.L`
Complementation	`NOT.B`	`NOT.S`	`NOT.L`

Register shortening works with the single-operand instructions in exactly the same way as it does with two-operand instructions: the unused high-order part of the register is disconnected for the duration of the operation so it neither affects the result nor is it affected in any way. For example, suppose a register contains

$$11100000 \quad 10101010 \quad 11001100 \quad 11110000$$

If the register content were to be rotated leftward one bit, it would contain

after ROL.L, 11000001   01010101   10011001   11100001, or
after ROL.S, *11100000   10101010*   10011001   11100001, or
after ROL.B, *11100000   10101010   11001100*   11100001.

All the above instructions except NOT permit a small integer argument n to be specified, a number in the range -16_{10} to $+16_{10}$ but excluding zero. This argument specifies the number of bit positions to be rotated or shifted in ROL, SHL and SHLA, or the amount by which the operand is to be incremented in the case of INC. To illustrate,

`SHL.L R2, 3`

causes the low-order two bytes of register R2 to be shifted left three places, so that the erstwhile content of bit 0 is copied into bit 3, bit 1 into bit 4, and so on. Bits 0, 1, and 2 are filled with zeros; the initial content of bits 13, 14, and 15 is lost. The argument is not an operand; it is always an actual numeric value, never a register number or other symbolic designation.

While some computers have separate *shift left* and *shift right* instructions, Simian accomplishes both in one. There is only a left shift instruction but it permits both positive and negative, i.e., leftward and rightward, shifting; likewise for rotation. Incrementation may also involve either a positive or a negative amount so that there is no need for a separate *decrement* instruction. For example, the register content

    11100000 10101010 11001100 11110000

will become

11000001	01010101	10011001	1110000**1**	if rotated +1,
00000101	01010110	01100111	10000**111**	if rotated +3,
00001110	00001010	10101100	11001111	if rotated −4.

Rotations or shifts greater than 16 bits cannot be accomplished by a single instruction. If required, they can be done by two successive instructions.

Two kinds of shifting instructions are provided in Simian, *logical* and *arithmetic*. The logical shift operation SHL is straightforward enough. It simply shifts the operand leftward the required number of bits, i.e., it moves every bit toward the most significant end of the register. Digits shifted out of the register are discarded. Bit positions vacated by the shift (the least significant digits in a left shift, the most significant in a right shift) are filled with zeros. For example, the instruction

    SHL.S R2, −3

signifies that the two low-order bytes of R2 are to be shifted right three places. Bits 15 through 13 will be filled in with zeros in this operation.

The arithmetic shift operation SHLA is a little more complicated, in that it performs *sign extension*. In an arithmetic *left* shift, the low-order digits are filled with zeros, exactly as they would be in a logical left shift. However, in an arithmetic *right* shift (SHLA with a negative argument), the vacated high-order bit positions are filled with copies of the original high-order bit, which is the sign bit in twos complement notation. Thus the word

    11100000 10101010 11001100 11110000

placed in, say, R7 will become, on performing a succession of one-bit arithmetic right shifts,

11110000	01010101	01100110	01111000	after SHLA.L R7, −1,
11111000	00101010	10110011	00111100	after a second shift,
11111100	00010101	01011001	10011110	after another.

However, the word

    01110000 10101010 11001100 11110000

subjected to the same operations will contain

00111000	01010101	01100110	01111000	after SHLA.L R7, −1,
00011100	00101010	10110011	00111100	after a second shift,
00001110	00010101	01011001	10011110	after another.

A right shift by three bits would, of course, have exactly the same effect as three successive one-bit shifts.

Having two kinds of right shift simplifies twos complement arithmetic, where the most significant bit of an integer indicates its sign. Arithmetic right shifts do not alter the leftmost bit, so they preserve the signs of twos complement numbers. Shifting right one place is therefore equivalent to dividing by 2, shifting left is equivalent to multiplying by 2, with the signs correctly handled in all cases. For the same reason, the carry bit C is made to participate in arithmetic shifts. The bit shifted out of the register (i.e., the most significant bit in a left shift, the least significant bit if shifting right) is not simply discarded, but is copied into the carry bit. On examining the carry bit, it is then immediately clear whether a remainder was created in division, or a carry generated in multiplication.

Incrementation with INC is a quite straightforward operation: the destination operand is increased by the specified small integer argument. This operation is probably most often used in counting applications. Having an incrementation operation is certainly not essential, for incrementation cannot do anything that cannot be done by the ADD operation. However, it is a single-operand instruction so it takes a little less time to execute. Counting is an extremely frequent activity in digital computing, so the effective operating speed of practical computers can often be increased by endowing them with INC as well as ADD instructions.

Basic Simian architecture

Although the central processor is certainly an essential part of a digital computer, it is a part just barely able to operate on its own. Other major components invariably need to be added so as to obtain a useful machine. The selection of components to make up a computer, and the manner in which these components are interconnected, is referred to as the *architecture* of a computer.

Memory organization

Simian possesses a single memory which serves to house both program instructions and data. This memory is connected to the central processing unit by a connecting *bus*, a multiwire connection, as indicated in Fig. 4.4. The bus contains 32 *data lines* so that a full register content can be moved between the memory and a working register at one time. It also contains 32 *address lines* used to specify the location in memory from (or to) which a data transfer is desired. The

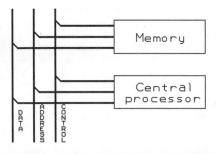

Fig. 4.4. Data transfers between memory and working registers take place along the bus data lines while the address lines specify memory location.

address lines lead to the address decoder circuits of the memory unit, where they determine which row and column select lines in memory are set. The bus structure also contains various control lines; at the very least, it must possess an additional line to indicate the direction of data transfer, i.e., whether reading or writing to memory is to take place. In almost all computers, however, the bus also serves to connect to various subsystems besides memory and central processor, such as terminal connections and communication lines to the outside world. These may also require control lines. The total number of connection lines on the bus of a 32-bit computer can therefore easily exceed 100.

Because the byte is the smallest unit of data that Simian registers can manipulate, Simian memory is addressable on a byte basis. In other words, all the available memory consists of units of eight bits and all memory addresses refer to byte units. A byte-oriented memory organization like that described here, or one much like it, is the basis for the majority of digital computers in existence today. It is generally easy to combine bytes into larger entities such as words, harder to break up long (e.g., 48-bit or 60-bit) words into subunits.

The bytes in Simian memory are numbered with unsigned integers, beginning at 0 and continuing to $FFFFFFFF_{16}$. Addresses are commonly specified in hexadecimal notation, although, in principle, decimal notation could be used instead. Memory may be regarded as a one-dimensional array of bytes, which are sequentially numbered as in Fig. 4.5. It may seem at first glance that this form of numbering is "left-handed," since numbers increase from right to left. However, it is

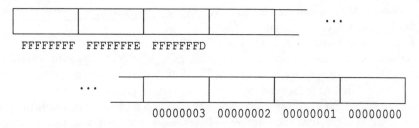

Fig. 4.5. Byte numbering in memory proceeds from high to low addresses in Simian.

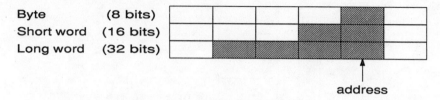

Byte   **(8 bits)**
Short word   **(16 bits)**
Long word   **(32 bits)**

address

Fig. 4.6. All data units are identified by their least significant byte addresses.

consistent with the scheme of numbering bits in a word, which is also "left-handed" in the same sense.

Because addresses are stored in registers 32 bits wide, the largest address possible in Simian is $2^{32} - 1$ or 4294967295.This limit is commonly known as the *address space* of a computer. Of course, not every computer necessarily contains enough physical memory to fill its address space, in fact most practical machines contain a good deal less. Large address spaces are thought desirable nevertheless, because the address space effectively limits the amount of memory that can be installed. Machines with small address spaces are unable to make use of large amounts of memory, even if price were no object.

Every memory address in Simian is in fact a byte address. When referring to *short* words or *long* words, the convention is used that *every data entity is addressed by giving the address of its least significant byte*, as shown in Fig. 4.6.

Any particular byte address is simply a number, so it is clearly impossible to distinguish whether a long word, a short word, or a byte is being addressed. The address of any data item should really be regarded as a *starting* address, with the data continuing for 1, 2, or 4 bytes from there. Whether data are stored in short or long words is not really a matter of memory structure, but of the user's intentions. The memory after all only stores bytes and does not care whether they are intended to represent parts of long numbers or not.

Instruction formats

Up to now the instructions that Simian can execute have been stated in a notation consisting of letters and numbers chosen so they are easy to remember (they are said to have *high mnemonic value*). Although this notation is easy for people to read and understand, it is not usable by computers because computers only deal with binary information. All instructions must therefore be encoded in binary form so they can be stored in memory and manipulated in the same way that all other digital information is handled.

Every Simian instruction is encoded in two bytes, organized into four fields as shown in Fig. 4.7. The operation code field simply gives an operation number, e.g., 0000 to denote ADD, 0001 to signify SUB, and so on. A full table of operation codes, including several not yet discussed, is given in Appendix 2. The operand length for each operation appears in bits 5 and 4 of the 16-bit instruction word. It is given as the number of bytes less 1, encoded in unsigned integer form. In other words,

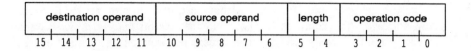

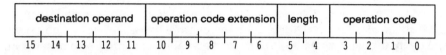

Fig. 4.7. Two-operand and single-operand instruction encoding in Simian: the format is always two bytes.

length = 00 signifies byte operands
01 signifies short (2-byte) operands
11 signifies long (4-byte) operands.

There are no three-byte operands in Simian. Consequently, 10 is considered an invalid length indicator, an error which will prevent the instruction from being executed.

Both the source and destination operand fields of two-operand instructions contain information encoded in the form shown in Fig. 4.8. Each contains three subfields: the register number and two one-bit flagging fields. Register numbers are always given as unsigned integers. Both flagging bits must be reset for straightforward register addressing of the sort discussed so far.

To see in some detail how a Simian instruction is stored, consider for example

    SUB.S R5, R3

This instruction says, translated into inelegant English, "subtract from the two-byte integer in the least significant half of R5 the integer in R3." Its machine encoding runs as follows:

Operation: SUB	. . . . 0 0 0 1
Two-byte instruction, S	. . . . 0 1 . . . .
Source register: R3,	. . . . 0 1 1 . . . . . .
mode bits reset	. . . . . 0 0 . . . .
Destination register: R5	. . 1 0 1 . . . .
mode bits reset	0 0 . . . .
Putting it all together,	0 0 1 0 1 0 0 0 1 1 0 1 0 0 0 1
or, in hexadecimal form,	2 8 D 1

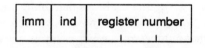

Fig. 4.8. An operand field in a Simian instruction.

In those single-operand instructions that permit an argument, ROL, SHL, SHLA, and INC, the argument is placed in the five-bit field occupied by the source argument in two-operand instructions. The argument is encoded in sign and magnitude form, as a four-bit unsigned integer with a separate sign bit. The coding is unusual in that the magnitude placed in the operand field is *lower by one* than the value intended; in other words, +0 in the operand field is understood to mean +1, −0 in the operand field is taken to mean −1, and so on. A zero argument cannot be requested in these instructions. This restriction causes no harm, for there would be little sense in a rotation or shift by zero bits, nor in incrementation by zero. On the other hand, this form of notation permits shifts and rotations by 16 bits in either direction.

A typical example of single-operand instruction encoding is the rotation instruction

```
ROL.L R6, -9
```

Again taking the details one at a time, its machine encoding runs as follows:

Operation: ROL	 0110
Four-byte instruction, L	. . . . 11 . . . .
Argument magnitude = 9,	. . . . . . 1000 . . . . . .
sign = negative.	. . . . . 1 . . . .
Destination register: R6	. . 110 . . . .
mode bits reset	00 . . . .
Putting it all together,	0011011000110110
or, in hexadecimal form,	3 6 3 6

In the NOT instructions, which take no argument, the operation code extension must always be set to 00000. Any other value will not lead to correct complementation.

The program counter

Like most other general-purpose digital computers, Simian uses one single physical memory to house both the program instructions and the data to be operated on. This arrangement has many advantages, not the least of which is economy.

Programs are normally executed in a computer one instruction at a time and instructions are placed in memory in the order of their execution. To keep track of which instructions have been executed and which one should be executed next, Simian has a special register, the *program counter*. Whenever Simian is ready to execute an instruction, it fetches two bytes (one instruction) from that place in memory where the program counter points, then interprets the instruction and executes it.

The address in the program counter is always that of the low-order byte of the instruction word, so the bytes fetched are the one pointed to by the program counter, and the next higher numbered byte. For example, the instruction SUB.S R5, R3 has the hexadecimal form 28D1 and is stored in two bytes:

D1 in byte 00000030
28 in byte 00000031

To fetch the instruction properly, the program counter must contain 00000030. When fetched, the instruction is placed into the *instruction register*, where decoding circuitry will have access to it.

After every instruction fetch, the program counter is incremented by two bytes. Simian instructions are two bytes long, so incrementation by 2 automatically makes the program counter contain the address of the *next* instruction. Thus, Simian normally runs in the following fetch-decode-execute cycle:

1. Fetch a two-byte instruction from the location pointed at by the program counter. Increment program counter 2 bytes.
2. Decode the instruction, i.e., analyze it to determine what action is required.
3. Execute the instruction.
4. Go to step 1. above, and continue.

This cycle continues eternally—or until the HALT instruction is encountered. The latter, whose full binary representation is 11111111 11111111, halts the processor.

Incrementation after the fetch is always by *two* bytes because all Simian instructions are two bytes long. During the execution of an instruction, the program counter invariably points at the byte following the location of the instruction itself. If the program code is *purely linear*, i.e., if one instruction always follows another, the program counter therefore points at the low-order byte of the next instruction. Where it is necessary to execute instructions in other than a sequential order, means are required for altering the program counter content. These will be dealt with next.

Branch instructions

During program execution, the next instruction to be decoded and executed is always taken from whatever place in memory is newly specified by the program counter, so a change in the sequence of instructions is readily achieved by changing the program counter content. Instructions that cause program counter contents to be changed are called *branch instructions*, because the replacement of program counter content by some noncontiguous address causes program execution to *branch* from the straight linear course it would otherwise have followed.

There are quite a few different branch instructions in Simian, all alike in one respect: their action is to add a specified amount to the program counter content. In other words, they bear some rough resemblance to INC.*x* instructions, with the difference that they act not on a general register, but on the program counter. The amount to be added may be positive or negative; it is specified by a short (two-byte) integer in twos complement notation. This number is called the *offset* of the branch instruction. The offset is always placed in memory immediately following the branch instruction. Every branch instruction thus takes up four bytes of memory: two bytes containing the instruction proper, followed by another two bytes that specify the offset.

Aside from a few exceptions yet to be discussed, branch instructions are *conditional* instructions; they are executed only if a logical condition, the *branching condition*, is met. The fundamental mechanism is simple: when a branch instruction is executed, the program counter content is increased by the offset, but *only if the branching condition is met*. Branching conditions are actually prescribed settings of the processor status register flag bits, so branching takes place if the status bits match the desired pattern. The sequence of execution of a branch instruction is therefore as follows:

1. Fetch the instruction.
2. Increment the program counter 2 bytes.
3. Decode the instruction and identify it as a branching instruction. Fetch the two bytes pointed to by the program counter (the offset value).
4. Increment the program counter 2.
5. Examine the processor status flag bits to see whether the branching condition is met.
6. If the branching condition is met, add the offset to the program counter contents.

If the branching condition is not met, program execution simply continues in the ordinary way with the instruction next following the stored offset. If the condition is met, the next instruction will be fetched from a memory location whose address depends on the offset.

There are many branch instructions, one corresponding to each of the possible patterns of the five status bits. All Simian branch instructions have the same basic operation code 1100, but they do not need to use the two five-bit operand fields for register addressing because they have no operands (they are said to be *zero-address instructions*). Because there are five condition code flags VCNLZ in the processor status register, the corresponding five distinct conditions can be prescribed separately. The instructions are therefore encoded by using one of the two available five-bit operand fields to specify the bit settings desired, the other to identify those bits whose settings are of no interest (the *don't care* settings), as shown in Fig. 4.9. Bits 4 and 5 are always reset for branching instructions; they have special uses discussed in due course.

Each distinct branch instruction is made up by specifying the desired settings

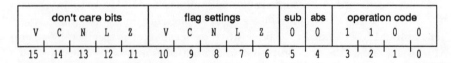

Fig. 4.9.   Branch instructions specify the flag bit settings in the processor status register.

of the processor status bits VCNLZ. For example, the instruction (written in binary form for clarity)

11010   11011   00   1100

means: *If the N bit is reset and the Z bit is set, increase the program counter content by the offset value in the two bytes immediately following this instruction; do so regardless of what values the V, C, and L bits may have.* The binary coding of this condition is actually quite simple: the three set bits in the first group of five (bits 15, 14, and 12) occupy positions corresponding to the status bits V, C, and L and thereby indicate that the values of these three bits are of no interest. In the second group, the N and Z bit positions are shown as 0 and 1, respectively, to indicate what condition is to be looked for.

Common branching instructions

Certain branch instructions are used very frequently, so it is a good idea to adopt a special set of names for these. Six basic forms of branch instruction, and a few others, merit such special treatment. The basic six, with their corresponding settings of *don't care* and status bits, are the following:

BR	Branch no matter what	11111	11111
BZ	Branch on zero	11110	11111
BN	Branch on negative	11011	11111
BL	Branch if lesser	11101	11111
BC	Branch if carry set	10111	11111
BV	Branch on overflow	01111	11111

These instructions, of course, only exist in register transfer notation, as notational simplifications; at the machine-code level, they are indistinguishable from their general equivalents. For example, BZ is represented in machine language as

Operation: branch	. . . . 1 1 0 0
Two-bit special field	. . . . 0 0 . . . .
Flag bit settings, VCNLZ	. . . . . 1 1 1 1 1 . . . . . .
Don't care bits, VCNLZ	1 1 1 1 0 . . . .
Putting it all together,	1 1 1 1 0 1 1 1 1 0 0 1 1 0 0
or, in hexadecimal form,	F 7 C C

In addition to the above six basic instructions, there are five others which examine the same flag bits, but take action if the condition is *not* met:

BNZ	Branch on nonzero	11110	11110
BNN	Branch on nonnegative	11011	11011
BNL	Branch if greater or equal	11101	11101
BNC	Branch if carry clear	10111	10111
BNV	Branch on no overflow	01111	01111

Because there are five condition code flags, each of which may take on three values (1, 0, or *don't care*), there are in principle $3^5 = 243$ different possible branch instructions. Fortunately, their number is a good deal smaller because some combinations of flag bit settings simply cannot occur. For example, the N and Z bits cannot both be set. Although it is technically quite proper to create a branch instruction that says *branch if N and Z set*, such an instruction really means *branch never*. It actually does nothing, aside from introducing a time delay.

Absolute value conversion

A brief example may serve to show how branch instructions are put to work in practical computing. Suppose that register R3 contains a 32-bit twos complement integer and it is desired to replace it by its absolute value. The process may be stated in symbolic form as follows:

```
CMP.L R3, R0        ; Compare R3 to 0: if
BNN 4               ; nonnegative skip 4.
NOT.L R3            ; Otherwise complement,
INC.L R3, 1         ; increment to negate.
HALT                ; Halt processor.
```

To determine whether the number in R3 is negative or not, it must be compared to zero. For convenience, R0 will be assumed to have been cleared to all zeros, providing a standard for comparison. After the comparison, the branch instruction BNN (branch if not negative) examines the N bit; if appropriate, it increases the program counter content four bytes, thereby skipping the next two instructions. In full machine-language detail, the instructions read

Operation: CMP.L	. . . . 1 1 0 0 1 0
source register R0	. . . . . 0 0 0 0 0 . . . . . .
destination register R3	0 0 0 1 1 . . . .
Putting it all together,	0 0 0 1 1 0 0 0 0 0 1 1 0 0 1 0
or, in hexadecimal form,	1 8 3 2
Branch	. . . . 0 0 1 1 0 0
if not negative	1 1 0 1 1 1 1 0 1 1 . . . . . .
Putting it together,	1 1 0 1 1 1 1 0 1 1 0 0 1 1 0 0
or	D E C C
followed by the offset	0 0 0 0 0 0 0 0 0 0 0 0 0 1 0 0
or in hexadecimal	0 0 0 4
Operation: NOT.L	. . . . 1 1 1 0 0 1
requires no argument	. . . . . 0 0 0 0 0 . . . . . .
register 3	0 0 0 1 1 . . . .
Putting it all together,	0 0 0 1 1 0 0 0 0 0 1 1 1 0 0 1
or, in hexadecimal form,	1 8 3 9
Operation: INC.L	. . . . 1 1 1 0 1 0
argument (less 1)	. . . . . 0 0 0 0 0 . . . . . .
direct to register 3	0 0 0 1 1 . . . .
Putting it all together,	0 0 0 1 1 0 0 0 0 0 1 1 1 0 1 0
or, in hexadecimal form,	1 8 3 A
Finally, to HALT,	1 1 1 1 1 1 1 1 1 1 1 1 1 1 1 1
or	F F F F

As it is stored in Simian memory, this program segment occupies a set of contiguous byte locations. Supposing for the moment that the first instruction were located at address 003A, the layout in storage would be as follows:

Object code	Address	Mnemonic instruction	Comments and explanatory remarks
18 32	; 003a	CMP.L R3, R0	; Compare R3 to 0: if
DE CC	; 003c	BNN 4	; nonnegative skip 4.
00 04	; 003e		
18 39	; 0040	NOT.L R3	; Otherwise complement,
18 3A	; 0042	INC.L R3, 1	; increment to negate.
FF FF	; 0044	HALT	; Halt processor.

Every instruction (and every data item) stored in memory is always addressed at its low-order byte address. The memory addresses indicated above are therefore the addresses of the *rightmost* bytes belonging to the corresponding memory contents.

The program as shown above is ready to be executed. To run it, it is stored in memory at the addresses shown. The address 003A is then placed in the program counter and the machine is permitted to proceed with its normal cycle of fetching and executing instructions.

The Simian simulator

Although there is no physical Simian computer consisting of logic circuits, Simian does exist as a computer simulator. A simulator consists of a set of programs that make a general-purpose computer act as if it were something different. The physical machine executing the simulator program is called the *host* computer, while the machine being simulated—in this case Simian—is known as the *target* computer.

Computer simulation

Simulators are widely used in the design of digital computers and in the development of computer programs for machines not yet in production. Simulation allows the hardware engineer to check designs and to explore the effects of changes, without the expense and delay that usually accompany hardware modifications. System programmers also use simulators, partly to save time, but more often because development of new hardware and new software are closely interrelated, with hardware structure dependent on software requirements and vice versa. Being able to write and run programs on a machine not yet built permits spotting possible design flaws at a time when the design is still open to modification.

A simulator, in general, is a program that makes one computer behave as if it were another. Like a complete physical computer, it must allow communication with the outside world in two ways: through its front panel control switches, and

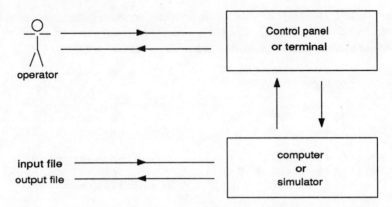

Fig. 4.10.   The computer operator controls the machine through its console switches, while programs and data are communicated via input and output file ports.

through its input and output devices that handle programs and data. In the Simian simulator, the computer control panel—the various readouts, indicators, and switches—is simulated by the terminal keyboard and screen. As represented by Fig. 4.10, its operation closely parallels the operation of a physical computer.

It is useful to distinguish between the computer *operator*, who controls and manages the computing machine through its control panel, and the computer *programmer*, who causes operations to be performed on data by placing instructions into the computer memory. While the programmer specifies *what* sequences or logical operations are to be performed, control by the operator typically involves telling the computer system *how* to go about it. The operator obviously must be able to make the machine run when necessary, and to halt when that is appropriate. Operator actions also include some more sophisticated possibilities: "copy the input file into memory beginning at location *xxxxxxxx*," "display the contents of all registers," and so on. These commands are different from executable *processor instructions*, in that they concern the manner in which the system itself works, not what computing work is actually done by the central processor.

Operator commands are frequently issued to computer systems by means of control panel switches. For example, there is often a *run/halt* switch. When running a simulator, analogous commands are entered at the terminal keyboard. These correspond directly to the front panel control switches of a physical computer and effect such actions as displaying register contents on the screen, starting and stopping the processor, examining memory contents.

An important aspect of simulators is that a well-designed simulator permits the operator easy access to almost any internal quantity. For example, the Simian simulator displays all register contents on screen at all times, and shows all the memory contents currently in use. In a physically "real" machine, register and memory contents would ordinarily be visible only with some difficulty.

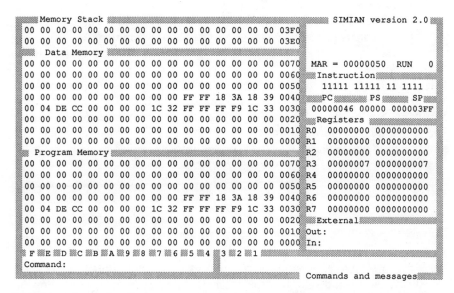

Fig. 4.11. The Simian display screen is organized as a set of individual windows, with the memory on the left, registers at the right, and communications along the bottom edge.

Manual operation of Simian

When Simian is first started, its memory and registers are cleared and their contents are displayed on the terminal screen. The screen is subdivided into ten separate windows, as shown in Fig. 4.11. Two small windows (along the bottom screen edge) act as an operator's console: the left-hand small window and keyboard accept user commands, the right-hand window replies with system messages. The remaining eight windows convey information about the internal state of Simian.

Although the amount of memory installed in the Simian simulator is much smaller than the 2^{32} bytes possible in its address space, there is insufficient room on the screen to show all the contents of its entire memory. Memory display is therefore organized in three display windows corresponding to the three major uses of memory: program storage, data manipulation, and stack (temporary storage) use. Simian chooses the window placement so that most operations take place in the middle of a display window. The program memory window, for example, is automatically altered when necessary to keep the program counter pointing into the memory area currently on display. The register display windows, which show the contents of all registers (in hexadecimal and decimal format), are also kept up to date as their contents change.

A simple program, such as the absolute value conversion routine discussed earlier, can be loaded into Simian memory from the keyboard. The simulator is first told to clear its memory by means of the operator command

clear

This command is typed in at the keyboard; it shows in the small command window at the lower left of the screen. On pressing RETURN at the end of the command, Simian clears the memory and shows the new values on the screen. The program is next loaded into memory one byte at a time, using the operator command *put* which places the given content into a specified memory byte:

put 32 3a
put 18
. . . .
put ff
put ff
put 3a pc

Here the first *put* command places the value 32 into memory location 0000003A, the second one puts the value 18 into the immediately following byte, and so on. (If no place is shown in the command, *put* puts bytes into sequential locations so that only the beginning memory location 0000003A need be specified.) The last *put*, after the program has been loaded, sets the program counter to the beginning of the program.

To run the program, the desired numbers are inserted in registers R3 and R0—again with the *put* command—and the *run* command is issued:

run 2

The program will run until two instructions have been fetched and executed, then stop. At the end of each step the screen is updated to show what changes have taken place to the memory or register contents. To see precisely how the program steps are executed, it is best to run only one step at a time. A blank line (i.e., a RETURN keystroke alone) is understood to mean *run 1*, so it is possible to "walk" through a program one instruction at a time, by simply pressing RETURN for every step.

When the task is finally finished, or the user grows tired, the simple command

quit

exits from Simian. A detailed description of these and other Simian commands may be found in Appendix 2. Brief *aides-mémoire* for most Simian commands can be obtained quickly in the message window, by requesting help with the *help* command.

Program loading

Like most computers, Simian permits byte-by-byte manual loading of registers and memory. However, this process is far too tedious and time-consuming for all but the shortest programs. Any larger program is normally placed in a machine-readable file as an image of the required memory contents, then read into the correct memory locations from the file. File reading and memory loading is accomplished by a program called a *loader*. A loader is permanently built into Simian so that loading large programs is quite easy.

To continue the previous example, the absolute value program can be entered into a file with some reasonable name, say *absval.ob*. The file content might be as follows:

```
.LOAD 3A
18 32
DE CC
00 04
18 39
18 3A
FF FF
.PROG 3A
.FINI
```

This file is made up exactly like any other text file, using the normal computer editing facilities. It is then loaded into memory by giving Simian the operator command

load absval.ob

The Simian loader reads through the file and loads the bytes in it into sequential locations, exactly as would be done in manual loading. When the loader stops, the memory contents are displayed in the appropriate screen windows.

The loader file *absval.ob* differs a little from the previous program text. It contains three items not present earlier:

```
.LOAD 3A
.PROG 3A
.FINI
```

These three curious statements are *loader directives*; they tell the loader how to go about its business. The first instructs the loader to begin loading at address 003A and to continue in successive byte locations. The second instructs the loader to put 003A in the program counter; the last informs the loader that it can stop work, it has reached the end of the loadable text and nothing further is desired from it. Loader directives do not place anything visible into the Simian memory. They control *how* loading is done, not *what* is loaded.

The Simian loader differs from most loader programs in one major respect: it accepts program files readable by the unaided human eye. Almost all other loaders strive to save file space by storing the machine text in compact binary form very hard to read. Simian, on the other hand, is designed to make almost all of its internal work visible; Simian object files are therefore written using only printable characters. As a further help, the Simian loader stops reading any input line when it encounters a semicolon (i.e., it ignores anything to the right of the semicolon). Program comments, proposed memory locations, indeed any other messages, can therefore be included in the object file along with the machine code; they will not hinder loading in any way, provided they are separated from the loadable machine text by a semicolon. Consequently, the following file will be loaded into exactly the same memory locations and will produce exactly the same effect as the hexadecimal byte sequence shown above:

```
.LOAD 3A
18 32 ; 003a    CMP.L R3, R0      ; Compare R3 to 0: if
DE CC ; 003c    BNN 4             ; nonnegative skip 4.
00 04
18 39 ; 0040    NOT.L R3          ; Otherwise complement,
18 3A ; 0042    INC.L R3, 1       ;   increment to negate.
FF FF ; 0044    HALT              ; Halt processor.
.PROG 3A
.FINI
```

The lines containing loader directives may not contain any comments. Comments, preceded by a semicolon, may be placed at the right of any line which contains material that will actually be loaded into memory.

There is no restriction on the number of .LOAD directives in an input file. An arrangement such as

```
.LOAD 5A
```

  . . . program code

```
.LOAD 1B2
```

  . . . data

```
.PROG 5A
.FINI
```

permits using widely separated parts of memory for program and data, for example. Resetting the loading locations in this way is not merely permissible, it should be regarded as sound practice. At the other extreme, loader directives may be omitted; the Simian loader then assumes that

```
.LOAD 20
```


  . . . program code

```
.PROG 20
.FINI
```

was meant and acts accordingly.

Just as the .LOAD directive specifies locations without causing Simian to run, so the .PROG directive loads the program counter but does not start Simian running. Consequently, the .PROG directive may be placed anywhere in the input file, although it is usually placed immediately before the end of file marker .FINI. The .FINI directive causes the loader to stop reading, so it should be physically the last line of the file.

Simian also has a built-in dumping program, which can be invoked with the *dump* command. It produces a file containing the current memory contents and the current program counter reading. The file format is such that a subsequent *load* command can reload the memory content. This facility is useful when working on moderately large programs, for it allows various states of work to be recorded and subsequently recovered.

Once Simian has started running, there is no way of making it pause, and no way of stopping it without destroying memory contents. To avoid inconvenience, the *run* command makes Simian run, but only for a limited number of program steps. An alternative way of controlling program execution is the technique known as *breakpointing*. Simian possesses a hardware register called the *breakpoint register* whose content can be set by the *break* command. When the breakpoint mechanism is enabled, the program counter content is compared to the breakpoint register at every instruction fetch. The processor is halted when the program counter and breakpoint register contents match. Breakpointing is normally turned off, but can be enabled by the *break* command.

Addressing modes and techniques

The Simian instructions discussed so far can manipulate register contents but they make little use of data stored in memory. Most computers permit operands to be stored either in memory or in registers, and Simian is no exception to this rule. Its several ways to access data are described in this section.

Register indirect addressing

Simian instructions may use register contents as operands; alternatively, operands may be taken from memory. In the latter case, the data locations are usually specified by storing their memory addresses (*not* their arithmetic values) in registers and informing the processor where these addresses may be found.

Suppose that an instruction specifies a register content as the operand, as for example

    LD.L R3, R1

This instruction says, in effect, "replace the content of register R3 by the content of R1." The operands, the long words contained in R1 and R3, are said to be *register direct* addressed. (Alternatively, they are sometimes said to be accessed in a *register direct addressing mode*.) It may happen, however, that a number is not located in a register, but in some memory location. If the address of that memory location is placed in R1, then the instruction

    LD.S R3, [R1]

will cause the number to be fetched from memory and copied to R3. To be precise: the content of R1 is considered to be not the operand itself, but the *address of the memory location where the operand is located*. This instruction is read as "load R3 with the short word located at the memory address in R1." All four bytes in R1 are taken to constitute a memory address; the short word located at that address is fetched and copied into R3. A two-byte operand is required by the LD.S instruction, so that two bytes are fetched and operated on; but all four bytes in R1 are used as the operand address, since *all addresses in Simian are four bytes long.* This form of operand addressing is called the *register indirect* addressing mode.

The principle of register indirect addressing should be familiar from many everyday indirect inquiries for information. For example, to call Joe Frenette in Milwaukee, telephone number unknown, one dials Directory Assistance at 715–555–1212. It would be surprising to find Joe at that number; one calls it not in the expectation of finding Joe, but of finding out Joe's telephone number. Joe Frenette is reached by calling *the number that one obtains by calling 715–555–1212*; Joe is not reached directly by calling 715–555–1212. In exactly the same way, one looks into R1 for the address of the operand, not for the operand itself.

Simian instructions which employ indirect addressing are generally similar to instructions with direct addressing. However, every indirectly addressed operand must be identified as such. In each indirectly addressed operand reference, the next-to-highest bit of the operand group (bit 9 for source operands, bit 14 for destination operands) is set, to show that indirect addressing is intended. For example,

```
SUB.S R5, [R3]
```

says, translated into somewhat tortuous English, "subtract, from the two-byte integer in the least significant half of R5, the integer whose memory address is in R3." Its machine encoding runs as follows:

Operation: SUB	. . . . 0 0 0 1
Two-byte instruction, S	. . . . 0 1 . . . .
Source register: R3,	. . . . 0 1 1 . . . . . .
indirectly addressed	. . . . . . 1 . . . .
through the register	. . . . . . 0 . . . .
Destination register: R5	. . 1 0 1 . . . .
directly addressed	. 0 . . . .
to the register	0 . . . .
Putting it all together,	0 0 1 0 1 0 1 0 1 1 0 1 0 0 0 1
or, in hexadecimal form,	2　　A　　D　　1

Each five-bit operand group in the instruction has its own indirect addressing bit, which may be set or reset independently of the other operand. Indirect addressing may thus be specified for one of the two operands, or both, or neither; two-operand instructions may mix addressing modes quite freely. It is said that *addressing modes are associated with operands,* not with instructions. For example, the instructions

```
LD.B R5, R2
LD.B [R5], [R2]
LD.B [R5], R2
LD.B R5, [R2]
```

are all perfectly valid though different. In fact, the references may even be to the same register;

        LD.L R6, [R6]

is valid. It says "replace the content of R6 by the content of the memory location whose address is now contained in R6." And finally,

        LD.S [R2], [R2]

is valid as well, but unlikely to be useful, for it does nothing at all.

Summation of series

Indirect addressing permits building programs otherwise difficult or even impossible to create. In the following example indirect addressing is essential to success.

Suppose it is desired to find the sum of a string of numbers (small integers, occupying one byte each) stored in Simian memory. For the sake of concreteness, let there be 12 numbers altogether, beginning at location 0120. The process itself is simple enough. The sum is accumulated in register R0. This register is cleared initially. Each of the 12 numbers is added to it in turn, by placing the address of each number in register R2 and adding:

        ADD.B R0, [R2]   ; Add item to sum.

This instruction causes the content of R0 to be augmented by the amount contained *in the memory location whose address is in* R2. Adding 12 numbers is accomplished by executing this instruction 12 times, with register R2 pointing to a different one of the 12 each time.

Given that the 12 operands reside in memory in their proper sequence, adding them only requires that R2 be incremented by 1 each time (thereby making it point to the next byte in the sequence). The whole program to do the adding, including data, thus reads as follows:

```
.LOAD 30
;   Sum in R0, number of items in R1,
;                  first address in R2.
;
02 80 ; 0030       ADD.B R0, [R2] ; Add item to sum.
0C 1A ; 0032       INC.S R1, -1   ; Decrement number,
F7 CC ; 0034       BZ 6           ;   quit if done.
00 06
10 3A ; 0038       INC.L R2, 1    ; Point to next one
FF CC ; 003a       BR -E          ;   and restart.
FF F2
FF FF ; 003e       HALT
.LOAD 120
04 03 02 01
08 07 06 05
0C 0B 0A 09
.PROG 30
.FINI
```

To run the program, it is loaded into Simian memory and the three working registers are initialized: 0 in R0 (the sum accumulator), 0C (hexadecimal 12, the number of items) in R1, and 0120 in R2. The sample data given with the program obviously represent the first 12 integers, so the correct answer, when Simian stops running, should be 78 (decimal) in R0.

It is worth noting that the program as given counts *down* from the number of items to zero. In other words, R1 does not count the number of terms that have been added; it counts the number still to come. Down-counting is common in programs because it is a little more economic than up-counting. Counting up and determining whether all 12 ($0C_{16}$) terms have been added requires storing the number 0C in a register, say in R3, and comparing it with the count in R1 at each step:

```
INC.S R1, 1            ; Increment number,
CMP.S R1, R4           ; compare with 12,
BZ 6                   ;   quit if all done
```

The CMP.S operation serves to set the Z flag if the required total of 12 has been reached. The flag is set in down-counting by

```
INC.S R1, -1           ; Decrement number,
BZ 6                   ;   quit if all done.
```

but this way one less instruction is required. To state the matter another way: down-counting is economical because Simian has a built-in flag (the Z bit) to show that 0 has been reached, but it does not have a status flag to signal that the value 12 has been reached. Arranging the computation to detect that 12 has been reached therefore takes a CMP.S instruction, while detecting a zero takes no instructions at all.

Although none are needed in the summation program, Simian programs may contains indirect addressing in single-operand as well as two-operand instructions. The operand encoding and instruction format follow the principles already stated, with the *indirect* bit set in the five-bit destination operand group that represents the single operand.

Immediate addressing modes

In Simian instructions, the field allocated for specifying operands is five bits wide. The low-order three bits in the operand field serve to identify a general register, as shown in Fig. 4.8, while the next higher numbered bit distinguishes between direct and indirect addressing. The remaining high-order bit in each operand field is the *immediate* bit, which indicates whether normal addressing through the general registers is intended or whether it is desired to use a different addressing mode not involving registers at all.

In the *immediate* addressing mode, the general registers are ignored; instead, the operand is sought at the address currently in the program counter. Keeping in mind that the program counter always points to the byte immediately following the current instruction, this means the operand is located in memory immediately following the instruction itself. Immediate addressing is commonly available in modern computers because it permits individual data bytes or data words to be embedded in the program code, adjoining the instructions themselves. Having permanently fixed data incorporated in the program itself makes both program coding and subsequent program reading easy. Avoidance of program errors is one desirable result. In some machines (not in Simian), operation speed may increase as well.

To illustrate how immediate addressing works, suppose it is desired to add the 16-bit decimal number 129 to the memory location pointed to by register 2. The instruction and data as encoded in machine representation will then have the following form:

```
Operation: ADD                    . . . . . . . . . . . . 0 0 0 0
Two-byte instruction, S           . . . . . . . . . . . 0 1 . . . .
Source: immediately addressed     . . . . . . 0 0 0 . . . . . .
directly addressed,               . . . . . . 0 . . . . . . . . .
not through a register            . . . . . 1 . . . . . . . . . .
Destination register: R2          . . 0 1 0 . . . . . . . . . . .
indirectly addressed              . 1 . . . . . . . . . . . . . .
in a register mode                0 . . . . . . . . . . . . . . .
```

Putting it all together,   0 1 0 1 0 1 0 0 0 0 0 1 0 0 0 0
or, in hexadecimal form,   5   4   1   0

In the next two bytes, 129 =   0 0 0 0 0 0 0 0 1 0 0 0 0 0 0 1
or, in hexadecimal,   0   0   8   1

Since no register is used, no general register number is now required in the source field of the instruction. The three bits ordinarily used for general register numbers are therefore reset to zeros. The instruction itself occupies two bytes, as do all Simian instructions; but the address of the operand is obtained from the program counter instead of a general register. The sequence of operations in executing the above is thus

1. Fetch the instruction.
2. Increment the program counter 2 bytes.
3. Decode the instruction. Set
      source operand address := program counter content,
      destination operand address := address in register 2.
4. Fetch data pointed to by program counter.
5. Increment program counter 2 (since the data word is 2 bytes long).
6. Add and store the result in the memory location pointed to by register 2.

The program counter is incremented twice in this process. The first incrementation takes it to the first address beyond the present instruction; the incrementation is by 2, because all Simian instructions occupy two bytes. The second incrementation is by 2 also, but this time because the operand, which is known to be immediately adjacent to the instruction, is two bytes long. Had the instruction been ADD.B, on the other hand, this second incrementation would only have added 1, the operand length.

In the register transfer notation usually employed to describe Simian operations, the symbol # denotes immediate addressing. For example,

```
ADD.S [R2], #81
```

is read "add to the number addressed by register 2 the short number 81_{16}," or perhaps "add short to R2 indirect the number 81_{16}." Using this notation, the absolute value calculation program can be made more sophisticated by including actual addresses:

```
.LOAD 2E
1C 33 ; 002e    LD.L R3, #138         ; Put address in R3
00 00 01 38
5C 33 ; 0034    LD.L [R3], #FFFFFFF9  ; Load into memory.
FF FF FF F9
5C 32 ; 003a    CMP.L [R3], #0        ; Compare to 0 if
00 00 00 00
DE CC ; 0040    BNN 4                 ; nonneg. skip 4.
00 04
58 39 ; 0044    NOT.L [R3]            ; Complement, then
58 3A ; 0046    INC.L [R3], 1         ;  increment.
FF FF ; 0048    HALT                  ;  Halt processor.
.PROG 2E
.FINI
```

The assumption that R0 would be cleared and used for comparison is no longer needed—the comparison is done directly between R3 and a four-byte zero stored as an immediate operand just after the CMP.L instruction itself. Similarly, the need for manual loading of R3 has been eliminated (perhaps a bit more artificially) by inserting the number to be negated FFFFFFF9 as an immediate operand. Note the distinction between the first two LD.L commands: the first says that the address 00000138 is to be placed into register R3, the second specifies the data value to be loaded into memory at that place.

The immediate addressing mode always communicates a numeric or character *value* and can therefore never be used for data to be modified, only for data to be read from memory. Thus it is proper to specify an immediate operand as the *source* operand in, say, an ADD.S operation; but an immediate-addressed operand cannot appear as the *destination,* because the numeric value must not be overwritten.

Absolute addressing

Immediate addressing may also be indirect. In that case, it is called *absolute* addressing, because the bytes immediately following the instruction contain not the operand value, but rather the address where the operand is stored. Suppose, for example, that the number FFFFC100 is located in memory immediately following an ADD.L instruction. If the immediate operand is directly addressed, as in

```
ADD.L R3, #FFFFC100
```

the instruction means that the numeric *value* FFFFC100$_{16}$ is to be added to the destination content. On the other hand, indirect addressing would imply that the number *stored at the address* FFFFC100 is to be added. The term *absolute* refers to the fact that an absolute address, in this case FFFFC100$_{16}$, is given for the source operand. In the register transfer notation usual for describing Simian operations, the symbol / denotes absolute addressing. Thus

ADD.L R3, /FFFFC100

is read "add to the number in register 3 the long integer at address FFFFC100" or "add long to R3 the number at FFFFC100."

The instruction is always followed by an *address*, never by an operand value, when absolute addressing is used. The second incrementation of the program counter therefore always increases the counter reading by 4 bytes; the increment must match the length of a Simian memory address, not the length of the oper-and. On the other hand, the first incrementation must match the instruction length, so it increases the program counter content by 2 regardless of addressing mode.

It is perfectly proper for both operands to be immediately addressed in some two-operand instructions. If such is the case, then the instruction will be fol-lowed by the immediate operand which acts as the *destination* and that will in turn be followed by the *source* operand. Such an instruction, including its oper-ands, may be up to ten bytes long: two bytes to house the instruction proper, followed by two operands of up to four bytes each.

An interesting point should be noted about the absolute value program: although it is shown as loadable at address 2A, it could just as well be loaded at any other address and executed with equal success, provided of course the .PROG directive is also altered to have execution begin at the new address. (Skeptics should feel free to try it!) This property of *position independence* in memory is a valuable one for programs to have, for it implies that several pro-gram sections, independently developed, can easily be loaded into memory and made to work together, without any worry about conflicting addresses. Position independence here comes about for two reasons. One is the use of immediate operands, which are relocated along with the program instructions. A second way position independence comes about in this program is inherent in the way *branch* instructions work. Branchings only specify *offsets* to addresses, not abso-lute addresses themselves. Consequently, relocation of the entire program means relocation of both the branch instructions and their target addresses by equal amounts, so they work just as well when loaded at address 00000170 as at address 0000002A.

Programs that work equally well no matter where in memory they are loaded are said to be written in *position independent code*. Because position indepen-dence is a desirable quality of machine code, almost all computers have instruc-tion sets organized to make the creation and execution of position independent code reasonably easy.

Copying character strings

A modest example of how computations are carried out in Simian is furnished by the following short but realistic program. Its purpose is to copy the string of 16 characters in memory locations 0FA–109 (hexadecimal!) to locations 0DF–0D0, reversing their order in the copying process.

The copying can be accomplished by using the LD.B instruction to copy a single character from its source location to its destination; the 16 characters are copied by repeating this action 16 times. To ensure that there are exactly 16 repetitions, a *counter* is used, a register which contains at all times the number of characters remaining to be copied. Every time a character is copied, this character counter must be decremented, to take account of the character just moved. In other words, the fundamental scheme is

> set character counter to 16;
> **while** count > 0 **do**
> **begin**   copy a character from old to new location;
>   decrement the character counter **end**.

Continuing while the count runs down to zero implies, of course, that the counter must be checked after copying each character, to see whether any more remain to be moved. It should be noted that *down-counting* is used in this example, just as in the number-summing program discussed earlier. Up-counting from 0 to 16 could be used, but it would be necessary to include an explicit CMP.B instruction to check whether the full count had been reached. Down-counting saves an instruction, so both execution time and program space are reduced.

Every character is copied in its turn from its *source* location to another, its *destination*.The source address (the memory location where the character is taken from) and the destination address (where to) are most conveniently stored in two general registers. If R0 is used as the counter, R1 as the source address register, and R2 as the destination address register then the process can be stated as follows:

```
.LOAD 42
52 43 ; 0042      LD.B [R2], [R1]      ; Copy one character.
04 0A ; 0044      INC.B R0, -1         ; Decrement counter,
F7 CC ; 0046      BZ 8                 ; branch if 16 done.
00 08
08 3A ; 004a      INC.L R1, 1          ; INC source pointer
14 3A ; 004c      INC.L R2, -1         ;    and destination.
FF CC ; 004e      BR -10               ; Back for next one!
FF F0
FF FF ; 0052      HALT                 ; Halt processor.
.LOAD FA
48 47 46 45 44 43 42 41                ; First 16 letters
50 4F 4E 4D 4C 4B 4A 49                ;    of the alphabet.
.PROG 42
.FINI
```

This scheme will only work if the three registers are set up to contain the correct values in the first place. Their values can be inserted by hand; however, it is more convenient do have the program do so, particularly if repeated execution is envisaged (as it necessarily is during program testing). Hence, it is necessary to precede the above with a process of initialization:

```
.LOAD 33
04 03 ; 0033        LD.B R0, #10       ; Count = 16 in R0,
10
0C 33 ; 0036        LD.L R1, #FA       ; Source addr = 0FA
00 00 00 FA
14 33 ; 003c        LD.L R2, #DF       ; Destin addr = 0DF.
00 00 00 DF
52 43 ; 0042        LD.B [R2], [R1]    ; Copy one character
04 0A ; 0044        INC.B R0, -1       ; Decrement counter,
F7 CC ; 0046        BZ 8               ; branch if 16 done.
00 08
08 3A ; 004a        INC.L R1, 1        ; INC source pointer
14 3A ; 004c        INC.L R2, -1       ;   and destination.
FF CC ; 004e        BR -10             ; Back for next one!
FF F0
FF FF ; 0052        HALT               ; Halt processor.
.LOAD FA
48 47 46 45 44 43 42 41                ; First 16 letters
50 4F 4E 4D 4C 4B 4A 49                ;   of the alphabet
.PROG 33
.FINI
```

An alternative way of organizing the computation might be to do all incrementations and decrementations first, then to check whether to continue:

```
LD.B [R2], [R1]    ; Copy one character
INC.L R1, 1        ; INC source pointer
INC.L R2, -1       ;   and destination.
INC.B R0, -1       ; Decrement counter,
BNZ -C             ; Back if not 16 yet!
HALT               ; Halt processor.
```

The resulting program takes just a little longer to execute, because it performs the two pointer incrementations even the seventeenth time, when the pointers will no longer be used. However, there is only one branch instruction so a little memory is saved. It illustrates in a very small way a frequent problem of program design: is it better to save space or to gain speed? The answer invariably depends on the application of the program. If memory is in short supply, which is sometimes the case in large programs, the choice that economizes on memory is the correct one. In some circumstances, for example in industrial control systems, execution time may be critical so the faster program version may be preferred. Trading memory for execution time in this manner is a common way to optimize computing systems for specific purposes.

Jump instructions

The branching instructions of Simian give the programmer very considerable flexibility. However, they do not suffice to give full control over the sequence of instruction execution. There are two shortcomings:

1. Branch instructions are followed by 16-bit offsets, so branching over long distances within the 32-bit address space of Simian is not practicable.
2. Branch instructions can never branch to specified absolute addresses, only to addresses given as offsets relative to the program counter.

The comparatively short range of branch instructions is not a major obstruction to writing small programs because most branches in practical computer programs cover very short spans of addresses anyway. In fact, several widely used computers have branching instructions with 8-bit offsets, which permit branching over a span of only 127 bytes either way! Difficulties may arise, however, when it is necessary to link together large program segments.

To alleviate problems that may arise in branching, Simian provides a group of *jump* instructions, that resemble branch instructions but communicate absolute addresses. A jump instruction is always followed by four data bytes that contain a 32-bit address stored as an unsigned integer. When a jump instruction is executed, the program counter content is replaced by that address. The next machine instruction is then fetched from the location specified in the jump instruction. The difference between a branch and a jump is that a branch instruction *adds* an offset to the program counter, a jump instruction *replaces* the program counter content. The branch therefore guides program execution to continue at an address determined *relatively* to the program counter, the jump forces execution to continue at a specified *absolute* address.

Jump instructions are similar to branch instructions, in fact they even share the operation code 1100 with the branches. Like branches, jump instructions are subject to conditional execution: jumps only occur if the prescribed conditions apply. The machine representation of jump and branch instructions is similar, the difference being that bit 4 in the instruction word (see Fig. 4.9) is reset for a branch, set for a jump. To return to an earlier example, the machine instruction

$$11110 \quad 11111 \quad 00 \quad 1100$$

is a branch instruction. It means: If the Z bit is set, then *add to the present program counter content the offset value in the two bytes immediately following this instruction*, regardless of what values the V, C, N and L bits may have. Correspondingly,

$$11110 \quad 11111 \quad 01 \quad 1100$$

is a jump instruction. It says: If the Z bit is set, then *replace the present program counter content by the address in the four bytes immediately following this instruction*, regardless of what values the V, C, N, and L bits may have.

Every jump instruction is followed by the address to which the jump is to be made. Because Simian addresses are always four bytes long, the amount by which the program counter is incremented during execution of a jump instruction differs from the corresponding branch instruction: two bytes for branches, four for jumps. For a jump instruction, the execution sequence is therefore as follows:

1. Fetch the instruction.
2. Increment the program counter 2 bytes.
3. Examine the processor status flag bits to see whether the branching condition is met.
4. If the branching condition is met, fetch the four byte spointed to by the program counter, and place them in the program counter.
5. If the branching condition is not met, increment the program counter by 4.

Some jump instructions occur far more frequently than others, just as some branch instructions are more common than the rest. The unconditional jump and the most common conditional jumps are therefore assigned special mnemonic codes:

> JM   Jump no matter what
> JZ   Jump if zero
> JN   Jump if negative
> JL   Jump if lesser
> JC   Jump if carry set
> JV   Jump if overflow

The corresponding negated-condition codes are handled in much the same way as their branching counterparts, by including the letter N to signify negation:

> JNZ   Jump if nonzero
> JNN   Jump if nonnegative
> JNL   Jump if greater or equal
> JNC   Jump if carry clear
> JNV   Jump if no overflow

As with the branch instructions, the number of theoretically possible conditions is $3^5 = 243$, but not all possible combinations of flag bits in the processor status register actually make sense. The number of reasonable jump conditions is substantially lower and most programmers in fact get along very well using only the half-dozen or so most common ones.

Assembler language translation

Register transfer notations are commonly used to describe computing processes, for although it is perfectly possible to state all the machine actions in terms of binary instructions, people find register transfer notation much more agreeable and make fewer mistakes when using it. When register transfer notations are extended to cover not only data movement between registers but decisions and control as well, they result in *assembler languages*. These are programming languages for specifying data movement and manipulation explicitly in terms of registers and memory locations, just exactly like the binary machine instructions; but they do so in a symbolic rather than machine-code form.

Automatic translation

Numerous examples have already been given of how binary instructions (as they are actually understood and executed by Simian) can be represented in a symbolic form far preferable for human purposes. To suit the machine, the symbols must of course be translated into binary text. Every symbolic instruction corresponds to one, and only one, binary instruction, so that translation is always unambiguous and follows a precisely defined set of rules. Indeed the examples shown so far have done just that, for example in establishing that INC.L R3, 1 corresponds to binary 0001100000111010.

Because the translation rules for transforming symbolic into binary instructions are quite precise, it is possible to write computer programs to perform the translation. Consequently, people only rarely translate any substantial amounts of symbolic code into binary form; almost all the translation is done in real situations by a translation program called an *assembler*. The process of translation is generally termed *program assembly*, or *assembling the program*, while the binary output issuing from the assembler is called the *machine language program* or *object code*.

The Simian simulator is accompanied by an assembler called Simile. Simile accepts as input a file containing assembler language text, in the format already described, and issues the corresponding object program in a format acceptable to the Simian loader. Simile is an entirely autonomous entity, it is not connected to Simian in any way. It understands assembler language and produces machine instructions suitable for Simian, but it neither knows nor cares whether a Simian simulator is available at the same computing installation.

Although writing programs in assembler language is much easier and much less error-prone than writing binary code by hand, it would be unrealistic to expect programmers never to make mistakes; *errare humanum est*. Common errors include mistypings and misspellings, which may be understood as requests for nonexistent operations; for example, keying in BNX instead of BNZ. To allow the programmer to find such errors, the assembly process routinely produces two forms of output: a neatly formatted printout or screen display containing a listing of the assembler-language text with errors flagged, and a machine readable file containing object code. Of course, no object code at all may be produced if so severe errors are encountered as to prevent translation. It is thus usual for the programmer alternately to assemble and correct program errors, as indicated in Fig. 4.12, until no more errors are detected. Only after error-free translation has been achieved is execution attempted.

Simile differs from most conventional assemblers in having only one output stream. Because the Simian loader permits comments to accompany the object program (an unusual arrangement for loaders), Simile combines the two con-

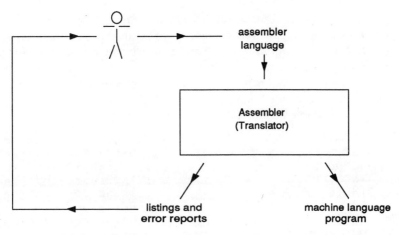

Fig. 4.12. Assemblers often produce two forms of output: object code for machines, error reports and listings for the programmer.

ventional output streams into one. It begins each line with machine instructions, then inserts as comments a reformatted listing of the original program and any messages from the assembler itself. The program listings already shown, as well as those to follow, are in the form produced by Simile.

Symbolic address references

People are unable to interpret machine code without first deciphering it into a more nearly verbal form, so most machine-level programming is done in assembler languages. For example, the following program segment, which copies characters as already discussed in detail, is more or less readable and understandable:

```
LD.B [R2], [R1]        ; Copy one character.
INC.B R0, -1           ; Decrement counter,
BZ 8                   ; branch if 16 done.
INC.L R1, 1            ; INC source pointer
INC.L R2, -1           ;    and destination.
BR -10                 ; Back for next one!
HALT                   ; Halt processor.
```

Comprehension of such instruction sequences is particularly easy when they are accompanied by verbal commentary. But the corresponding binary or hexadecimal code is so hard to understand that it is hardly worth writing down.

Unfortunately, even the symbolic form given here is not very good. Although it is much more readable than binary text, it still requires the programmer to determine the exact number of bytes occupied by the instructions and data, so as to be able to specify the offsets of all branching instructions correctly. This process, which probably yields more machine-language programming errors than any other, can be avoided by introducing *symbolic address references*. The principle is simple: instead of forcing the programmer to find out how large a span of bytes a branching instruction requires, a symbolic label is employed to identify the memory locations *to* which and *from* which the branch instruction transfers control. The assembler, not the programmer, is then given the task of counting bytes and subtracting so as to find the right number of bytes. This is just exactly the kind of job computers excel at! Using symbolic labelling, the program segment above might read

```
START:  LD.B [R2], [R1]          ; Copy one character.
        INC.B R0, -1             ; Decrement counter,
        BZ DONE                  ; branch if 16 done.
        INC.L R1, 1              ; INC source pointer
        INC.L R2, -1             ;   and destination.
        BR START                ; Back for next one!
DONE:   HALT                    ; Halt processor.
```

Here START and DONE are symbolic references to addresses. The branching instructions say, in effect, "branch whatever number of bytes is necessary to reach the memory location labeled DONE." It must be emphasized that these two program segments are not merely equivalent when assembled; they are *identical*. (Try it!)

The use of symbolic labels simplifies the task of program preparation enormously. Of course, it also creates a significant additional task for the assembler and makes the assembler itself more complicated. This additional complexity arises from the need to correlate symbolic references with instruction and data lengths. Consider again the program segment for copying a character string. The symbolic program and its machine-language version as stored in memory will have the following form:

Object code	Address	Mnemonic instruction	Comments and explanatory remarks
04 03 10	; 0033	LD.B R0, #10	; Count = 16 in R0,
0C 33 00 00 00 FA	; 0036	LD.L R1, #FA	; Source addr = 0FA
14 33 00 00 00 DF	; 003c	LD.L R2, #DF	; Destin addr = 0DF.
52 43	; 0042 START:	LD.B [R2], [R1];	Copy one character
04 0A	; 0044	INC.B R0, -1	; Decrement counter,
F7 CC 00 08	; 0046	BZ DONE	; branch if 16 done.
08 3A	; 004a	INC.L R1, 1	; INC source pointer
14 3A	; 004c	INC.L R2, -1	; and destination.
FF CC FF F0	; 004e	BR START	; Back for next one!
FF FF	; 0052 DONE:	HALT	; Halt processor.

The right-hand part of this listing gives the original assembler language input text, the hexadecimally expressed object code (machine language) appears on the

```
Symbol table

Total labels = 2

START      0042
DONE       0052
```

Fig. 4.13.   The symbol table associates symbolic memory references with locations within the program.

left. Addresses, where they appear, give the locations of the rightmost bytes in each line.

As translation proceeds, actual values must be substituted for symbolic location references. For example, the instruction BR START can only be translated if, at the time translation is attempted, it is known that START refers to byte 0042. In other words, the procedure for translating BR START requires two steps,

1. Translate BR START into its numeric equivalent BR -10,
2. Translate BR -10 into the equivalent binary instruction.

The second step is straightforward enough; it follows the techniques already discussed in detail. The first step is possible, indeed simple, if the symbolic references and their byte number locations within the program, are available in a *symbol table*, illustrated in Fig. 4.13. In general, a symbol table will contain at least the labels and the memory locations they represent. It may also contain other information, e.g., the number of times a label is referred to in the source program, and from what locations.

Locations given in the symbol table refer only to byte counts from the beginning of the program itself, not to any actual memory addresses. In fact, actual memory addresses are never needed to compute the offsets in branch instructions, for branch instructions always specify offsets *relative* to the program counter, never to actual memory addresses.

Two-pass assembly

The process of translating assembler language text into machine instructions normally proceeds on a line-by-line basis. As the assembler reads each line it must perform an analysis to determine

1. Whether the instruction is followed by data, and if so, how many bytes the data occupy.
2. Whether the instruction includes a symbolic location, and if so, what is the actual address or offset.

To determine the offsets, every assembler must compile a symbol table. As it reads the source text, the assembler maintains a *current location counter* which

counts locations within the program. Whenever a branch instruction is encountered, its offset is determined by taking the difference between the location of
the symbolic reference as given in the symbol table and the current location
counter, then adjusting for the length of the instruction itself. In the example
shown above, the current location counter contains 0051 when the instruction
BR START is analyzed, so that the correct offset is 0042 (the value of START
shown in the symbol table) less 0052, or -10_{16}. Similarly, the correct numeric
offset for BZ NEXT is 0055 less the instruction length of 4 bytes, less the location
counter reading 0046 when the instruction is analyzed: $00525 - 4 - 00469 =$
8.

When offsets are negative, i.e., when branching backward in a program, translation by lookup in the symbol table causes no difficulty. Such is the case for the
instruction BR START; when it is analyzed, the value of START already exists
in the symbol table, so that the task of translation is straightforward. Forward
references, however, cannot be translated on a first reading of the program text.
In the example given immediately above, the instruction BZ DONE is impossible to translate initially, because the instruction itself precedes the symbolic
location DONE, so the value of DONE is not yet listed in the symbol table at
the time it is needed. This problem is fundamental, and can be fully resolved
only by reading and analyzing the assembler language code *twice*: once to set up
a complete symbol table and to effect partial translation, then once more to complete the translation and insert values in place of symbolic references. Assemblers which take this course—and that includes almost all assemblers in practical use—are known as *two-pass assemblers*.

The first pass of a two-pass assembler need not do much beyond generating
the symbol table. This task is not altogether trivial, because it involves keeping
count of the number of bytes occupied by program code from the beginning of
the program to the place where the label actually occurs; that in turn requires at
least partial analysis of the assembler-language text. Simian instructions can be
followed by immediate operands, amounting to as little as one byte, and possibly
involving as many as eight bytes. The only way to determine the amount of
space taken by each is to analyze the instruction in some detail. There is little
point in doing the same work twice, so many two-pass assemblers do a major
part of the translation in the first pass, then fill in the missing portions in the
second.

Simile, like most two-pass assemblers, effects a partial translation on the first
pass. Everything that can be translated is translated immediately, but forward
references are left unresolved. The incompletely translated text is left in a temporary file called *simile.tmp*. It will be instructive to compare this temporary file
with the final result; both are written in an easily readable character form.

It should be mentioned that there also exist *single-pass* and *three-pass* assemblers. Practically all are really two-pass assemblers. The so-called single-pass
assemblers actually read the program text twice, but do so only over a restricted
range of program lines; they are therefore limited to short branching offsets or

to small programs; but they often run very fast. Most three-pass assemblers are fancier versions of two-pass assemblers, with the third pass serving to correlate all available information regarding errors and to prepare a full listing of the assembler language text, with an extensive identification of errors and detailed analysis of their probable sources.

Assembler syntax

Programming in assembler language is much more agreeable than using binary machine instructions. But although a given computer has only a single set of machine instructions, several assembler languages could be devised to correspond to the same binary machine codes. Each could clothe the same binary content in different instruction names and arrangement of operands. The range of operations that can be described, usually referred to as the *semantics* of a language, is determined by the underlying machine structure and its binary instruction codes. On the other hand, the form of expression, the *syntax* of the assembler language, is open to choice. This distinction between *syntax* and *semantics*—form and meaning—is perhaps best illustrated by Lewis Carroll's well-known lines

> 'Twas brillig, and the slithy toves
>   Did gyre and gimble in the wabe;
> All mimsy were the borogoves
>   And the mome raths outgrabe.

This little verse obviously satisfies all the formal rules of English: the clauses are clearly identifiable, the parts of speech are in their right places, the meter and rhyme correct for verse. It is syntactically correct, even though it does not mean anything.

The rules of syntax for assembler languages are much simpler than for English. They are principally concerned with how a line of code containing an instruction should be entered at the keyboard or in a machine-readable file. The syntax rules of an assembler language define the formal appearance of program statements, but they need to show no more regard for their meaning in the underlying machine language than shown by Carroll for English—happily so, for although there are many widely different machine instruction sets, syntax rules common to all can (and have) been embodied in published standards.

Following the IEEE Computer Society standard for assembler languages, two distinct types of statement are allowed in programming Simian: *instructions* and *directives*. Instructions are translated into actual machine code, while directives only tell the assembler how to go about translating; they do not themselves give rise to any machine instructions.

Each assembler-language instruction must be placed on a separate line. Each instruction may contain the following fields:

label, followed by a colon (the : character);
instruction name;
operand(s)—destination first, then source;
comment, preceded by a semicolon (the ; character).

All four fields are optional, in the sense that no line must necessarily contain any one of the four. Even a blank line is syntactically correct. The sequence of fields, on the other hand, is quite inflexible; whichever fields do exist must be placed in the order shown. Despite the requirement of fixed order, any field may begin at any place in the line. The presence (or absence) of a colon determines whether the first character string in the line is a label or an instruction mnemonic. Blank characters separate the instruction from any operands; if there are several operands, they are in turn separated by commas. The translatable part of a line is considered to be terminated by a semicolon or by the end of the line, whichever comes first.

Directives must be placed one to a line also, but the syntax rules are much simpler. Every line containing a directive begins with the period (the.character) at the left edge. The directive itself must follow immediately after the period, there may not be any intervening space. Nothing other than the directive itself may appear in any line that contains a directive.

In practically all assembler languages, symbolic references are strings of characters which must begin with a capital letter and may contain a mixture of numbers and capital letters thereafter. This fact occasionally causes problems. It is usual for assemblers to accept symbolic references but also to permit actual numeric values to be used instead. Where numbers are restricted to be given in decimal or octal notation, the distinction between numerals and letters is clear enough. But if the machine structure is such that hexadecimal numeric notations are the natural ones to use—as is the case with Simian—then it is not always obvious whether the characters ABCDEF are intended to denote the first six letters of the alphabet or the hexadecimal numerics following 9. Consequently, it may be impossible to tell whether such character combinations as F100, BABA, or DEAD are intended to be symbolic labels or numbers. Various conventions are used. The rule used in Simian programs is that all numeric values must begin with a numeral character or a sign. Thus a number may be prefixed by a sign or may begin with a zero, resolving any possible ambiguity. Under this convention, 0BABE and +BABE are understood to be hexadecimal numbers, but BABE is interpreted as a symbolic label. Unlike more sophisticated assemblers, Simile does not provide the programmer a choice of numeric notations; everything is expected to be hexadecimal.

The *mnemonic abbreviations* or *mnemonics* for the various machine instructions are probably the least standardized part of assembler languages—indeed they cannot be completely standardized because all possible machine instructions cannot be catalogued, computer designers are much too inventive for that! However, published standards do prescribe the abbreviations for the most common types of instruction. Small instruction sets, such as that of Simian, are almost entirely made up of operations for which standardized abbreviations exist.

Assembler directives

To translate assembler-language text, also known as *source code*, into object code successfully, an assembler must read the input text two or more times. This requirement raises a problem: how is the assembler to know that it has come to the end of the input text? Simply running on until there is no text left is not always satisfactory. The solution is to embed an *assembler directive* in the source text, to tell the assembler that the end of translatable text has been reached. Not unreasonably, this directive is .END.

In addition to .END, Simile recognizes the assembler directive .ORG, which indicates that the next instruction to be translated is to be assigned a specified memory location. For example,

```
.ORG 137
```

indicates that the next memory location to be used in translation should be 00000137. This directive is particularly useful if several segments of a program must be located at predetermined places in memory. An assembler language text file may contain as many .ORG directives as desired, so it is not necessary that all the segments of a program be presented to the assembler in the same sequence as they are to be placed into machine memory eventually.

Like .ORG, the assembler directive .DATA resets the location counter to a new value. Unlike .ORG, it turns off translation, so that segments of numeric code may be included in the assembler language listing. Use of both the .ORG and .DATA directives can achieve this purpose:

```
.ORG 33
        LD.B R0, #10        ; Count = 16 in R1,
        LD.L R1, #FA        ; Source addr = 0FA
        LD.L R2, #DF        ; Destin addr = 0DF.
START:  LD.B [R2], [R1]     ; Copy one character.
        INC.B R0, -1        ; Decrement counter,
        BZ DONE             ; branch if 16 done.
        INC.L R1, 1         ; INC source pointer
        INC.L R2, -1        ;    and destination.
        BR START            ; Back for next one!
DONE:   HALT                ; Halt processor.
.DATA FA
48 47 46 45 44 43 42 41     ; First 16 letters
50 4F 4E 4D 4C 4B 4A 49     ;    of the alphabet
.END
```

The .DATA directive permits numeric or alphabetic data to be inserted wherever desired. The byte values that follow the .DATA directive are simply copied into the object program, byte for byte. Perhaps more interestingly, maverick machine instructions for which no conventional assembler language mnemonics are available (e.g., *branch if V and L are set and C is reset*) can be included in this way. Placement next to given instructions is feasible without having to count bytes by using the asterisk (the * character) as an address, as in

.ORG *

and

.DATA *

which merely turn assembler translation on and off, respectively, without affecting the location counter.

Simian object programs may, indeed usually do, contain loader directives so that program loading and execution can be controlled. Simile does not recognize loader directives, but it generates most of the required ones—.LOAD, .PROG and .FINI—so that object files created by Simile can be loaded and executed without further editing. For the most part, .ORG and .DATA assembler directives will give rise to .LOAD loader directives with similar addresses. Because it does not know anything about the Simian computer on which the programs will be executed, Simile does not report all possible errors in directives. By way of illustration, suppose the programmer had inserted an impossible address in a .ORG directive. This situation can easily occur;

.ORG 1200

is a valid request for a Simian computer containing 2000_{16} = 8192 bytes of memory, but it could not be executed by a Simian with only 1000_{16} = 4096 bytes of memory installed because the directive would ask for loading to begin at an address where no memory is installed. Simile considers this request perfectly proper because it is only interested in formal correctness of language, not the context in which execution will be attempted. The translation will be effected correctly because the .ORG directive is syntactically correct, but execution will fail because the directive may be semantically unacceptable—unless, that is, execution is attempted on a Simian machine with sufficiently large memory.

Problems

1. Numerous computer instruction sets include, in addition to left and right shifts, a *rotate through carry* instruction, which resembles rotation as defined in Simian but moves the most significant bit into the carry bit and the carry bit into the least significant position (if rotating left). What sequence of Simian operations is equivalent to a *left rotate through carry*?

2. Define a set of rules for examining two unsigned integers and deciding which is larger, without performing a subtraction. The rules should lend themselves to implementation in combinational logic circuits, and to programming in the Simian language. Give a circuit and a program, either able to accomplish this task.

3. Define a set of rules for examining a character and deciding whether it is printable. The rules should lend themselves to implementation in a combinational

logic circuit, and to programming in the Simian language. Give at least one circuit and a program, either able to accomplish this task.

4. The Simian instruction set as defined does not permit double indirection. In other words, LD.B R3, [[R4]] meaning *load into R3 the byte whose address is in the memory location pointed to by R4* is not included as an admissible instruction. Why not? Could it be included? How?

5. Give the binary form of the Simian instruction ROL.S [R1], 1. What is its hexadecimal representation?

6. The program counter of a Simian computer contains 0000018A before the instruction SHL.S R5, 3 is executed. What does it contain after execution?

7. Trace the event sequence, step by step, of fetching the instruction, executing it, and incrementing the program counter, for the instruction LD.L [R4], # 001A02DD.

8. Give the binary and hexadecimal forms of the Simian instruction LD.L [R4], # 001A02DD. How many memory bytes does it occupy?

9. A program is intended to be loaded in Simian beginning at location 008A. It includes the branching instructions BNN −6 and BNV 1A. If the program is loaded at location 0090 instead, how must the branching instructions be modified? Why?

10. Register R5 of Simian contains 0A21F00F before SHL.S R5, 3 is executed. What does it contain afterward? What does the processor status register contain?

11. The Primate computer has an instruction set similar to Simian, and resembles it structurally, but it does not have an L bit in the processor status register. State a set of rules for performing a comparison of two unsigned 32-bit integers to determine which is larger, and flow chart a program for carrying out the comparison.

12. Which combinations of condition codes do not make up sensible combinations for branch and jump instructions? How many distinct instructions are there in reality? (It may be convenient to enumerate them using a Pascal or Fortran program.)

13. To identify data transmission errors, 8-bit bytes are often formed out of 7-bit ASCII characters by giving the extra bit (bit 7) the value 1 if the 7-bit character contains an even number of bits set to 1. The extra bit *P* is called the *parity bit* and the transmission scheme is said to have *odd parity encoding* because every byte always has an odd number of bits set to 1:

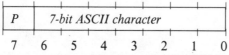

Write and test a segment of Simian code to produce an odd parity encoded 8-bit character out a 7-bit character placed in register R0.

14. A character with odd parity encoding (as in the preceding problem) is placed in register R0. Write and test a segment of Simian code that will replace the parity encoded character by a 7-bit ASCII character (with bit 7 reset to 0) and set the zero flag if a parity error was detected. This scheme is often used to spot data transmission errors.

15. Which two-operand instructions in the Simian language may have both operands immediately addressed? Which ones may have both operands absolutely

addressed? Which ones may have one immediately and one absolutely addressed operand? Why?

16. An ASCII character is placed in register R0. Write and test a segment of Simian code to determine whether the character is a valid hexadecimal numeral. The character in R0 should remain unaffected but the zero flag should be set if the character is acceptable, reset if it is not.

17. An ASCII character is placed in register R0. Write and test a segment of Simian code to examine this character and to convert any lower-case letter into its upper-case equivalent. If the conversion is performed, the zero flag should be set to indicate that fact.

18. In one particular 16-bit date representation *date(S)*, bits 15–9 are used to house the year (less 1900), bits 8–5 for the month, bits 4–0 for the day. Write and test a Simian program to place into registers R3, R2, R1 the full year, month, and day corresponding to a 16-bit date placed in register R0.

19. Write and test a Simian program to invert the representation of the above problem, i.e., to compute and store in register R0 the compact (16-bit) date representation corresponding to the year, month, and date in registers R3, R2, and R1.

20. Register R2 of a Simian computer contains a floating-point number encoded in the *float(S)* notation discussed earlier. Write and test a Simian program to place a twos complement integer corresponding to its mantissa in register R0 and a twos complement integer that represents the corresponding power of 2 in register R1.

21. Register R0 of a Simian computer contains a twos complement integer that represents the mantissa of a floating-point number, while R1 contains the corresponding exponent of 2. Write and test a Simian program to place the *float(S)* representation of this number into register R2.

22. A sequence of K bits is said to be *bitonic* if it contains zero or more 0s, followed by zero or more 1s, followed by zero or more 0s. (For example: 00001110, 00000000, 11111111, 00011111 are bitonic sequences, but 01100111, 11110001 are not.) Write and test a Simian program to determine whether the low-order byte in register R0 is bitonic, and to set the content of R0 to 1 if it is bitonic, 0 if it is not.

5
Digital computer structure

Digital computing processes are inextricably linked to the machines that carry them out; *how* data manipulation is done and *what* devices are required to do it cannot be considered separately. This chapter examines both the *how* and the *what*. It begins by developing the digital circuits necessary to perform the basic manipulative operations of digital computing, then examines how these operations can be coordinated and controlled to form sequential processes.

Arithmetic and logical operations

Addition, subtraction, counting, and other arithmetic processes are all closely related through the many elementary operations which they share. Similarity of processes, however, implies similarity of the digital circuits used to perform them. Arithmetic and logical operations are commonly carried out by a combined digital circuit referred to as an *arithmetic and logic unit*. The most complex operation that the arithmetic and logic unit must be able to perform, even in the simplest computer, is addition. This section, therefore, begins by looking rather closely at how addition is performed, then generalizes to the other logical and arithmetic operations.

Adding two words

The most fundamental arithmetic operation is undoubtedly the addition of two unsigned binary integers such as $a = 0101$ and $b = 0001$. The conventional pencil-and-paper technique is to write one number beneath the other, then to apply the basic rules of addition to each digit in turn. Thus

$$a = 0\ 1\ 0\ 1$$
$$b = \underline{0\ 0\ 0\ 1}$$
$$s = 0\ 1\ 1\ 0.$$

Beginning with the rightmost, each sum digit is formed from three components: the corresponding digit a_i of the addend, the corresponding digit b_i of the augend, and the *carry* c_i from the previous digit. A conventional full adder circuit implements the addition rules, producing from these three input arguments two outputs: the sum digit and a carry to be propagated leftward. Consequently, N full

217

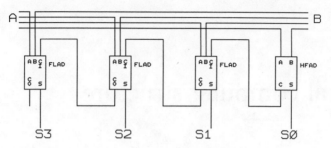

Fig. 5.1.   Four-bit ripple-through parallel adder.

adder circuits can be connected together to perform additions of the above type. An addition circuit suitable for 4-bit words is shown in Fig. 5.1.

The circuit shown in Fig. 5.1 is called a *parallel* adder because the addend, augend, and sum are all available on parallel (word-width) sets of signal lines, exactly as would be the case for a parallel register. It is called a *ripple carry* or *ripple-through* adder because any carry propagating from the right moves across from right to left in much the same fashion as do the carries in a ripple counter. In fact, comparison of Fig. 5.1 with the circuit of a ripple counter shows that there is considerable similarity.

The ripple carry adder and the ripple counter resemble each other in both circuitry and operation. Consequently, one might well expect their operating characteristics to be related as well. Indeed, so they are; both take time proportional to the number N of bit positions to be counted or added. If a time T_d is required for a full adder cell to perform a single-bit addition, the time to add N bits in a ripple adder is NT_d. Because carries are propagated from right to left, adder cell i cannot compute the ith digit correctly before all the preceding $i - 1$ digits are known, so that the carries will have rippled through the preceding $i - 1$ adders.

Improved adder performance can be achieved in much the same manner as improved counter performance, keeping in mind that the adder circuit is always a little more complicated. The necessary modifications are not difficult and can be deduced easily by examining the logical operations performed by a full adder cell.

Carry generation and propagation

An investigation of circuits able to carry out arithmetic and logic operations is best begun by reexamining the full adder. The conventional full adder cell has three inputs: the addend and augend digits a_i and b_i, and the carry in c_i. It has two outputs: the sum digit s_i and the carry out c_{i+1}. The outputs are related to the inputs by the following truth table:

c_i	a_i	b_i	c_{i+1}	s_i
0	0	0	0	0
0	0	1	0	1
0	1	0	0	1
0	1	1	1	0
1	0	0	0	1
1	0	1	1	0
1	1	0	1	0
1	1	1	1	1

The carry out c_{i+1} may be written in sum-of-products form as

$$c_{i+1} = c_i' a_i b_i + c_i a_i' b_i + c_i a_i b_i' + c_i a_i b_i$$

This expression can be simplified in an interesting way by first introducing two duplicates of the final right-hand term (as permitted by the principle of idempotence),

$$c_{i+1} = c_i' a_i b_i + c_i a_i b_i$$
$$+ c_i a_i' b_i + c_i a_i b_i$$
$$+ \qquad c_i a_i b_i' + c_i a_i b_i$$

then combining terms in pairs:

$$c_{i+1} = (c_i' + c_i) a_i b_i + c_i (a_i' + a_i) b_i + c_i a_i (b_i' + b_i)$$
$$= a_i b_i + c_i b_i + c_i a_i$$
$$= a_i b_i + (a_i + b_i) c_i$$

It is convenient to define two auxiliary functions

$$g_i = a_i b_i,$$
$$p_i = a_i + b_i,$$

so that the carry out is given by the expression

$$c_{i+1} = g_i + p_i c_i$$

The function p_i is known as the *propagation* function, because if p_i is true, an incoming carry will propagate further. Similarly, g_i is called the *generation* function, for it signals that a carry has been newly generated at digit i. Both functions are easy to implement in combinational logic, as indicated in Fig. 5.2.

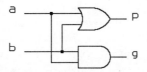

Fig. 5.2.   Logic gates to implement the generation and propagation functions g_i and p_i.

The sum s_i can be dealt with in a similar fashion to the carry, again beginning with the sum-of-products form derived directly from the truth table:

$$s_i = c_i' a_i' b_i + c_i' a_i b_i' + c_i a_i' b_i' + c_i a_i b_i$$

Combining terms, this expression is quickly simplified,

$$s_i = (a_i' b_i + a_i b_i')c_i' + (a_i' b_i' + a_i b_i)c_i$$

The first term clearly contains an exclusive-or function. Further simplification then hinges on rewriting the second right-hand term,

$$
\begin{aligned}
a_i b_i' + a_i b_i &= [(a_i b_i')' \cdot (a_i b_i)']' \\
&= [(a_i + b_i) \cdot (a_i' + b_i')]' \\
&= (a_i a_i' + b_i a_i' + a_i b_i + b_i b_i')' \\
&= (a_i b_i' + b_i a_i')'
\end{aligned}
$$

Substituting above, there quickly results

$$
\begin{aligned}
s_i &= (a_i' b_i + a_i b_i')\, c_i' + (a_i' b_i + a_i b_i')'\, c_i \\
&= a_i \oplus b_i \oplus c_i
\end{aligned}
$$

where the sign $\oplus$ denotes the exclusive-or function. This expression says, in a slightly roundabout fashion, that the sum digit s_i will be set if any one of the arguments a_i, b_i, c_i is set, or if all three are set.

To restate the sum bit s_i in terms of the generation and propagation functions, return to the expression

$$a_i \oplus b_i = a_i b_i' + b_i a_i'$$

and use the development immediately above to rewrite it as

$$
\begin{aligned}
a_i \oplus b_i &= (a_i + b_i) \cdot (a_i b_i)' \\
&= g_i p_i'.
\end{aligned}
$$

Negated propagation function terms can be avoided if the right-hand side is extended by null terms,

$$
\begin{aligned}
a_i \oplus b_i &= g_i p_i' + a_i a_i' \, b_i b_i' \\
&= g_i p_i' + (a_i' b_i')\,(a_i b_i).
\end{aligned}
$$

Applying De Morgan's theorem once more,

$$
\begin{aligned}
a_i \oplus b_i &= g_i p_i' + (a_i + b_i)\,(a_i b_i). \\
&= g_i p_i' + g_i' p_i \\
&= g_i \oplus p_i.
\end{aligned}
$$

Hence

$$s_i = g_i \oplus p_i \oplus c_i.$$

This expression is implemented easily, using a single exclusive-or gate with three inputs as shown in Fig. 5.3a. The carry bit c_{i+1} is equally easy; it requires one AND gate and one OR gate, as in Fig. 5.3b.

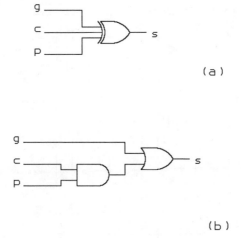

(a)

(b)

Fig. 5.3.   Sum and carry derived from the generation and propagation functions: (a) sum, (b) carry.

The circuit given in Fig. 5.3a for the sum s_i may be combined with that of Fig. 5.2, to yield a partial adder circuit that does not generate a carry, but instead produces the sum, generation, and propagation functions. Such a circuit appears in Fig. 5.4. It is a partial adder in the sense that it provides the intermediate functions p_i and g_i but requires the help of other circuits to compute the sum and carry out.

The conventional full adder is obtained from the partial adder circuit of Fig. 5.4 if the simple carry generator circuit of Fig. 5.3b is included. Chaining together four such cells, the ripple-carry adder of Fig. 5.1 is obtained, as shown in Fig. 5.5. It should be noted that the circuit of Fig. 5.5 is not different from that of Fig. 5.1; it is the same circuit drawn using an altered graphic notation.

The reason for recasting the full adder in terms of generation and propagation functions instead of sums and carries lies in the ease with which algebraic manipulations can be applied to these two functions. The algebraic manipulations then permit modifying the carry circuit, to produce different forms of adders.

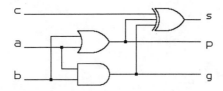

Fig. 5.4.   Partial adder circuit to yield generation and propagation functions instead of sum and carry.

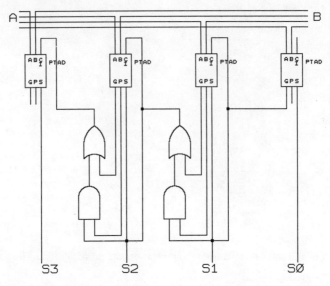

Fig. 5.5.   Four-bit ripple carry adder redrawn using partial adders and separate carry circuits.

Ripple adder performance

To check on the timings obtainable from a ripple-through adder, it is interesting to simulate a ripple-through adder and examine its speed of operation. A 4-bit adder, similar to Fig. 5.5, but including full provisions for carries out of bit 3 and into bit 0, is described by the following simulation:

```
    /* Four-bit ripple adder */
circuit ripladdr:
    {
    or:  a0, b0 > p0;
    and: a0, b0 > g0;
    and: c0, p0 > tmp1;
    xor: c0, p0, g0 > sum0;
    or:  g0, tmp1 > c1;
    or:  a1, b1 > p1;
    and: a1, b1 > g1;
    and: c1, p1 > tmp2;
    xor: c1, p1, g1 > sum1;
    or:  g1, tmp2 > c2;
    or:  a2, b2 > p2;
    and: a2, b2 > g2;
    and: c2, p2 > tmp3;
    xor: c2, p2, g2 > sum2;
    or:  g2, tmp3 > c3;
    or:  a3, b3 > p3;
    and: a3, b3 > g3;
    and: c3, p3 > tmp4;
    xor: c3, p3, g3 > sum3;
```

```
     or: g3, tmp4 > c4;
     }
output:
     {
     c4, sum3, sum2, sum1, sum0, a3, a2, a1, a0;
     time = 192;
     }
input:
     {
     a0 = 0 (12) 24;
     a1 = 0 (24) 48;
     a2 = 0 (48) 96;
     a3 = 0 (96) 192;
     b0 = 1; b1 = 1; b2 = 0; b3 = 1;
     c0 = 0;
     }
```

Here the input word b is fixed at 1011 while input a is cycled through all possible
four-bit values; the carry in c_0 to the low-order bit is kept fixed at zero.

Partial results of the adder simulation are shown in Fig. 5.6. The ripple effect
of successive carries is immediately visible in the right-hand half of this display.
At $t = 60$, a_0 changes value and triggers a cascade of carries lasting 8 time units,
with the final carry out c_4 being established at $t = 68$. A similar, though more
complex, set of events begins at $t = 48$. Here $a_{2,} a_1$ and a_0 all change value, so

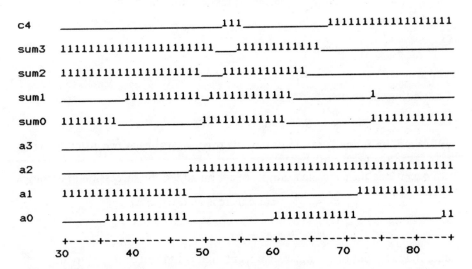

Fig. 5.6.   As carries propagate through the bit positions of a ripple carry adder, sum and carry
bits fluctuate.

successive digit adders in the chain are presented with new inputs before the corresponding carries arrive. As a result, the output (*sum* preceded by the carry out c_4) changes several times, first to 01001, then successively to 01011, 00011, 10111 and 11111, before finally settling on the stable result 01111. Settling to a stable result once again takes 8 time units.

Carry propagation in the ripple adder is clearly linear in time. The total delay is therefore proportional to the number of digits added; an 8-bit adder would take twice as much time as the 4-bit configuration investigated here. Thus the ripple carry adder grows less and less attractive as word length is increased. A second practical problem involves the short-lived false sums generated while the carries ripple through. These might become troublesome if other circuits draw on the output of the adder before the addition has been fully carried out.

Carry look-ahead adders

A fast adder can be built in a manner analogous to the synchronous (carry look-ahead) counter, by anticipating when carries will occur. Why and how to modify the circuits is best seen from an examination of the algebraic expressions for carries. Consider again the general expression for carries,

$$c_{i+1} = g_i + p_i c_i.$$

The key point to observe is that this expression is *recursive*: it defines c_{i+1} in terms of c_i. Stepping back one digit, an expression may be written for the preceding carry bit,

$$c_i = g_{i-1} + p_{i-1} c_{i-1}.$$

Substituting c_i as given by the latter expression into the former, there results

$$c_{i+1} = g_i + p_i(g_{i-1} + p_{i-1} c_{i-1})$$

which may be rearranged to read

$$c_{i+1} = g_i + g_{i-1} p_i + p_i p_{i-1} c_{i-1}.$$

Continuing the recursion,

$$c_{i+1} = g_i + g_{i-1} p_i + g_{i-2} p_{i-1} p_i + p_i p_{i-1} p_{i-2} c_{i-2}$$

and so on, until finally at the ith step the carry c_{i-1} vanishes because there is no carry in to the least significant digit.

To continue the concrete example of a 4-bit adder, the succession of carries is

$$c_1 = g_0 \quad \text{(since there is no carry in c_0)},$$
$$c_2 = g_1 + g_0 p_1,$$
$$c_3 = g_2 + g_1 p_2 + g_0 p_1 p_2,$$

and, if a carry out of the most significant digit is thought to be of any interest,

$$c_4 = g_3 + g_2 p_3 + g_1 p_2 p_3 + g_0 p_1 p_2 p_3.$$

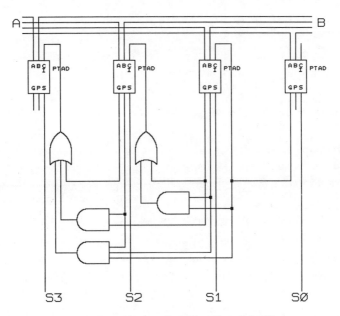

Fig. 5.7. Four-bit carry look-ahead parallel adder.

The generation and propagation functions do not involve any carries; they are computed from the addend and augend bits only. Using the circuits of Fig. 5.3, all the g_i and p_i are therefore computed at once. The important point in the final expressions given for the carries is that no term anywhere on the right-hand sides involves any quantity except the various g_i and p_i; all the carries may therefore be found simultaneously and independently by appropriate logic circuits.

A possible circuit configuration for determining the carries independently is shown in Fig. 5.7. It clearly resembles the carry circuits used in carry look-ahead counters, for the very good reason that carries must be determined in both cases. A counter, after all, could be thought of as merely a rather specialized adder. By analogy, the adder circuit of Fig. 5.7 is therefore known as a *carry look-ahead* adder.

Carry look-ahead performance

Performance of the carry look-ahead adder can be determined by simulation exactly like that given for the ripple carry adder. For a 4-bit adder similar to Fig. 5.7, but allowing for carries in and out of bits 0 and 3, the simulation description reads

```
    /* 4-bit carry-look-ahead adder */
circuit lookahd:
    {
    or: a0, b0 > p0;
```

```
    and: a0, b0 > g0;
    xor: p0, g0, c0 > sum0;
    or: a1, b1 > p1;
    and: a1, b1 > g1;
    xor: p1, g1, g0 > sum1;
    and: p1, g0 > tmp11;
    or: tmp11, g1 > c2;
    or: a2, b2 > p2;
    and: a2, b2 > g2;
    xor: p2, g2, c2 > sum2;
    and: p2, g1 > tmp21;
    and: p2, p1, g0 > tmp22;
    or: g2, tmp21, tmp22 > c3;
    or: a3, b3 > p3;
    and: a3, b3 > g3;
    xor: p3, g3, c3 > sum3;
    and: p3, g2 > tmp31;
    and: p3, p2, g1 > tmp32;
    and: p3, p2, p1, g0 > tmp33;
    or: g3, tmp31, tmp32, tmp33 > c4;
    }
input:
    {
    a0 = 0 (12) 24;
    a1 = 0 (24) 48;
    a2 = 0 (48) 96;
    a3 = 0 (96) 192;
    b0 = 1; b1 = 1; b2 = 0; b3 = 1;
    c0 = 0;
    }
output:
    {
    c4, sum3, sum2, sum1, sum0, a3, a2, a1, a0;
    time = 197;
    }
```

The circuit here is substantially that shown in Fig. 5.7; the inputs and outputs, however, are identically the same as for the ripple adder simulation: $b = 1011$ while a is cycled through all values. Results will therefore be directly comparable. This simulation produces the output shown (in part) in Fig. 5.8.

At $t = 60$ in Fig. 5.8, a_0 changes value and causes a carry to be propagated through all bit positions. In contrast to the ripple carry adder, it does not take a fixed time per bit position for the ripple to propagate; whatever is known about carries at any bit position is immediately communicated to all higher positions. No carries are in fact *propagated*; the only carries for which the higher-order bit adders need to wait are new ones *generated* at lower positions. The waiting time therefore consists of one fixed delay (independent of the number of bit positions) during which both operands and all propagated carries are added, then another similar time delay during which any newly generated carries are taken care of. In Fig. 5.8 these delay times amount to 2 time units each, for a total of 4.

```
                        4-bit carry-look-ahead adder

c4            _____1111111111111111111111

sum3     1111111111111111111111111111111111111_____

sum2     1111111111111111111__1111111111111_____

sum1     _____1111111111111111111111111_____

sum0     11111111_____1111111111111_____111111111111

a3            _____

a2            _____11111111111111111111111111111111111111111111

a1       11111111111111111_____1111111111111

a0       _____1111111111111_____111111111111_____11

         +----+----+----+----+----+----+----+----+----+----+----+
            30        40        50        60        70        80
```

Fig. 5.8.   The carry look-ahead adder driven by signals identical to Fig. 5.6. Short-lived false sums still appear, but time to stabilize is faster than in Fig. 5.6.

While the carry look-ahead adder stabilizes, false sums can appear briefly just as they do in the ripple-through adder. Between the altered excitation at $t = 60$ and stability at $t = 64$, the apparent sum traverses the values 01100 and 11100 on its way to 10000. In a similar way, the input alteration at $t = 48$ makes the sum pass through 01011 on its way to the correct value 01111. Here too stability is achieved at $t = 52$, four time units after the arguments were supplied to the adder.

Adders of mixed type

Both the look-ahead carry adder and the ripple carry adder are valuable, but both have serious disadvantages. These are readily discerned by examining their circuit diagrams or the corresponding algebraic expressions.

The algebraic expressions for successive carries in a look-ahead carry adder show that the carry bit c_k can be generated by a circuit made of one OR gate with $k + 1$ inputs and k AND gates whose numbers of inputs range from 2 to $k + 1$. To build an N-bit adder of this type, the number N_g of logic gates required is

$$N_g = \sum_{k=0}^{N} (1 + k) - 1 = N(N + 1)/2 - 1 = N^2/2 + N/2 - 1$$

This number can be reduced a little if the carry propagated out of the most significant bit position is not of interest. The gate count then becomes

$$N_g = \sum_{k=0}^{N-1} (1 + k) - 1 = N(N - 1)/2 - 1 = N^2/2 - N/2 - 1$$

For any but small values of N, the number of logic gates is very nearly $N^2/2$ in either case, because the term $N^2/2$ is dominant over the others in either expression. For large values of N, the number of gates is thus proportional to N^2. It is said that the circuit complexity is of order N^2, or that *the circuit has $O(N^2)$ complexity*. The speed of operation of the carry look-ahead adder, on the other hand, does not vary with the number of bits; the time taken to find the sum of two numbers of any length is twice the delay time of a combinational logic gate plus twice the delay time of a partial adder cell.

The ripple-through carry adder, in contrast to its carry look-ahead counterpart, does not grow in complexity as the word length is increased, but its operating time does. Operating speed can thus be bought at the price of circuit complexity. This choice, termed *space-time tradeoff*, is often faced by the digital hardware designer. Such tradeoffs, as well as other operating characteristics of the various adders, are perhaps best explored by simulation. Examples will be omitted here, however, because of their close similarity to the simulation of counters, a topic already treated in detail.

The main characteristics of the two adder types shown in Figs. 5.5 and 5.7 are summarized in Table 5.1. As is usual in such cases, the complexity is given in terms of the rate of growth of one variable with another. Thus the notation $O(N^p)$, which is read "of order N^p," indicates that the variable in question is proportional to the pth power of N. It should be obvious that the look-ahead carry adders are fast, but that they become very complicated for large word-lengths because the logic gate count rises as the square of the number of bits in the word.

In computers with long word lengths, such as 32 bits, both types of adder appear unattractive: one is very slow, the other very complicated. Furthermore, the carry look-ahead adder in this case requires gates with 32 input lines, which are both difficult to obtain and difficult to use because the number of connections to be made is large. Fortunately it is possible to construct hybrid circuits that represent a compromise between the speed of the carry look-ahead adder and the simplicity of the ripple-through carry adder. To construct a compromise adder a carry look-ahead adder of moderate size, say 4 bits, is first built. It is

Table 5.1. Principal characteristics of adders

Significant characteristic	Ripple-through	Look-ahead
Time to add	$O(N^1)$	$O(N^0)$
Number of logic gates	$O(N^1)$	$O(N^2)$
Maximum fan-in	$O(N^0)$	$O(N^1)$

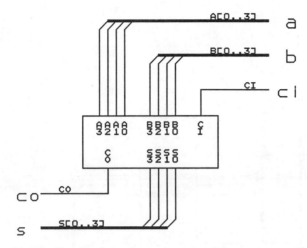

Fig. 5.9. Four-bit full adder. The input data paths *a*, *b* and the output *s* are all four bits wide; *ci*, *co* are one-bit carries in and out.

configured as a multibit full adder; in other words, provision is made for two 4-bit operands *a* and *b*, a 4-bit sum *s*, a carry in bit *ci*, and a carry out bit *co*. Such an adder is often symbolically represented as shown in Fig. 5.9: the 4-bit data paths are simply shown as broad lines, labeled with the number of bits they represent. The internal structure of a 4-bit adder could well resemble Fig. 5.7, except for the more fully developed carry provisions.

Several short-length carry look-ahead units with full carry provisions, as in Fig. 5.9, can be connected together in the fashion of a ripple-through carry adder. This form of circuit is shown in Fig. 5.10, which illustrates a 12-bit adder constructed by chaining three 4-bit cells. Additions are executed in each 4-bit unit very quickly, because each unit works in the carry look-ahead fashion. The complexity of each unit, however, is relatively low.

The circuit of Fig. 5.10 could be termed a *ripple carry combination of look-ahead adders*. It is also possible to construct a carry look-ahead combination of ripple-through units. In the latter case, each 4-bit unit would be of the ripple-through carry type internally, but the three units would be connected together in the carry look-ahead manner. This form of adder, however, is not quite so simple as the design in Fig. 5.10 because the look-ahead circuits to deal with 4-bit adders are more complicated than those for 1-bit full adders.

Adder circuits are important to computers because addition is a fundamentally important arithmetic operation and accounts for much of the total time taken in actual programs. Machine performance is thus significantly affected by how well additions can be carried out. Equally important, however, is the fact that addition circuits form the basis on which other operations are built. Some of these are explored in the sections to follow.

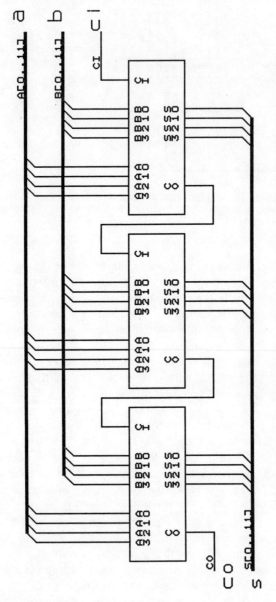

Fig. 5.10. Twelve-bit adder of mixed design. Carries ripple through three carry look-ahead adder units.

Subtraction

In twos complement arithmetic, on which all of the discussion to follow is based, subtraction is achieved by complementation and adding. That is to say, the difference d between the minuend m and subtrahend s,

$$d = m - s,$$

is obtained by forming the logical (ones) complement of s, incrementing by 1 so as to obtain the negative of s in twos complement notation, then adding:

$$d = m + (-s).$$

This technique of subtraction can clearly be carried out by any machine capable of performing addition and bitwise complementation. However, subtraction is quite easy to implement directly in hardware and is required often enough to justify the additional expenditure.

A subtraction circuit can be obtained by modifying one of the various adders. As compared to addition, subtraction requires two additional operations: bitwise complementation and incrementation. Bitwise complementation can be accomplished easily by including the requisite number of NOT gates in the input lines that carry the subtrahend. The complexity of the circuit is increased only slightly thereby; an N-bit subtractor is obtained from an N-bit adder by means of an extra N gates. Incrementation is even simpler to achieve than complementation: to add 1 it is only necessary to set the incoming carry bit to the adder circuit. A 4-bit subtraction circuit based on this argument has the form shown in Fig. 5.11. The heart of the operation remains the adder cell. Although a carry look-ahead adder is shown in Fig. 5.11, any other kind of adder would work equally well.

To keep down the complexity of computing systems, designers usually strive to combine various functions in the same hardware units. Addition and subtraction are closely related operations, so there is strong incentive to search for

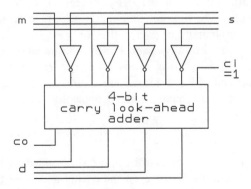

Fig. 5.11. Four-bit subtractor constructed implementing negation and addition directly in logic circuits.

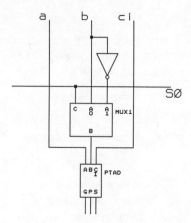

Fig. 5.12. Add/subtract cell built around a partial adder. Select line s_0 determines the operation.

ways to combine both in a common functional unit. Both can in fact be combined in an adder/subtractor cell of the form shown in Fig. 5.12.

The operation to be performed by the cell of Fig. 5.12 is chosen by the *select line* s_0. When the select line s_0 is reset, the multiplexer which it controls establishes a direct connection between input b_i and the partial adder. The cell then acts as a straightforward adder. On the other hand, if s_0 is set then the multiplexer connects b_i to the partial adder through an inverter so that subtraction results, provided the carry in to the lowest-order bit in the adder is also set. In other words, line s_0 acts to select the operation to be performed. It is therefore known as a *select line* or *control line*.

Logical operations

Still attempting to keep hardware units from becoming too numerous, computer designers usually attempt to combine logical operations with arithmetic ones in a single hardware unit. The fundamental operations of logical sum and product are very simple to implement, of course; they only require a single gate per bit and there are no carries, nor any other information transfers, between the various bits of a word. In fact, if it is desired to incorporate these operations into the bit add/subtract cell of Fig. 5.12, the job is already as good as done, for the partial adder produces the generation and propagation functions

$$g_i = a_i \cdot b_i,$$
$$p_i = a_i + b_i.$$

These are exactly the logical operations desired. Provided that select line s_0 is set, so that the correct arguments reach the partial adder, all that needs to be done is to channel the correct signal to the output of what has now become a multifunction cell. That can be done by inserting another multiplexer to choose

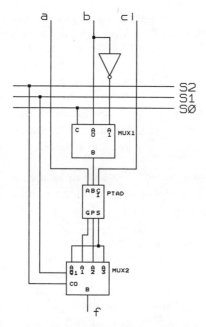

Fig. 5.13. Combining a single-bit add/subtract cell with logical operations yields a flexible processing unit.

one of the three adder outputs as the cell output f_i. The selection is governed by two select lines s_1 and s_2. Two select lines provide four choices, not three; to avoid having any indeterminate signal settings, the fourth choice is made identical to the first so that two of the four settings of the select lines return the cell to a simple add/subtract function. This configuration is shown in Fig. 5.13.

The single bit cell of Fig. 5.13 is controlled by three select lines s_0, s_1, s_2 and the carry in ci, which may be regarded as a a fourth select line (although it is actually connected to only one bit cell). If a processing device capable of acting on N-bit words is to be built, N such cells must be connected together through logic gates that propagate carries between cells. The carry connections could of course be either of the ripple or look-ahead type. To make the composite unit work, the select lines must all be driven from a common control unit, so that all the N cells perform the same function. Only the rightmost carry in signal $ci = c_0$ is externally controllable in the same way as the select lines. In principle, the select lines could be considered independent, so that the cascade of N cells is able to execute $2^4 = 16$ different operations. However, many of the possible operations are not particularly interesting; setting $s_0 = s_1 = s_2 = 1$, for example, results in subtraction if $c_0 = 1$, in nothing directly useful if $c_0 = 0$. To avoid inclusion of such unprofitable cases, the relationships between signals on the select lines can be constrained to include only those operations deemed worthwhile by the circuit designer. Such constraints are often implemented in a control circuit composed of combinational logic gates. There need only be one control circuit for the entire set of all N bit cells, however, because the select lines are common to all.

Shifting operations

With the additive and bitwise logical operations all incorporated in the cell of Fig. 5.13, the main digital data processing operations are provided in a single unit. Of the processing operations normally considered necessary, the missing ones are *shifting* and *rotation*.

Shifts and rotations are easily taken care of by means of a shift register, if a carry-around provision is made so that the high-order digit is shifted to or from the least significant position in rotations. However, it is often convenient not to employ a set of combined cells of the variety shown in Fig. 5.13 to effect some operations, and a separate shift register unit to accomplish the others. The obvious course is to incorporate the shifting operations into the general cell structure also. There are in principle two approaches by which this goal can be accomplished. Additional circuitry can be used to alter the flip-flop interconnection structure, so as to turn the addition/subtraction unit into a shift register on demand. Alternatively, a shifting network can be provided so that the general processing cell is fed from an offset (shifted) input. The latter approach is very easily implemented by including one multiplexer per bit, and an extra set of select lines, as in Fig. 5.14.

The additional select lines in Fig. 5.14 choose one of a_i, a_{i+1} or a_{i-1} as input to the bit cell, according to the settings of s_3 and s_4: $[s_4,s_3] = [0,0]$ selects a_{i+1}, $[0,1]$ chooses a_i, and $[1,0]$ corresponds to a_{i-1}. To avoid the problems that may arise from an undefined input, the setting $[1,1]$ is connected to yield the same result as $[0,1]$.

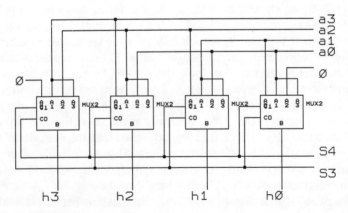

Fig. 5.14.   Four-bit shifting network to select a_i, a_{i+1} or a_{i-1} as input h_i to the ith processor cell. The input is augmented by zero bits in positions a_{-1} and a_4.

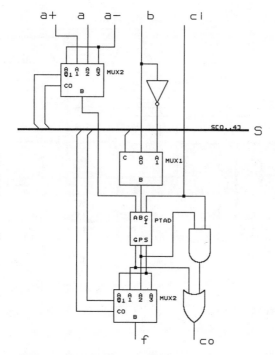

Fig. 5.15. Bit cell for an arithmetic and logic unit, including provision for ripple-through carry.

An arithmetic and logic unit

The various component circuits described up to now may be combined into a single whole, to form a *bit cell* of an arithmetic and logic unit. Such a circuit appears in Fig. 5.15. With appropriate signals applied to its five independent control lines, it is capable of addition, subtraction, complementation, incrementation, and left or right shifting; in other words, it can do all the ordinarily required arithmetic and logical operations needed to perform data manipulation. In addition to the normal operations, such as logical products and sums, it can also execute a number of combined operations: for example, it can compute the logical product of B with A shifted left one bit, or subtract B from A shifted right one bit.

To produce a complete working processor cell, two extra logic gates have been included in Fig. 5.15 to generate carries. These appear in the lower right corner of the drawing: one AND gate and one OR. To keep matters simple, a ripple-through carry adder is assumed. Other types of carry treatment are possible, of course; they only require replacing the two gates at the extreme lower right of Fig. 5.15 by other circuits suitable to the task. For example, the arrangement of Fig. 5.7 is readily generalized to deal with an ALU cell such as shown in Fig.

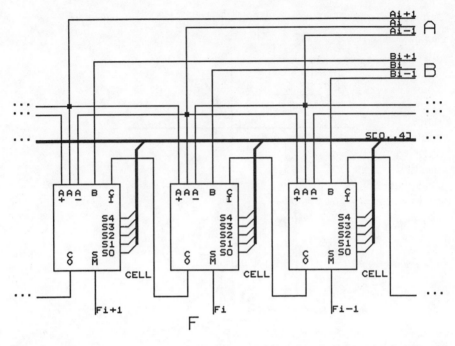

Fig. 5.16. Three bit cells from a ripple-through arithmetic and logic unit, showing cell interconnection.

5.15, instead of the simple full adders shown in Fig. 5.7. The result will be a look-ahead carry arithmetic and logic unit.

A bit cell of an arithmetic and logic unit naturally can only include circuits that deal with a single bit. The set of logic gates to perform the look-ahead carry function cannot be attached to a single cell—it belongs to the whole arithmetic and logic unit because it must *look ahead* over several cells. In exactly the same way, the overflow, sign, zero and carry-out flag bits, which programmers expect to find in reasonably designed computers, cannot be attached to a single cell; they belong to the whole unit. They are therefore not shown in Fig. 5.15, indeed there is no way they could be.

Combining numerous cells to form a complete arithmetic and logic unit is an easy task. If the ripple-through carry configuration is assumed, then it is only necessary to interconnect the carries, the carry out of one bit cell becoming the carry in to the next. Arithmetic and logic units of any length may be built in this way. A segment out of such a unit is shown in Fig. 5.16.

The control lines that select the function to be performed by the arithmetic and logic unit are common to all the cells in Fig. 5.16. It is worth noting, however, that the interconnection of the input lines a_i is more complicated. Each cell must in fact have access to three such lines: its own, and those of the cells to its left and right, so that shifting operations may be performed.

A ripple-through ALU

Through a sequence of modifications and reconnections, the simple ripple carry adder of Fig. 5.1 has now grown to the full-fledged arithmetic and logic unit of Figs. 5.15 and 5.16. This unit is able to carry out the basic data processing operations expected of any computer, and can do a few others besides. How well it performs, and how it might be further modified to obtain both better performance and a greater range of operations, are largely matters to be studied by simulating an actual arithmetic and logic unit. Such a simulation is comparatively lengthy because the circuits have grown rather more complex than the straightforward adders treated earlier; but aside from length, it is not more complicated. A 4-bit arithmetic and logic unit of the ripple carry type, as sketched out in Figs. 5.15 and 5.16, is simulated by the following Apodix circuit description:

```
        /*  4-bit ripple carry ALU   */
circuit alu4bit:
        {
        not:   b0   >   nb0;
        not:   b1   >   nb1;
        not:   b2   >   nb2;
        not:   b3   >   nb3;
        mux:   nb0, b0, s0, enb   >   bb0;
        mux:   nb1, b1, s0, enb   >   bb1;
        mux:   nb2, b2, s0, enb   >   bb2;
        mux:   nb3, b3, s0, enb   >   bb3;
        mux:   a1, a0, zero, a1, s3, s4, enb   >   h0;
        mux:   a2, a1, a0, a2, s3, s4, enb   >   h1;
        mux:   a3, a2, a1, a3, s3, s4, enb   >   h2;
        mux:   zero, a3, a2, zero, s3, s4, enb   >   h3;
        not:   s0   >   c0;
        or:    h0, bb0   >   p0;
        and:   h0, bb0   >   g0;
        and:   c0, p0   >   tmp0;
        xor:   c0, p0, g0   >   sum0;
        or:    g0, tmp0   >   c1;
        or:    h1, bb1   >   p1;
        and:   h1, bb1   >   g1;
        and:   c1, p1   >   tmp1;
        xor:   c1, p1, g1   >   sum1;
        or:    g1, tmp1   >   c2;
        or:    h2, bb2   >   p2;
        and:   h2, bb2   >   g2;
        and:   c2, p2   >   tmp2;
        xor:   c2, p2, g2   >   sum2;
        or:    g2, tmp2   >   c3;
        or:    h3, bb3   >   p3;
        and:   h3, bb3   >   g3;
        and:   c3, p3   >   tmp3;
        xor:   c3, p3, g3   >   sum3;
        or:    g3, tmp3   >   c4;
        mux:   sum0, g0, p0, sum0, s1, s2, enb   >   f0;
```

```
mux:   sum1,  g1,  p1,  sum1,  s1,  s2,  enb   >   f1;
mux:   sum2,  g2,  p2,  sum2,  s1,  s2,  enb   >   f2;
mux:   sum3,  g3,  p3,  sum3,  s1,  s2,  enb   >   f3;
}
```

Testing this circuit is in principle no different from any other: first one establishes exactly what it is expected to do, then one devises tests to determine
whether it really does that.

The five select lines of Fig. 5.15 control at least the following elementary
functions:

Function	Value	s_4	s_3	s_2	s_1	s_0	Remarks
Addition	$f = a + b$	1	0	0	0	1	Arithmetic
Subtraction	$f = a - b$	1	0	0	0	0	Arithmetic
logical OR	$f_i = a_i + b_i$	1	0	0	1	1	Logic
logical AND	$f_i = a_i \cdot b_i$	1	0	1	0	1	Logic
shift right	$f = a \gg 1$	0	0	1	1	1	$b = 0$
shift left	$f = a \ll 1$	0	1	1	1	1	$b = 0c$

One acceptable way of testing the arithmetic and logic unit is to choose a pair
of operand values a and b, then to run the select lines through a sequence of
settings which at least include the six operations in the above list. Allowing 40
time units for each setting, the following input specification is arrived at:

```
input:
    {
    zero = 0;
    a0 = 1; a1 = 0; a2 = 1; a3 = 1;
    b0 = 1 (160); b1 = 0; b2 = 1 (160); b3 = 0;
    s4 = 1 (160);
    s3 = 0 (200);
    s2 = 0 (120);
    s1 = 0 (80,120,160);
    s0 = 1 (40,80);
    enb = 1;
    }
output:
    {
    s4, s3, s2, s1, s0, f3, f2, f1, f0;
    time = 240;
    }
```

Here the input word b is held until $t = 160$, then reset to all zeros so as to test
the select line combinations that require $b = 0$ at $t = 160$ and $t = 200$. The
select line signals shown in the simulation amount to little more than a transcription of the tabular columns above; they are obtained by tracing the table
and requesting a value alteration whenever one occurs in the table.

The simulation requested here appears in Fig. 5.17, with the time scale compressed fourfold. To save space, the input words a and b are not shown. The

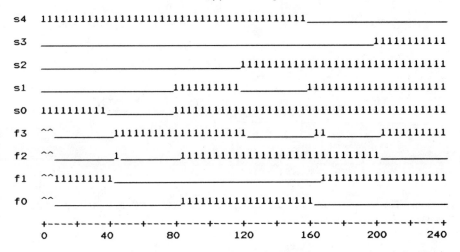

```
                    4-bit ripple carry ALU
s4  11111111111111111111111111111111111111111_____

s3  _____11111111111

s2  _____1111111111111111111111111111111

s1  _____1111111111_____1111111111111111111111

s0  1111111111_____1111111111111111111111111111111111111111111

f3  ^^_____1111111111111111111_____11_____1111111111

f2  ^^_____1_____111111111111111111111111111111111_____

f1  ^^111111111_____1111111111111111111

f0  ^^_____1111111111111111111111_____

    +----+----+----+----+----+----+----+----+----+----+----+----+
    0         40        80        120       160       200       240
```

Fig. 5.17.   Simulation of the 4-bit ALU. The six principal functions are tested, each for 40 time units.

augend *a* has the value 1101 throughout the simulation. The addend *b* equals 0101 until $t = 16$, then drops to 0000.

Taking the leftmost time interval first, $0 < t < 40$, addition appears to work satisfactorily: $1101 - 0101 = 0010$. This 4-bit ripple carry arithmetic unit is closely related to the 4-bit ripple carry adder investigated earlier, so it is to be expected that here, as before, it will take eight time units for carries to propagate; in fact, the result turns out to be correct as of $t = 7$. Similarly, subtraction seems to work correctly: $1101 + 0101 = 1000$ (modulo 16, for this is a 4-bit arithmetic unit!), and appears stably within eight time units of the input signals being presented. Not unexpectedly, similar results hold for the AND and OR operations.

Perhaps the more surprising results are obtained when the right and left shifting operations are tested. The shifts are correctly executed: 1101 becomes 0110 on shifting right, 1010 on shifting left. The shifts take eight time units, just like the other operations, even though the shifting is done by rerouting signals through multiplexers, hence almost instantaneously. Although the shifting is done at the input to each arithmetic cell, all signals must still pass through the cell and must wait to have a zero correctly added. Because the signal path for every operation is the same as for any other operation, total execution times are the same for all operations.

The central processing unit

The arithmetic and logic unit of any computer is its primary working tool, the device that actually carries out the various operations it is capable of. It alone,

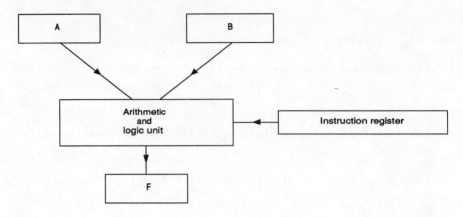

Fig. 5.18.   The arithmetic and logic unit derives its input data as well as control signals from registers.

however, does not suffice to do useful work; the *central processing unit*, or *CPU*, of a computer must include more than the ability to perform manipulative tasks. It must be able to fetch and store data, so it must contain some components able to remember data. It must understand instructions in order to carry them out, and must therefore also possess means for instruction decoding and control. These requirements are not particularly hard to satisfy, but unless attention is paid to them, the result will be a hand calculator, not a computer. To illustrate the difference, a typical simple CPU structure will now be examined, paying particular attention to how that structure affects the work of the computer user or programmer.

Central processor registers

The arithmetic and logic unit of a computer is purely a combinational logic circuit. It possesses no memory at all, so although it is able to form, for example, the sum of two integers A and B, some other device must be provided to maintain the two numbers in existence. Suitable devices for this task are of course *registers*, the word-width storage devices discussed earlier. To perform a two-operand manipulation, the sequence of activities must thus be

> select control signals of the ALU for *add*,
> load register A with the number A,
> load register B with the number B,
> accept result $A + B$ into result register F.

In the first step, "select" means that the control lines are to be set or reset in the correct combination, and kept at those values at least until after register F has been loaded with the result. In other words, the control lines themselves need to be connected to a register IR, usually called the *instruction register*. To provide the function $F(A,B)$ at its output, the arithmetic and logic unit therefore needs to be coupled to at least three registers, and preferably four. The connection scheme is sketched out in Fig. 5.18.

Three or four registers being the absolute minimum requirement, it is usual for computers to be built with at least some half a dozen registers in the central processing unit. Eight or 16 registers are commonly provided. The number may be larger, but it rarely exceeds 30–40 registers, although there do exist some specialized machines with as many as 8000.

In principle, the three steps of loading the registers A, B, and IR could be carried out simultaneously, for the register contents are independent so none of the three loading operations need wait for any other to be completed. In practice, computers vary in this regard: some permit concurrent data transfers to several registers, others do not. The reasons that lead to one choice or the other arise mainly from structure of interconnections within the central processor, as discussed next.

The CPU bus

The arithmetic and logic unit of a modern computer is a flexible and sophisticated device able to perform a large variety of operations. However, it requires the support of at least a few registers, and for full flexibility to be maintained it must be possible to transfer data from any register to any other. The least complicated way to move data from one register to another is to provide a direct path from every register to every other. If the registers are N bits wide, the data paths would normally take the form of N parallel wires leading from the output of one register to the input of the other, and another N parallel wires connecting output to input in the opposite direction. This approach to data transfer, however, is impractical because the number of connections required is excessively large. If there are p processor registers, each one connected to the $p-1$ others, the total number of possible connections between registers is clearly $p(p-1)$ $= p^2 - p$. This number grows unmanageably large very rapidly as p is increased, becoming excessive even at the rather modest levels needed for small computers, say $p = 8$ or 16. This situation would resemble a telephone system with a direct connection between every pair of telephones—an impractical idea because there is not enough copper on earth to make the necessary quantity of wire!

The usual solution to the interregister communication problem is the same as adopted by both telephone and highway engineers. Instead of providing a direct connection for every conceivable origin–destination pair, a single trunk connection is built and all possible users are given access to it. In computers, this general-purpose connection is called a *bus*; it usually consists of a set of N or more parallel wires to which various connections can be made. No attempt is made to connect any registers to each other directly, all communication is via the bus. Such an arrangement is illustrated in Fig. 5.19.

Using a central processor with the structure shown in Fig. 5.19, only one data

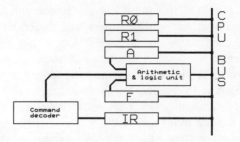

Fig. 5.19.   All registers of the CPU communicate via a single shared central processor bus.

item may be moved between registers at a time because only one bus is available for data transfers. Thus the operation of adding two general register contents, ADD.L R0, R1, is dealt with by first setting the select lines of the arithmetic and logic unit to perform an addition, then carrying out the following sequence of steps:

Step	Activity	Bus signal
1	connect R1 output to bus	R1
2	load register A from bus	R1
3	connect R0 output to bus	R0
4	load register F from ALU	R0
5	connect F output to bus	F
6	load register R0 from bus	F

Interestingly, there is no need to have two special operand registers just to furnish input data to the arithmetic and logic unit. It suffices to have one operand register connected to the ALU directly, for the second operand can be communicated to the arithmetic and logic unit through the bus. Any register anywhere may therefore be used for the second operand.

At various times, the bus carries the content of R1, the content of R0, or the content of register F. Although the contents of R1 and R0 are both available at the initial moment, two separate steps are required for supplying the two input arguments to the adder because only one signal can be present on the bus at any one time. Thus the advantage of using a bus to communicate between registers is the small number of interconnections; the disadvantage is the relatively slow transfer of data, because each item must wait its turn. Nevertheless, the slowing is minor but the saving of interconnections is very great, as compared to point-to-point connections. Bus-based computer structures are therefore very common.

Three-state logic devices

Connecting individual registers or devices to the bus, then disconnecting them again, is a process impossible to achieve with normal logic gates but can be

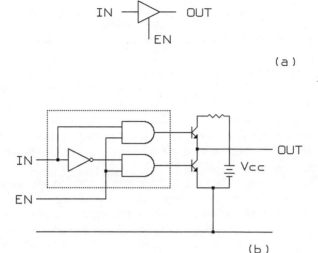

(a)

(b)

Fig. 5.20. (a) Three-state buffer symbol. (b) One form of buffer, often called the *totem-pole* circuit.

effected readily with *three-state devices*. All the logic gates discussed so far possess truth tables with defined outputs, so that their output lines are always either set or reset, depending on the inputs. If any register is connected to the bus by way of normal logic gates, those gates will attempt to control the voltages on the bus under all circumstances. Multiple connections to the bus will therefore result in conflicting signals and erratic behavior is bound to result.

To ensure that only one register output is connected to the bus at a time, three-state logic gates are used in much the same way as discussed in connection with memory cells. The principle is simple: a disconnect switch is provided at the output side of each register, so that the register can be isolated from anything connected to its output. Several register outputs can then be connected to the input of a single device; they will not interfere with each other provided the circuit timing is so arranged that only one output connection is enabled at any given moment.

The simplest and perhaps most widespread three-state device is a circuit possessing one input line and one output line, whose output exactly echoes its input if (and only if) the enable line EN is set. Such devices are denoted by the symbol shown in Fig. 5.20a, similar to the symbol for a three-state NOT gate but lacking the inversion bubble on the output side. They are known as *three-state buffers* or *three-state bus drivers*. One possible circuit for a three-state buffer is shown in schematic outline form in Fig. 5.20b. When the EN line is high in this circuit, the AND gates echo their inputs; in other words, base current flows in the upper transistor when the input is high, but the lower transistor is cut off. The output voltage therefore rises to nearly V_{CC}. Conversely, when the input is low the upper transistor is cut off but the lower one acts essentially like a short circuit: the output voltage falls to near zero. If the EN signal is low, on the other hand, both AND gates are forced to have low outputs. No base current flows in either transistor; both are essentially open circuited. The output terminal is thereby isolated in much the same way as it might be by a mechanical switch.

In Fig. 5.19 it is assumed that all the register outputs are connected to the bus through three-state devices. Bus control is exercised by means of the EN lines, ensuring that at most one register output is actually connected to the bus at any one time. There may even be times when none of the register outputs is actually tied to the bus. The bus voltages at such times cannot be predicted because they depend on the relative imperfection of the "open" switches formed by the three-state devices.

The loading of registers from the bus must be controlled also, to ensure that register contents are not altered at the wrong times. There are several good ways to doing so. Three-state devices may be used, in the same way as for outputs. Alternatively, ordinary logic gates may be employed. For example, if the register in question is built of edge-triggered delay flip-flops, it suffices to disable its clock line. Most normal register designs provide for this requirement, by inserting a two-input AND gate in the clock input signal line, the second input being driven by an external *LOAD* signal. In other words, the register will be loaded from its available input signal only if *LOAD* = 1. The register input may therefore remain physically connected to the bus at all times; unless the *LOAD* signal line is asserted, no change will take place in the register contents at the next rising edge of the clock signal. From a practical engineer's point of view, the three-state bus drivers used in this case must be able to furnish substantial amounts of output current, because quite a large number of gates may remain connected to the bus lines permanently.

Register access from the bus

In the simple central processor of Fig. 5.19 there are several registers, so controlling register access to the bus means selecting which register is to have its output placed on the bus. The *enable* lines of the various three-state buffers allow individual register outputs to be controlled; what remains is to ensure also that only one register can be connected to the bus at a time.

One possible way of arranging for bus access control is illustrated in Fig. 5.21, which shows one of the four registers in a hypothetical 4-bit central processing unit. The output of this register is connected to the four data lines of the bus through a set of three-state buffers, all controlled by a single enable line. This line is connected to one of the four register select lines (the right-hand group of four lines in Fig. 5.19). Each of the four processor registers is connected to a different select line in the group. The group of lines is controlled by a 2-to-4 decoder, so only one select line can be asserted at a time. Placing a register number (0 through 3) as a 2-bit signal at the decoder input, the decoder will assert

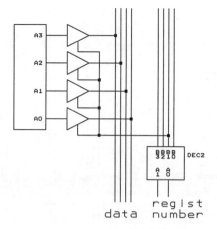

Fig. 5.21. Register 2 of four registers in a 4-bit CPU provides signals to bus data lines if it is selected.

the corresponding select line and thereby connect one (and only one) register output to the bus data lines.

The arrangement of Fig. 5.21 guarantees that only one CPU register furnishes the bus signals. It requires a bus structure with as many data lines as there are bits in a register, and as many register select lines as there are registers. A b-bit machine with r registers thus requires b data lines and r register select lines. To be precise, these should be termed *source* register select lines, for they determine the bus signals by choosing one register to act as a signal source; they do not indicate which register is to serve as the data recipient.

Register loading from the bus can be controlled in much the same way as connecting register outputs to the bus. In fact, the task is simpler because there is no physical reason why two register inputs cannot be connected to the bus simultaneously; three-state devices are therefore not required. A simple but effective scheme is to include *destination register select* lines within the bus structure, in the same way as source register select lines were introduced: there is one line per register and the whole group is controlled by a decoder so only one line can be asserted at a time. These select lines are connected to the *LOAD* lines of their respective registers, as shown in Fig. 5.22. When a register number is placed at the input of the destination decoder, the latter asserts one of the destination select lines. It thereby asserts the *LOAD* signal of the corresponding register, causing that register to be loaded from the bus data lines. This arrangement has the advantage of simplicity, with input and output circuitry very similar. It suffers from the mild disadvantage that several registers cannot be loaded from the bus at the same time.

It goes without saying that the bus line arrangement of Fig. 5.22 is not the only one possible. Another method, economically attractive in small computers,

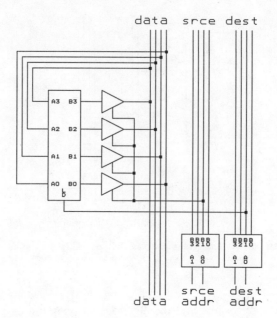

Fig. 5.22.   Source and destination register select lines control the access of register 2 to bus data lines.

uses the same set of register select lines to carry both source and destination register numbers, one after the other. This can be done if an extra register is attached to the bus data lines themselves, so data can be retained on the bus even when no register output is connected to the bus lines. (In Fig. 5.22 such a register could be placed at the foot of the bus data lines, next to the source decoder.) To transfer data, the selected source register is connected to bus data lines; the data values are loaded into the bus register and the source is disconnected. The destination register number is next placed on the single set of select lines and that register is loaded from the bus data lines. Loading data onto the bus and taking it from the bus thus constitute two distinct register transfer operations, in which the bus register is essentially used as a mailbox. This scheme uses only half as many register select lines as the method of Fig. 5.22, but it can at best transfer data only half as fast. It also requires more complicated logic circuits and more precise timing.

Simian CPU architecture

The internal organization of the Simian computer closely follows the principles implicit in Fig. 5.22. Simian possesses eight general registers and three special registers, as detailed in the previous chapter. It also incorporates an arithmetic and logic unit (ALU) which has two registers A and F associated with it, as shown in Fig. 5.23.

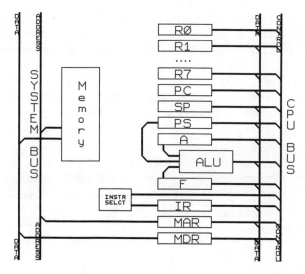

Fig. 5.23. Data transfers between CPU registers use the internal bus; memory is accessed over the system bus.

As may be seen in Fig. 5.23, the Simian central processor contains the expected eleven registers (eight general plus three special) with which the programmer is expected to be acquainted. In addition, it contains five others to which the programmer does not have direct access: two for memory control, two for ALU servicing, and the instruction register IR. The latter always contains the instruction currently being executed. The full set of 16 Simian registers appears in Table 5.2.

The arithmetic and logic unit is shown in Table 5.2 as sharing the number 1100 with the F-register. There is fortunately no danger of confusion, for as may be seen from Fig. 5.23, the F-register can only be connected to the internal bus

Table 5.2. Bus-accessible registers in Simian

| Register | | Purpose |
Number	Name	
0000	R0	General register 0
0001	R1	General register 1
...	...	.....
0111	R7	General register 7
1000	PC	Program counter
1001	SP	Stack pointer
1010	PS	Processor status
1001	A	A-register
1100	F	ALU and F-register
1101	MAR	Memory address register
1110	MDR	Memory data register
1111	IR	Instruction register

on its output side, its input lines being permanently connected to the ALU; conversely, the ALU output lines are permanently connected to the F-register and only its input side is ever connected to the bus. So far as anyone could tell by examining bus signals, the arithmetic and logic unit thus appears to constitute a single unit with the F-register.

The arithmetic and logic unit actually possesses a direct connection to the processor status register, an exception to the general rule that register-to-register data movements always use the bus. The status bits VCNLZ of the processor status register always reflect the outcome of the most recent operation of the ALU, so every ALU operation must be followed by transfer of these five status bits. Transfer over the bus could certainly be arranged; but precisely the same data transfer is required over and over again, after every instruction involving the ALU. The effective speed of the CPU can be increased considerably by allowing the status bits to be moved over a specialized direct connection at the same time as some other data transfer takes place over the bus.

Because Simian registers are all 32 bits wide, its central processor bus obviously must contain 32 data lines so that a full register content can be communicated in parallel over the bus. In addition, it must contain two sets of 16 address lines, for it is necessary to control 16 different registers from or to which data may move. Control of data movement within the central processor thus follows the general principles already discussed, with separate register select lines for the source and destination registers in each data transfer. This form of organization implies that every register-to-register data transfer takes place within the time of a single system clock pulse. The example of an addition instruction ADD.L R0, R1, sketched out above in general terms, then takes the following specific form:

Step	Register select		Bus signal
	Source	Destination	
1	R1	A	R1
2	R0	F/ALU	R0
3	ALU/F	R0	F

Because the ALU and the F register share a single register number, the register select lines are effectively interchanged from step 2 to step 3.

Of the full set of 16 central processor registers in Simian, most have already been dealt with in considerable detail. What purposes the others serve, however, may still remain obscure. At least two of the still unexplained registers will therefore be taken up next.

Accessing memory

To understand how Simian operates it is vital to realize that the central processor bus, which provides a communication path between the various registers and the ALU, is not the same bus as that connecting central processor and memory. The latter furnishes a data path between major units of the computer system—the processor, memory, and other major devices like disk drives—and is therefore usually called the *system bus*. The former, on the other hand, is contained entirely within the central processing unit and is called the *CPU bus*. The terms *external* and *internal* bus are sometimes used, to emphasize that one connects the CPU with the external world, the other is purely internal to the central processor itself. The external bus must be able to move data to memory locations, which in Simian always have 32-bit addresses. It must therefore contain 32 address lines as well as 32 data lines and some others, not shown in Fig. 5.23, to carry control signals. By contrast, the internal bus only needs to distinguish between the CPU internal registers; four lines suffice for this task.

When a data transfer takes place from the central processor to memory, two items of information must be transmitted from the internal to the external bus: the data word or byte itself, and the address to which it is to be sent. Movement of data to and from memory therefore requires two processor registers accessible from the CPU bus: a *memory address register* and a *memory data register*. These appear in Fig. 5.23, labeled MAR and MDR, respectively. Data transfers are effected by placing the desired data address in the memory address register and the data in the memory data register, then informing the memory that the direction of data transfer is to be from CPU to memory ("writing") rather than the other way around ("reading"). The memory address register is connected to the address lines of the external bus, which in turn connects to the address decoder of the physical memory unit. It thus serves, as its name implies, to direct the flow of data to specific memory locations. The memory data register, on the other hand, merely serves as a temporary storage area for data in transit to or from memory.

To transfer data from one of the processor registers, say R6, to a memory location whose address is in another register, say R5, the following steps are required.

Step	Register select		Bus signal	Activity
	Source	Destination		
1	R5	MAR	R5	MAR ← R5
2	R6	MDR	R6	MDR ← R6

In plain words, the memory address to which data are to be written is placed in the memory address register and the content of R6 is copied into the memory data register. The symbolic notation in the right-hand column of this table is commonly used to denote register transfers; the left-pointing arrow serves as a reminder of the transfer direction.

The memory data register is accessible from both the internal (processor) and external (system) buses, so that data can next be moved from that register into the memory itself over the system bus. Because the system bus is separate from the processor bus, data transfers can take place on the two buses independently and concurrently; the processor can manipulate data at the same time as a data transfer is taking place on the system bus. In other words, the memory address decoder attached to the external bus can identify the desired memory location during step 2, at the same time as the memory data register is being loaded. Similarly, the data transfer from the memory data register to the address indicated can take place in the next clock time period following step 2, while the central processor is doing something else. So far as the CPU is concerned, there is no such thing as writing into memory location M; all it recognizes is the pair of registers MAR and MDR.

When writing to memory, the central processor considers its task completed when the two registers have been loaded. It finds itself in precisely the position of a gentleman sending a letter to his friend: it writes the message (into the memory data register), affixes the address (in the memory address register), and hopes it will be properly delivered to the right place while he attends to other matters. However, he is usually not wise to assume that the letter will be delivered instantaneously. Much the same applies to memory data transfers. Memory chips are usually slower than the circuits used in the processor itself, for excellent economic reasons. It can therefore happen that the central processor wishes to write or read memory faster than the memory is able to respond. Difficulties are avoided by permitting an additional communication channel between the central processor and memory, perhaps only one bit wide, to serve as a "busy" flag to show that the last memory function requested has not yet been completed. Timing considerations of this sort introduce inessential complications; for present purposes, they will be avoided by assuming that Simian memory is able to react as quickly as its central processor may require.

Memory is an essentially passive device; it remembers data, recalling it as and when requested; but it does not initiate action. Actions on memory (reading or writing) are always initiated by the central processing unit, so that memory addresses are always specified by the CPU. For this reason, the memory address register is shown in Fig. 5.23 as being unidirectionally connected. Data transfers, on the other hand, may proceed in either direction, as indicated by the bidirectional arrows attached to the memory data register.

Instruction selection

Data transfers along the central processor bus can proceed between registers. However, data may also be transferred from a register to the arithmetic and logic unit. So long as the ALU has a structure similar to that outlined in Figs. 5.15 and 5.16, its output register F will always be loaded with some function F of the two inputs to the ALU, the content A of register A in Fig. 5.23 and the bus data B supplied to the ALU along the bus lines. What function of A and B is actually placed in F depends entirely on the setting of the ALU select lines; a certain set of values will result in the arithmetic sum being computed, another will yield the logical product, and so on. That is,

$$F = F(A, B, c)$$

where *c* denotes the *control word*, i.e., the string of control bits placed on the select lines. These must be determined and communicated to the arithmetic and logic unit in the manner indicated in Fig. 5.19. The current instruction is housed in the *instruction register*, whose content is available to instruction decoding circuits capable of understanding each instruction and asserting the control lines of the arithmetic and logic unit accordingly. For example, if the operation code bits in a Simian instruction are 0000 (denoting ADD), the control lines that govern the shifting network of the ALU must be set to indicate *no shift* and the control lines that govern arithmetic and logical operations must enable the addition operation. Because Simian permits operations with three different word lengths, its ALU must also include enabling gates that will permit the temporarily superfluous bit cells to be simply turned on or off. These gates must be controlled in accordance with the word length indicated in the instruction. The combinational logic network required to decode instructions and to set the control lines is quite straightforward in principle. Its detailed structure may nevertheless become fairly complicated. Even though the tasks to be carried out are not very complex, especially in so simple a computer as Simian, the relatively large number of possible instructions means that quite a few logic gates must be included in the circuit.

Before an instruction can be decoded at all, it must reside in the CPU instruction register. Instructions are invariably stored in memory, so the actual execution of instructions must alternate with a *fetch sequence*. The latter is a simple action sequence in which the next instruction is fetched from memory and deposited in the instruction register, the program counter being at the same time incremented 2 so that it will point at the memory address of the next instruction, ready to be fetched from memory when its time comes. The actions that make up the fetch sequence are thus the following:

	Register select		Bus		ALU
Step	Source	Destination	signal	Bus Transfer	Instruction
1	PC	MAR	PC	MAR ← PC	?
2	MDR	IR	MDR	IR ← MDR	?
3	PC	ALU/F	PC	ALU ← PC	inc 2
4	F/ALU	PC	F	PC ← F	?

While register-to-register transfers not involving the ALU are carried out, the settings of the ALU control lines have no effect. They are therefore denoted by question marks in the above action sequence, to indicate that the values placed on them do not matter. Only while the next instruction address is being calculated (i.e., while the program counter content is incremented by 2) must the ALU control lines be set for the appropriate arithmetic function. It is assumed here that the memory itself is able to respond fast enough to fetch data from storage almost instantly. In practical situations that may not be the case; if so, progress from step 1 to step 2 may involve an enforced wait until the expected data word has been deposited in the memory data register.

Microinstructions and microprograms

All the actions that take place in the central processing unit of a computer rely on data transfers between registers, possibly accompanied by setting of ALU control lines. Clearly, execution of even a very simple machine instruction such as LD.L R7, R4 requires a whole sequence of such more elementary actions, including the fetching and understanding of the machine instruction itself. These elementary activities are generally known as *microoperations*, and their descriptions in any reasonable formal notation are known as *microinstructions*. A sequence of microinstructions, as for example the set of four actions necessary to fetch an instruction from memory, is known as a *microprogram*.

A common formalism for expressing microprograms is the register transfer notation used in the examples above, augmented with the ability to indicate actions of the arithmetic and logic unit. The transfer of information between registers is denoted by a left-pointing arrow,

$$MAR \leftarrow PC$$

while the modification that may occur during a transfer involving the arithmetic and logic unit is indicated in an algebraic or functional notation,

$$F \leftarrow incr(PC,2)$$

or

$$F \leftarrow or(A,R1).$$

In Simian, functional expressions of this sort are only applicable to transfers in which F serves as the destination register, for only in this case does information become available for modification by passing through the ALU. Expressed in this notation, the sequence of actions for fetching an instruction reads

$$MAR \leftarrow PC$$
$$IR \leftarrow MDR$$
$$F \leftarrow incr(PC,2)$$
$$PC \leftarrow F$$

Notations of this sort for expressing microprograms are widely used in computer engineering. They are not well standardized, however, for the sufficient reason that they are very closely related to the details of machine hardware. Every computer differs from all others in some crucial detail; consequently, their microinstruction notations usually differ at least a little as well.

Simian instructions are generally two-address instructions: they include the description of an operation (by means of an operation code and a word length specification) and the register numbers of up to two operands. The instruction decoding circuit must therefore do more than merely set the ALU control lines, it must also determine from and to where the operands are to be transferred. For example, to execute the Simian instruction ADD.L R1, R0 the instruction itself must first be fetched from memory for decoding; thereafter, the control lines must be set and the register transfers necessary for executing the instructions must be carried out. The microprogram in this case will consist of two simpler microprograms executed in sequence: the instruction fetch and the actual addition itself. In detail, they are as follows:

	Step	Register select Source	Register select Destination	Bus signal	Bus Transfer	ALU Instruction
fetch:	1	PC	MAR	PC	MAR ← PC	?
	2	MDR	IR	MDR	IR ← MDR	?
	3	PC	ALU/F	PC	ALU ← PC	inc 2
	4	F/ALU	PC	F	PC ← F	?
add:	5	R1	A	R1	A ← R1	?
	6	R0	F/ALU	R0	ALU ← R0	add
load:	7	ALU/F	R0	F	R0 ← F	?

In a microprogramming notation suitable for Simian, this sequence reads

> **fetch:** MAR ← PC
> IR ← MDR
> F ← *incr*(PC,2)
> PC ← F
> **add:** A ← R1
> F ← *add*(A,R0)
> **load:** RO ← F

If an instruction requires register indirect addressing, the sequence is a little more complicated because the effective address of the indirect operand must be determined before any action can be taken. For example, the Simian instruction ADD.L R0, [R1] requires bringing the source operand value from memory before adding. Addition must therefore be preceded by an operand fetch similar to the instruction fetch, but simpler because no address incrementation needs to be done. The register serving as a pointer to memory is in this case R1, not PC as in the instruction fetch. The microoperation sequence for ADD.L R0, [R1] therefore includes an additional step:

> **fetch:** MAR ← PC
> IR ← MDR
> F ← *incr*(PC,2)
> PC ← F
> **bring:** MAR ← R1
> **add:** A ← MDR
> F ← *add*(R0)
> **load:** RO ← F

Simian instructions involving immediate operands need still longer microprograms. To illustrate, consider ADD.L [R1], #FF. Here the source operand must be fetched from the place where the program counter PC points, followed by incrementation of the program counter. The destination operand is indirectly addressed, necessitating another memory access. The microoperations are therefore as shown in the following:

fetch:	MAR	← PC
	IR	← MDR
	F	← *incr*(PC,2)
	PC	← F
immed:	MAR	← PC
	F	← *incr*(PC,4)
	PC	← F
	A	← MDR
bring:	MAR	← R1
add:	F	← *add*(MDR)
load:	MDR	← F

Complicated addressing schemes can obviously stretch out microprograms to quite considerable lengths. Nevertheless, every one of the arithmetic and logical operations in the Simian machine language can be carried out by an appropriate sequence of microoperations—register transfers and concurrent manipulations of ALU control (operation select) lines.

Processor control

The various elementary operations that a central processing unit is capable of carrying out—transferring data between registers and setting control lines on the ALU as well as both machine buses—combine to form the much more sophisticated activities that constitute the machine language of the entire computer. Indeed it can be said that the conventional machine instructions are the commands stored in memory and transmitted along the memory bus, whereas microinstructions are the commands that the central processor knows how to deal with. The next line of inquiry, therefore, is to ask how the central processor hardware actually manages to perform the sequences of actions that constitute microprograms.

Control paths in the processor

In addition to the data paths that tie them together, the various processor registers are interconnected by a set of control lines. Several of these have been mentioned briefly; for example, a pair of lines is necessary to control the effective register length. Others, such as the source and destination register enabling lines of Fig. 5.22, have been described at length. Taken together, they form a set of interconnections whose layout roughly parallels that of the data flow paths in the processor. Figure. 5.24 shows an outline sketch of the information flow in the central processor of Simian, including data as well as control signals.

Of particular note in Fig. 5.24 is the organization of control signal paths. Like

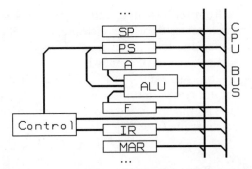

Fig. 5.24. Register transfers are controlled by the contents of the processor status and instruction registers.

data, control signals in the central processor are distributed to all registers over a set of bus lines. In Simian, these must include at least the following:

Source register identification	16 lines
Destination register identification	16 lines
ALU select signals	5 lines
Argument value for increment or shift	5 lines
Word length specification	2 lines
Clock signal	1 line
Run/wait signal	1 line
Other control signals	? lines
Total	46 + ? lines.

The control signal count as calculated here is actually a fairly strict lower bound. There are often additional control lines, yet in some processor designs one or two of the lines listed here may be missing—not because they are unnecessary but because the signals are communicated through point-to-point wiring instead of over the bus. The ALU select signals, for example, are of no use to most registers, so they could be omitted from the bus structure and connected directly from the control circuitry to the ALU instead.

All processor control functions are exercised by the control circuits of Fig. 5.24 on the basis of information derived from two sources: the instruction register and the processor status register. At the conclusion of each instruction fetch sequence, the instruction register contains the next instruction to be executed: word length, source and destination register addresses, and instruction code. These are processed by the control circuits and appropriate bus signals are asserted. Processing in some cases is trivial; the word length bits of a Simian instruction, for example, can be simply copied to a two-bit register that will hold their values on a pair of bus lines. The proper signals to be placed on the ALU control (function select) lines, on the other hand, are related to the 4-bit instruction code in a more complicated manner.

A fundamental point to observe is that the instruction register content is always a word copied from the machine main memory via the memory data register. It generally corresponds to a whole microprogram, not just one microinstruction. The single machine instruction must therefore be mapped into a microinstruction sequence. This task cannot be performed by combinational logic alone, for the microinstructions must be executed in their correct time sequence—clearly a job for clock-controlled sequential logic circuits. Thus, the next problem to tackle is how to create and time a sequence of microinstructions to correspond to a particular machine instruction.

Microinstruction sequences

To see how microinstruction sequences can be carried out by a central processing unit, it is instructive to begin by examining a particular microprogram. Almost all machine instructions in fact require execution of at least two microprograms: one to carry out the actions indicated by the instruction and another to fetch the instruction from memory in the first place. Because the instruction fetch sequence is so frequently needed, it may be appropriate to begin with a detailed examination of the microoperations involved in it:

$$\textbf{fetch: } \text{MAR} \leftarrow \text{PC}$$
$$\text{IR} \leftarrow \text{MDR}$$
$$\text{F} \leftarrow incr(\text{PC},2)$$
$$\text{PC} \leftarrow \text{F}$$

Each microinstruction in this sequence is executed by placing a certain set of signals on the ALU control lines and on those processor bus lines which determine register selection. The microinstruction is thus representable as a string of bits, one corresponding to each of the relevant bus lines. There are four microinstructions, hence four distinct bit strings that must be be presented to the central processor in turn.

Most present-day digital computers are controlled by placing the microprograms to be executed, such as the fetch sequence above, in a read-only memory which forms part of the control circuit of the central processor. This memory area is not connected to the external bus and is therefore entirely separate from the main memory of the computer; it is usually called the *control memory* or the *microprogram memory*. Typically, a read-only memory chip or circuit has N address (input) lines and M data (output) lines, arranged so that whenever an N-bit binary number is presented to the input, the M-bit word stored at the corresponding control memory address appears at the output. Suppose for the sake of simplicity that only the four-step sequence above needs to be executed—in other words, that a computer is to be built which never executes any instructions but merely keeps on fetching new ones to ignore. In this admittedly oversimplified case, a control memory capable of storing exactly four control words suffices. The word width, as already indicated, must be at least 46 bits if the machine is to be similar to Simian in structure. A four-word memory requires only two address lines, of course, because the addresses in such a memory device

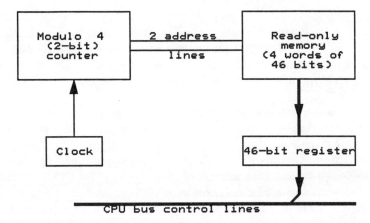

Fig. 5.25. Microinstructions stored in read-only memory are presented to the bus control lines sequentially.

will lie in the range 00_2 to 11_2. For the microinstructions to be executed in their proper fixed sequence, the addresses must be presented to the control memory in the corresponding sequence also. This need is easily met by deriving the addresses from a modulo-4 counter, driven by a clock. A suitable arrangement is shown in Fig. 5.25; although a 46-bit control word is assumed, any other reasonable number could be used instead.

The operation of this scheme is quite straightforward. As the clock runs, the counter counts clock pulses and places the appropriate counts on the address lines of the read-only memory. This memory contains four words, the control bit strings that correspond to the four microinstructions:

ROM address	Microinstruction
00	MAR ← PC
01	IR ← MDR
10	F ← *incr*(PC,2)
11	PC ← F

As each address is presented to the read-only memory in turn, it responds by placing the corresponding string of 46 control bits (each corresponding to a microinstruction) on its output lines. The output values are secured by latching them into a register whose output side drives the control lines of the CPU bus. Whenever the counter reaches its maximum count of 11_2 it "wraps around" to the beginning of its counting cycle and starts over again from 00, so the successive counts run 00, 01, 10, 11, 00, 01, ...Because these counts are communicated to the read-only memory as addresses, the data lines will correspondingly show the contents of memory word 00, memory word 01, word 10, word 11, word 00, . . . , in an unending cyclic sequence. The central processing unit must execute microinstructions exactly as they are presented, so it will continue to fetch instructions from successive memory locations forever.

Just fetching instructions forever without executing them is not particularly useful, so the mechanism shown here must next be expanded so that the fetching is followed by action. The necessary details are added and embellished in the next few sections of text, building up more complex operation sequences and allowing a variety of different operations to fit within the framework of "continuing forever."

It is important to underscore that the read-only memory in which microinstructions are stored resides in the central processing unit, it does not form part of the computer main memory. Because it is entirely separate from main memory, the microprogram memory need not have the same word length. Its word length is selected to match the number of control lines in the CPU internal bus, whereas the word length of main memory is chosen to suit the needs of applications programs. Because the control memory serves a very specialized purpose, rather odd word lengths can and do occur, such as 46 or 157 bits. One very widely used minicomputer type, for example, uses 99 bits.

Branching in microprograms

In a real computer, various different microinstruction sequences need to be executed. These are most conveniently stored in a single read-only memory device, for most sequences are quite short, perhaps just three or four microinstructions each. If the control memory contains several independent sequences, however, simple clocked execution of microinstruction sequences is not adequate because it would cause all the stored microinstruction sequences to be executed in the order of their storage. Provision must therefore be made to vary the order of microinstruction execution.

In machine languages, the order of instruction execution is controlled by branch instructions. A similar approach to sequence control is possible in microprograms. Branching in a microprogram, like any other program, requires two things: a condition that prescribes whether to branch or not, and an alternative address to which to branch. The branching addresses of course refer to the microprogram memory, not to the main memory. The branching conditions to be examined will include the processor status bit settings, just as in machine-language programs; but there may be others, as for example a bit to indicate that the memory read/write operation last requested is not yet complete.

Unlike programs in high-level languages, most microprograms are quite short and contain very simple actions. If branch microinstructions are provided, following the pattern of machine language, then a large percentage of all the instructions in a typical microprogram will be branch microinstructions. Recognizing these and taking action as necessary requires one or two clock cycles each, so that a significant part of total machine time will be devoted to interpreting branch microinstructions. A scheme preferred by many computer designers is to use a single word of microprogram memory for each microinstruction and to include the possibility of branching in each and every word. In other words, every microinstruction is composed of two parts: an action part (the bits to be placed on the CPU control lines) and a decision part. The microinstruction word for a Simian-like computer in this case takes the following form:

control word bits	condition	branch address

This microinstruction word constitutes a sort of embryonic program in itself. It may be understood as a request for the following actions, all carried out simultaneously:

1. Execute the action (the register transfer) shown in the control (bus line setting) bits.
2. Examine the condition bits in the microinstruction word. If they request an unconditional branch, use the branch address as the next address in the microprogram counter.
3. If the condition bits unconditionally forbid branching, allow the microprogram counter to advance to the next microprogram instruction.
4. If conditional branching is indicated, compare the appropriate condition bits with the bit settings requested in the microinstruction. Branch if the prescribed condition is met, otherwise continue to the next microinstruction.

These steps can be embedded directly in logic circuits. However, the structure shown in Fig. 5.25 is not up to the task because it contains neither a provision for checking status bits nor any mechanism for branching. A more complicated layout, along the lines of Fig. 5.26, is therefore necessary.

The operation of the circuits in Fig. 5.26 is reasonably straightforward. The central processor bus control lines are directly connected to the *microinstruction*

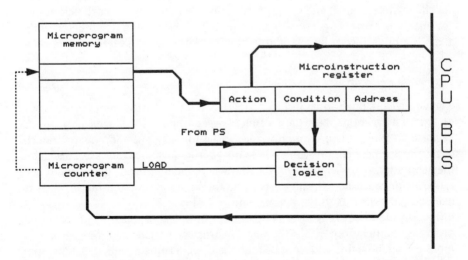

Fig. 5.26. Branching is achieved by loading the microprogram counter, which otherwise counts linearly.

register, which always contains a copy of the current microinstruction word as stored in *microprogram memory*. This is a read-only memory much like that in Fig. 5.25 but having a word width sufficiently enlarged to contain condition codes and branching addresses. The *microbranching logic unit*, a combinational logic circuit, examines condition bits to determine whether to branch. Depending on the outcome, it may then assert the *LOAD* line of the microprogram counter. Enabling this line loads the microprogram counter from the branching address field of the microinstruction register, thereby forcing a branch; otherwise, microinstructions are taken sequentially as the microprogram counter reading increases. Success of this scheme requires that every microprogram terminate in an unconditional jump to the instruction fetch sequence.

Condition codes for the Simian microinstructions may be set up in much the same way as in Simian machine language. In fact, the machine language instructions must include conditional microinstructions as the mechanism of decision. The number of condition bits is therefore at least ten—five to indicate processor status register flag settings and five to flag "don't care," as appropriate. In most cases it is actually higher, for there are usually some additional condition codes that do not interest the programmer at the machine language level. In contrast to the machine instruction level, branching addresses in microcode are absolute, i.e., they are analogous to the *jump* instructions of machine language, with actual microprogram memory addresses specified rather than address offsets.

The width of the microprogram memory word depends on several factors. There must be room for the control line settings—at least 46 bits—and at least ten bits must be allowed for branching conditions. The amount of space required for microprogram addresses depends on the number of microinstructions to be stored in the microprogram memory. Allowing 12 bits for microprogram addresses implies a microprogram memory of $2^{12} = 4096$ words, certainly ample for the relatively small and simple instruction set of Simian (though perhaps not for machines with larger instruction sets). The microprogram memory must therefore have a word length of at least $46 + 10 + 12 = 68$ bits.

Instruction execution

The control circuits shown in Fig. 5.26 are able to deal with complex sequences of microinstructions but they cannot execute machine-language programs because no mechanism is provided for initiation of a specified instruction. In other words, these circuits can execute microprograms once they are started, but they contain no provision for finding out where the microcode corresponding to a particular machine instruction is to be found. This shortcoming is cured by extending the circuits in the manner shown in Fig. 5.27.

The key element in Fig. 5.27 is the set of multiplexers able to load the microprogram counter from either the microinstruction register or from an *address table*. To see how this additional circuit element permits flexible machine operation, consider again the register transfer sequence for the instruction ADD.L R0, R1 discussed in detail previously:

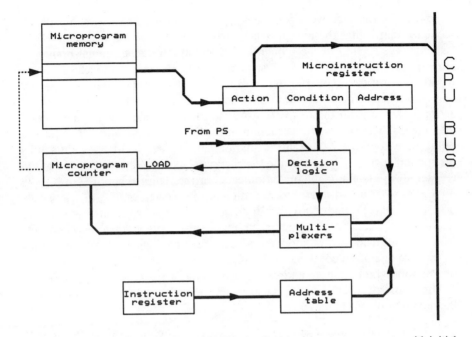

Fig. 5.27. Machine instructions are initiated by loading the microprogram counter with initial addresses determined by the instruction register content.

$$
\begin{array}{rl}
\textbf{fetch:} & \text{MAR} \leftarrow \text{PC} \\
& \text{IR} \leftarrow \text{MDR} \\
& \text{F} \leftarrow \textit{incr}(\text{PC,2}) \\
& \text{PC} \leftarrow \text{F} \\
\textbf{add:} & \text{A} \leftarrow \text{R1} \\
& \text{F} \leftarrow \textit{add}(\text{R0}) \\
\textbf{load:} & \text{R0} \leftarrow \text{F}
\end{array}
$$

Turning this sequence of register transfer instructions into a microprogram requires attaching a set of conditions to each transfer operation and specifying branch addresses. In an informal notation which avoids the detail of binary encoding, the above becomes

Symbolic location	Required action	Branching condition	Branch address
fetch:	MAR ← PC	*branch never*	?
	IR ← MDR	*branch never*	?
	F ← *incr*(PC,2)	*branch never*	?
	PC ← F	*branch never*	?
add:	A ← R1	*branch never*	?
	F ← *add*(R0)	*branch always*	load
load:	R0 ← F	*branch always*	fetch

To begin at the end: every completed instruction must be followed by a fetch sequence that brings the next instruction into the instruction register IR. The last microinstruction in the sequence is therefore an unconditional branch to **fetch**, the address where the fetch sequence starts. Because the machine always works in a two-step sequence (fetch–execute–fetch–execute–fetch– ...), every instruction fetch must be followed by some action to be executed. What the action is depends on the instruction just fetched—indeed it *is* the instruction just fetched. The last microinstruction in the fetch sequence must therefore be followed by a branch to whichever microprogram corresponds to the machine instruction currently stored in the instruction register IR. Now the instruction register always contains the operation code for the required action, but it gives no hint as to where in microprogram memory the corresponding microinstruction sequence is located. The correspondence between machine instructions and microprogram addresses is established by consulting the *microprogram address table*, a small read-only memory (or a combinational logic circuit) that accepts a symbolic operation code as input and responds by furnishing the corresponding microprogram memory address at its output.

After a microinstruction has been executed, one of three factors will determine the next microinstruction address:

1. No branching is indicated; the microprogram counter advances to the next control memory address.
2. A branching within the current microprogram is indicated. The microprogram counter must be loaded with a new address taken from the address field within the microinstruction register.
3. Branching is indicated to a new microprogram, corresponding to a new machine instruction. The microprogram counter is loaded with a new address taken from the microprogram address table.

The two sorts of branches differ fundamentally. When branching *within* a microprogram, the next action to be performed is known because it is specified as part of the microprogram itself. When branching to a *new* microprogram, the current microprogram cannot know what comes next. It must be told; that is precisely the purpose of the instruction register IR and its associated microprogram address table. On the other hand, the microprogram can be made to know perfectly well whether a branch to an internally known address is required, or a branch to one supplied externally. One simple way of having it know is to extend the microinstruction word by an extra bit, to flag that an externally supplied address is expected.

Mechanisms suitable for implementing this scheme of address control are incorporated in Fig. 5.27. Here the condition codes in the microinstruction words are assumed to contain the extra flagging bit necessary to distinguish externally supplied branch addresses from internal ones. If set, this bit causes a multiplexer to be loaded from the microprogram address table instead of using the address given in the microinstruction register. If no branching is indicated, the *LOAD* line of the microprogram counter is not asserted and the multiplexer setting is irrelevant anyway.

Although the main outlines of microinstruction control are shown in Fig. 5.27, a great deal of detail has been suppressed. The design of control circuits is perhaps one of the most complex aspects of computer design, so it would be inappropriate to pursue it here at any great length. The essential point, common to all computing machines, is that every machine-language instruction is representable as a sequence of still more elementary microinstructions, with the individual microinstruction simple enough to allow direct implementation in logic circuit components.

Microprogramming and emulation

The control memory circuits and microinstruction set chosen for a computer system are almost invisible to their users. It is probably fair to say that users never write microcode, rarely look at machine language (binary) code, occasionally program in assembler language, and frequently employ a high-level language like Pascal or C. Computer hardware is incapable of actually executing anything but microinstructions, so programs written in any other form must undergo one or more stages of translation before being executed. A typical cascade of translation, from Pascal to machine execution, is outlined in Fig. 5.28.

If machine users never write microcode, they are not likely to know—or care—what microinstructions are actually executed by the hardware. This raises two intriguing possibilities. First, a single physical computer can be made to execute two or more different machine instruction sets by altering the contents of its control memory but leaving the machine otherwise unaltered. Second, two or more physically different computers can be made to appear identical to the programmer by suitably altering their control memories. The first possibility is often called *emulation* of one machine by another. It is valuable when changing from an old computer to a new one, for if the new machine can execute two

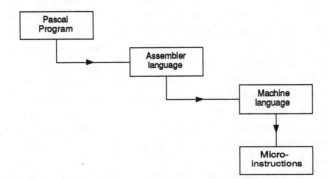

Fig. 5.28. Computer programs undergo successive stages of translation; only microcode can be executed by hardware.

different instruction sets, then users can take advantage of the new machine without altering any already existing programs written for the old one. The second, complementary, possibility has been exploited by several major computer manufacturers to produce entire ranges of computers, from quite small to very large, made of different components using different technologies, but indistinguishable from each other so far as the programmer is concerned because they share a common machine instruction set. Because their machine languages are identical, all machines in the range are able to execute the same programs, though obviously at different speeds and data capacities.

Computers instruction sets are often designed to suit a wide audience of users. If the computer is intended for a narrowly defined set of users, on the other hand, machine performance can often be improved by redesigning the instruction set. For example, computers intended for scientific use are usually programmed in Fortran, Pascal, C, or other languages that make heavy use of looping structures such as

```
for i := 1 to n do
    begin this(x, y, i);
          that(x, y, i) end
```

or

```
        DO 2 I = 1, N
        CALL THIS(X, Y, I)
    2   CALL THAT(X, Y, I)
```

Each time around such a loop, several machine instructions of a housekeeping nature must be executed:

1. Increment the loop counter i (probably kept in a register).
2. Compare i to the final value n.
3. Branch out of the loop if $i > n$.

In Simian or any comparable machine, this loop control will appear as three machine instructions (increment–compare–branch if zero); if the loop index is counted downward, two will suffice (decrement–branch if zero). Each time around the loop, two or three instructions must be fetched from main memory, decoded, and executed. Speed can be increased by creating a single "decrement and branch if zero" instruction because only one memory fetch cycle will be needed and the number of other register transfers can be reduced as well. Knowing the characteristics of scientific programs thus permits modifying the machine to do this one class of jobs better.

Some computers are designed with instruction sets containing several unused operation codes and have at least part of their control memories made of read-write memory. In other words, certain machine instructions are permanently built-in parts of the microprogram memory but others are left undefined, with blank microprogram memory into which users are free to write their own machine instruction definitions. Users are thus free to create machine instructions and thereby to redesign the computer to be better suited to their own purposes! Computers that permit their instruction sets to be reconfigured in this way are said to have *writable control memory* or to be *microprogrammable.*

Making effective use of microprogramming is a complicated task. Not only is microprogramming itself tricky and error-prone, it usually requires alteration of a great deal of supporting software as well. Microprogramming is of interest mainly to makers of specialized computer systems, only rarely to applications programmers or computer users.

Problems

1. Build a 4-bit ripple-through parallel adder, using the Apodix simulator. Determine experimentally the longest and shortest times for the correct result to appear.
2. Build a 4-bit carry look-ahead adder, using the Apodix simulator. Determine experimentally the longest and shortest times for the correct result to appear.
3. Verify the algebraic description of a single full adder cell,

$$c_{i+1} = a_i b_i + (a_i + b_i)c_i$$
$$s_i \;\; = a_i b_i \oplus (a_i + b_i) \oplus c_i,$$

by writing a program in Fortran or Pascal to generate the complete truth table corresponding to these expressions.
4. An MN-bit adder is built by connecting M carry look-ahead adders of N bits each, in the manner of Fig. 5.10. Find the maximum time required for an addition to be performed.
5. A ripple carry adder like that in Fig. 5.7 generates short-lived false sums while the circuit is still settling down. Devise circuits to ensure that the output of such an adder is not made available on the *sum* lines until the sum and carry out have been correctly computed. Test these by means of simulation.
6. A 16-bit adder is built by combining four units in the ripple carry manner, each unit being a 4-bit carry look-ahead adder. Draw a circuit diagram of such a circuit. How do its speed and complexity compare with a 16-bit carry look-ahead unit?
7. Find the complete truth table of a single-bit add/subtract cell such as shown in Fig. 5.12. How many functions can it perform? What are they?
8. An arithmetic and logic unit is built out of individual bit cells. What signal must be provided as *carry in* to the rightmost cell so as to make addition and subtraction possible?
9. An arithmetic and logic unit is built out of individual bit cells. What must be provided as *carry out* of the leftmost cell and *carry in* to the rightmost cell so as to make both arithmetic and logical shifts possible?
10. Design a combinational logic circuit that will accept as input the binary numbers 000 to 111 and cause, by appropriately setting its control lines, the following actions to be performed by the ALU of Figs. 5.15 to 5.17:

000 add A and B	100 shift right
001 subtract B from A	101 shift left
010 logical sum	110 shift A left, add B
011 logical product	111 shift A right, subtract B

Incorporate this combinational circuit in the arithmetic and logic unit simulation of Fig. 5.17 and test it.

11. Modify the arithmetic and logic unit of Fig. 5.17 to permit left and right rotations. Test the resulting ALU and prove that it works correctly.

12. The arithmetic and logic unit of Figs. 5.15 to 5.17 has five select lines so there are $2^5 = 32$ possible combinations of line settings. List them and tabulate the functions obtainable using all the 32 combinations of line settings. Verify by simulation. Which ones are useful in computing?

13. Construct a full arithmetic and logic unit with look-ahead carry, analogous to the ripple carry unit of Fig. 5.17. Simulate this unit so as to obtain results analogous to Fig. 5.17. In what respects, if any, is its performance superior to the ripple carry unit of Fig. 5.17?

14. A set of four 3-bit registers is connected to a bus structure comprising data lines, source select lines, and destination select lines, much like Fig. 5.22. Determine the sequence of operations required to copy the content of register 1 into register 3. Simulate this sequence of operations and prove that it works correctly for any data word placed in register 1.

15. Trace the precise sequence of register transfers required to execute the Simian instruction ADD.S R1, R0.

16. Specify the microprogram that corresponds to the Simian instruction OR.L [R6], /0D300.

17. Processor status register flag bits are affected by most Simian machine instructions. Which elementary register transfers should be permitted to affect the status flags? Why? How can these operations be distinguished so as to avoid resetting of flags by other microinstructions?

18. In addition to a central processing unit, many digital computers possess a *hardware multiply unit*. This device is a special-purpose processor with three externally accessible registers: the multiplier M and the multiplicand Q, each of k bits, and the product P, of $2k$ bits. Define the hardware architecture and microinstruction set for a multiplier unit usable with Simian.

19. *The circuit of Fig. 5.10 may be regarded as a 3-digit fifteens-complement adder.* Is this statement true? Amend it in any way that may be necessary to make it true. Redraw the figure in a notation or representation better suited to this statement.

20. Adding two integers in a programming language such as Fortran or Pascal may be regarded as equivalent to using an adder circuit of appropriate word length. Using the general structure indicated in Fig. 5.10, devise a method for adding two integers of 50 decimal digits each. Write a program in Fortran, Pascal, or C to implement this method, and show by means of appropriately chosen experiments that it works correctly for all integers within its number range.

21. Obtain from your library a manual for the model 6502 microprocessor that gives details of its instruction set. How does this instruction set compare with that of Simian? What main differences in processor structure are necessary to account for the differences in the instruction sets?

22. Write the microcode necessary to endow Simian with an additional instruction that strips the parity bit (bit 7) from a character placed in the low-order byte of its arithmetic and logic unit. How can you test the microcode steps to be sure they are correct, without access to Simian microcode?

6
Programming the Simian computer

Programs written in machine code or assembler language are useful only for a specific type of computer, for they describe the required computational steps in terms of the instruction set applicable to a specific machine. Conversely, the hardware structure of the machine is determined by the instruction set which it must be able to execute. The software and hardware thus affect each other through the instruction set and and through the register configuration which the machine makes available to the programmer. This chapter shows how the techniques of programming Simian are related to its registers and its instruction set; and conversely, how the hardware structure is tailored to suit the needs of the programmer.

Programming in assembler language

Very few programs are ever written in binary machine code. Indeed there is rarely any reason to do so, for the assembler language programmer has full control over the choice of registers and memory locations; the assembler only removes the drudgery of binary notation and location counting. This situation contrasts with programming in high-level languages, such as Pascal or Fortran, where the programmer is far removed from the hardware details and cannot even tell how many registers the processor has—if any! Programming in assembler language is therefore sometimes loosely called "programming in machine language."

The techniques of programming in assembler languages resemble those of programming in high-level languages, but they also include some peculiarities that arise from the programmer's more intimate contact with the machine.

Flow charting

Professional programmers often use *flow charts* to describe the structure of computer programs. Flow charts are graphic representations of control flow, showing the program steps in diagrammatic form. They consist of three main graphic figures:

> *rectangles,* which represent some *action,*
> *diamonds,* which represent *decision* and branching,
> *circles,*   which represent *terminal* points.

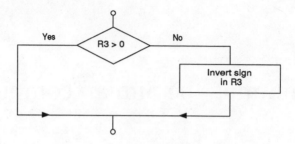

Fig. 6.1.   Flow chart representation of a program fragment to replace R3 content by its absolute value.

The rectangle, or *action*, always has exactly one entry point and one exit point—that is to say, it must always represent a sequence of operations which can only be entered in one way, and from which exit is possible at only one place. The *decision* diamond has one entry, and exactly two exit points; it always represents a pure decision and performs no actions that alter any data. The circles or *terminals* indicate entry and exit points, so the circular symbols themselves must have exactly one exit (at an entry terminal) or one entry (at an exit) but never more. These rules are illustrated by a simple example in Fig. 6.1, which shows a graphic representation of the program fragment discussed earlier by way of example: replace the content of register R3 by its absolute value. The entry and exit points are shown by circles. Which is the entry point, and which the exit, is ordinarily evident from context. Furthermore, it is conventional to show direction of flow on the chart by means of arrowheads, to obviate any possibility of misunderstanding.

Flow charts provide a convenient way of describing what programs do, without drowning the reader in details. Program listings are often hard to read, because they present all the details of a program without first indicating what its general outline is. Flow charts can exhibit structure without detail, and can do so at many levels. For example, it takes quite a few lines of assembler code to carry out a multiplication of two numbers; but in a flow chart, multiplication may be indicated by a single rectangular box. What is more, in the flow chart of a really large program the multiplication itself may be considered an unnecessary detail within a box called "compute velocity."

The most evident benefit of flow charts is that they permit program development by gradual refinement. Initially, the program designer may break down the overall job into a few rather complicated subsidiary jobs, each represented by an action box in a flow chart. Each action is then defined in more detail as a set of simpler actions and decisions, effectively replacing each action box by a flow chart that shows how the action is carried out. The actions in this refined flow chart are then refined in their turn, the stepwise refinement being continued until the individual boxes represent actions comprising only a few machine instructions. For example, the simple task of copying a string of 16 characters could be sketched out initially in a flow chart as shown in Fig. 6.2a, then coded

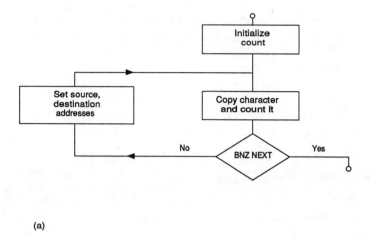

(a)

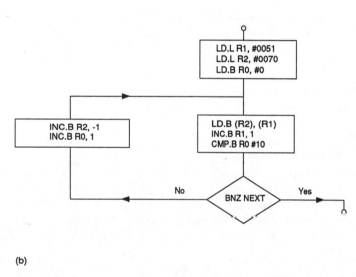

(b)

Fig. 6.2. Flow charts for the character copying task. (a) Verbally expressed. (b) Fully programmed.

as a program by defining each step in terms of machine instructions, as in Fig. 6.2b.

Flow charts have one major shortcoming as programming tools: they are graphical and therefore do not lend themselves readily to inclusion in program listings. They usually have to form a separate document, and some pains must be taken to ensure that any revisions or alterations in the program are correctly entered in the chart. If such updating is not conscientiously carried out, or if any mistakes are made in the process, the chart may conflict with the program list-ing, confusing the reader. This situation can easily be worse than having no flow chart at all!

In spite of their shortcomings, flow charts are useful design tools, particularly for large programs. It is rare indeed to find large programs designed without graphic aids. Even if the final program listings do not contain the flow charts, the charts do form part of the design process, and should therefore appear in the notebooks or design notes that record how the design came about in the first place.

An example: binary multiplication

Multiplication of two eight-bit numbers is a sufficiently complicated task to serve as an example of the program design process. The basic principle of integer multiplication by machine is the same as the principle of manual (pencil and paper) multiplication; any complications arise mainly in details and embellish-ments. To multiply two numbers by hand, say 01101010 and 00110001, the two are written down and the multiplicand is multiplied by every digit of the mul-tiplier in turn:

$$
\begin{array}{r}
01101010 \quad \times \quad 00110001 \\
\hline
00000000 \\
00110001 \\
00000000 \\
00110001 \\
00000000 \\
00110001 \\
00110001 \\
00000000 \\
\hline
001010001001010
\end{array}
$$

To mimic this process in a computer is not a good idea because eight inter-mediate results need to be stored. A better method is to accumulate the partial results into a total as soon as each partial result becomes available. Suppose M_1 and M_2 are the multiplier and the multiplicand, respectively, while A is the accu-mulated result. The above process can be modified, with A updated at every step:

$$
\begin{array}{ccc}
M_1 & M_2 & A \\
01101010 \quad \times \quad 00110001 & & \\
\hline
00000000 & & 00000000 \\
00110001 & & 001100010 \\
00000000 & & 0001100010 \\
00110001 & & 00111101010 \\
00000000 & & 000111101010 \\
00110001 & & 0100000001010 \\
00110001 & & 01010001001010 \\
00000000 & & 001010001001010 \\
\hline
& & 001010001001010
\end{array}
$$

The partial results at the left are now added into A as soon as they are computed. No further use is made of them. But they are never used again so there is no need to store them; they can be discarded as soon as they have been added to A. The result, of course, is the final value of A, the same value as obtained by the manual technique. To guarantee that A will not overflow the space available for it, the register in which A is stored must be twice as wide as the registers used to store the two factors M_1 and M_2.

The manual procedure for multiplication, modified as described, is readily adapted to machine computation. Suppose that the factors M_1 and M_2 are initially placed in registers R1 and R2, respectively, and that register R0 is used to accumulate the partial results A:

R0	R1	R2	
00000000	01101010	00110001	Starting values
00000000	*01101010*		Add 0 times R2 to R0;
00000000	*00110101*		shift R0 and R1 right.
00110001	*00110101*		Add 1 times R2 to R0;
00011000	*10011010*		shift R0 and R1 right.
00011000	*10011010*		Add 0 times R2 to R0;
00001100	*01001101*		shift R0 and R1 right.
00111101	*01001101*		Add 1 times R2,
00011110	*10100110*		shift again, . . .
. . . . . .	. . . . .		. . . .,
00010100	*01001010*		and shift the last time.

The steps in the work can then proceed as follows. The factor in R2 is multiplied by the trailing digit in R1 and added to R0. Then the *combination* of R0 and R1 is shifted right. The low-order bit in R1 is now the next multiplier digit to be taken care of, and the cycle is repeated: multiply the content of R2 by the low-order bit in R1, add to R0, then shift the combination of R0 and R1 right. This process is repeated as many times as there are bits in each register. It can be stated graphically as a flow chart, as shown in Fig. 6.3.

The multiplication shown in Fig. 6.3 places the resulting product in two registers, with R1 containing the low-order bits and R0 the high-order ones. Low-order digits of the multiplier are no longer needed once they have been used, so nothing is lost by shifting them out of R1. On the other hand, every shift lengthens the space available in R1 by one bit, so that the room available for the partial result (which must lengthen by one bit at each step) grows at just the right rate as the number of leftover digits in the multiplier diminishes. With this technique, a product twice the register length is formed. Multiplication of 32-bit numbers will therefore yield a result 64 bits long.

Flow charting the multiplication

Once a computing process is defined in outline form, as in Fig. 6.3, details need to be filled in. These are usually dependent on the machine instruction set to a

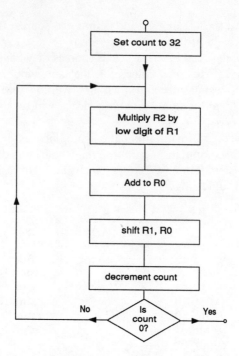

Fig. 6.3.   The 32-bit integer multiplication algorithm expressed as a flow chart.

much greater degree than the initial flow chart. The initial flow chart concentrates on recording *what* needs to be done, while the more detailed charts to follow must show *how* it is to be done. This progression is quite natural, for the design process must eventually lead from a broad idea about the method to actual lines of machine code.

Creation of increasingly detailed flow charts always follows the same path: action boxes are replaced by flow charts that break down the action into sequences of smaller actions and decisions. The obvious candidate for subdivision in Fig. 6.3 is the first action in the main loop, which actually performs the multiplication by a single digit. Multiplication by 1 is actually accomplished by merely copying the multiplicand, while multiplication by 0 amounts to doing nothing at all. The essential part of each multiplication step is therefore to decide whether to add the multiplicand to R0 or not. The basis for decision is the value of the least significant bit in R1: R2 is to be added to R0 if its value is 1, not otherwise. The simple box of Fig. 6.4a is thus refined into the details of Fig. 6.4b.

When the multiplicand digits are added to R0, a carry may propagate out of the high-order bit. The C bit must therefore be checked after addition so it can be restored after shifting if necessary. If not, negative products will be calculated incorrectly. To have the C bit correctly set after addition, zero is added to R0 if the multiplier digit is 0. The point is that *adding zero is not equivalent to doing nothing*. Doing nothing has no effect on the carry bit, whereas adding zero will reset it. Fig. 6.4b therefore shows additions in both its left and right branches.

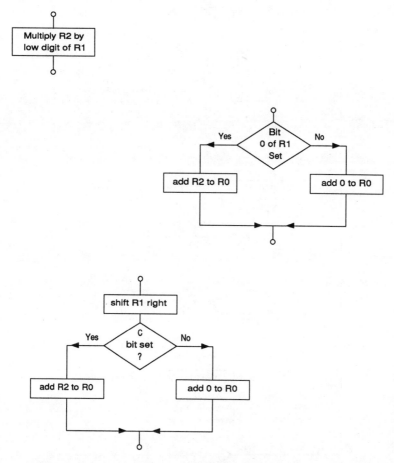

Fig. 6.4.   Successive refinement of an action block. (a) The need stated. (b) Two different add operations are required. (c) Value of the least significant bit of R1 is determined by examining the Z bit after shifting.

The next refinement of Fig. 6.4b is to ask how the decision regarding bit 0 of R1 is to be taken—in other words, to ask what more detailed figure should replace the decision diamond. All Simian branch instructions are conditional on settings of the processor status flags, so a way must be devised to set at least one flag so as to reflect the value of bit 0. Of the various ways, the simplest may well

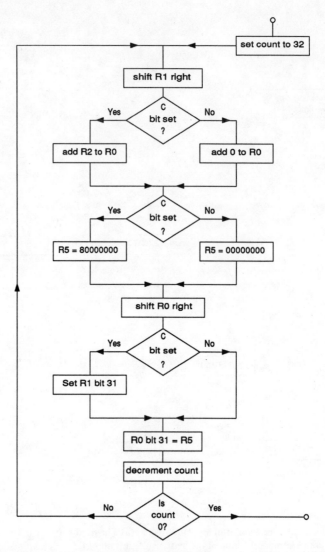

Fig. 6.5. The 32-bit integer multiplication algorithm, flow charted in sufficient detail for coding.

be to shift R1 right one bit position. All shifting operations in Simian give the C bit the same value as the last bit shifted out of the destination operand, so after

$$\text{SHL.L R1, -1}$$

the C bit will have the desired value. The flow chart of Fig. 6.4c incorporates this operation.

Shifting R1 to determine the proper multiplier digit alters its content, so it is next necessary to determine whether the content of R1 is required in any subsequent operation in Fig. 6.3. Fortunately, it is not; but R1 does enter into the joint shift of R1 and R0. Figure 6.4c therefore requires alteration of Fig. 6.3 to reflect that shifting R1 is no longer required. The box labeled "shift R1, R0" must therefore be replaced by one labeled "shift R0 and transfer its least significant bit into the most significant bit of R1." Following the same logic as above, such a transfer is actually rather easy. Shifting R0 right moves its least significant bit into the carry bit C, permitting branching: the high-order bit of R1 is set if C is set. These flow chart refinements (and others that remain to be discussed) finally lead to Fig. 6.5, which is at a level of detail quite sufficient for writing code.

The flow charts shown here apply to 32-bit integers, while the numerical example worked out above showed multiplication of eight-bit integers. The same procedure is clearly applicable to any other word lengths as well. The maximum length of the product is always twice the length of the factors, so two registers must invariably be treated as a unit. Because multiplication is a fairly common operation, especially in machines intended for scientific computing, some computers are actually built so that two registers can be chained as a double-length pair and handled with special instructions that address the pair.

From flow chart to code

The final flow chart of Fig. 6.5 is quite detailed, each action rectangle corresponding to no more than one or two machine instructions. It therefore permits almost direct transcription into code. Choosing registers and symbolic labels more or less arbitrarily, the following program results:

```
;       Multiplication of 32-bit twos complement integers.
;
;       Factors are placed in R1 and R2, result is in R0
;       (high order digits) and R1 (low order digits).
;       R4 and R5 are used as temporary storage registers.
;
.ORG 30
        LD.B R4, #20        ; Counter R4 = 32 bits.
MORE:   SHL.L R1, -1        ; Shift R1 so C = bit 0,
        BNC ZERO            ;     branch if it is 0.
        ADD.L R0, R2        ; Add factor to R0 if 1,
        BR CHEK             ;     else get C bit right
ZERO:   ADD.L R0, #0        ;     by adding zero.
CHEK:   LD.L R5, #0         ; Clear R5, then
        BNC SHFT            ;     check carry bit C.
        LD.L R5, #80000000  ; If C, set bit 31 of R5.
SHFT:   SHL.L R0, -1        ; Shift R0; C shows bit 0.
        BNC HIGH            ; Do nothing if no C, else
        OR.L R1, #80000000  ;     set bit 31 in R1.
```

```
HIGH:  OR.L R0, R5          ; Transfer R5 carry to R0.
       INC.B R4, -1         ; Count this round and
       BNZ MORE             ;   go back for the next!
       HALT                 ; Stop when finished.
.END
```

One interesting point in the flow chart of Fig. 6.5 is the handling of carries in addition. When the multiplicand in R2 is added to R0, a carry out of the most significant bit may occur. The extra bit does actually belong to R0 *as shifted right*, but it must be temporarily housed somewhere else until the shift takes place. In Fig. 6.5 it is dealt with by copying the value of the C bit into bit 31 of R5, restoring it to R0 later.

The flow chart shown here is not unique; neither is the corresponding assembler language program. Other ways of organizing the same fundamental method can lead to different charts, and different programs, with differing memory or computing time requirements. The program as shown takes approximately 650 machine cycles in the course of a 32-bit multiplication, about 20 each time around the main loop. Software designers spend considerable effort to economize on time in computations used so frequently as multiplication. Saving one or two instructions times is not a petty economy, not in an often-used program anyway. One instruction time saved in the main loop of a multiplication program amounts to a 5 percent increase in speed—or what is often equivalent, a 5 percent reduction in the cost of computation! (However, the same argument can obviously not be applied to programs used infrequently.) For example, loop control is here exercised by counting down from 32 to zero. As discussed previously, the alternative of up-counting would require an extra CMP.B operation and thus slow down the process.

Seemingly minor differences in the instruction sets of computers can make a great deal of difference in their operation. Consider, for example, a computer whose instruction set is identical to that of Simian except for one detail: it does not alter the carry bit when executing shifting (SHL or SHLA) instructions. The integer multiplication process must then use some other way of ascertaining and using the least significant bit of R1. One reasonable way is to make a copy of the number in R1 and to mask it so only its least significant bit survives:

```
       LD.L R3, R1          ; Make working copy of R1.
       AND.L R3, #1         ; Mask off bit 0.
```

The AND.L operation sets the Z bit if a zero results. Because the leading bits of R3 are known to be zero, the Z bit must now be the inverse of the least significant bit of R1. It can be tested and subsequent operations steered accordingly:

```
       BZ ZERO              ;     branch if zero.
       ADD.L R0, R2         ; Add multiplicand if not Z,
       BR CHEK              ;    else get C bit right
ZERO:  ADD.L R0, #0         ;    by adding zero.
CHEK:  ... whatever comes next ...
```

The same treatment can be given to R0 subsequently. The resulting multiplication program is much like that of Fig. 6.5, but involves four extra instructions!

It is worth noting that the comments accompanying the machine instructions in this example indicate, among other things, which registers have been used in carrying out the work. This practice is generally a good one, for code segments of general use are often employed by people other than their original programmers. Knowing which register contents are likely to survive unaltered, and which ones will likely be destroyed, allows the user to secure any data that might be needed after the multiplication has been carried out.

Comments and documentation

Assembler language programs by their very nature are lengthy. They usually contain many instructions, each of which performs only some very minor piece of work. They are therefore very hard to read, for even if every single instruction is crystal clear, the overall purpose of a program can still be very difficult to discern. Verbal comments included with the program text are therefore an extremely important part of any assembler language program. Because the individual program steps are simple, a competent programmer might even prefer a full set of line-by-line comments without instructions than the instructions without comments! It can be easier to recreate the program from comments than to decipher and understand uncommented code.

Good commenting of programs really amounts to good writing, since the comments are directed to human readers only. Some good programmers indeed say that comments should be nothing more than flow charts expressed in words, and back up this view by writing the comments first, then filling in code afterward! Commenting should ideally be done on two levels: line-by-line and block-by-block. The latter should state what a particular block of code is intended to do, and how. The line-by-line comments should clarify why actions are being taken, not just what is being done. For example, in the program segment

```
;       Initialization: Set up source and destination
;       addresses   and use R0 as a character counter.
;
        LD.L R1, #0051      ; Source array starts at 0051,
        LD.L R2, #0070      ; destination array at 0070.
        LD.B R0, #0         ; Counting starts at zero.
```

the commentary says something about why the instructions do what they do. On the other hand, in the computationally identical program segment

```
;       Initialization: Set up R1 and R2 with correct
;       values to start and clear R0 before beginning .
;
        LD.L R1, #0051      ; Place #0051 in R1, then
        LD.L R2, #0070      ; place #0070 in R2 to start.
        LD.B R0, #0         ; Clear R0 to zero.
```

the comments only repeat the code itself. Such commentary really contributes nothing to understanding the program. It might just as well not be there at all.

In this very brief example, there are as many lines devoted entirely to comments as there are lines containing code. This proportion is quite appropriate to much longer programs as well. Clarifying comment-only lines are an excellent form of descriptive documentation. It is sometimes tempting to write clarifying comments on printed program listings by hand, especially while the process of catching and correcting errors is still going on. Unfortunately, the handwritten comments do not survive reprinting, while all comments entered into the file in machine-readable form do.

A sad fact of life is that very few programmers, even highly experienced professionals, are able to read uncommented code—including their own code written only a few weeks ago! Comments are therefore a vital part of programming. An unreadable program is most often an unusable program, and can be worse than worthless because it may appear to satisfy requirements without actually doing so.

String concatenation

Alphabetic text is often stored in the form of *character strings*, sequences of characters with a known beginning address but unknown length, terminating in a null byte. The character string "*a dog*" might be stored, for example, as

Hex	ASCII	address
61	a	0047
20		0048
64	d	0049
6F	o	004a
67	g	004b
00	null	004c

It would be ordinarily referred to as "the string beginning at address 47" or simply as "the string at 47."

Computer-based text processing involves various operations on strings. One common operation is *concatenation*, which produces a single string out of two by placing them end to end. (The next most common is probably the *comparison* of two strings, to determine which should take precedence in an alphabetic ordering.)

Concatenation of two strings can be carried out in the obvious way, by copying characters out of the first string until it is exhausted, then copying characters from the second until no more remain. To consider a concrete example, suppose the address of one string (say *S1*) resides in register R1, the address of the second (*S2*) is in R2. The resulting string *S0* is to be located at the address in register R0. One way of proceeding is to regard the operation as two successive character copying tasks, as sketched in Fig. 6.6. Here string *S1*, *without its terminating null character*, is copied to the output first, *S2* thereafter.

The flow chart of Fig. 6.6 contains two quite similar action boxes that append a string to an existing one. These can be refined in turn, as in Fig. 6.7.

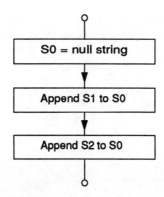

Fig. 6.6. String concatenation involves two successive character copying operations.

Instead of refining the flow chart until it becomes large and cumbersome, many programmers prefer to leave program segments like that shown in Fig. 6.7 in separate charts and to code these directly, then build up the whole program out of segments. The code for Fig. 6.7 reads

```
        LD.L R4,  destination string
        LD.L R3,  source string address
REPT:   LD.B [R4], [R3]        ; Move one character.
        CMP.B [R4], #0         ; Check if it's null.
        BZ NEXT               ; Copy no more if so,
        INC.L R3, 1           ;   or else increment
        INC.L R4, 1           ;   both pointers and
        BR REPT              ;   keep repeating.
NEXT:
... whatever comes next ...
```

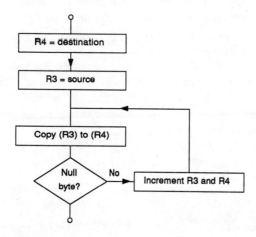

Fig. 6.7. Building a composite string by appending one string to another.

Repeating this segment twice, initializing at the beginning and appending the terminating null byte at the end, the code for string concatenation then becomes

```
;                    String concatenation program
;
;           Forms a character string, beginning at the
;           address in R0, out of the string beginning at
;           the addresses in R1 and R2.    Uses R3 and R4
;           as working registers.
.ORG 30
        LD.L R4, R0              ; Start output string.
        LD.L R3, R1              ; First input string.
REP1:   LD.B [R4], [R3]         ; Move one character.
        CMP.B [R4], #0          ; Check if it's null.
        BZ NEXT                 ; Copy no more if so,
        INC.L R3, 1             ;   or else increment
        INC.L R4, 1             ;   both pointers and
        BR REP1                 ;   keep repeating.
NEXT:   LD.L R3, R2             ; Second input string.
REP2:   LD.B [R4], [R3]         ; Move one character.
        CMP.B [R4], #          ; Check if it's null.
        BZ DONE                 ; Copy no more if so,
        INC.L R3, 1             ;   or else increment
        INC.L R4, 1             ;   both pointers and
        BR REP2                 ;   keep repeating.
DONE:   HALT                    ; All finished!
.END
```

One key to success in this program is that the destination address is kept in register R4 on a running basis. It does not need to be reset after the first string has been copied; only the source register address is changed (in the line labeled NEXT).

The concatenation program spends almost all of its time in one or the other of two similar loops, which typically execute six instructions. The processor throughput (the amount of useful work it can do in unit time) can be increased by reducing the number of instructions per loop. One way of doing so is to design the machine instruction set cleverly. For example, were the LD.B instruction to manipulate the Z bit (it does not do so in Simian), one CMP.B instruction could be saved per character copied, a speed increase of about 17 percent. Another way, not dependent on the instruction set, is to reorganize the program loop. As shown above, the loops contain two branching instructions. Only one can be made to serve:

```
        INC.L R4, -1            ; Destination pointer R4:
REPT:   INC.L R4, 1             ; Increment destination,
        LD.B [R4], [R3]         ;   move one character.
        INC.L R3, 1             ; Increment source.
        CMP.B [R4], #0          ; If it wasn't null,
        BNZ REPT                ;   keep repeating.
```

This approach increases speed by another 17 percent (one instruction in six). An extra instruction INC.L R4, −1 is needed before looping, however, because incrementing R4 *before* the character is moved means that R4 must be started with a value one lower than the true address. (An initial decrementation of R3 is not needed because R3 is incremented *after* each character is moved.) However, this extra instruction is only executed once, not once for every character.

Data input and output

Most computers need to communicate frequently with the outside world. Although some special-purpose machines rarely transfer data to external devices, they are really the exceptions that prove the general rule: *computation always implies communication.* Any serious examination of computers must therefore include the processes of moving data into computers and out again, processes usually referred to as *input–output operations.*

Input–output operations are probably the most diverse area of computer technology, for many different kinds of input and output devices are commonly used with computers.

Input and output units

Most computers possess at least one input and one output unit, so data can be moved into the machine as well as out. Input units may be manually operated, as keyboards or graphics tablets are; or they may serve for reading machine-accessible information only, as magnetic tape readers do. Output units may be intended for the human eye (printers, display screens), may produce computer-readable records (magnetic tapes or disks), or may even be of a highly specialized nature (traffic lights, door latches, fire alarm sirens). General-purpose computers normally possess at least a keyboard and a display screen or printer, and possibly other devices. Specialized computers may communicate in strange ways indeed; for instance, the tiny computer embedded in a digital watch ordinarily has one or two push buttons for input, while its output consists of a numeric display that operates in a mixed-base notation (partly base 12, partly base 60)! Input–output devices are commonly also called *peripheral devices,* implying that they are attached to the external *periphery* of the computer system, while the central processing unit and memory occupy the *central* position in processing and moving data.

Simian is a general-purpose computer and receives its input from an input device which furnishes a stream of characters. Whether the physical input unit is a keyboard or some device capable of reading files matters little to the computer designer; the main issue is that it is a *character-oriented device.* The main characteristics of importance are (a) one character arrives at a time and (b) it is not possible to predict how long an interval will elapse between characters. The

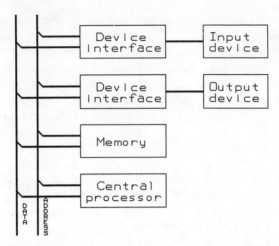

Fig. 6.8.   Many small and medium computer systems use a single system bus for internal communication as well as for external device interfacing.

Simian output unit may be character printer or a file writing device; again, its key distinguishing characteristic is its ability to accept and print one character at a time. Many computers are able to communicate also with other kinds of device, but these will not be discussed in this section.

Every physical input or output unit is connected to Simian (or to any other computer) through a set of electronic circuits termed the *interface logic*, or the *device interface*. This set of circuits monitors all communications between computer and peripheral device, to ensure error-free transfer of data. Each peripheral device is connected to the central processor through a separate interface, designed to suit that particular device. In small computers, device interfaces are usually connected to the system bus (external bus), as shown in Fig. 6.8. As already discussed in detail, the system bus comprises address, data, and control lines. Device interfaces connected in this fashion may take data directly from the bus, or supply data to the bus. Communication between device interfaces and the bus itself is bidirectional, as in Fig. 6.8, even where the physical input or output unit is not. Bidirectional information flow is necessary for controlling data transfer. For example, a printer might serve as the output device in Fig. 6.8. Although no input can be expected from a printer, the device interface still must be able to report how data transfers are proceeding, at least to the extent of notifying the CPU the printer has been turned off and is not printing at all!

When several device interfaces share a bus with the central processing unit, memory, and possibly other internal units, a pleasingly simple way of identifying input–output units is to assign them memory addresses, just as if they were memory locations. Addresses are then placed on the bus address lines to identify not only the actual computer memory, but also any other devices. In fact, in some computer handbooks the addresses of memory locations are not referred to as memory addresses but as *bus addresses* to emphasize this point. Because two distinct devices cannot share the same address, any addresses allocated to the peripheral devices cannot be used for memory as well. This reduction in the total number of available addresses is rarely a problem, for even a large computer system is unlikely to include more than a few hundred peripheral devices, while memory address spaces typically range from many thousands to billions.

The single-bus scheme of Fig. 6.8 is simple in physical construction and convenient to the programmer. Its main disadvantage is that the system bus also serves as the CPU-to-memory data transfer path, so traffic on the bus can become quite congested if input, output, and memory operations all need to take place at the same time. Many large computing systems avoid such problems by using two or more separate buses. Two or more independent data transfers may then be able to take place concurrently. Of course, there is a price to be paid in both complexity and cost.

Printing characters with Simian

Simian peripheral device interfaces are connected to the system bus and assigned bus addresses, so every peripheral device appears to the central processor as if it were memory. For example, the Simian output device (printer) interface is able to accept exactly one byte at a time, for the printer is only able to deal with single characters; this one-byte information channel replaces the memory byte at address 0000000C. The instruction

```
LD.B /0C, R6
```

appears merely to copy the content of register R6 into memory, but actually causes the low-order byte of R6 to be sent to the output. In other words, it causes the ASCII character whose binary representation resides in the low-order byte of R6 to be printed. In the Simian simulator, output is displayed on the screen and also written into an output file which can be printed later, echoing exactly the printing actions that would have taken place with a direct printer connection. However, using a file as an intermediate medium provides a major advantage: all characters written into the file can be examined individually, even if they are not printable and would therefore not show up in printed output.

Writing into byte 0C of Simian causes the relevant character to be printed as soon as the printer is able to do so—which in most practical cases means as soon as it has finished printing the previous character. The output interface logic circuit detects the arrival of a new character at 0C, enables it for output, and notes that it has been printed so as to ensure it is not printed a second time when the printing mechanism next becomes available.

Printing single characters is not a common task. It is much more usual to print out whole words or lines of text. Printing out a string of characters is of course equivalent to printing a sequence of individual characters, so that a line of (say) 52 characters is printed by successively moving each of the 52 characters into memory location 0C. Suppose, for example, that the 52 characters represent the upper and lower case alphabets, useful for a printer test, and that they are placed in memory locations 050 to 084 (hexadecimal). They may be loaded into 0C in succession (in other words, printed out) by the following program segment.

```
.LOAD 10
04 03 ; 0010           LD.B R0, #34       ; 2 alphabets = 52,
34
0C 33 ; 0013           LD.L R1, #50       ;     start at 050.
00 00 00 50
C2 43 ; 0019 NEXT:     LD.B /C, [R1]      ; Send character,
00 00 00 0C
08 3A ; 001f           INC.L R1, 1        ; point to next,
04 0A ; 0021           INC.B R0, -1       ; count.
F7 8C ; 0023           BNZ NEXT           ; Back if not done!
FF F2
FF FF ; 0027           HALT
.LOAD 50
48 47 46 45 44 43 42 41                   ; The uppercase
50 4F 4E 4D 4C 4B 4A 49                   ;   alphabet is
58 57 56 55 54 53 52 51                   ;   at A = 041.
66 65 64 63 62 61 5A 59                   ; Small letters
6E 6D 6C 6B 6A 69 68 67                   ;   go from a =
76 75 74 73 72 71 70 6F                   ;   061 up to z
7A 79 78 7                                ;   at 07a.
.PROG 10
.FINI
```

The programmer who tries this scheme is likely to be disappointed, for after execution of the code segment above, only a part of the expected run of characters will appear printed on the paper! The flaw is not in the programming, but rather in the failure to observe *machine timings*.

Central processor instructions are executed, on the average, in about 5–10 clock cycles (also called *clock ticks*) each. In present-day small and medium computers, with clock speeds in the range 5–50 MHz, an instruction may thus be executed in half a microsecond or a microsecond. Sending a single character to memory location 0C takes four machine instructions (LD.B, INC.L, INC.B, BNZ) and therefore consumes about three microseconds in a typical computer. On the other hand, a medium-speed character printer is able to print some 100 characters per second, i.e., one character every ten milliseconds. These speeds are quite different; the program shown above moves all 52 characters to the printer in 52 times $3 * 10^{-6}$ seconds, or 0.15 millisecond—about one-sixtieth of the time actually needed to print one of them! The characters follow so fast on each other's heels that the printer will be unable to deal with more than the first and the last; the last character is transmitted while it is still busy beginning to print the first one.

The Simian simulator behaves in much the same manner as a real computer, but on a different time scale. Simian typically executes one instruction per second, so it runs about 10^6 times slower than the real computer. Slowing down character output by a corresponding amount would mean printing one character every 10^4 seconds (roughly, one character every four hours). To avoid wasting time, the Simian output device is made very fast, able to operate in about the time needed to execute five or ten machine instructions. Loading the above program into Simian and running it produces the output

`BEKLMOPRSTVWefghiklpqwx`

instead of two complete alphabets. More than half the characters are lost because even a fast output device is unable to keep up with the central processor. A typical character printer as used with small computers, a much slower device, might yield

`Az`

because the printer would proceed to deal with A as soon as it arrived, and would find z waiting when it had finished with A!

Speed matching

The small case study shown above illustrates the major problem of practically all input–output operations in computers. Every peripheral device, as well as the central processor, has its own natural working speed, and no two devices can communicate successfully unless they are prepared to do so at a speed and rhythm agreeable to both. Working speeds can only be made equal by slowing down the faster device of the communicating pair. It must be slowed enough to lock the faster device into synchronism with the natural working speed of the slower one. There are various techniques for doing so. The simplest of these is very straightforward: the faster device is made to wait whenever the slower one is busy.

A printing device or terminal operates relatively slowly and can only keep up with the central processor if the processor is held back long enough after each character to allow time for printing. For example, the printing sequence in the above example can be made successful by forcing the central processor to send out characters several times slower than it naturally would. It is not possible to have the processor do nothing at all for a predetermined time; but it can be made to perform some fixed sequence of harmless actions, such as counting. For example, the printer of the above example can be made to print successfully by making the processor count down from 8 to 0 after transmitting each character, as follows:

```
04 03 ; 0010        LD.B R0, #34     ; 2 alphabets = 52,
34
0C 33 ; 0013        LD.L R1, #60     ;    start at 060.
00 00 00 60
C2 43 ; 0019 NEXT:  LD.B /C, [R1]    ; Send character.
00 00 00 0C
14 03 ; 001f        LD.B R2, #8      ; Idling counter:
08
14 0A ; 0022 IDLE:  INC.B R2, -1     ; decrement count,
F7 8C ; 0024        BNZ IDLE         ; for 8 steps.
```

```
FF FA
08 3A ; 0028        INC.L R1, 1        ; Point to next,
04 0A ; 002a        INC.B R0, -1       ; count.
F7 8C ; 002c        BNZ NEXT           ; Back if not done!
FF E9
FF FF ; 0030        HALT
```

Character transmission with this scheme is successful with Simian.

This scheme is not often used in practice because it has two serious shortcomings. It is device dependent: a time delay that suffices for one printer may not be enough for another. Perhaps more seriously, the scheme is inefficient in its use of both the processor and the printer, because the time delay must be chosen to allow for the *worst* possible case. For example, if the printer employs a moving type-wheel, the delay time must at least equal the time taken for the *longest* movement of the printing element. If the printer uses a moving carriage (similar to a typewriter), the slowest motion is usually the carriage return movement that precedes a new line; the delay must allow for that relatively slow process. In this way, the average speed of operation is certain to be slower than the average speed the printer is capable of achieving. It is interesting to experiment with Simian to see how low the idling count can be dropped before characters are lost. But even at its best, the printing is still painfully slow.

Device status

Although a fast central processor inevitably needs to wait for a slow peripheral device to complete its work, it is nonetheless desirable to make the waiting time the shortest practicable. A common way to minimize waiting time is to pass a signal between the two communicating devices so that the slower partner can request the faster one to send information when, and only when, it is ready to receive. This way of controlling the waiting times requires a second communication channel, along which information can be transmitted about the *status* of the slower device; it typically accounts for the two-way arrows in Fig. 6.8.

For successful control of a simple printer, only one binary signal is required, in addition to the eight-bit channel that transmits the actual character itself. In Simian, the byte at address 0D is employed as the output device *status register*, with bit 0 the only bit actually used; it is set to 1 if the printer is busy, reset to 0 if the printer is ready to accept a character. Before sending any character to the printer, the program that does the sending is expected to check whether the printer is ready. In other words, the processor uses 0C as the register into which to write data, and memory location 0D as an acknowledgment channel along which printer status information is communicated. The content of the *printer data register* 0C is only ever altered by the processor whereas the content of 0D, the printer status register, is altered by the printer interface electronics without any action by the processor. In fact, from the programmer's point of view 0D probably should be thought of as read-only memory! With this arrangement, a typical hardware event sequence during printing runs as follows.

Status	*Data*	*Event*
— 0D —	— 0C —	
00000000	????????	Interface can receive, shows *ready*
00000000	00100001	Processor writes data to 0000000C.
00000001	00100001	Interface shows 0000000D to be *busy.*
00000001	00100001	Printing: continued *busy*
00000000	00100001	when finished, interface shows *ready*
00000000	00100100	Processor writes next character,
00000001	00100100	interface changes 0000000D to *busy.*

The program mechanism used to achieve waiting is in principle similar to that used above, where time delays were fixed: the processor simply idles in a short program loop until ready. This time, however, there is no need to do any counting. Instead, the wait loop repeatedly compares the content of location 0D to zero, then initiates action as soon as the printer is no longer busy:

```
04 03 ; 0024         LD.B R0, #34        ; 2 alphabets = 52,
34
0C 33 ; 0027         LD.L R1, #50        ;    start at 050.
00 00 00 50
C4 02 ; 002d WAIT:   CMP.B /0D, #0       ; Output busy?
00 00 0D 00
00
F7 8C ; 0034         BNZ WAIT            ; Loop if yes.
FF F5
C2 43 ; 0038         LD.B /C, [R1]       ; If not, send,
00 00 00 0C
08 3A ; 003e         INC.L R1, 1         ; point to next,
04 0A ; 0040         INC.B R0, -1        ; count.
F7 8C ; 0042         BNZ WAIT            ; Back if not done!
FF E7
FF FF ; 0046         HALT
```

Halting as shown here is actually not a good idea, for exactly the same reasons of timing as required a waiting loop in the first place: there is no guarantee that the *last* character to be printed will have been printed successfully by the time the processor halts. It is therefore wise not to terminate abruptly with a HALT instruction, but to wait in a test loop until the last character has been printed:

```
C4 02 ; 0052 WAIT:   CMP.B /0D, #0       ; Printer ready?
00
00 00 00 0D
F7 8C ; 0057         BNZ WAIT            ; If not, ask again.
FF F5
FF FF ;0059          HALT
.PROG 20
.FINI
```

Here halting is delayed until all the printer reports that all activity has ceased.

The form of communication control illustrated here is usually referred to as *polled input/output* operation, because the device interface is interrogated or *polled* at intervals to determine whether it is prepared to receive data. Alternatively, it is referred to as *program-controlled input/output*, because data transmission timing is controlled by the program itself.

Extended simulator facilities

The Simian simulator allows polled output techniques to be investigated experimentally. In real computing environments, printing is *asynchronous* with computation—there is no way to know exactly how long the printer will take to output any given character. Simian goes some way toward realism in this regard, by making the printer response time vary randomly within a moderate range. Its mean delay is about five instruction times but the actual times taken can vary both up and down from that value. This variation is clearly evident in the experiment described above, where successive characters are simply loaded into the Simian output data byte. Over half the characters are lost, but there is no clear pattern to which are lost and which transmitted. On some occasions, the delays are short and successive characters are actually printed; at other times the delays are longer and several characters in a row are lost.

Simian shows the output that actually reaches the external world in a one-line display in its *external* window. The line initially begins with a highlighted arrow, so that blanks appearing in the output are discernible even if not preceded by any other character. As the window fills, the arrow eventually disappears; the effect is similar to reading ticker tape. Larger quantities of output can be captured for later examination or processing by attaching a writable file to the output port. Simian permits file attachment with the *file* command, as in

file out *filename*

where *filename* is any valid file name. A similar command, but with the file name omitted, detaches the file subsequently. Whenever an output file is attached, its name is displayed in the Simian status window.

Nonprintable characters—indeed any bytes whatever—are accepted by the Simian output and written into the output file, but any byte that does not represent a printable character is displayed as the commercial *at*-sign @ in the output window. Output files, on the other hand, will contain all line feed, form feed, and other control characters exactly as they are produced at the output data port, so that a subsequent listing of the file will have precisely the appearance intended by the programmer.

Simian input follows general principles similar to those that apply to output. There is a one-line display a few characters long and files may be attached to the input data port. Input will be dealt with in later sections; for the moment, it will suffice to note that in most respects Simian provides comparable facilities for both input and output.

Number conversion

The Simian output device writes each outgoing character to a file and also displays it on the terminal screen. Like a common character printer, this device can only handle one character at a time. It is therefore only able to write out data arranged in character format. Much of the work done by digital computers, however, deals with numbers, encoded in one of several forms. For numbers to be printed out by the printer, they must first be converted into character strings. The details of doing so vary with the type of numeric encoding, and are perhaps best explained by means of an illustrative example.

Suppose bits 15–0 of register R0, interpreted as a 16-bit unsigned integer, are to be printed out in octal notation. The output device, in other words, will need to be sent a sequence of six 8-bit characters, one corresponding to each octal digit, with the most significant digit first. Binary to octal conversion is easy; it suffices to take the bits of the integer three at a time, and to substitute the appropriate octal digit for each group of three bits. For example,

the binary number	0	010	100	101	010	011
in octal notation is	0	2	4	5	2	3

The printer thus needs to be fed the ASCII character codes for the numeral characters 0, 2, 4, 5, 2, 3 in that order. The leading octal digit corresponds to only one bit, so it can only have the value 0 or 1.

Octal numbers are represented using the numerals 0 through 7. The ASCII character representations of these eight are as follows:

$$0 \text{ is represented as } 00110000 \text{ or } 48_{10} = 30_{16}$$
$$1 \text{ is represented as } 00110001 \text{ or } 49_{10} = 31_{16}$$
$$\cdots \cdots$$
$$7 \text{ is represented as } 00110111 \text{ or } 55_{10} = 37_{16}.$$

It is easy to see that the ASCII code for each octal digit may be obtained by adding 30_{16} to the numeric value of the digit. Thus, only a very simple numeric manipulation is required. This suggests that the conversion can be carried out by separating the number into 3-bit groups, and adding each three-bit group in turn to 30_{16}. Of course, the groups must be taken *from the left*, i.e., the most significant digits first, for that is the conventional sequence of printing. Furthermore, the very first digit must be given special treatment; it contains only a single binary digit, for a 16-bit number cannot be subdivided into three-bit groups exactly.

Details of a program to achieve binary to octal conversion are given in Fig. 6.9. The essence of this process is that the number in R0 is rotated so as to bring successive three-bit groups into the low-order bit positions, and the content of R0 is then copied to R1. Register R1 is then cleared except the three low-order bits, the ASCII character is formed by adding 030. The digits are counted as they are printed, the process being stopped after the sixth digit. The maverick first digit is dealt with separately. The number in R0 is obviously corrupted as successive rotations take place, but since the total amount of leftward rotation for the six octal digits amounts to exactly 16 bits, R0 regains its original content by the time the printing is finished. R1 is used as a processing register, sometimes also referred to as a *scratch* register, and contains nothing useful when the job is

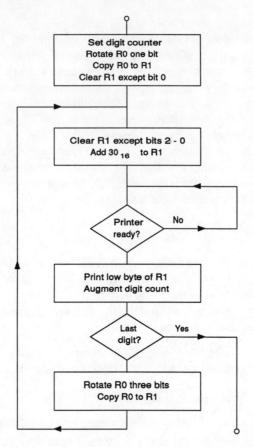

Fig. 6.9.   The character conversion process for printing out short unsigned integers in octal notation.

done; similarly for R2, which is used as a counter for the digits. It might be noted that the content of R2 is never compared to zero as work proceeds; that is unnecessary, for the incrementation instruction will affect the Z bit anyway. The assembler code for this task runs as follows:

```
.LOAD 20
; Print unsigned short integer in R0 as 6 octal digits.
;
14 03 ; 0020          LD.B R2, #6      ; Digit counter,
06
;                          Set up bit 15:
00 16 ; 0023          ROL.S R0, 1      ; Rotate high to low,
08 13 ; 0025          LD.S R1, R0      ; copy work register.
0C 14 ; 0027          AND.S R1, #1     ; Clear all but bit 0
00 01
```

```
;                                        Main computation:
0C 14  ; 002b CHAR: AND.S R1, #07     ; Clear high bits,
00 07
0C 10  ; 002f        ADD.S R1, #30    ;   add 30 for ASCII.
00 30
C4 02  ; 0033 WAIT: CMP.B /0D, #      ; Printer ready?
00
00 00 00 0D
F7 8C  ; 003a        BNZ WAIT         ; If not, ask again.
FF F5
C0 43  ; 003e        LD.B /0C, R1     ; Move the character,
00 00 00 0C
14 0A  ; 0044        INC.B R2, -1     ;   count it;
F7 CC  ; 0046        BZ EXIT          ;   exit if done.
00 08
00 96  ; 004a        ROL.S R0, 3      ; Position next 3
08 13  ; 004c        LD.S R1, R0      ;   for printing
FF CC  ; 004e        BR CHAR          ;   and go do it.
FF D9
FF FF  ; 0052 EXIT: HALT
.PROG 20
.FINI
```

Of course there is no need to stop the processor at the exit point; other useful actions may be required after the octal number has been printed.

Full-length (32-bit) unsigned integers, or byte-length integers, can be dealt with in a similar fashion. Printing in hexadecimal or decimal notations follows the same general principle, but involves more processing; so does the printing of signed integers, which must be represented in sign and magnitude notation. The octal conversion is probably the easiest of all; for other number bases, a slightly longer run of code will be needed.

Data input

Input procedures used by Simian follow the same principles as output. There is a difference, however: in one case the slower device is the receiver, in the other case the sender. When sending output, the central processor is responsible for establishing synchronization and it does so by simply withholding information from the printer whenever necessary.The corresponding form of input control requires the input device, which is now the sender, to withhold information from the central processor. But the input device, which might typically be a key-board, has no processing ability so it cannot establish waiting loops or time delays; it cannot hold back information but must instead ask the central processor to curb its appetite for data. Status messages may therefore need to flow in both directions, not only from receiver to sender. Why and how is probably best seen by considering Simian input in some detail.

The input device available to Simian is a character reader that extracts individual characters from a file and presents them to the processor one at a time.

It resembles a keyboard in many respects: characters are available one at a time and each one remains available only until the next arrives. Simian uses two one-byte registers for handling input. These appear to the processor as memory locations: a data register at 0A and a status register at 0B. Although they have memory addresses, these locations are actually not bytes in main memory but registers in the input device interface. The interface circuits place characters into the data byte and flag their arrival by setting the least significant bit of the status byte at 0B, much as their output counterparts remove characters from the data byte at 0C and flag their departure by resetting the least significant bit of 0D.

When printing output, the receiving unit must declare to the sender (i.e., the printer must tell the central processor) when it is ready to receive the next character; the sending unit must not transmit it until the receiver is ready. To do likewise with input requires two distinct information channels. One is needed for informing the sending device (the keyboard or reader) that the receiving device (the processor) is unoccupied and ready to accept input. The other channel is required to inform the receiver that a new character is available. A third channel is usually employed as well, to signify exceptional conditions; the most usual of these is an end of file, with no input remaining. Because all three messages are of a yes–no nature, one bit in the device status register suffices for each. Bits 2, 1, and 0 of the status byte serve these three functions; they are called the *enable* bit, the *end-of-file* bit, and the *character available* bit. When set, the character available bit signifies that an as yet unprocessed (i.e., newly arrived) character is located in the data register; reading that register also resets the character available bit. When printing, the printer must remind the device interface when it is ready to deal with a new character; no information corresponding to the enable bit is necessary or visible to the central processor. When taking input, however, it is precisely the central processing unit that must inform the device interface whenever another character is desired. It must therefore manipulate the *enable* bit so as to control the sequence of events. A typical character transfer therefore proceeds somewhat as follows:

Status	*Data*	*Event*
— 0B —	— 0A —	
00000100	????????	CPU sets enable bit to ask for data.
00000001	00100001	Interface has character, shows *ready*.
00000000	00100001	After reading interface resets bit 0.
00000100	????????	CPU sets enable bit to ask for data.
00000001	00100101	Interface has new character, . . .

The enable bit is reset by the device interface at the same time as the character available bit is set. By this means, the device interface ensures that only one character is transferred each time the central processor requests one. Thus the enable bit is normally set by the central processor, reset by the device interface. In contrast, the character available bit is always updated by the device interface, never by the central processor.

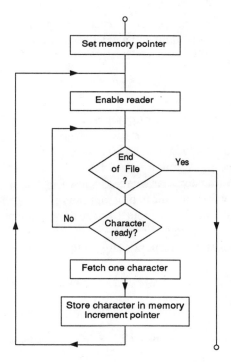

Fig. 6.10. Basic form of the character read-and-store program. Note that end-of-file must be checked before attempting to read characters.

Character reading

To illustrate the techniques followed in accepting input, consider the following example. A file of characters is to be read from the Simian input device, the characters being stored in sequential memory locations beginning at 05A. The input file is short, about 50 bytes, so there is no need to check whether memory has been exhausted.

The principle of operation here is simple. One character is read at a time and placed in memory, at a location pointed to by an addressing pointer; the pointer is then incremented. This action is repeated until the file is exhausted. A rough outline flow chart of this process appears in Fig. 6.10. As already discussed, the reader is automatically disabled when a character is brought from the input file. The reader therefore needs to be explicitly enabled to read a character, but no steps need be taken to disable it. Once enabled, the reading mechanism proceeds to fetch a character from file and place it in the input data register. This is a comparatively slow process and may take an unknown amount of time, so the central processor is obliged to wait for its completion to be flagged.

Waiting for the incoming character is accomplished in precisely the same way as during output: a waiting loop is made to check for character availability over and over again, until an input character shows up. To enable the reader, bit 2 in the input status register must be set. This is accomplished by taking the logical sum of the status register content and a mask containing 00000100 (hexadecimal 04). In other words,

OR.B /0B, #4

enables the reader.

Exiting from the input-reading program is a little trickier. The end-of-file condition is detected by the reader interface and flagged by setting the exception bit (bit 1), *but no character is read at this time* because there is no character available any longer. The right time to check for end of file is therefore before any attempt is made to transfer characters, as shown in Fig. 6.10. In fact the flow chart of Fig. 6.10, which for most programmers should represent at least the second (and probably the third or fourth) stage of refinement, is detailed enough to be turned into program code directly.

The following program corresponds closely to the flow chart of Fig. 6.10.

```
.LOAD 20
;    Reads characters and places them in memory, from
;    address 5A.
04 33 ; 0020        LD.L R0, #5A    ; Establish pointer.
00 00 00 5A
C4 05 ; 0026 NEXT: OR.B /0B, #4    ; Enable reader.
04
00 00 00 0B
C4 02 ; 002d WAIT: CMP.B /0B, #2   ; End of file?
02
00 00 00 0B
F7 CC ; 0034        BZ FINI         ; Get out if yes!
00 17
C4 02 ; 0038        CMP.B /0B, #1   ; Character ready?
01
00 00 00 0B
F7 8C ; 003f        BNZ WAIT        ;   Wait if not.
FF EA
46 03 ; 0043        LD.B [R0], /0A  ; move character in.
00 00 00 0A
00 3A ; 0049        INC.L R0, 1     ; Increment pointer,
FF CC ; 004b        BR NEXT         ;   go get more.
FF D7
FF FF ; 004f FINI: HALT
.PROG 20
.FINI
```

Reader delays in Simian average about half a dozen instructions, but their actual durations vary randomly. The four-instruction wait loop shown here will usually be traversed about two or three times between characters. It is not known at what time during this loop the actual arrival of a character will occur; but when it does arrive, the character available bit will flag that event. However, this bit is only tested, and the presence of a character will only be noted, after the CMP.B instruction.

Because the Simian reader is fast, it sometimes manages to fetch a new character during just one execution of the wait loop. Particularly on those occasions, the enabling–disabling mechanism is vitally important; were the reader permitted to fetch characters at its own pace, it could overrun the ability of the processor to take care of them. If the physical input unit is a keyboard, on the other hand, difficulties are unlikely. Even very fast typists only manage to produce keystrokes at intervals of 150–200 milliseconds.

The electric typewriter

An electric typewriter could be viewed as a device for reading incoming characters from a keyboard and printing the characters on a printer as they arrive. Building a typewriter is therefore a matter of programming a Simian computer to perform interlaced input and output operations, as shown in the flow chart of Fig. 6.11. The essence of this chart is that the input reading program just discussed has been joined to a simple character printing program. After capturing a character from the keyboard, the program waits until the printer is available, then prints it. This process continues forever, or at any rate as long as the computer is not turned off.

The typewriter of course "prints" the *carriage return* and *line feed* characters, in the sense that it responds to the former by moving the print head to the left edge of a print line, and moves the paper up one line in response to the latter.

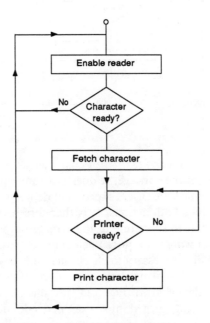

Fig. 6.11. The electric typewriter alternately reads characters at the keyboard and prints them.

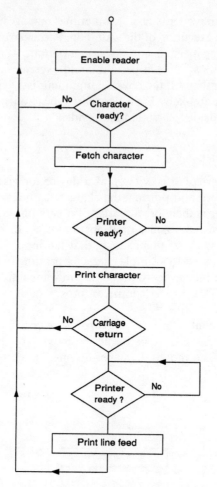

Fig. 6.12.   The complete electric typewriter. It echoes all characters and adds line feeds to carriage returns.

It should be noted that the *carriage return* character as defined in the ASCII character set *only* returns the carriage, it does not move the paper up a line. However, experienced typewriter users expect that depressing the *return* key on the keyboard will produce both actions. It is therefore necessary to recognize each *return* keystroke and to substitute in the printed output the pair *carriage return–line feed*. In other words, it is not sufficient merely to echo keyboard characters as received; it is also necessary to check each one to see whether it was a carriage return, and to follow it up with a *line feed* if it was. This additional modification turns the flow chart of Fig. 6.11 into the more refined version of Fig. 6.12. The latter is readily turned into assembler code, since each step in the chart is very nearly the equivalent of one or two program lines.

```
.ORG 20
NEXT:    OR.B /0B, #4           ; Enable reader.
READ:    CMP.B /0B, #2          ; End of file?
         BZ FINI                ; Get out if yes!
         CMP.B /0B, #1          ; Character ready?
         BNZ READ               ;   Wait if not,
         LD.B R0, /0A           ;   else get it in.
PRNT:    CMP.B /0D, #0          ; Output busy?
         BNZ PRNT               ; Loop if yes.
         LD.B /C, R0            ; If not, print.
         CMP.B R0, #0D          ; Carriage return?
         BNZ NEXT               ; No, go get more.
PTLF:    CMP.B /0D, #0          ; Output busy?
         BNZ PTLF               ; Loop if yes,
         LD.B /0C, #0A          ; else print LF,
         BZ NEXT                ; go for next.
FINI:    HALT
.END
```

The scheme shown here is likely to be entirely satisfactory for a typewriter, but it may leave something to be desired in other applications. The flow chart of Fig. 6.12 contains a hidden assumption: it only works reliably if the input device (keyboard) is slower than the output device (printer), so that the processor will need to wait for the next character. Examination of Fig. 6.11 will show that keyboard input fast enough to deliver a character while the last one is being printed is acceptable; but should two characters arrive while Simian waits for the printer, the first of the pair will be lost. Simple character printers are able to print about 40–50 characters per second; an expert typist can only key in about 5–6 characters in the same time. Loss of characters might just possibly occur in the design of Fig. 6.12 if a particularly slow printer motion (e.g., returning the carriage to the beginning of a new line) coincides with a letter combination likely to be typed exceptionally fast. (For example, many expert typists deal with the *th* pair of *the* in practically a single motion.) A similar fetch–wait–print arrangement might not be satisfactory with faster input devices such as magnetic tape drives or disks.

The electric typewriter program is probably best studied experimentally. Its behavior, incidentally, will be a little different if it is tested with text files (rather than actual keyboard input) under the Unix operating system. In Unix text files the new-line character 0A by itself stands for the combination of a carriage return character and a new-line character. Typists, of course, expect just the opposite: the carriage return 0D alone should imply both. Thus the program will work satisfactorily with ordinary Unix text files if the 0A and 0D characters are interchanged:

```
         CMP.B R0, #0A          ; Carriage return?
         BNZ NEXT               ; No, go get more.
PTLF:    CMP.B /0D, #0          ; Output busy?
         BNZ PTLF               ; Loop if yes,
         LD.B /0C, #0D          ; else print LF,
```

A full-fledged typewriter program should probably be able to take care of such additional items as *tab* characters, *form feed* characters that request a new page to be started, and perhaps other special characters as well. The technique, however, remains the same for every one.

Subroutines

Printing of characters, converting numerical data to ASCII character strings or character strings to numbers, as well as a host of other input–output programming tasks, come up very frequently in computer programming. So do various mathematical operations, like multiplying or dividing two numbers, adding real fractions, or computing square roots. It would be a waste of computer memory to store essentially the same program code at every place where similar functions are required. Consequently, most computer systems make provision for storing the program code for character printing (or other function) in one place only, branching to that segment of code and away from it again whenever required. These reusable program segments are called *subroutines*.

Subroutines are very useful also in organizing the work of program design and program coding. They permit logically distinct tasks to be separated from each other, thereby allowing large programs to be segmented into distinct, easily distinguishable, units. Subroutines can be, and very often are, written, assembled, and tested independently of the programs with which they are to be used eventually. Subroutines of wide general use are in fact accumulated into *subroutine libraries* on which programmers can draw for such very common operations as character printing or binary–octal conversion.

Branching to subroutines

Subroutines are programs no different from any other in principle. However, a subroutine may be used by one program several times. For example, the simple electric typewriter program contains substantially the same segment of code in two places,

```
PRNT:   CMP.B /0000000D, #0    ; Printer ready for next?
        BNZ PRNT                ;    If not, ask again!
        LD.B /0000000C, R1      ;    Otherwise print it.
```

Instead of repeating the same code two or more times, the subroutine is placed into memory only once, and executed whenever required. Doing so, however, raises two distinct problems:

1. How to branch to the subroutine, and back out again to the right place.
2. How to pass any required numerical or character data (parameters) to or from the subroutine.

There are many possible solutions to both problems. The difficulty is in fact less one of inventing good ways, than of finding ways easy to standardize. After all, little work is saved by accumulating subroutine libraries if every library routine requires a different method for its use!

Getting into a subroutine may superficially appear the simplest thing in the world—since the memory location of the first instruction of the subroutine is known, any branch instruction should do the job! But this simple solution only deals with the easy half of the problem, for it is also necessary to return from subroutine execution to the right place to continue. If a subroutine is entered from two different places in a program, as would be the case if character printing were to be segmented off as a subroutine in the electric typewriter example, how is one to know which of the two places to resume work from?

The problem of subroutine entry and exit is solved in most computers by hardware means, or at least with a strong hardware assist, and Simian is no exception in this regard. Subroutine entry is effected by means of specially tagged branch instructions, the *branch to subroutine* instructions. These arrange for branching in exactly the same fashion as ordinary branch instructions, but in addition they save the program counter content immediately prior to the branching taking place. Because the program counter in Simian always points to the *next* instruction during instruction execution, the address saved is therefore the address following the branching instruction. Having saved the address when branching to the subroutine, return to the right place is easily possible by retrieving the saved address from its temporary storage location.

The *branch* and *jump* instructions have already been discussed in some detail. In that discussion, however, it was assumed throughout that bit 5 in every branch or jump instruction was reset to 0. The *branch to subroutine* instructions of Simian are encoded in exactly the same way as the ordinary branch instructions, but bit 5 is set to 1, to identify that branching to a subroutine is meant. The decoding and action sequence for branching instructions is therefore in fact just a little more complex than shown earlier:

1. Fetch the instruction.
2. Increment the program counter 2 bytes.
3. Fetch the offset pointed to by the program counter.
4. Increment the program counter 2.
5. Examine the processor status flag bits. If the branching condition is met, then
   5.1. Examine bit 5 of the instruction. If it is set, save the program counter content.
   5.2. Add the offset to the program counter content.

As in the case of ordinary branching instructions, program execution simply continues with the next following instruction if the branching condition is not met. But if the condition is met, the location of the next instruction is saved, so as to be able to return to it after subroutine execution, and the program counter is loaded with the first instruction location of the subroutine.

In assembler language notation, branch-to-subroutine instructions are identified similarly to the ordinary branch instructions, but the mnemonic abbreviation CALL is used instead of BR. CALL may be followed by a condition specification in exactly the same way as BR. For example, the *branch if not negative* and *branch to subroutine if not negative* are constructed similarly; they differ only in bit 5 of the binary code:

| BNN | 11001 11011 **00** 1100 | DE CC |
| CALLNN | 11001 11011 **10** 1100 | DE EC |

The second instruction is usually read *call subroutine if not negative.* Because the CALL instructions are like the BR instructions, differing only in bit 5, exactly parallel families of instructions can be built up. The Simile assembler language has special abbreviations for a few of the most commonly used conditional subroutine calls:

CALL	Branch to subroutine no matter what
CALLZ	Branch to subroutine if zero
CALLN	Branch to subroutine if negative
CALLL	Branch to subroutine if lesser
CALLC	Branch to subroutine if carry set
CALLV	Branch to subroutine if overflow

A corresponding modification applies to the negated-condition codes:

CALLNZ	Branch to subroutine if nonzero
CALLNN	Branch to subroutine if nonnegative
CALLNL	Branch to subroutine if greater or equal
CALLNC	Branch to subroutine if carry clear
CALLNV	Branch to subroutine if no overflow

Just as for the straightforward branching instructions, there are $3^5 = 243$ possible combinations of conditions. Not all of these make good sense, so that the total number is not quite so huge as might at first glance seem the case.

After a subroutine has been executed, it is usually necessary to return to the calling program, at the point where the subroutine was called. Because the CALL instructions all save the program counter content at the moment they are invoked, returning to the right place is now easy; it suffices to retrieve the saved value and place it into the program counter again. Program execution will then resume with the instruction following the CALL. The precise mechanism for saving and retrieval of subroutine return addresses remains to be discussed in greater detail. For the moment, it will suffice to know that the address can be retrieved and the program counter content reestablished by the instruction RET, whose binary form is 0000 0010 0111 1111.

The electric typewriter revisited

To illustrate the manner in which the subroutine call and return instructions are used, consider the electric typewriter program again. This time, the character-printing and character-reading tasks are removed from the program proper and are made to constitute separate subroutines:

```
.LOAD 20
;                    The Electric Typewriter
;  Perpetually reads and prints keyboard characters.
;  Appends line feeds to all incoming carriage returns.
;
FF EC ; 0020 TYPW: CALL READ         ; Read keyboard,
00 16
FF EC ; 0024       CALL PRNT         ;    then print.
00 2C
04 02 ; 0028       CMP.B R0, #0D      ; New line?
0D
F7 8C ; 002b       BNZ TYPW          ; No, go get more.
FF F1
04 03 ; 002f       LD.B R0, #0A       ; Yes, send LF
0A
FF EC ; 0032       CALL PRNT         ;    to printer,
00 1E
F7 CC ; 0036       BZ TYPW           ;    go for next.
FF E6
;
;        Subroutine to read character into R0.
C4 05 ; 003a READ: OR.B /0B, #4      ; Enable reader.
04
00 00 00 0B
C4 02 ; 0041 LOOP: CMP.B /0B, #1     ; Character ready?
01
00 00 00 0B
F7 8C ; 0048       BNZ LOOP          ;    Wait if not,
FF F5
06 03 ; 004c       LD.B R0, /0A       ;    else fetch it.
00 00 00 0A
02 7F ; 0052       RET
;
;        Subroutine to output character in R0.
C4 02 ; 0054 PRNT: CMP.B /0D, #0     ; Output busy?
00
00 00 00 0D
F7 8C ; 005b       BNZ PRNT          ; Loop if yes.
FF F5
C0 03 ; 005f       LD.B /C, R0        ; If not, print.
00 00 00 0C
02 7F ; 0065       RET
.PROG 20
.FINI
```

The key point here is that the character printing subroutine is entered twice, once from the CALL PRNT instruction at location 0024 and once from location 0032. When it is called from location 0024, the program counter has advanced to 0028 and points at the next instruction. The CALL instruction causes the program counter content, which is at that time 00000028, to be saved, and 0000005B to be substituted. The instructions to be executed next are therefore those at 005B, 005F, and 0065. The last of these is RET. While it is being executed, the program counter points at 0067; RET, however, causes that value to be overwritten with 00000028 so the next instruction to be executed is CMP.B R0, #0D. In other words, the CALL–RET pair allows the sequence of program steps to be sidetracked to the subroutine, then resumed after subroutine completion. In exactly the same way, CALL PRNT at 0032 causes the instructions at 0054, 005b and 005f to be executed, then the instruction at 0036.

The character reading subroutine is only called once, so it may seem unnecessary to separate it from the main typewriter program. If the subroutine is to be drawn from a library created at another time and place, however, the separation is useful.

Text file conversion

Text files under the Unix system do not normally contain the carriage return–line feed pair of characters at the end of each text line; the Unix convention is to signal line breaks by single *new-line* characters. The new-line character, ASCII 0A hexadecimal, is identical to the *line feed* character; for some reason that no one seems to know, it is always referred to as a *new-line* in literature dealing with the Unix system. Converting a Unix text file into a standard text file acceptable to most microprocessor operating environments can therefore be accomplished by a program analogous to the electric typewriter, but different in two respects. First, the text will now contain single 0A characters which must be *preceded* by carriage-returns 0D. Second, the program must halt gracefully when it reaches the end of the input file.

Stopping work when a file-end is reached is a subtle matter. When the end of file is reached, a character cannot be read so the reading subroutine cannot be executed successfully. In fact, the reading subroutine shown in the electric typewriter example is totally unacceptable because at the end of the file it will enter the waiting loop and remain in it forever. To exit when the file ends, it is necessary to check *first* whether there is anything left to read, only thereafter to attempt reading. Simian flags an end of input file by setting bit 1 of the reader status byte, so data exhaustion can be detected by examining this bit before entering the reader wait loop.

```
;     Character read subroutine with EOF detection
;
READ:   OR.B /0B, #4          ; Enable reader.
        LD.B R1, #0           ; Assume: not EOF.
LOOP:   CMP.B /0B, #2         ; End of file?
        BNZ CHAR              ; Go on if not;
        LD.B R1, #1           ;   if EOF flag R1
        RET                   ;   and return.
CHAR:   CMP.B /0B, #1         ; Character ready?
        BNZ LOOP              ; Retry if not, or
        LD.B R0, /0A          ;   else fetch it.
        RET
```

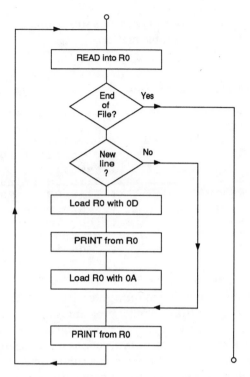

Fig. 6.13. Text file processing to replace new-line characters by carriage return–line feed combinations.

One important advantage of organizing programs as coordinated sets of subroutines is evident from this example. Although the program itself is fairly long, the character reading subroutine is short enough to be read and understood easily. Isolating the character reading task to be performed by the subroutine means that a programmer can alter the reading procedure with only an outline understanding of the whole program.

The test for end-of-file yields a result that must be communicated to the remainder of the program in some way. The means chosen here is to place the character into R0 if there is one, and to return 1 in R1 if the character in R0 is meaningless (i.e., if an end of file was encountered). The calling program can then examine R1 to determine whether to take the contents of R0 as a text character or not.

Preceding each 0A character by 0D is easily done. It is only necessary to print the 0D character first, then to print 0A. Printing is effected in a way similar to that of the electric typewriter: loading the desired character into register R0, then calling the printing subroutine. The arrangement shown in Fig. 6.13 accomplishes this goal in a reasonably compact fashion.

It is worth noting that the flow chart of Fig. 6.13 implicitly relies on the use of subroutines. Every action block in the chart in fact represents either a very small fragment of code, one or two lines, or a subroutine call. As a result, coding the program becomes a very simple matter:

```
;                     The File Processor
; Reads input characters and prints them until EOF.
; Puts carriage returns ahead of incoming line feeds.
;
FILE:   LD.B R1, #0          ; R1 is EOF flag.
TEXT:   CALL READ            ; Read input.
        CMP.B R1, #0         ; Check for EOF,
        BNZ FINI             ;    quit if EOF.
        CMP.B R0, #0A        ; New line?
        BNZ SKIP             ; Skip CR if not.
        LD.B R0, #0D         ; Else CR in R0
        CALL PRNT            ;    and print.
        LD.B R0, #0A         ; Then LF in R0
SKIP:   CALL PRNT            ;    and print.
        BZ TEXT              ;    go for next.
FINI:   RET                  ; At end, return.
```

To make its use convenient, the file processor itself has been structured as a subroutine! All that is required is to substitute a RET instruction for HALT, and to provide the entry point FILE so other programs can refer to it. FILE can now be called from another program. This example illustrates a common programming practice: a subroutine contains instructions for branching to another subroutine, or, as the matter is usually phrased, a subroutine *calls* another. There is nothing wrong with doing so. In fact, the possibility of having subroutines call subroutines which in turn call other subroutines permits creating programs of great complexity while still retaining a good grasp of overall structure and purpose.

Jumping to subroutines

Subroutine calls as implemented in Simian are a form of branch operation, hence position independent. However, one important lack persists in the structure of subroutines: it is not possible to branch to a subroutine beginning at a known absolute address in memory. This ability is important because some subroutines are so frequently used that they are left permanently memory-resident, for use by all programs.

Access to subroutines beginning at absolutely known addresses is obtainable through *jump to subroutine* instructions. Just as the ordinary branching instructions are turned into *jump* instructions by setting bit 4 in the instruction word to 1, so the branch-to-subroutine instructions can be altered into *jump to subroutine* instructions by setting that same bit. Jumping to a subroutine differs from straightforward jumping in the same way that the corresponding branching instructions differ. When a simple jump instruction is executed, the indicated address is simply placed in the program counter, while the jump to subroutine involves the additional step of saving the previous program counter content. In this way, a return to the same place becomes possible after subroutine execution.

In Simile assembler language, jump-to-subroutine instructions have similar mnemonic codes to the ordinary jump instructions, but the letter S appears instead of M. The unqualified jump to subroutine is called JS, others are made up by concatenating JS and the condition label. For example,

JS   Jump to subroutine no matter what
JSZ   Jump to subroutine if zero
JSN   Jump to subroutine if negative
JSNN   Jump to subroutine if nonnegative
JSNV   Jump to subroutine if no overflow

Most user-written programs will employ branching instructions rather than jumps, to ensure that the object code remains position-independent. Jumps to subroutine are employed most often for access to system-provided routines. Such routines may be located in read-only memory, therefore always at the same absolute addresses.

System stack management

When a subroutine is called, its return address needs to be saved so as to permit returning to the right place in the calling program after the subroutine has completed its task. For this purpose, many computers provide a set of special storage locations called the *system stack*. A detailed investigation of how subroutines work and what they can do therefore requires some acquaintance with the stack and stack management.

The system stack

To return successfully from a subroutine it suffices to know a single address, that of the instruction following the subroutine call. Enough storage area must thus be provided to save this return address. But if subroutines are allowed to call other subroutines, which in turn may call others, a single storage location for the return address is not enough. If a program calls some subroutine, say TEXT, the return address must be saved; if TEXT then calls another subroutine READ, it is necessary to save the return address within TEXT. If subroutines are deeply nested, the list of return addresses could grow quite long.

In Simian, as in many modern computers, a special mechanism is provided for temporarily storing lists of data, such as subroutine return addresses: a large proportion of unused memory is allocated to a temporary storage area called the *system stack*. By convention, programs are loaded into Simian at low address locations, and the stack is placed at the high end of memory. As larger programs are loaded, the upper bounding address of the program memory area rises; as more items are stored in the stack area, the stack grows from high addresses toward lower ones. The allocation of memory addresses in a Simian computer with 1024 bytes of read/write memory installed is then as shown in Fig. 6.14. It

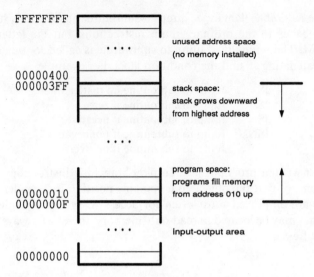

FFFFFFFF

.... unused address space
(no memory installed)

00000400
000003FF

stack space:
stack grows downward
from highest address

....

program space:
programs fill memory
from address 010 up

00000010
0000000F

.... input-output area

00000000

Fig. 6.14. Memory allocation in a Simian computer with less than maximum possible memory installed.

will be noted that some very low addresses are reserved for input-output unit services, such as the data and status bytes for the character reading and writing units.

As arranged in Simian, the stack is merely the high end of user-accessible memory. Whenever a subroutine is called, its return address is placed in the next-to-highest four bytes in stack memory, 03FE through 03FB in a Simian machine with 1024 bytes of memory. (The highest-addressed byte is left blank, for reasons to be taken up directly.) If the subroutine calls another, the corresponding return address is placed in the next four bytes, and so on. The addresses are written in order (downward from the highest memory location) and are retrieved in the opposite order when needed, the most recent one last. Saving the return addresses is done automatically by the CALL or JS instruction that accesses the subroutine.

To keep track of how far the stack has grown, Simian uses a special purpose register, the *stack pointer*. When Simian is first started, the stack is empty and the stack pointer is set to contain the address of the highest-numbered byte of the available memory, 03FF = 1024_{10} in the example above. Every time an address is *pushed on the stack* (i.e, when it is saved), the stack pointer is decremented four bytes. The stack pointer then actually points at the least significant byte of the return address, just like any other address pointer. Conversely, whenever an address is *popped from the stack* (i.e., when it is removed), the stack pointer is incremented four bytes. In this way, after one item has been pushed onto the stack, the stack pointer in the above example contains 03FB, when two addresses have been pushed on the stack it contains 03F7, and so on. The stack pointer therefore always points at the address currently on top of the stack.

Saving subroutine return addresses on the stack means that subroutines can be nested very deeply indeed; unless the program crowds memory space very badly, there is plenty of space for return addresses. Furthermore, the available space is always used efficiently, in the sense that no space is ever reserved but not actually used.

Stack management: an example

The system stack is a particular case of *last-in-first-out* memory. A good visual image of such an arrangement is a stack of cards. If it is imagined that subroutine return addresses are written on file cards, the cards stacked one on top of the other, then return addresses will always be taken up in the right order. To demonstrate this sequence of events concretely, consider the following simple example. Suppose a program calls subroutine LETT, which calls subroutine TEXT, which in turn calls subroutine READ:

```
.ORG 20
;      Return address management demonstration
DEMO:   NOP                   ; DEMO program
        CALL LETT             ; calls LETT and
        BR DEMO               ; nothing else.
;
.ORG 30
;      Demonstration subroutine LETT
LETT:   NOP                   ; LETT program
        CALL TEXT             ; calls TEXT and
        RET                   ; returns.
;
.ORG 40
;      Demonstration subroutine TEXT
TEXT:   NOP                   ; TEXT program
        CALL READ             ; calls READ and
        RET                   ; returns.
;
.ORG 50
;      Subroutine to read character into R0.
READ:   OR.B /0B, #4          ; Enable reader.
LOOP:   CMP.B /0B, #1         ; Character ready?
        BNZ LOOP              ;   Wait if not,
        LD.B R0, /0A          ;   else fetch it.
        RET
```

The READ subroutine is directly copied from previous examples. The others are artificial; they just waste one machine instruction time doing nothing, then call another subroutine.

Initially, the stack pointer of Simian is set to 03FF; the stack contains nothing. When LETT is called, the program counter contains 00000026 (the next instruction address after CALL LETT). This is the return address for LETT; it is placed on the stack, into locations 03FB to 03FE. The stack pointer now contains 03FB, indicating where the return address is. When LETT in turn calls TEXT, the return address 00000036 within LETT is placed on the stack and the stack pointer is advanced to 03F7. Continuing, at a moment when subroutine READ is actually being executed, the stack will contain

00	00	00	26	at location	03FB
00	00	00	36		03F7
00	00	00	46		03F3

and the stack pointer will contain 03F3, the address of the last item pushed on the stack. This last location is always referred to as the *top of the stack*, in keeping with the image of a stack of file cards—despite the fact that the memory address of the "top" is actually the smallest address used!

When READ terminates work the address 00000046 on the top of the stack is used to return from it. Control, therefore, returns to TEXT. The stack must then contain

00	00	00	26	at location	03FB
00	00	00	36		03F7

Return from the TEXT subroutine is again effected by popping its return address from the stack. The sequence of events in calling and returning is actually best followed by running and watching Simian itself; tracing program execution with pencil and paper is a pale substitute at best. A session with Simian is most warmly recommended at this point!

Recursive subroutines

With subroutine addresses placed on the stack, it is permissible for a subroutine to call itself, provided of course that it does so only a finite number of times. The return addresses associated with successive calls are likely to be the same, but the right number of them is pushed onto the stack, and the right number popped in due course, so that no confusion can arise. Subroutines that call themselves are called *recursive*. They are widely used almost everywhere in programming.

To illustrate how such repeated subroutine calls may be employed profitably, suppose it is desired to form the sum of all integers equal to or smaller than the number N,

$$s = \sum_{k=0}^{N} k$$

This work may be organized in several ways. One is to rewrite the summation as

$$s = N + \sum_{k=0}^{N-1} k$$

and to regard the task as having been reduced in complexity to that of summing only the integers smaller than $N - 1$. In other words, the task of summing N

integers can be carried out effectively provided one can find a way of summing
$N - 1$ integers! This statement is not silly; it actually provides the clue to solution. The sum of the first *zero* integers is obviously zero, and the solution for
any larger number can be reduced to a series of additions to that zero.

Computation of the sum of integers is best carried out by creating a subroutine
SUM to do one of two things, depending on the value of N: declare the sum to
be zero if N is zero, or else add N to the value obtained by calling SUM. The
value N is placed in some convenient register, say R1; the sum of N and all
smaller nonzero integers is accumulated in R2. The subroutine reads as follows:

```
;         Recursive subprogram to sum N integers
SUM: ADD.L R2, R1                 ; Add number to R2,
     INC.L R1, -1                 ; next number in R1;
     CALLNZ SUM                   ; call SUM unless
     RET                          ;    next N is zero.
```

To do the summing, little is necessary beyond setting up initial values in both
registers before calling SUM and halting execution afterward. For $N = 8$, the
program as loaded then reads as follows:

```
.LOAD 20
0C 33 ; 0020          LD.L R1, #8       ; Put N = 8 in R1,
00 00 00 08
14 33 ; 0026          LD.L R2, #0       ; zero sum to start.
00 00 00 00
FF EC ; 002c          CALL SUM          ; Compute sum.
00 02
FF FF ; 0030          HALT
;
;           Recursive subprogram to sum N integers
10 70 ; 0032 SUM:     ADD.L R2, R1      ; Add number to R2,
0C 3A ; 0034          INC.L R1, -1      ; next number in R1;
F7 AC ; 0036          CALLNZ SUM        ; call SUM unless
FF F8
02 7F ; 003a          RET               ;    next N is zero.
.PROG 20
.FINI
```

When this program is executed, SUM is called and the return address
00000030 is pushed on the stack. SUM then adds 8 to R2 and reduces the number N to 7 (in R1). It then calls itself! The return address this time is 0000003A,
the return point within SUM. The second call adds 7 to R2, reduces the content
of R1 to 6 and calls SUM again. The result is to accumulate a sequence of return
addresses on the stack, all alike. After the sequence has grown to eight (00000030
and seven copies of 0000003A), the next number N is zero and CALLNZ is not
executed any longer. The machine action then consists of a whole string of RET
instructions, one for each subroutine call. Each one pops one copy of the return
address 0000003A off the stack and restores it to the program counter. Finally,
the return address to the calling (main) program is popped and the sequence
terminates. The arithmetical result, of course, remains in R2.

Recursive employment of subroutines is frequently of use in mathematical computation as well as in character processing and system management. Only rarely are tasks encountered that cannot be done in any other way than recursion; but in many cases recursive programming provides for elegant, short, and efficient programs. Recursion clearly cannot be used if the number of repeated steps is so large as to use up all the available stack space. Aside from this shortcoming, however, the method is attractive in many applications.

Special register instructions

The instruction RET used for returning from a subroutine really performs a very simple action: it pops the top address from the stack and places it in the program counter. It thus resembles the LD.L instruction, except that it moves data between special registers, not the general ones. RET is actually just one of a whole family of instructions that move data to and from the special registers. Others include the CALL and JS instructions, which move data to the stack. They have already been dealt with in detail; the RET instruction has been used in several programming examples. There are several others of value, so an examination of their action is worth the trouble.

Leaving aside CALL and JS, three distinct families of Simian instructions transfer the contents of special registers. One group allows data to be copied from a special register to a general (register or immediate) operand; one group allows transfers from a general operand to a special register. The binary operation codes for these groups are 1101 and 1110, respectively. The third group, to which RET belongs, permits data to be copied from one special register to another. The binary operation code corresponding to this group of instructions is 1111. Only a few instructions in each group are of any major interest and assembler language mnemonics exist for only that handful. The remainder, should they be needed, can of course always be inserted in programs in their hexadecimal form, using the .DATA and .ORG assembler directives.

The special register transfer instructions follow the same binary format conventions as do all other Simian instructions. Each one contains the operation code in its least significant four bits, followed by a two-bit operand length and two five-bit operand description fields. When reference is made to a normal operand, the usual conventions apply: three bits serve to identify the register, the other two to distinguish indirect or immediate addressing. Reference to a special register is made by a somewhat different use of the operand bits. Because there are only three special registers, only two bits are needed to identify them; the third (most significant) register identification bit is simply reset. Indirect addressing makes sense with special registers, but immediate addressing does not; the immediate addressing bit is therefore always reset. The operand field thus has the form

0	ind	0	register

where the register numbers are 00 for the program counter, 01 for the stack pointer, and 10 for the processor status register.

To furnish a simple example, suppose it is desired to retrieve an address from the stack and to place it into the program counter—in other words, to return from a subroutine. Here the transfer is from one special register to another—from SP to PC—with the first one addressed indirectly, the second directly. The operand length must be 4 bytes (because all Simian addresses are four bytes long), so the instruction is composed as follows:

Operation: special to special	. . . . 1 1 1 1
Four-byte word length	. . . . 1 1 . . . .
Source register: SP	. . . . 0 0 1 . . . . . .
indirectly addressed	. . . . . 0 1 . . . .
Destination register: PC	. . 0 0 0 . . . .
directly addressed	0 0 . . . .
Putting it all together,	0 0 0 0 0 0 1 0 0 1 1 1 1 1 1 1
or, in hexadecimal form,	0 2 7 F

This instruction is very widely used and is therefore given the mnemonic abbreviation RET. A total of 36 special register to special register copying instructions can be constructed in this way; however, only a minority are of common enough use to merit assembler-language mnemonics. Some are technically possible but devoid of any sense, such as indirect addressing through the processor status register!

Two other special cases within the 1111 operation code family are valuable and therefore have mnemonic abbreviations recognized by Simile. One, called SAVE, fetches the least significant byte of the processor status register (i.e., the set of processor flag bits) and pushes it onto the stack. The other one does precisely the opposite: it pops one byte off the stack and places it in the processor status register. It is called REST (for *restore*), for it restores the processor condition codes as they were at some previous time. Both use a single-byte operand, for the high-order bits of the PS register are not used to flag processor events. SAVE clearly amounts to a data transfer from PS (addressed directly) to SP (addressed indirectly); its hexadecimal representation is 488F. REST, by a similar argument, translates into 124F.

The HALT instruction is a member of the 1111 operation code family. Simian takes *any* 1111 family operation with two identical operands as meant to halt the processor. Simile makes doubly sure by translating HALT as 11111 11111 11 1111. Formally, this bit string denotes a vacuous operation (data transfer from a special register to itself) performed on a nonexistent register using an impossible addressing mode!

PUSH and POP

Indirect addressing is only useful with reference to one special register, the stack pointer. For the other two special registers, it is either not very useful or else completely meaningless. When applied to the program counter, indirect addressing can make sense, but it is of no use because the program counter invariably points at the next instruction anyway. The processor status register can never contain an address, so indirect addressing through the status register makes no sense at all. Indirect addressing through special registers is therefore considered permissible in Simian only with reference to the stack pointer.

The stack pointer always contains the address of the operand at the top of the stack. Data movement from a location indirectly addressed through the stack pointer therefore means data movement from the top of the stack; conversely, data movement *to* such an indirect address means data movement *to* the top of the stack. Because the stack inherently works on a last-in-first-out basis, two special assembler-language instructions are provided for stack management, POP and PUSH. These store data on the stack in the same way as the CALL and JS instructions store addresses. However, they take one operand of the regular sort. For example,

```
PUSH.S #0af
POP.B [R4]
```

make good sense. In general, all the normal addressing modes are permissible; so are all three conventional operand lengths. When PUSH and POP instructions are executed, the stack pointer is modified by exactly the same number of bytes as the operand length; it is *incremented after* data movement *from* the stack (the POP instruction), and it is *decremented before* data transfer *to* the stack (the PUSH instruction). In this way, operands of byte, short, or long lengths can be placed on the stack, with the stack pointer always moved exactly the correct amount.

The PUSH.*x* and POP.*x* instructions belong to the 1110 and 1101 operation code families, respectively. For PUSH, the source operand is a normal Simian register operand while the destination is a special register; POP works the other way around. Thus POP.B [R4] is represented as

Operation: special to general	. . . . 1 1 0 1
Two-byte word length	. . . . 0 1 . . . .
Source register: SP	. . . . 0 0 1 . . . . . .
indirectly addressed	. . . . . 0 1 . . . .
Destination register: R4	. . 1 0 0 . . . .
indirectly addressed	. 1 . . . .
in register mode	0 . . . .
Putting it all together,	0 1 1 0 0 0 1 0 0 1 0 1 1 1 0 1
or, in hexadecimal form,	6 2 5 D

The PUSH operation, as well as POP operations with different destination operands, are encoded in an analogous manner.

A detail of stack management mentioned briefly but not yet discussed concerns the highest stack address. Because the stack is empty at least part of the time, some value of the stack pointer content must signify *empty*. In Simian, this value is chosen to equal the highest-numbered byte of memory actually available. This choice makes the topmost byte of memory unavailable as stack space; were it used, there would be no way of distinguishing an *empty* stack from a stack that contains exactly one byte of data. An alternative convention, adopted in some computers, is to signify emptiness by pointing at an address one byte higher than the top of memory. This choice has a flaw as well: if a full complement of memory is installed, the stack pointer register cannot point to an address above the top of memory. The only way to point at a higher address is to use a stack pointer one bit longer than the other machine registers. This choice would clearly cause havoc in the design of bus data paths so it is very unattractive indeed.

It is interesting to note that the convention by which words are assigned memory addresses at their least significant byte locations is *not* altogether arbitrary, but that it is on the contrary essential to make stack management work. Were they addressed at their most significant byte locations, it would not be possible to know exactly how far the stack extends. Because the stack grows from the top end of memory downward, the least significant byte of the data item last placed on the stack is also the final byte actually occupied by the stack. Hence, the pushing and popping of intermixed bytes, short words, and long words is possible.

String reversal

Character strings are commonly stored by placing the characters in sequential memory locations and appending a null byte to the string after its last character, to show that the string has ended. The string itself is then referred to by giving its beginning address. For example, suppose the character string ABCD were to be stored in Simian memory beginning at location 050. It could be placed in memory by including

```
.DATA 50
00 44 43 42 41
```

in the assembler language file (the source code). This string would usually be referred to as "the string beginning at address 050," or simply as "the string at 050."

Suppose it is desired to replace the string beginning at 050 with its own inverse. For example, if the string originally stored were ABCD, inversion would produce DCBA. This task is easily carried out by first pushing the entire string on the stack, character by character, and then popping it back into its original locations. The stack is a *last-in-first-out* memory structure, so if the characters were first pushed on the stack in their natural order A-B-C-D, they would be popped in the order D-C-B-A, which is exactly what is desired. A program to accomplish this task could have the structure shown in Fig. 6.15. One possible assembler-language implementation of this flow chart runs as follows:

```
.LOAD 20
;       Reverses character string at 050 in place.
04 33 ; 0020        LD.L R0, #50        ; String pointer
00 00 00 50
```

```
18 33 ; 0026         LD.L R3, R0        ; copied to R3.
5C 02 ; 0028 STOW: CMP.B [R3], #0      ; End of string?
00
F7 CC ; 002b         BZ DONE            ; Return if yes.
00 08
4A CE ; 002f         PUSH.B [R3]        ; Push character,
18 3A ; 0031         INC.L R3, 1        ;   move pointer,
FF CC ; 0033         BR STOW            ;   do the next.
FF F1
18 31 ; 0037 DONE: SUB.L R3, R0        ; Length in R3,
10 33 ; 0039         LD.L R2, R0        ; pointer in R2.
52 4D ; 003b REVS: POP.B [R2]          ; Pop character,
10 3A ; 003d         INC.L R2, 1        ; move pointer,
1C 3A ; 003f         INC.L R3, -1       ; up the count.
F7 8C ; 0041         BNZ REVS           ; Go for next
FF F6
FF FF ; 0045         HALT               ;   or quit!
.LOAD 50
00 44 43 42 41
.PROG 20
.FINI
```

Here the pointer to the string is initially placed in R0 and is left there through-out; no manipulation is carried out on that register. The string is first pushed onto the stack by the loop at label STOW. Each time through this loop, a character pointed to by R3 is pushed on the stack and the pointer moved on to the next; the loop is satisfied when a null byte is encountered. Next, the length of the string is calculated; it must be the difference in pointers R3 (which now

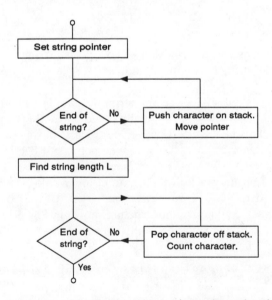

Fig. 6.15. String reversal accomplished by copying to the stack and back again.

points to the end of the string) and R0 (which points to its beginning). The loop at label REVS is then used to pop successive characters from the stack, placing them at the locations pointed to by R2. The loop is controlled by R3; characters are counted as they are popped, by decrementing R3. When R3 reaches zero, the last character must have been popped off the stack and the program halts.

Like several examples shown previously, this one is probably easier to study at the terminal than at a desk. A trial run with Simian is therefore recommended.

Subroutine linkages

It is common practice in computer programming to write and maintain large libraries of subroutines, linking together subroutines as required in building new programs. Writing correct programs and certifying them to be correct requires a great deal of hard work, so it is generally considered wise to profit from past work by making subroutines reusable.

When large programs are written as collections of subroutines, how subroutines communicate is an important matter. Some of the standard ways of arranging coordination and data exchange are therefore discussed in this section.

Parameter passing

When a subroutine is called, data must usually be passed to it for processing. Data items communicated from calling program to subroutine or conversely are called *subroutine parameters* or *subroutine arguments*. There are various ways of passing subroutine parameters, all used from time to time.

The simplest scheme for parameter passing is undoubtedly the method used in almost all subroutine examples so far: the parameter values are left in general registers, for the called routine to collect and use. Any information which the subroutine may be required to return to the calling program can be returned in the same fashion, by leaving the *output arguments* in one or more general registers. This scheme is simple and makes for short programs; it is also straightforward and not very likely to give rise to many programming errors. However, it has at least one very serious shortcoming. If one subroutine calls another, and both need to use the same registers, the data used by one will likely be destroyed by the other. In the case of recursive computations, in which a subroutine is allowed to call itself, such destruction is almost certain. Worst of all, this method of parameter passing makes it difficult to use subroutines written by other programmers or at other times without careful reading to determine which registers are used by the subroutine for its own ends. Because the calling program and the subroutine may put registers to conflicting uses, parameter passing through registers is not generally used, and then only for subroutines so short that they can be read and register use examined quickly.

A second technique of passing parameters between programs, which is also fairly straightforward, is for the calling program to push parameter values on the stack, for the subroutine to fetch. This method has shortcomings as well. The subroutine return address is pushed on the stack by the CALL or JS instruction that invokes the subroutine, so the data to be transferred to the subroutine end up on the stack *below* the return address; but the input data will be needed before the return address is used. The result is that programs become complicated. In most cases, it is necessary for the subroutine to pop its own return address from the stack, use whatever data may reside on the stack, and finally to restore the return address. A second shortcoming is closely related to this first one: because the stack is a last-in-first-out storage mechanism, the subroutine arguments must be placed on the stack in exactly the order in which the subroutine will require them.

The third conventional method of passing parameters was already introduced by the string reversal subroutine. In this technique, the subroutine is handed not the actual argument *values*, but the *addresses* of the data items. This is the technique most commonly used, and it will be described in more detail in the following section.

Saving the working environment

Few, if any, useful subroutines actually manage to do any work without using some of the general registers and without affecting some of the flags in the processor status register. The most effective use of subroutines, on the other hand, is achieved if the CALL instructions in a program have the appearance of single instructions without any hidden side effects. In other words, subroutines are best written so that few if any register contents are altered and no unexpected condition flags are manipulated. More succinctly, it is sometimes said that a subroutine should not alter its *working environment*—the set of register contents and condition codes that surround it.

To illustrate both the problems and some of their solutions, consider once again the problem of printing an unsigned integer as a string of octal digits. Because this task is one likely to be encountered often, the program originally written to perform it is now turned into a subroutine:

```
;         Subroutine to print unsigned short integer in R0
                                  ;
OCTL:     LD.B R2, #6             ; Digit counter,
                                  ; Set up bit 15:
          ROL.S R0, 1            ; Rotate high to low,
          LD.S R1, R0            ; copy work register.
          AND.S R1, #1           ; Clear all but bit 0.
                                  ; Main computation:
CHAR:     AND.S R1,  #07          ; Clear high bits,
          ADD.S R1, #30           ;    add 30 for ASCII.
WAIT:     CMP.B /0D,  #0          ; Printer ready?
          BNZ WAIT               ; If not, ask again.
```

```
          LD.B /0C, R1        ; Move the character,
          INC.B R2, -1        ;   count it;
          BZ EXIT             ;   exit if done.
          ROL.S R0, 3         ; Position next triple
          LD.S R1, R0         ;   for printing
          BR CHAR             ;   and go do it.
EXIT:     RET
```

This routine works nicely; it is only necessary to load the number to be printed into register R0 and to execute the instruction CALL OCTL. However, it may cause problems for other computations, possibly done by other subroutines. First, this octal printing subroutine uses R1 and R2 as temporary working registers. Any data the calling program might have left in these two registers before calling the subroutine will certainly be lost. Second, the subroutine contains both arithmetic and comparison operations, all certain to manipulate the status flags in the processor status register. The status before subroutine entry will certainly be destroyed, and the status upon return will be unrelated to any events relevant to the *calling* program.

The usual method for dealing with this problem is to establish a rule: *except as otherwise clearly specified, every subroutine will restore the processor status and the working register contents* to their values at the time of entry to the subroutine. The easiest way of doing so is to save on the stack a copy of the processor status register, and of each working register actually modified by the subroutine. These are then restored just before returning to the calling program. Under this rule, the octal printout subroutine becomes just a little longer:

```
;         Subroutine to print unsigned short integer in R0
                              ;
OCTL:     PUSH.L R1           ; Save registers for
          PUSH.L R2           ; later restoration,
          SAVE                ; also status flags.
          LD.B R2, #6         ; Start digit count.
                              ; Set up bit 15:
          ROL.S R0, 1         ; Rotate high to low,
          LD.S R1, R0         ; copy work register.
          AND.S R1, #1        ; Clear all but bit 0.
                              ; Main computation:
CHAR:     AND.S R1, #07       ; Clear high bits,
          ADD.S R1, #30       ;   add 30 for ASCII.
WAIT:     CMP.B /0D, #0       ; Printer ready?
          BNZ WAIT            ; If not, ask again.
          LD.B /0C, R1        ; Move the character,
          INC.B R2, -1        ;   count it;
          BZ EXIT             ;   exit if done.
          ROL.S R0, 3         ; Position next triple
          LD.S R1, R0         ;   for printing
          BR CHAR             ;   and go do it.
EXIT:     REST                ; Exit: restore flags
          POP.L R2            ;   and registers as
          POP.L R1            ;   they were before.
          RET
```

Three lines have been added at the beginning and three at the end. Those at the start push register contents and status on the stack, those at the end pop them in the opposite order. So far as any calling program is concerned, OCTL now operates invisibly—it leaves the register contents and the processor status entirely unaffected!

Standard subroutine linkages

Simian subroutines are always entered by means of CALL instructions, which store the return address on the system stack. Returning from a subroutine should always be done through a RET instruction, so that the return address is taken from the system stack and the stack restored to its status prior to subroutine entry. The hardware implementation of these instructions establishes how subroutine entry and exit should be arranged. However, it does not even suggest how parameters should be passed. Where only a small amount of information needs to be communicated, arguments can simply be passed through registers, as illustrated by the octal printout routine above. This simple technique fails, however, if there are many arguments or if they are of a complex kind. Concatenation of two character strings, for example, involves an amount of data that cannot even be known beforehand.

A common argument passing convention, applicable to Simian subroutines, employs one general register as a *subroutine linkage register*. This register serves as an address pointer to identify the memory location where the list of subroutine arguments may be found. This list consists of the following:

1. One byte, containing the number N of parameters as an unsigned integer.
2. N addresses, the starting addresses of each of the N arguments.

The scheme is symbolically illustrated in Fig. 6.16. Only one linkage register is required no matter how many arguments the subroutine may require and how

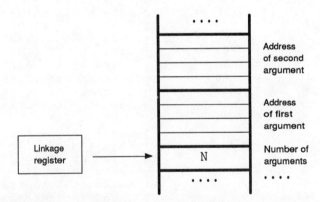

Fig. 6.16. The subroutine linkage register points at the address of the subroutine argument list, which in turn contains the argument addresses.

complicated their structure might be. The register used for this purpose in Simian subroutines is R7. This choice is arbitrary, there is no reason of hardware design to single out R7 and any other general register would serve equally well. It is important, on the other hand, to stick with this choice once it has been made, just as it is important that everyone drive on the same side of the road even though the choice of left or right side is in principle arbitrary.

An *argument* referred to in the subroutine argument list may be a single number, an array of numbers, a character string, or any other data structure, provided only that it can be identified uniquely by a single address. The argument list does not distinguish between the various possible kinds of input or output data; it merely communicates addresses and leaves it to the programs to do with them as their creators saw fit.

The process of building and using conventional subroutine linkages may be illustrated by constructing a subroutine to replace an integer by its absolute value. The task itself only requires the rather simple actions shown in the flow chart of Fig. 6.1: examine the number to determine its sign, then either invert its sign (if negative) or not (if positive). A program fragment to do so was already developed in an earlier chapter:

```
       CMP.L [R3], #0      ; Compare argument to 0,
       BNN SKIP            ;   do nothing if > 0,
       NOT.L [R3]          ;   otherwise complement
       INC.L [R3], 1       ;   and increment.
SKIP:  NOP
```

Register R3 here serves as an address pointer; it contains the address of the argument.

A complete subroutine to accomplish this task must first fetch the integer from wherever the subroutine argument list specifies, then return it after numeric conversion to absolute value. In addition, the subroutine must secure its working environment, by saving register contents and status at the moment of entry, restoring afterward. The resulting structure is shown in the flow chart of Fig. 6.17.

The main arithmetic action here requires R3 to contain the argument address. In the present case, the argument list must consist of just two ingredients: the number 1 (showing how many arguments there are) and the address of the integer operand. At the moment of entry, R7 points to the number of arguments. Hence incrementing it (by 1, since the number of arguments occupies one byte) makes it point to the address of the one and only operand:

```
       INC.L R7, 1         ; Find argument address,
       LD.L R3, [R7]       ;   load it into R3.
       INC.L R7, -1        ; Restore R7 as before.
```

If R3 is to be used as a working register, its prior content must be saved at subroutine entry and replaced afterward; similarly, the processor status must be saved and restored. Translation of Fig. 6.17 into code is thus reasonably direct:

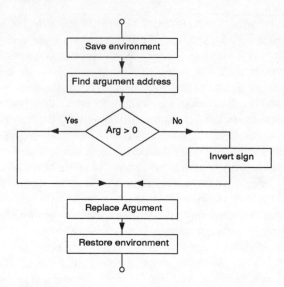

Fig. 6.17.   Subroutine structure for replacing a number by its absolute value. R7 is used as the subroutine linkage register.

```
;              Absolute value subroutine
;
;     Replaces long integer with its own absolute value.
;
.ORG 40
ABSV:  PUSH.L R3            ; Save R3 contents,
       SAVE                ;   also status flags.
       INC.L R7, 1         ; Find argument address,
       LD.L R3, [R7]       ;   load it into R3.
       INC.L R7, -1        ; Restore R7 as before.
       CMP.L [R3], #0      ; Compare argument to 0,
       BNN SKIP            ;   do nothing if > 0,
       NOT.L [R3]          ;   otherwise complement
       INC.L [R3], 1       ;   and increment.
SKIP:  REST                ; Exit: restore flags
       POP.L R3            ;   and registers R3.
       RET
.END
```

Using a subroutine such as this naturally requires setting up the argument list appropriately. For example, the program fragment

```
....
LD.B /3B, #1            ; There is one argument,
LD.L /3C, #70           ;   its value is at  070.
LD.L R7, #3B            ; R7 points to arg. list
CALL ABSV              ; Call for replacement!
....
```

sets up the argument list (in the three LD instructions), then branches to the subroutine with a CALL.

Typical subroutine libraries include hundreds, in some cases thousands, of routines. Because their number is large, and because it is essential to ensure that any combination of library routines can be used without mutual interference, it is vital to standardize the manner in which subroutines are entered and in which arguments are passed. Where the subroutine only performs some very simple action, as is the case here, the subroutine linkage exceeds the action itself both in the amount of code and in the processor time taken; yet most programmers and system analysts consider this apparent waste of resources worthwhile, for what is being saved is the human effort of any alternative coding. Where the subroutine performs a large quantity of work, of course, the linkage code still amounts to only a half a dozen or a dozen lines. It then makes up a small fraction of the whole and appears economic of machine resources as well.

String concatenation

A realistic example of subroutine linkage construction is furnished by converting into subroutine form the string concatenation program considered earlier. As in the simpler examples of this chapter, segments of linking code are placed at the beginning and end of the existing code so as to create a linkage in standard form. The linking code includes, first of all, a half-dozen lines that save the working environment at subroutine entry and restore it at exit time. In addition, the addresses of all three strings—one output and two input—are now communicated by an argument list, not by placing them in registers. The program thus becomes a little longer. In the following listing, a vertical bar at the right marks every line which is not identical to its counterpart in the original program:

```
;              String concatenation subroutine
;
;         Forms a character string, beginning at the
;      first argument address, out of the strings at
;      the second and third argument addresses.
;
.ORG 50
CONC:   PUSH.L R3            ; Save registers for        !
        PUSH.L R4            ;    later restoration,      !
        SAVE                 ;    also status flags.      !
        INC.L R7, 1          ; Find output string,        !
        LD.L R4, [R7]        ; set pointer to it.         !
        INC.L R7, 4          ; Find first input,          !
        LD.L R3, [R7]        ;    set pointer to it,       !
        INC.L R7, 4          ;    find second string.      !
REP1:   LD.B [R4], [R3]      ; Move one character.
        CMP.B [R4], #0       ; Check if it's null.
        BZ NEXT              ; Copy no more if so,
        INC.L R3, 1          ;    or else increment
        INC.L R4, 1          ;    both pointers and
        BR REP1              ;    keep repeating.
```

```
NEXT:   LD.L  R3, [R7]        ; Second input string.    !
REP2:   LD.B  [R4], [R3]      ; Move one character.
        CMP.B [R4], #0         ; Check if it's null.
        BZ DONE               ; Copy no more if so,
        INC.L R3, 1           ;   or else increment
        INC.L R4, 1           ;   both pointers and
        BR REP2               ;   keep repeating.
DONE:   REST                  ; Exit: restore flags     !
        POP.L R4              ;   and registers as       !
        POP.L R3              ;   they were before,      !
        INC.L R7, -9          ;   restore R7 also.       !
        RET.                  ;                          !
.END
```

The addressing of operands here is worth noting: it is multiply indirect. Register R7 contains the address of the argument list, so at various places in the subroutine (after incrementation) it actually contains the argument addresses. The arguments, however, are themselves addresses, pointers to the places where the character strings begin.

To use the string concatenation subroutine, the calling program must once again establish the subroutine parameters and ensure that the input data are available. These tasks are accomplished by a relatively small amount of program code:

```
;           Program which calls concatenating subroutine
;
.ORG 30
        LD.B  /3B, #3        ; There are three arguments.
        LD.L  /3C, #F0       ; Output starts at 0F0.
        LD.L  /40, #D0       ; First input string is at 0D0.
        LD.L  /44, #E0       ; Second input string at 0E0.
        LD.L  R7, #3B        ; R7 points to argument list.
        CALL CONC            ; Concatenate strings.
        HALT
;
;           String concatenation subroutine
;
        ... as shown above ...
;
.DATA D0
00 47 46 45 44 43 42 41
.DATA E0
00 4E 4D 4C 4B 4A 49 48 47 46
.END
```

The data accompanying this program are not particularly imaginative or useful, but they should be sufficient for initial program testing.

Using standard linkages

The point of working subroutines through standard linkages is to minimize restrictions on the number and kind of arguments passed to the subroutine. The standard linkage convention uses a single byte to pass the number of arguments, thereby limiting their number to 255! There is no need, however, for any subroutine to have a fixed number of arguments, nor need every argument be just a single number, as illustrated by the next example.

A subroutine is shown further below to examine a list of small integers and decide whether any of them are negative. The number of integers may be different every time the subroutine is called. The need for such a routine may arise, for example, to check for frost danger in an orange grove where an alarm needs to be sounded if *any* temperature reading anywhere falls below 0°C. Obviously, only very simple arithmetic work is required: every temperature in its turn is checked and the alarm is raised (by returning a nonzero number as an output argument) if a negative sign is encountered at any point. The argument list for this routine is organized as follows:

> Byte   0:   number of arguments = 3;
> Bytes   4 – 1:   address of number of temperatures;
> Bytes   8 – 5:   address of output variable (alarm);
> Bytes 12 – 9:   address of first temperature.

Any number of temperatures can be placed in adjacent memory locations, forming linear array of arbitrary (although specified) length. Although the subroutine has three arguments, one of the arguments is an array of arbitrary size so the amount of information to be conveyed is unlimited.

Suppose that in one particular circumstance ten temperatures are furnished to the subroutine, stored as single bytes at addresses 00E0 through 00E9. The number of temperatures is also given, as a number located at 00D0. The subroutine linkage is then set up by the following main program, and the actual work is executed by the subroutine that follows it:

```
;         Program to check for negative numbers.
;
.ORG 40
          LD.B /20, #3      ; There are 3 arguments.
          LD.B /21, #D0     ; Number of temperatures at 00D0
          LD.L /25, #100    ; Output placement at 0100
          LD.L /29, #E0     ; First temperature is at 00E0.
          LD.L R7, #20      ; R7 points to argument list.
          CALL CHEK         ; Check temperatures.
          HALT
;
;         Negative checking subroutine
;
CHEK:     PUSH.L R0         ; Save register contents
          PUSH.L R1         ;    on the system stack
          PUSH.L R2         ;    for later
          PUSH.L R7         ;    restoration,
          SAVE              ;    also status flags.
          INC.B R7, 1       ; Get address of 1st argument,
          LD.L R0, [R7]     ;    set pointer to it.
```

```
          LD.L R0, [R0]      ; Set up counter.
          INC.L R7, 4        ; Find output address,
          LD.L R1, [R7]      ;    set pointer to it.
          INC.L R7, 4        ; Find first temperature
          LD.L R2, [R7]      ;    set pointer to it.
NEXT:     CMP.B [R2], #0     ; Compare temperature to 0.   |
          BN YES             ;    get out if negative.     |
          INC.L R0, -1       ; If not decrement counter.   |
          BZ NO              ; Get out if all done, else   |
          INC.L R2, 1        ;    get next temperature      |
          BR NEXT            ;    and go back.              |
YES:      LD.L [R1], #1      ; If any negative, output 1   |
          BR EXIT            ;    and exit.                 |
NO:       LD.L [R1], #0      ; If all positive, output 0   |
          BR EXIT            ;    and exit.                 |
EXIT:     REST               ; Exit: restore flags,
          POP.L R7           ;    machine register
          POP.L R2           ;    contents as they
          POP.L R1           ;    were before
          POP.L R0           ;    subroutine call.
          RET                ; Back to calling program.
.DATA D0
0A                           ; Number of readings
.DATA E0
 23 33 15 10 22             ; The temperature readings.
10 45 12 08 FF
.END
```

About ten instructions (marked by a vertical rule in the program listing) perform data manipulation or arithmetic; the rest, around 20 or 30 instructions, are concerned with subroutine linkage management. This number is almost independent of the amount of work done by the subroutine and of the amount of data transferred to or from it. In other words, entering a subroutine and returning from it entails an essentially fixed cost in both memory space and computing time. This cost is relatively high if the subroutine involves only a few working instructions; it is negligible in larger subroutines.

Standard subroutine linkages always take the same form, as illustrated by the examples in this chapter. The calling program must set up the argument list in proper form; the subroutine must save the volatile environment (status and register contents) before beginning work and restore it afterward. The code required, especially within the subroutine, is simple enough to be produced automatically by a computer program, it does not need to be written by hand! Entering and leaving a subroutine are very simple matters in high level languages, such as Pascal, Fortran, or C, because the register saving and argument list construction are handled automatically. In fact, subroutines are handled by high level languages in almost exactly the manner described here; the process *looks* simple to the programmer, however, because the creation of subroutine linkages is a part of translating the Pascal or Fortran code into machine language and remains invisible to the system user.

Problems

1. Show that the multiplication algorithm of Fig. 6.3 works for negative numbers as well as for mixtures of negative and positive numbers. Over what range of inputs is it satisfactory?
2. Devise a multiplication algorithm to multiply two floating-point numbers. What does it have in common with the integer multiplication algorithm of Fig. 6.3?
3. Many high-level programming languages provide for multiway branching (e.g., the Pascal **case** or the Fortran *computed GO TO* statements). Show that a flow chart can always be drawn for a multiway branch that only involves two-way branches, hence that the rectangle, diamond, and circle figures suffice to represent computing processes in flow charts.
4. Describe by means of flow charts a method for performing binary integer division.
5. Experiment with Simian to determine how long an idling loop is needed (without device status checking) to have a high probability of printing all 52 characters of the lower and upper case alphabets.
6. Give an algorithm for number conversion in which the content of a machine register is put into hexadecimal notation for printing (or for other input–output operations). Use a scheme similar to the octal conversion program, with appropriate amounts added to bit groups to form ASCII character representations.
7. Give an algorithm for number conversion in which the characters read from a keyboard are interpreted as hexadecimal numbers for loading a machine register.
8. An ordinary printing terminal mechanism can respond to *carriage return* and *line feed* characters. The *form feed, new-line* and *tab* characters are not acted upon. Design a program which will send to this printer (a) any printable ASCII character in its natural form, (b) the *carriage-return* and *line-feed* characters in their natural form, and (c) sequences of ASCII characters, including carriage control characters, that simulate the actions of *tab, form feed, new-line*. Provide full design documentation, including flow charts and precise specifications.
9. Code and test the program described in Problem 8.
10. Modify the integer multiplication program described so as to make it appropriate to short (16-bit) integers. Test this program and give evidence that it works satisfactorily. Over what range of input values is it usable?
11. Flow chart, write, and test a subroutine to print out *any* ASCII character (including the nonprinting ones) as an octal number.
12. Flow chart, code, and test a subroutine to print out any ASCII character as a two-digit hexadecimal number.
13. Design a subroutine to compare two character strings. The output should be a one-byte integer, positive if the first input string is the greater, negative if the second is the greater, and zero if the strings are identical. A string is considered greater than another if it precedes it in alphabetic ordering. If the whole of the shorter string exactly matches the beginning part of the longer (e.g., *DOG* and *DOGS*), the longer string is considered to be the greater. Provide sufficiently detailed flow charts and descriptive material to allow someone else to proceed with the actual coding.
14. Construct, test, and document the subroutine described in Problem 13. What tests must be made to verify that it works in all cases? How can the test data be designed to ensure that *all* parts of the program have actually been tested?

15. Flow chart, code, and test a subroutine to print out a character string. The string begins at a location specified in the subroutine calling sequence; it terminates with a null character. Use the standard form of subroutine linkage through R7 as a linking register.

16. In data transmission, ASCII characters are often *parity encoded*: the seven bits of the ASCII characters are placed in bits 6–0 of an eight-bit byte, while bit 7 is given such a value that the total number of set bits in the byte is odd. Write a Simian subroutine to turn a 7-bit ASCII character (an input argument) into a parity-encoded character (an output argument). Use a standard subroutine linkage through register R7 as the linking register.

17. Parity encoding (as defined in Problem 16) is often used to spot data transmission errors: if a received message has lost a bit in transmission, the byte to which it belongs will not have the parity bit (bit 8) correctly set. Write a Simian subroutine to produce a 7-bit ASCII character (an output argument) and a parity error number (another output argument) out of a parity-encoded character (an input argument). Use a standard subroutine linkage through register R7 as the linking register.

APPENDIX 1

Apodix circuit simulator

Apodix is a logic circuit simulator with simple input and output arrangements, designed to run under the MS-DOS operating system. This Appendix serves as a user manual to Apodix. It contains details of language syntax and procedures of use. For examples, the reader should consult the appropriate chapters of the main text.

The Apodix circuit simulator

The Apodix simulator is available in the form of MS-DOS diskettes appropriate to the IBM PC or equivalent computers. It uses little memory and requires no hard disk, so it can be run even on minimal machine configurations. Speed and convenience of operation improve, however, if a hard disk is available. A coprocessor serves little purpose, since logic simulation involves few operations that benefit from its presence.

There also exists a version of Apodix designed for the Unix time-sharing system. Its use differs slightly from the MS-DOS version because of differences in the computer operating systems. However, the internal characteristics of both versions (the available logic elements, error messages, etc.) are identical.

Apodix structure

The Apodix package consists of three parts which are most often used together but can be used separately:

1. *Apodixis*, a language processor that reads an Apodix input file and produces an output file in a format usable by Apogee.
2. *Apogee*, a simulation package that carries out the specified simulation and writes the results into an intermediate file usable by Apograph.
3. *Apograph*, a display package that permits examination of the simulation results in quasigraphical form.

The intermediate files are written in printable ASCII characters only, so they can be read and edited. However, they are in a format hard to read without machine aids so few users ever bother to.

Apodix operation

Apodix is normally run from a keyboard terminal and sends its output to the terminal screen. Its three constituent programs are usually run together automatically, by the MS-DOS command

`A> APODIX` *inputfile*

where A> is the MS-DOS system prompt and *inputfile* is a file name acceptable to MS-DOS. The Apodix manager program passes the *inputfile* to Apodixis, which in turn delivers its output to Apogee and eventually to Apograph. Apograph is an interactive program, so its principal output stream is the terminal screen; it does permit the user, however, to write snapshots of the screen content into a file.

The three individual components of Apodix may be run separately. For example, an input file can be examined for syntax errors without carrying out the simulation, by

`A> APODIXIS <` *inputfile*

Similarly, a neat printout of the file can be produced by redirecting the screen output to a file,

`A> APODIXIS <` *inputfile* `>` *outputfile.*

The redirection arrows are necessary because Apodixis takes input from its standard input stream and sends output to the standard output stream, usually the keyboard and screen. Redirection arrows are not used when all three programs are run together under Apodix, because Apodix takes care of redirection.

Apodixis creates an intermediate file called APODIX.TM and leaves it for use by Apogee. After running Apodixis, it suffices to run Apogee,

`A> APOGEE`

to carry out the simulation. Apogee, however, does not create an output display, it merely writes an output file called APOGRAPH.TM. To make the file visible, Apograph is run by

`A> APOGRAPH`

or

`A> APOGRAPH` *filename.*

Apograph looks for APOGRAPH.TM if no file name is given; otherwise it tries to read *filename.*

Apodix does not include any provision for creating or editing input files; they are plain text files so any normal text editor or word processing program (e.g., WordStar, WordPerfect, or *vi*) may be used. Some popular MS-DOS word processors (notably WordStar) use bit 7 of each character as a formatting control flag. Such word processors should be used in an editing mode (sometimes called *nondocument mode*) in which automatic line justification and blank character padding is never done. If difficulties are encountered, the TIDYUP.EXE program (supplied on the MS-DOS program diskette) can be used to strip bit 7 from all characters in a text file. This program reads its standard input and writes to its standard output, so it is usually run by specifying redirection from and to files:

A> TIDYUP < *inputfile* > *outputfile*

The input and output file names must be different, it is not possible to have TIDYUP replace a file by another of the same name.

TIDYUP is able to perform a few reformatting and tidying tasks besides taking care of bit 7. The options available from TIDYUP are best determined by asking,

A> TIDYUP -h

where the h (for *help*) must be in lower case. A screen display of the available options results.

Error handling

Error handling is almost exclusively a matter for Apodix because the input files to Apogee and Apograph are prepared by other programs; if they exist at all, they may be presumed correct. Apodix reads the input file and checks it first for syntax errors, i.e., for input errors that violate the language rules of Apodix and therefore make the input either incomprehensible or ambiguous. It then checks a few major semantic points as well.

Syntax checks by Apodix are all produced as the input file is read; Apodixis does not read ahead and then analyze. It knows only those parts of the input that have already been read, not those yet to come. When a syntax error is encountered, Apodixis reports its location by giving the physical line number in the input file as well as the statement number. The statement number is arrived at by counting statement ends (semicolons); the line number is obtained by keeping count of line-ends in the original input file (*not* the reformatted printout that Apodixis produces). Along with the line and statement numbers Apodixis also reports the last word read before the error was discovered. This word need not necessarily be in error; Apodixis may object to its being there at all, or it may think something is missing (perhaps a closing brace or a semicolon).

Semantic checking by Apodixis mainly consists of verifying that all logic elements have consistent numbers of inputs and outputs. This check is run only after the circuit has undergone syntax analysis, so an input file with numerous syntax errors may produce no semantic error messages at all. In fact, running a semantic check is impossible in principle if the file does not obey the syntax rules; for if the file cannot be understood at all, how can Apodixis know what to check?

File naming

Apodix simulations are generally quick to execute, but can only carry out one experiment at a time. As a result, reasonably serious investigation of even a simple circuit can easily lead to a large number of small files. To manage these effectively, the following file naming convention is suggested.

1. A name of 8 or fewer characters, preferably the same as the circuit name declared in the file itself, is chosen (e.g., *EXAMPLE*).
2. All Apodix input files as manually prepared are given the generic file name, with the suffix *.AP* appended (e.g., *EXAMPLE.AP*).
3. Reformatted printouts, as produced by Apodixis, should be identified by the *.PR* suffix (e.g., *EXAMPLE.PR*).
4. Graphic image output taken from Apograph always has *.IM* appended as an identifying suffix; Apograph itself always produces a file called *APOGRAPH.IM*.
5. Temporary files generated by Apodix all carry the *.TM* suffix. To avoid conflict, this suffix should not be used for other purposes.

This file naming convention is primarily a matter of user convenience, the Apodix software does not require that it be adhered to.

Apodix simulations

An Apodix program is called a *simulation*; it describes exactly one experiment. Simulations are written in a form reminiscent of some general-purpose programming languages. However, the Apodix input language is *object-oriented*, i.e., it describes an experimental setup and the desired results, it does not specify the computational steps to be taken in simulating the experiment. Every Apodix input file contains four parts, that must be presented in the prescribed order:

> title
> circuit description
> input description
> output description

The rules applicable to each part are outlined informally in this section, along with general rules applicable to all parts.

General rules

Apodix input files are written in free format. A statement may be placed anywhere in an input line, and an input line may contain more than one statement. Statements must always be terminated by the semicolon character. The semicolon serves as a statement *terminator*, not as a statement *separator*; in other words, a semicolon must follow every statement, even the last one.

Blanks, tab characters, line ends, and commas are regarded as *white space*. Every word must be separated from its neighbors by white space or by a permissible punctuation mark. It is not important which white-space characters are used. A statement may continue over several lines, for Apodix views the line ends as equivalent to blanks.

User-defined names may use upper or lower case letters, numerals, or mixtures of these. The first character of any name must be a letter, succeeding ones may be letters or numbers. Names may be at most 8 characters long.

Apodix is case sensitive; upper and lower case letters are viewed as entirely separate, indeed unrelated, entities. For example, *Fred, FRED, fred* are all distinct. Case sensitivity extends to both user-defined names and to predefined recognized symbols such as gate names. Thus *jkff* will be recognized as the name of a J–K flip-flop, *JKFF* will not.

Title

Every Apodix simulation must have a title. The title must be on the first line of the input file (except for any blank lines that may precede it) and must occupy a separate line. Apodix regards failure to provide a title as being just as serious as failure to provide a circuit to analyze, and the result is the same: no simulation.

Titles may be up to 40 characters long. They may contain upper or lower case letters, numerals, blanks, and punctuation marks. The title must always be preceded by the character pair /* and the character pair */ must always follow it. (There is no way of including the character pair */ as part of the title.) If the title as given is excessively long, Apodix truncates it to the maximum permissible length.

Circuit description

A circuit is defined in terms of its components and their interconnections. The circuit description must begin with the word *circuit* followed by the circuit name and a colon. The description of the circuit components is enclosed in braces, as

```
circuit example:
    { and: a, s > y;
      not: s  > t;
      and: b, t > z;
      or: y, z > x; }
```

Each statement enclosed by braces begins with a keyword that identifies a logic gate or other circuit element. The element name, followed by a colon, is followed by the names of its input signals; these are followed by a right-arrow > and the output or outputs available from that gate. The signal names in each list are separated by commas, optionally followed by any number of blanks.

Apodix recognizes numerous different element types. These include all the conventional elementary logic gates and an assortment of more complicated combinational logic circuits such as adders and multiplexers. The basic flip-flop types are included, as are a few larger-scale sequential circuits. The available elements are summarized in Tables A1.1 and A1.2. They are described in detail at the end of this Appendix.

Input definition

The inputs to be applied to the circuit are identified by the word *input:* (the colon is obligatory) and are placed in braces:

```
input: {S = 1 (5) 10; T = 0 (7,14); u = 1;}
```

The input definition consists entirely of statements that assign values to signals applied to specified nodes. At $t = 0$ the signal is assigned the value that follows the equal sign. The signal is negated at each of the times listed in parentheses; thus, in the above example, signal u has the value 1 forever, while T begins with value 0, then switches to 1 at $t = 7$, and back to 0 again at $t = 14$. If a number T_N follows the closing parenthesis, it signifies that the signal is periodic and has the same values for any time t in $T_N < t < 2T_N$ as it did in $0 < t < T_N$. S in the above example is periodic, with period 10 time units: $S(10) = S(0)$.

Output

Output definitions are placed in braces following the keyword *output:* (the colon is obligatory). Two types of assignment are permitted within the output definition: requests for variables to be recorded, and a definition of the running time. Variables to be recorded are given as a list, terminated by a semicolon. The total running time may be given in a time assignment statement. A typical output definition is thus

```
output: {S, T, u; time = 120;}
```

The time specification is optional. If it is omitted, Apodix chooses a default value and reports it in the reformatted output listing.

Reserved symbols

User-defined names for variables or circuits must not duplicate reserved words. These include all gate names known to Apodix (in *lower case*!) as well as the following:

circuit
input
output
time

These have special significance only if entered in lower case; their upper-case equivalents may be used for any purpose.

Where numeric input is expected by Apodix, decimal notation is always used. There is no provision for number entry in octal or hexadecimal notation. All numbers must be unsigned integers; Apodix does not understand the concept of sign.

Punctuation marks with special significance to Apodix include $=(){}:>$; as well as the /* */ character pairs.

Limitations of Apodix

Apodix is intended for rapid testing of small circuits and does not permit very large circuits to be analyzed. It places bounds on the memory used, through limitations on the number of variables and gates employed. It does not restrict the computer running time; time and disk storage space on the computer are controlled by the computer operating system, if at all. Restrictions on program files vary between program versions. Apogee displays the restrictions applicable as well as the current version number whenever it starts running.

In addition to the variables externally visible (number of logic elements, number of output channels, ...), Apodix maintains several internal lists to record interconnections of variables. It is possible, though unlikely, that the space available for one of these lists may become exhausted even though the restrictions displayed by Apogee have not been violated. In such cases, Apodix will report that the problem is unmanageably big, but it cannot suggest which user-accessible measure of bigness is at the root of the trouble.

The Apograph postprocessor

Apodixis and Apogee are simple programs to run—they take an input file, perform some operations on it, and produce an output file. The user's main involvement is input file preparation. Apograph, on the other hand, is an interactive program for examining the output produced by Apogee. In sharp contrast to the first two programs in the Apodix suite, Apograph yields little by way of output files but involves the user extensively.

Running Apograph

When Apograph is started, either as part of an Apodix run or by itself, it opens its input file, clears the terminal screen, and displays part of the output file. The initial display always consists of the first eight signals to appear in the output list of the simulation file, shown for the time span $0 < t < 55$. This action usually takes very little time and produces a screen display much like Fig. A1.1. After carrying out this initial step, Apograph awaits instructions from the user.

The user controls Apograph actions and displays by issuing keyboard commands. The commands appear in a small command window at the lower left of the screen; replies and system messages, if there are any, appear in a message window immediately to its right. The commands are simple. They permit the user to move the display forward and backward in time, by choosing the starting time and the calibration of the time axis; they also permit the display to be scrolled vertically if there are more signals than fit on the screen at one time. Screen images (similar to Fig. A1.1) may be written to a file at any time for later printing and examination.

Apograph uses the characters **1** and _ to denote logic *true* and *false* respectively; the caret or up-arrow character ^ stands for *unknown*. The asterisk * stands for variables that were never initialized, or have somehow acquired values other than *true*, *false*, or *unknown*. These can only result from errors; the most probable cause is that an input variable was never given a value.

Apograph commands

The full keyboard command repertoire of Apograph comprises six command verbs: *help, image, next, quit, start, step*. These are described precisely in the following. Commands may be typed in either lower or upper case; Apograph translates all characters to lower case internally and does not care which is typed at the keyboard. Any item in brackets [   ] is optional in the following.

```
┌─────────────────────────┐
│                         │
│          HELP           │
│                         │
└─────────────────────────┘
```

Syntax: HELP [<keyword>]

Action: Responds with a 37-character help message about the (optional) <keyword>. If no <keyword> is specified, HELP is assumed. The keyword may be either the name of a command verb, or one of the additional words listed with the command verbs in screen messages.

```
┌─────────────────────────┐
│                         │
│          IMAGE          │
│                         │
└─────────────────────────┘
```

Syntax: IMAGE <title>

Action: Writes a character-by-character image of the screen content to file *APOGRAPH.IM*. This file is always *appended* to, not overwritten; as a result, the file grows indefinitely and must be purged from time to time.

The screen image is identified by its <title>; to help further in identification, the date and time are written into the area normally used for system messages. Exactly one word is allowed in the title as given in the command. To obtain a

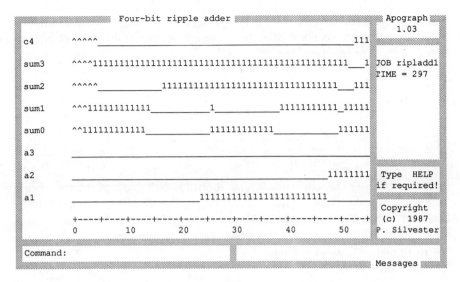

Fig. A1.1.   Screen display produced by the Apograph logic circuit postprocessor.

title consisting of several words, underscores may be used; they are translated into blanks when writing into the file. The title itself is translated into upper case. Thus a title such as

two_word_title

is altered to

TWO WORD TITLE

both on screen and in the file. The file contains printable characters and can be edited or printed with the usual text processing tools. Because the screen image is exactly the width of the full screen, some text processing software may insert extra blank lines.

NEXT

Syntax: NEXT [<number>]

Action: Rewrites the screen display, scrolled upward by <number> lines. If the simulation contains exactly a full screen or less, no action is taken. The scrolling is cyclic; continued redrawing of the screen moves lines off screen at the top and reinserts them at the bottom of the display.

If no <number> is given, the screen is scrolled by four lines (half the display). If <number> is given as zero, the screen is reset to the same configuration of lines as at program startup.

START

Syntax: START [<time>]

Action: Rewrites the screen display, positioned laterally so that <time> is the leftmost time value shown. The <time> may be omitted; it is then taken to be the value shown at the right edge of the screen (i.e., the display is moved left one screen width). Movement can be carried out only within the limits of times for which simulation data is available.

STEP

Syntax: STEP [<time>]

Action: Rewrites the screen display, compressed or expanded so that each time value plotted is greater than its predecessor by <time> units. The starting time value (left edge of the display) is kept fixed. If <time> is omitted, the time step is reset to its value at startup (normally 1 time unit).

QUIT

Syntax: QUIT

Action: Stops execution entirely, returns to operating system.

Syntax: <null line>

Action: A null line (i.e., a RETURN keystroke without any other keys having been pressed) is interpreted as equivalent to a *start* command with the starting time specified as the highest time value currently displayed. This default interpretation permits traversing the entire time axis from left to right by successive RETURN keystrokes.

Available element types

The circuit elements available in Apodix are described in detail in this section. In the following, *Italic* type denotes generic rather than literal information, e.g., *variable* denotes a variable name, not the specific character string *variable*. Items given in square brackets, as for example [this], denote optional items that may be omitted.

An apostrophe affixed to any variable name denotes negation, e.g., T' is the logical inverse of the variable T.

Description: Multiinput AND gate.

Inputs: Two or more inputs $in1,, in2, \ldots, inN$.

Output: One output, *out*.

Syntax: and: $in1, in2[, in3] \ldots [, in8] > out$;

Truth table:

in1	in2	out	in1	in2	out
0	0	0	?	?	?
0	1	0	?	1	?
1	0	0	?	0	0
1	1	1			

Limitations: Not less than 2 and not more than 8 inputs.

Description: Bidirectional N-bit shift/rotate register.

Inputs: Clear C, load L, clock *clk*, shift left/right *slr*, shift/rotate *shr*; bit values $x1, \ldots, xN$.

Output: Parallel available bit values $y1, \ldots, yN$.

Syntax: bsrr: $C, clk, L, slr, shr, x1[, \ldots xN] > y1[, \ldots yN]$;

Action: If $C = 1$, the register is reset to all zeros (regardless of the values of $x1$, $\ldots, xN$ and the setting of L) immediately. If $L = 1$ and $C = 0$, the register is loaded with $x1, \ldots, xN$ at the next rising edge of the clock pulse. If $L = C = 0$, the register contents are shifted left at every rising edge of the clock pulse if $slr = 1$ and shifted right if slr $= 0$, provided $shr = 1$. If $shr = 0$, left and right rotations result. In shifting, the endmost bit is shifted out and lost. In rotations it is replaced at the opposite end of the register.

Limitations: N must not exceed 8. $N = 1$ is acceptable.

```
┌─────────────────────────────┐
│                             │
│            cntr             │
│                             │
│                             │
└─────────────────────────────┘
```

Description: Parallel-load N-bit counter.

Inputs: Load L, enable *enb*, reset R, clock *clk*, parallel loadable bit values $x1, \ldots, xN$.

Output: Parallel available bit values $y1, \ldots, yN$.

Syntax: cntr: enb, R, *clk*, L, $x1[, \ldots xN] > y1[, \ldots yN]$;

Action: If $R = 1$, the counter is reset to all zeros immediately (regardless of the value of *enb* or L). If $L = 1$, the counter is loaded with $x1, \ldots, xN$ (regardless of the value of *enb*) at the next rising edge of the clock pulse. If $L = 0, R = 0$ and *enb* is set, the count is incremented at every rising edge of the clock pulse.

This counter must have parallel-load input lines available. If a counter without the parallel loading facility is required, the resettable counter *rcnt* should be used.

Limitations: N must not exceed 8. $N = 1$ is acceptable.

```
┌─────────────────────────────┐
│                             │
│            dec              │
│                             │
│                             │
└─────────────────────────────┘
```

Description: N-line to 2^N-line decoder

Inputs: $in1, in2, \ldots, inN$

Output: $out1, out2, \ldots, out2^N$

Syntax: dec: $in1, \ldots, inN > out1, out2, \ldots, out2^N$;

Truth table:

in1	in2	out1	out2	out3	out4
0	0	1	0	0	0
0	1	0	1	0	0
1	0	0	0	1	0
1	1	0	0	0	1

Limitations: Decoders are available for $N = 1, 2, 3, 4$.

```
+-----------------------+
|                       |
|          dff          |
|                       |
+-----------------------+
```

Description: Delay (D-type) flip-flop, rising edge triggered

Inputs: Principal input D, clock line *clk*; optionally, preset *ps*, preclear *pc*

Outputs: One output, Q

Syntax: dff: D, *clk*[, *ps, pc*] > Q;

Transition table:

D	old Q	new Q
0	0	0
0	1	0
1	0	1
1	1	1

Operation: Edge-triggered flip-flop; transitions take place at rising edges of the clock pulse. If the optional preset and preclear signals are not specified in the input, dff is precleared, i.e., placed in the state $Q = 0$, at time $t = 0$. The full transition table satisfied by this flip-flop, including undefined states, appears in Table A.1.3.

The preset or preclear line is asserted to establish the state of this flip-flop; when both are low, the circuit operates as prescribed by its transition table. Both *ps* and *pc* must not be asserted simultaneously; if they are, *pc* is given precedence, i.e., the output Q is reset.

```
+-----------------------+
|                       |
|          enc          |
|                       |
+-----------------------+
```

Description: 2^N-line to N-line encoder

Inputs: *in1, in2, . . . , in2^N*

Output: *out1, out2, . . . , outN*

Syntax: enc: *in1, . . . , in2^N* > *out1, out2, . . . , outN*;

Truth table:

out1	out2	in1	in2	in3	in4
0	0	1	0	0	0
0	1	0	1	0	0
1	0	0	0	1	0
1	1	0	0	0	1

Limitations: Encoders are available for $N = 1, 2, 3, 4$.

```
┌─────────────────────────────┐
│                             │
│            flad             │
│                             │
└─────────────────────────────┘
```

Description: One-bit full adder cell.

Inputs: Addend *in1*, augend *in2*, carry in *cin*.

Output: Sum *sum*, carry out *cout*.

Syntax: flad: *in1, in2, cin > sum, cout*;

Truth table: Condensed, noting that *in1, in2, cin* commute.

in1,	in2,	cin	sum	cout
0	0	0	0	0
0	0	1	1	0
0	1	1	0	1
1	1	1	1	1
0	0	?	?	0
0	1	?	?	?
0	?	?	?	?
1	?	?	?	?
?	?	?	?	?

Limitations: None.

```
┌─────────────────────────────┐
│                             │
│            hfad             │
│                             │
└─────────────────────────────┘
```

Description: One-bit half-adder cell.

Inputs: Addend *in1*, augend *in2*

Output: Sum *sum*, carry out *carry*.

Syntax: hfad: *in1, in2 > sum, carry*;

Truth table: Condensed, noting that *in1, in2* commute.

in1,	in2	sum	carry
0	0	0	0
0	1	1	0
1	1	0	1
0	?	?	0
1	?	?	?
?	?	?	?

Limitations: None.

```
┌─────────────────────────────┐
│                             │
│            jkff             │
│                             │
└─────────────────────────────┘
```

Description: J–K flip-flop, rising edge triggered.

Inputs: Principal inputs *J*, *K*, clock *clk* ; optionally, preset *ps*, preclear *pc*.

Output: One output *Q*.

Syntax: jkff: *J*, *K*, *clk*[, *ps*, *pc*] > *Q*;

Transition table:

J	*K*	old *Q*	new *Q*
0	0	0	0
0	0	1	1
0	1	0	0
0	1	1	0
1	0	0	1
1	0	1	1
1	1	0	1
1	1	1	0

Operation: Edge-triggered flip-flop; transitions take place at rising edges of the clock pulse. If the optional preset and preclear signals are not specified in the input, *jkff* is precleared, i.e., placed in the state $Q = 0$, at time $t = 0$. The full transition table satisfied by this flip-flop, including undefined states, appears in Table A1.3.

The preset or preclear line is asserted to establish the state of this flip-flop; when both are low, the circuit operates as prescribed by its transition table. Both *ps* and *pc* must not be asserted simultaneously; if they are, *pc* is given precedence, i.e., the output *Q* is reset.

```
┌─────────────────────────────┐
│                             │
│            mux              │
│                             │
└─────────────────────────────┘
```

Description: 2^N input, *N* controller, enabled multiplexer.

Inputs: Inputs *in1*, *in2*, . . . , controllers *c1*, *c2*, . . . , enable line *enb*

Output: One output line *out*

Syntax: mux: *in1*, *in2*, . . . *in*N, *c1*, . . . *c*N, *enb* > *out*;

Truth table:

in1	in2	c1	enb	out
0	0	0	1	0
0	0	1	1	0
0	1	0	1	0
0	1	1	1	1
1	0	0	1	1
1	0	1	1	0
1	1	0	1	1
1	1	1	1	1
x	x	x	0	0

Limitations: Multiplexers are available for $N = 1, 2, 3, 4$.

```
+-----------------------------+
|                             |
|            nand             |
|                             |
+-----------------------------+
```

Description: Multiinput NAND gate.

Inputs: Two or more inputs *in1,, in2, . . . , in*N.

Output: One output, *out*.

Syntax: nand: *in1, in2*[, *in3*] . . . [, *in8*] > *out*;

Truth table:

in1	in2	out	in1	in2	out
0	0	1	?	?	?
0	1	1	?	1	?
1	0	1	?	0	1
1	1	0			

Limitations: Not less than 2 and not more than 8 inputs.

```
+-----------------------------+
|                             |
|            nor              |
|                             |
+-----------------------------+
```

Description: Multiinput NOR gate.

Inputs: Two or more inputs *in1,, in2, . . . , in*N.

Output: One output, *out*.

Syntax: nor: *in1, in2*[, *in3*] . . . [, *in8*] > *out*;

Truth table:

in1	in2	out	in1	in2	out
0	0	1	?	?	?
0	1	0	?	1	0
1	0	0	?	0	?
1	1	0			

Limitations: Not less than 2 and not more than 8 inputs.

Description: Inverter (NOT gate).

Inputs: One input, *in*.

Output: One output, *out*.

Syntax: not: *in* > *out*;

Truth table:

in	out
0	1
1	0
?	?

Limitations: None.

Description: Multiinput OR gate.

Inputs: Two or more inputs *in1,, in2, . . . , in*N.

Output: One output, *out*.

Syntax: or: *in1, in2*[, *in3*] . . . [, *in8*] > *out*;

Truth table:

in1	in2	out	in1	in2	out
0	0	0	?	?	?
0	1	1	?	1	1
1	0	1	?	0	?
1	1	1			

Limitations: Not less than 2 and not more than 8 inputs.

Description: Parallel-load *N*-bit shift register.

Inputs: Set *S*, reset *R*, clock *clk*, load *L*, parallel-loadable bit values *x1*, . . . , *x*N.

Output: Parallel available bit values $y1, \ldots, yN$.

Syntax: plsr: $S, R, L, clk, x1[, \ldots xN] > y1[, \ldots yN]$;

Action: If $R = 1$, the register is reset to all zeros immediately (regardless of the values of $x1, \ldots, xN$ and the setting of L). If $S = 1$, the register is set to all ones immediately (regardless of the values of $x1, \ldots, xN$ and the setting of L). If $L = 1, R = 0$, the register is loaded with values $x1, \ldots, xN$ at the next rising edge of the clock pulse. If $L = 0, R = 0$, the register contents are shifted left at every rising edge of the clock pulse. The most significant bit is shifted out and lost; the least significant bit is replaced by 0.

Limitations: N must not exceed 8. $N = 1$ is acceptable.

rcnt

Description: N-bit (modulo 2^N) counter.

Inputs: Enable *enb*, reset R, clock *clk*.

Output: Parallel available bit values $y1, \ldots, yN$.

Syntax: rcnt: *enb*, R, *clk*, $> y1[, \ldots yN]$;

Action: If $R = 1$, the counter is reset to all zeros (regardless of the value of *enb*) immediately. If $R = 0$ and *enb* = 1, the count is incremented at every rising edge of the clock pulse. The count progresses modulo 2^N.

Limitations: N must not exceed 8. $N = 1$ is acceptable.

regs

Description: Parallel-load N-bit register.

Inputs: Reset R, clock *clk*, load L; parallel-loadable bit values $x1, \ldots, xN$.

Output: Parallel available bit values $y1, \ldots, yN$.

Syntax: regs: R, *clk*, L, x1$[, \ldots xN] > $y1$[, \ldots yN]$;

Action: If $L = 1$ and $R = 0$, the register is loaded with $x1, \ldots, xN$ at the next rising edge of the clock pulse. If $R = 1$, the register is reset to all zeros (regardless of the values of $x1, \ldots, xN$ and the setting of L) immediately.

Limitations: N must not exceed 8. $N = 1$ is acceptable.

```
┌─────────────────────────────┐
│                             │
│            sreg             │
│                             │
│                             │
└─────────────────────────────┘
```

Description: Serially loadable N-bit shift register.

Inputs: Set S, reset R, clock *clk*, serial data D.

Output: Parallel available bit values $y1, \ldots, yN$.

Syntax: sreg: $S, R, clk, D > y1[, \ldots yN]$;

Action: If $R = 1$, the register is reset to all zeros immediately. If $S = 1$, the register is set to all ones immediately. If $S = R = 0$, the register contents are shifted left at every rising edge of the clock pulse. The most significant bit is shifted out and lost; the least significant bit is replaced by the current value of the serial data line D.

Limitations: N must not exceed 8. $N = 1$ is acceptable. It is not permissible to make $S = R = 1$; if they are, R takes precedence, i.e., the register is reset.

```
┌─────────────────────────────┐
│                             │
│            srff             │
│                             │
│                             │
└─────────────────────────────┘
```

Description: S–R flip-flop, rising edge triggered

Inputs: Set S, reset R, clock *clk*; optionally, preset *ps*, preclear *pc*

Output: Principal output Q, secondary output $Qsec$

Syntax: srff: $S, R, clk[, ps, pc] > Q, Qsec$;

Transition table:

S	R	old Q	new Q
0	0	0	0
0	0	1	1
0	1	0	0
0	1	1	0
1	0	0	1
1	0	1	1
1*	1*	0	?*
1*	1*	1	?*

The asterisk * denotes an inadmissible state.

Action: Edge-triggered flip-flop; transitions take place at rising edges of the clock pulse. If the optional preset and preclear signals are not specified in the input, *srff* is precleared, i.e., placed in the state $Q = 0$, at time $t = 0$. The full transition table satisfied by this flip-flop, including undefined states, appears in Table A1.3.

The preset or preclear line is asserted to establish the state of this flip-flop; when both are low, the circuit operates as prescribed by its transition table. Both *ps* and *pc* must not be asserted simultaneously; if they are, *pc* is given precedence, i.e., the output *Q* is reset.

Limitations: The input $S = R = 1$ is not admissible. For any admissible input, the two outputs are complements of each other, $Qsec = Q'$. If inadmissible input is presented, *srff* yields undefined outputs, $Qsec = Q = undefined$.

```
+-------------------------------+
|                               |
|             tbuf              |
|                               |
+-------------------------------+
```

Description: *N*-bit three-state buffer

Inputs: input *in*, enable *enb*

Output: *out*

Syntax: tbuf: *enb, in1[, . . . , inN] > out1[, . . . , outN]*;

Truth table:

in	enb	out
0	0	
0	1	0
1	0	
1	1	1

Limitations: Not less than 1 and not more than 8 inputs; the number of outputs must match the number of inputs. The output echoes the input if and only if the enable signal is set. If the enable signal is cleared, the output is not set by this gate, its value will remain whatever it may have previously been.

```
+-------------------------------+
|                               |
|             xnor              |
|                               |
+-------------------------------+
```

Description: Multiinput exclusive-NOR gate.

Inputs: Two or more inputs *in1,, in2, . . . , inN*.

Output: One output, *out*.

Syntax: xnor: *in1, in2[, in3] . . . [, in8] > out*;

Truth table:

in1	in2	out	in1	in2	out
0	0	1	?	?	?
0	1	0	?	1	?
1	0	0	?	0	?
1	1	1			

Limitations: Not less than 2 and not more than 8 inputs.

```
┌─────────────────────────────┐
│                             │
│             xor             │
│                             │
└─────────────────────────────┘
```

Description: Multiinput exclusive-OR gate.

Inputs: Two or more inputs *in1,, in2, . . . , in*N.

Output: One output, *out*.

Syntax: xor: *in1, in2[, in3] . . . [, in8] > out*

Truth table:

in1	*in2*	*out*	*in1*	*in2*	*out*
0	0	0	?	?	?
0	1	1	?	1	?
1	0	1	?	0	?
1	1	0			

Limitations: Not less than 2 and not more than 8 inputs.

Table A1.1. Circuit elements recognized by Apodix

Name	Element description	Inputs	Outputs
not	Inverter (NOT gate)	1	1
and	N-input AND gate	2 to 8	1
nand	N-input NAND gate	2 to 8	1
or	N-input OR gate	2 to 8	1
nor	N-input NOR gate	2 to 8	1
xor	N-input exclusive-OR gate	2 to 8	1
xnor	N-input exclusive-NOR gate	2 to 8	1
hfad	Half adder (no carry in)	2	2
flad	Full adder cell	3	2
mux	2^N-input multiplexer, $N < 5$	$2^N + N + 1$	1
dec	N to 2^N decoder, $N < 5$	N	2^N
enc	2^N to N encoder, $N < 5$	2^N	N
tbuf	Three-state buffer, $N < 9$ lines	$N + 1$	N
srff	Set-reset flip-flop	3 or 5	2
dff	Delay flip-flop	2 or 4	1
jkff	J-K flip-flop	3 or 5	1
rcnt	Modulo 2^N counter, $N < 9$	3	N
cntr	Parallel-load N-bit counter	$4 + N$	N
sreg	Serial-load shift register	4	N
regs	Parallel-load register	$3 + N$	N
bsrr	Bidirectional shift/rotate	$5 + N$	N
plsr	Parallel-load shift register	$4 + N$	N

Table A1.2. Truth tables of combinational logic gates

a	b	and	or	xor	nand	nor	xnor	not(b)
0	0	0	0	0	1	1	1	1
0	1	0	1	1	1	0	0	0
0	?	0	?	?	1	?	?	?
1	0	0	1	1	1	0	0	1
1	1	1	1	0	0	0	1	0
1	?	?	1	?	?	0	?	?
?	0	0	?	?	1	?	?	1
?	1	?	1	?	?	0	?	0
?	?	?	?	?	?	?	?	?

Table A1.3. Transition tables of edge-triggered flip-flops

S	R	Q(0)	Q(1)	J	K	Q(0)	Q(1)	D	Q(0)	Q(1)
0	0	0	0	0	0	0	0	0	0	0
0	0	1	1	0	0	1	1	0	1	0
0	0	?	?	0	0	?	?	0	?	0
0	1	0	0	0	1	0	0	1	0	1
0	1	1	0	0	1	1	0	1	1	1
0	1	?	0	0	1	?	0	1	?	1
0	?	0	0	0	?	0	0	?	0	?
0	?	1	?	0	?	1	?	?	1	?
0	?	?	?	0	?	?	?	?	?	?
1	0	0	1	1	0	0	1			
1	0	1	1	1	0	1	1			
1	0	?	1	1	0	?	1			
1	1	0	?	1	1	0	1			
1	1	1	?	1	1	1	0			
1	1	?	?	1	1	?	?			
1	?	0	?	1	?	0	1			
1	?	1	?	1	?	1	?			
1	?	?	?	1	?	?	?			
?	0	0	?	?	0	0	?			
?	0	1	1	?	0	1	1			
?	0	?	?	?	0	?	?			
?	1	0	?	?	1	0	?			
?	1	1	?	?	1	1	0			
?	1	?	?	?	1	?	?			
?	?	0	?	?	?	0	?			
?	?	1	?	?	?	1	?			
?	?	?	?	?	?	?	?			

APPENDIX 2

The Simian simulator

This Appendix describes an implementation of the Simian computer in the form of a simulator and gives user instructions for running it. It is not intended as an introduction to Simian, but as a reference guide to its use. Programming notes and an extensive description of the Simian structure are given in the chapters dealing with Simian, to which the reader should refer for introductory matter.

Simulation

The Simian simulator permits programs to be written and tested for a Simian computer on various other physical computers. As described here, Simian is implemented under the MS-DOS operating system and will run on IBM-PC or PC-compatible computers of almost any system configuration. A hard disk is not required (although convenient) and a coprocessor, if present, will be used for very few operations. MS-DOS release 3.0 or above is recommended to ensure that all system services are available, even though Simian will run under most system versions above release 2.00. A version of Simian also exists for the Unix operating system.

The Simile assembler that translates Simian code is a separate entity, not part of this processor simulation. An immediate consequence of this separation is that Simian programs must be given to the simulator (via the loader) in object form. Simian, in other words, cannot accept assembler language programs; they must be converted into object code first, either manually or by means of Simile.

Running Simian

The Simian simulator is invoked by its name SIMIAN. In other words, typing its name in response to the MS-DOS system prompt, as in

`A> SIMIAN`

suffices to set the simulator running. Simian then displays a sign-on screen containing program identification. When any command is issued at the keyboard, the sign-on screen disappears and is replaced by the standard window layout, shown in Fig. A2.1, which remains unchanged for the duration of the simulator

349

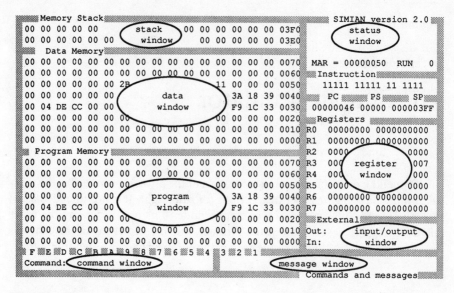

Fig. A2.1. Window layout for the Simian display. The display is updated after every instruction execution.

run. Once the window pattern has been established, Simian places the screen cursor in its command window and awaits keyboard instructions.

Simian communicates with the user through two one-line windows, both placed at the bottom of the screen display. Commands typed at the keyboard are echoed in the left window; the right window serves to communicate responses and messages from Simian to the user. Action in response to any user command is begun as soon as the keyboard line has been terminated by pressing RETURN. The keyboard cursor, however, is not returned to the left edge of the command window until the action is complete. The cursor position thus indicates whether Simian is working (cursor at right end of command line) or awaiting commands (cursor at left end of command line). The last keyboard line remains visible in the command window; it is not cleared until the first character of a new command line has been typed.

To exit from Simian, the *quit* command is used. Like any other command, it is issued when Simian is awaiting commands. No arguments or parameters are available with this command:

```
quit
```

This and other Simian command verbs are described in detail in this Appendix. Quick, although brief, memory-joggers on the command structure are also available by typing *help* while Simian is awaiting a command.

Simian screen display

The display used by Simian completely fills the terminal screen. It divides the screen into ten independent *windows,* as shown in Fig. A2.1. These are:

1. Status window. The state of Simian is shown. The current value of the memory address register is always shown, as is the number of program steps left to run; other information is only shown if currently relevant.
2. Instruction window. The last instruction executed is shown in this window at all times. The display format is binary, to make instructions reasonably easy to read.
3. Special register window. Current values of the program counter and stack pointer are shown, as well as bits 4 through 0 of the processor status register (the VCNLZ flags).
4. Register window. All general register contents are shown in hexadecimal as well as unsigned decimal interpretations.
5. Stack window. The region of memory immediately surrounding the stack pointer is displayed in this window.
6. Data memory window. The region of memory immediately surrounding the memory address register content is displayed in this window.
7. Program window. The region of memory immediately surrounding the program counter content is displayed in this window.
8. Input/output window. Characters sent out or in through the input/output ports are scrolled through this window, so the most recent 20 or so characters sent in or out are always visible.
9. Command window. Shows the last command entered, or (if at least one character has been typed at the keyboard) the command currently being entered.
10. Message window. Shows status messages, error messages, and responses to queries by the user.

All display windows are updated at the end of each instruction execution cycle. Where necessary, some windows are also updated during instruction execution.

Execution control

Simian maintains a *run counter* whose content is always shown in the status window. This counter is decremented at each instruction execution; when the counter reaches zero, the machine is halted. Control then returns to the keyboard and Simian awaits the next command. There is no way of halting execution from the keyboard until the run counter reaches zero.

Execution control may also be exercised by setting breakpoints. Simian maintains a *breakpoint address register* and a breakpoint flag. The register is initially set to 00000000 and the flag to OFF. Before every instruction fetch, the breakpoint register is examined and the run control counter is set to zero if the breakpoint has been reached, i.e., if the program counter content matches that of the breakpoint register or is 1 short of it. (The latter arrangement allows for the fact that instructions occupy two bytes.) In other words, the machine is halted before fetching and decoding the instruction at which the breakpoint is situated.

The status display area will show BREAK 00000000 if the breakpointing is enabled at 00000000; the corresponding area of the display will be blank if the breakpoint mechanism is not active.

Simulator commands

All Simian commands have the same general form. They always begin with the command verb itself; the verb is followed (in most cases) by one or more descriptive parameters:

command parameters *CR*

Every command line issued from the keyboard must always terminate in the carriage return *CR*, generated by means of the RETURN keystroke. All acceptable Simian command verbs are defined in the following. Words shown in CAPITAL LETTERS are commands or reserved words and must be entered in precisely the form shown (although lower case may be substituted). Words shown in angle brackets, as in <word> identify generic items; actual values or identifiers must be used and the angle brackets must *not* be typed. Words shown in square brackets are optional. For example, the BREAK command must always begin with the command verb itself, optionally followed by a memory address.

BREAK

Syntax: BREAK [<address>]

Action: A processor breakpoint is enabled, disabled, or reset. If the optional <address> is included in the command, the breakpoint register is set to <address> and the breakpoint mechanism is enabled. If BREAK is issued with no address, the breakpoint flag is toggled to its opposite state. The default breakpoint setting at startup is 00000000. The breakpoint address is shown in the status display if the breakpoint mechanism is active; if not, the status field shows a blank in that area.

Breakpoints are responded to when the breakpoint address (or 1 less than the breakpoint address) appears in the program counter. At that moment the machine is halted and brought back to its quiescent state, awaiting an instruction.

CLEAR

Syntax: CLEAR [<byte>]

Action: The entire memory of Simian is cleared so every byte contains the value <byte>, which must appear in the command in hexadecimal notation. If <byte> is not given, the memory is reset to all nulls. Registers, including the memory address register, are unaffected.

DUMP

Syntax: DUMP <filename>

Action: Writes an image of the memory contents and program counter content to <filename>. The memory content is dumped byte by byte, 16 to a line, followed by a semicolon and the trailing four digits of the rightmost address. Loader directives .LOAD, .PROG, and .FINI are included in the file as required, to permit later reading by the LOAD command.

FILE

Syntax: FILE <in/out> [<filename>]

Action: Connects files to the input or output stream, or disconnects them. The first argument, which must be present, must be either *IN* or *OUT*. The second argument gives the file name to be connected; if another file was previously connected, it will be disconnected before connecting the newly named file. If no file name is given, any currently connected file is disconnected.

HELP

Syntax: HELP [<keyword>]

Action: Responds with a 37-character help message about the (optional) <keyword>, which may be any command or reserved word. If no <keyword> is specified, HELP is assumed. Because the full list of command additional a 37-character line, two keywords are accepted, *verb* and *verb2*; these produce two (overlapping) partial verb lists.

```
┌─────────────────────────────┐
│                             │
│           IMAGE             │
│                             │
└─────────────────────────────┘
```

Syntax: IMAGE <title>

Action: Writes a character-by-character image of the screen content to file *SIMIAN.IM*. This file is always *appended* to, not overwritten; as a result, the file grows indefinitely and must be purged from time to time.

The screen is identified by its <title>; to help further in identification, the date and time are written into the area normally used for system messages. Exactly one word is allowed in the title as given in the command. To obtain a title consisting of several words, underscores may be used; they are translated into blanks when writing into the file. The title itself is translated into upper case only. A title such as

two_word_title

is altered to

TWO WORD TITLE

both on the screen and in the file. The file contains printable characters and can be edited or printed with the usual text processing tools. Because the screen image is exactly the width of the full screen, some text processing software may insert extra blank lines.

```
┌─────────────────────────────┐
│                             │
│           LOAD              │
│                             │
└─────────────────────────────┘
```

Syntax: LOAD <filename>

Action: Loads the content of <filename> into Simian memory. The file may have been manually prepared, or may be the output of the Simile assembler. Files created by the Simian DUMP command are also in the correct format for loading, so it is practical to dump memory when stopping work, then to resume later by LOADing the dumped file. Loading is a slow process, it can take as long as two or three minutes.

```
┌─────────────────────────────┐
│                             │
│           PUT               │
│                             │
└─────────────────────────────┘
```

Syntax: PUT <value> [<location>]

Action: A machine <location> is loaded with a <value>, a hexadecimal number. The <location> may be a memory address or an identifiable register name: R*n*, PC, PS, SP, MAR. The <value> must be one byte long (two hexadecimal characters) if a memory location is specified; it must be four bytes long (eight characters) if a register is specified.The <location> may be omitted; in that case memory will be loaded at the place pointed to by the memory address register and the memory address register will be incremented. No incrementation occurs if the <value> is loaded to a register. The memory address register content appears in the status display area at all times. Attempts to set PC, SP, or MAR to extremes of memory (highest or lowest possible location) are in some cases not permitted.

```
QUIT
```

Syntax: QUIT

Action: Stops execution entirely, returns to operating system.

```
RUN
```

Syntax: RUN [<number> [<time>]]

Action: Runs simulation of <number> instructions, taking approximately <time> seconds for each; <number> and <time> are given in decimal notation. The <time> option is only available in time-shared implementations of Simian, not under MS-DOS. A default number of steps is assumed if RUN is issued without any number. As the simulation runs, the number of steps remaining to the next processor halt appears in the status display. The basic running cycle comprises

> fetch a keyboard command
> decode it
> execute it
> refresh display

Single stepping is possible by asking for RUN 1. To simplify work, a null keyboard line (generated by simply pressing RETURN) is taken to mean RUN 1.

While running, the program counter controls the sequence of instruction execution and subsequent fetches. Running is halted if the run counter reaches zero, or if the breakpoint address shown in the status display area is reached by the PC, or if the PC attempts to access memory not existent in the computer.

SHOW

Syntax: SHOW <location> <format>

Action: Displays the content of <location>, which may be a register or a memory address, in the screen message area in the form prescribed by <format>. The format specification consists of one numeral and one letter, without any intervening space, e.g., 4D. The numeral may be 1, 2, or 4, to indicate the number of bytes to be shown. The letter may be C, D, O, U, or X, to request character, signed decimal, octal, unsigned decimal, or hexadecimal display. The specifying character is mandatory; the numeral is optional. If it is omitted, 4 is understood for registers, 1 for memory locations.

Character displays are shown in a field of four spaces for each character; the first is always blank, the third is occupied by a printable character. If the character to be displayed is printable, it is placed in this field. If it is not printable because it is a control character, the corresponding printable character is shown, preceded by ^ , as for example ^A. If it is not printable because bit 7 is high, the character is shown, followed by an exclamation mark ! as for example A! or A!. The DELETE character is shown as the letter pair *dl*. CAUTION: for internal reasons, the percent sign and the blank character are both shown as blank.

Syntax: <null line>

Action: A null line (i.e., a RETURN keystroke without any other keys having been pressed) is interpreted as equivalent to RUN 1. This default interpretation permits single-stepping through programs by successive RETURN keystrokes.

Instructions and effective addresses

Simian understands various machine-language instructions and addressing modes. Two, one, or zero operands may appear with each instruction; each instruction must be further qualified by an operand length argument. The general structure of instructions is

operand 2	*operand 1*	*length*	*operation*
5 bits	5 bits	2 bits	4 bits

The operand fields are encoded in four different ways, depending on the operation to be performed. The length field is encoded in either of two ways, depending on the operation. Operation codes are encoded in one way only.

Operand encoding

Operands appear as five-bit fields in the instruction word. There are four ways of decoding the operand references: register, special register, offset, or flags. Each occurs in a different context so there is never any ambiguity about which one is involved.

register: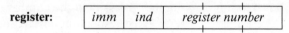

The register number is an unsigned binary number, 000 to 111, that identifies a general register. The *ind* and *imm* bits signify

$$
\begin{aligned}
ind &= 0 && \text{direct addressing} \\
&= 1 && \text{indirect addressing} \\
imm &= 0 && \text{register addressing} \\
&= 1 && \text{immediate addressing.}
\end{aligned}
$$

When immediate addressing is used, the register number is ignored. It should be set to 000 in hand-coded instructions.

special register:

The register number is an unsigned binary number, 00 to 10, which identifies a special register:

$$
\begin{aligned}
00 && \text{program counter} \\
01 && \text{stack pointer} \\
10 && \text{processor status register.}
\end{aligned}
$$

The *ind* bit signifies

$$
\begin{aligned}
ind &= 0 && \text{direct addressing} \\
&= 1 && \text{indirect addressing (stack pointer only!)}
\end{aligned}
$$

Immediate addressing is not available with special registers and indirect addressing is available only for the stack pointer.

offset: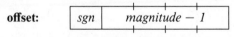

The offset is stored as a signed magnitude; *sgn* = 1 denotes negative offsets. The magnitude stored is actually 1 less than intended, so a zero offset cannot be stored.

flags:

V	C	N	L	Z

Each flag setting corresponds to one of the processor flag bits in the processor status register: 1 denotes set, 0 reset.

Lengths

Two ways exist for using the length field: as an operand length indicator or as a flagging argument for special register handling.

length:

The length is shown as a binary number, 1 less than the number of bytes to be handled by the operation: 00, 01, or 11 corresponding to 1, 2, or 4 bytes. An error is considered to have occurred for lengths of 3 (code 10).

displacement:

spc	lng

This form of use occurs in operand-free instructions such as BRANCH or CALL.

$lng = 0$		16-bit address displacement
$= 1$		32-bit address
$spc = 0$		no special register alteration
$= 1$		store program counter on stack

Instruction repertoire

Every one of the 16 possible instruction codes is understood by Simian as a request for some action. The actions are as given in Table A2.1.

In Table A2.1, status flags are left unaltered by an instruction wherever a blank is shown. The character x indicates that the flag is set to 1 if the condition is true, reset to 0 if false. The character y, which occurs for two entries with the CMP instruction, indicates that the flags are given the values they would have had for a twos complement subtraction with the same operands. In comparisons and subtractions, the procedure followed is to form the logical complement, increment, then add. The flags reflect the events occurring on that last addition.

Loader directives

The *load* command of Simian invokes a loader program which reads machine-language text from an input file and loads it into Simian memory. The loader is permanently embedded in Simian (in a hardware implementation of Simian, it would be placed in read-only memory). Loading is controlled by *loader directives* that instruct the loader where and how to load. These are placed into the machine-language text file in the appropriate places.

Loader directives issued to Simian are input lines that begin with a dot (period) character. They guide the loading of the program, not its execution; program execution is entirely controlled by the processor instructions contained within the program itself. Once the program has been loaded, the loader directives have already been acted upon and are no longer known to the simulator.

.FINI

Syntax: .FINI

Action: Informs Simian that the end of the object file has been reached; no more text remains to be loaded.

Remarks: The .FINI directive should must be physically the last line of the Simian input file. Anything following this directive will not be read and will not be loaded. If this directive is omitted, loading continues to the end of the object file.

.LOAD

Syntax: .LOAD <*address*>

Action: Directs the Simian loader to load the object text to follow into a set of sequential locations beginning at the memory address given in this directive. Loading in this fashion continues until some other directive is encountered. A .LOAD can be terminated by another .LOAD, so that strings of bytes can be loaded into different areas of memory if they are begun with separate .LOAD directives that give starting addresses of the contiguous strings of bytes.

Remarks: <*address*> must be a valid address value for Simian. It must be given in hexadecimal notation. There may be as many .LOAD directives as desired within any one program. If this directive is omitted, Simian assumes .LOAD 20 was meant and loads accordingly.

.PROG

Syntax: .PROG <*address*>

Action: Causes Simian to initialize the program counter with a given address. It thereby allows the user to specify the starting location for program execution.

Remarks: *<address>* must be a valid address value for Simian. It must be given in hexadecimal notation. There may be more than one .PROG directive in a program file, but only the last one will have any effect. The .PROG directive is usually placed at the end of the listing, but its location is not important. If no directive appears in the object file, the program counter content remains as it was prior to loading.

Implementation notes

Simian has one input device and one output device. The I/O units are memory mapped; their port addresses are normally

input data:	0000000A
input status:	0000000B
output data:	0000000C
output status:	0000000D

The available memory is 1024 bytes, located at addresses 00000000 to 000003FF.

These and other factual details may differ in some Simian versions. In all cases, they are always shown in the sign-on screen display whenever Simian starts up.

Table A2.1. Summary of Simian instructions

Hex	Bin	Mnemonic	Description	Operands		Length	V	C	N	L	Z
0	0000	ADD.x	add	reg	reg	lng	x	x	x	0	x
1	0001	SUB.x	subtract	reg	reg	lng	x	x	x	0	x
2	0010	CMP.x	compare	reg	reg	lng	y	y	x	x	x
3	0011	LD.x	load	reg	reg	lng					
4	0100	AND.x	logical product	reg	reg	lng					x
5	0101	OR.x	logical sum	reg	reg	lng					x
6	0110	ROL.x	rotate left	off	reg	lng					x
7	0111	SHLA.x	arithmt shift	off	reg	lng		x			x
8	1000	SHL.x	logical shift	off	reg	lng		x			x
9	1001	NOT.x	complement	00	reg	lng					x
a	1010	INC.x	increment	off	reg	lng	x	x	x	0	x
b	1011	NOP	no operation	00	00	0					
c	1100	BR	branch	flg	flg	0					
		CALL	call subroutine	flg	flg	2					
		JM	jump	flg	flg	1					
		JS	jump subroutine	flg	flg	3					
d	1101	POP.x	pop from stack	reg	09	lng					
e	1110	PUSH.x	push on stack	09	reg	lng					
f	1111	RET	return subrout	00	09	3					
		SAVE	push PS flags	09	02	0					
		REST	pop PS flags	02	09	0					
		HALT	halt processor	1F	1F	3					

APPENDIX 3

The Simile assembler

Simile is a simple assembler able to translate mnemonic instruction codes into Simian machine language. This appendix describes the syntax rules of the assembler language, the instructions available in it, and the assembler directives available for controlling the way translation is carried out.

Running Simile

Simile is a very simple, classical two-pass assembler. It accepts input from a file of assembler language text and translates it into Simian machine instructions. Unlike most assemblers, Simile produces only a single output file, combining the object code it produces with a listing of the assembler language program. This arrangement is convenient for checking code; it is made possible by the unconventional input format of the Simian loader, which accepts object code as hexadecimally represented byte images. Simile output files contain printable characters only, so they can be printed, displayed, and edited like any other text files.

Terminal commands

Simile is available on diskettes for the MS-DOS operating system. It is invoked by the command

```
A> SIMILE PROGRAM.AS PROGRAM.OB
```

where **A>** is the MS-DOS command prompt. The file *PROGRAM.AS* is the input file containing the source (assembler language) text; *PROGRAM.OB* is the output file containing the object code for Simian. In addition to the object file, Simile also produces a symbol table and a brief statistical report. These appear on the terminal screen. To place them in a file instead, it suffices to specify a third file name,

```
A> SIMILE PROGRAM.AS PROGRAM.OB PROGRAM.SY
```

If an object file is not immediately wanted (e.g., to check fragments of assembler language code for syntax errors without saving the object code), the object file name may be omitted:

```
A> SIMILE PROGRAM.AS
```

In this case Simile sends the object file the standard output stream, normally the terminal screen. It is also possible to omit the input file name,

```
A> SIMILE
```

Input is then taken from the standard input stream (normally the terminal keyboard). All output is placed in the standard output stream. This possibility can be of value for checking brief program fragments, for example, to find the binary form of one or two instructions.

File names

Neither the operating system nor Simile makes any assumptions about file names, so any file names acceptable to the operating systems will be accepted by Simile. However, file housekeeping is simplified if a consistent nomenclature is adopted. Programmers generally find it convenient to use the same name for related files, identifying its several derivatives by two-letter suffixes. Recommended suffixes are *.AS* for assembler language files, *.OB* for object files, and *.SY* for symbol table files.

Simile also produces an intermediate file containing the partly translated text passed from the first to the second pass of assembly. This file is always located in the current directory and is always called *SIMILE.TMP* under MS-DOS. This name must not be used for any other purpose.

Input preparation

A Simile input file is organized as a set of lines, with one instruction, directive, or set of data items per line. The file may contain the following elements:

> Assembler language instructions
> Simile assembler directives
> Numeric data items
> Blank lines

Input files may be prepared using any commonly available text editor, since the file contains nothing but printable characters. (Caution: WordStar and some other MS-DOS word processors use non-ASCII 8-bit characters internally.) A typical input file may have the following appearance:

```
.ORG 32
START:  LD.B [R2], [R1] ; Copy one character.
        INC.B R0, 1     ; Increment counter,
        CMP.B R0, #10    ;   compare it to 16.
        BZ NEXT         ; Branch to end if 16.
        INC.L R1, 1     ; Increment source and
        INC.L R2, -1    ; destination pointers
        BR START        ; and go for the next!
NEXT:   HALT            ; Halt processor.
```

```
.DATA 152
0a ab dd                        ; The data needed!
.END
```

Comments may be included in every line containing data or an assembler language instruction. Directives may not be accompanied by comments. The comment must be separated from the translatable text by a semicolon. Simile ignores the semicolon and any characters to the right of it, so comments may only be placed at the right-hand side of each line of assembler language text.

Embedded object code

Lines containing numeric data or object code may be included in assembler language text. Such text, however, is subject to restrictions. It must be organized in the same manner as Simile output, i.e., with every byte represented as a letter pair divided from its neighbors by a single blank. Bytes are loaded in sequence, with the rightmost byte in every line loaded first. For example, the following input file is similar to the last example, but with two bytes of literal text inserted:

```
.ORG 32
START:   LD.B [R2], [R1]  ; Copy one character.
         INC.B R0, 1      ; Increment counter,
         CMP.B R0, #10    ;   compare it to 16.
         BZ NEXT          ; Branch on 16 in R0.
         INC.L R1, 1      ; INC source and des-
.DATA *
9F DC                     ;              inserted data!
.ORG *
         INC.L R2, -1     ;   tination pointers,
         BR START         ;     return for more...
NEXT:    HALT             ; Quit if count = 16.
.DATA 152
0a ab dd                  ; The data needed!
.END
```

The bytes to be merged into the object code are preceded and followed by the assembler directives .DATA * and .ORG *. The first informs the assembler that the following text is to be passed on to the loader exactly as it stands. The second requests that translation be resumed. In these directives an asterisk replaces the memory address, indicating that sequential addresses are to be used.

Numeric data or embedded code lines may contain comments, set off by semicolons as usual.

Blank lines

Blank lines are of no significance to Simile, so they are weeded out on the first reading of the input text. They are ignored completely and are not even reproduced in the output. Blank lines are not the same thing as comment lines with no assembler language code (i.e., lines blank except for a single semicolon); the latter are reproduced in the output.

Labels

Symbolic labels may be used in branch and jump instructions in place of numeric values. Numeric values must be given as *signed* hexadecimal numbers, e.g., 8, −A, −F03. Confusion may arise between hexadecimal values and labels composed of alphanumeric characters (e.g., FAD could be either). Wherever ambiguity may exist, numeric values must be prefixed by a sign or a zero. Thus 0FAD and +FAD clearly represent numbers, FAD will be understood as a symbolic label.

Output file format

The output file format of Simile is designed to be directly loadable by Simian. However, it contains only printable characters so it may be read, edited, or printed with the usual text processing tools.

File layout

The Simile output file contains the assembled text and one or two levels of commentary. A typical file is laid out as follows:

```
; SIMILE version 1.02          Mon Jun 22 13:41:56 1987
; charactr.as
.LOAD 32
52 43 ; 0032 START: LD.B [R2], [R1]   ; Copy character.
00 0A ; 0034         INC.B R0, 1       ; Incr. counter,
04 02 ; 0036         CMP.B R0, #10     ;   compare to 16.
10
F7 CC ; 0039         BZ NEXT           ; Branch on 16 .
00 08
08 3A ; 003d         INC.L R1, 1       ; INC source, des-
14 3A ; 003f         INC.L R2, -1      ;   tin. pointers,
FF CC ; 0041         BR START          ;   return for more.
FF ED
FF FF ; 0045 NEXT:   HALT              ; Quit if count 16.
.LOAD 152
0A AB DD
.FINI
```

The file begins with a header showing the version number of Simile and the date of assembly. The second line of the header shows the name of the source file. Thereafter, the assembled code follows. Each line contains at its left the assembled object code, followed by the memory location of the rightmost byte of the code shown. The original assembler language text and the original comments are placed on the same line, but separated from all informative matter and comment by a semicolon. The Simian loader ignores everything to the right of the *leftmost semicolon* in each line, so that the source text, commentary, and memory locations are all treated as comments by the loader.

The source code is not reproduced by Simile in its original format; Simile reformats lines as it has read and understood them. In keeping with the IEEE assembler language standard as well as historical practice, Simile employs only upper case when echoing input text. The only exception to this rule is the original comments, which are reproduced as they were initially entered (including upper and lower case distinctions). Comments may be truncated if they are excessively long, and may be replaced by error messages if errors are encountered.

Additional lines

Simile source text is written one instruction to a line. When assembled, an instruction may produce from two to ten bytes of object code, because the two-byte instruction may be followed by from one to eight bytes of additional material, such as immediate operands, branch offsets, or addresses. Simile usually places these additional items on additional output lines.

When additional output lines are generated by Simile, up to four bytes are placed on each additional line. These bytes are displayed in the order they appear in memory, so a given additional line may or may not correspond to logical entities such as addresses or operands.

Comments are appended to additional lines only where errors are encountered by the second pass of the assembler. Except for forward branching references, the content of additional lines is generated in the first pass of assembly. Location counter values are always established at that time. In the case of branching statements with forward label references, the appropriate number of bytes is reserved but not used until the second pass. The intermediate file generated by the first pass includes instead an output line containing a plus or minus sign (to identify the line), the unresolved label, and the current location counter reading. These temporary entries are replaced by label values on the second pass, when the symbol table is complete.

Error messages

In common with most simple assemblers, Simile flags errors but does not attempt to produce extensive diagnostic messages. Each assembler language text line is ordinarily quite brief and simple, so the nature of an error is usually easy to determine once its existence and general character are known.

On the first pass of assembly, Simile produces an error code consisting of a single long integer, in which the six least significant bits are set to flag particular kinds of errors. They are:

> bit 0 Label missing, too long, or otherwise bad
> bit 1 Operation code missing, invalid or indecipherable
> bit 2 Operand length wrong, too long, or indecipherable
> bit 3 Destination operand too long or indecipherable
> bit 4 Source operand too long or indecipherable
> bit 5 Labels multiply defined, or too many labels

Bits 31 through 6 of the error word are always reset to zero.

Some errors are not of a localizable nature. For example, reference to an undefined label does not constitute a syntax error in the line where it occurs; it is rather a semantic error related to the entire program. Such errors are flagged with verbal messages. Consider, for instance, the following erroneous version of the last example program:

```
.ORG 32
START:  LD.B [R2], [R1]           ; Copy character.
        INC.B R0, 1               ; Incr. counter,
        CMP.B R9, #10             ;   compare to 16.
        BZ NEXT                   ; Branch on 16.
        INC.L R1, 1               ; INC source, des-
        INC.L R2, -1              ;   tin. pointers,
        BR START                  ;   return for more.
NMEXT:  HLAT                      ; Quit if count 16.
.DATA 152
0a ab dd                          ; The data needed!
.END
```

An attempt to assemble this program with Simile results in the output

```
.LOAD 32
42 03 ; 0032 START:  LD.B [R2], [R1]   ; Copy character.
00 0A ; 0034         INC.B R0, 1       ; Incr. counter,
04 02 ; 0035         CMP.B R9, #10     ; Error 0008
F7 CC ; 0036         BZ NEXT           ; Branch on 16.
-NEXT 36             ;    Error:  undefined label!
08 3A ; 003a         INC.L R1, 1       ; INC source, des-
14 3A ; 003c         INC.L R2, -1      ;   tin. pointers,
FF CC ; 003e         BR START          ;   return for more.
FF F0
FF FF ; 0042 NMEXT:  HLAT              ; Error 0002
.LOAD 152
0A AB DD                              ; The data needed!
.PROG 32
.FINI
```

Error messages replace comments in the source code listing wherever errors are encountered. Messages are brief, consisting of the word ERROR and may include the error code number (shown as hexadecimal).

To illustrate the makeup of error codes, suppose an assembler language statement has a bad label, an indecipherable operation code, and an incomprehensible source operand:

```
LAB%EL: ZAP.S [R3], R9
```

The error word will be made up as follows:

Bad source operand, R9	Bit 4	. . . 1 . . . .
Bad operation code ZAP	Bit 1	. . . . . . 1 .
Bad label LAB%EL	Bit 0	 1
All other bits are reset:		0 0 0 1 0 0 1 1

The hexadecimal equivalent of this unsigned binary number is 13; Simile will therefore report *Error 0013*.

Directives

A Simile assembler language program may include assembler directives. Assembler directives are used to control the assembly process. Simile also generates any loader directives that may be needed and passes them on to the Simian loader.

Assembler directives

Simian assembler directives may be inserted anywhere in assembler text. The effect of any directive is immediate, and continues in force until canceled or superseded by another directive. The three available assembler directives, with details of their use, follow.

```
.DATA
```

Syntax: .DATA *location*

Action: Stops translation and causes the following text to be interpreted as hexadecimally coded bytes, to be loaded into sequential memory locations beginning at *location*. The *location* may be a hexadecimal memory address, or it may be the asterisk character *, indicating that the locations to be used are those immediately following the already translated text.

Remarks: The data to be loaded must be presented as a set of hexadecimal byte images, either upper or lower case. Loading proceeds line by line, with the loading sequence *from right to left* within each line. The first byte will be loaded at address *location*, the second at the next higher memory location, and so on. As many .DATA directives as desired may be included in an assembler language program.

```
.END
```

Syntax: .END

Action: Terminates assembly.

Remarks: An .END directive is optional in Simile input. If there is one, it is converted into the .FINI loader directive; if there is none, a .FINI is generated when the input file has been exhausted. Any lines following .END are not read by Simile. A program may contain at most one .END directive.

```
                    .ORG
```

Syntax: .ORG *location*

Action: Resets location counter so that the next line assembled is assigned the new *location*. Initiates translation, so the lines to follow are regarded as source text. The *location* may be a hexadecimal memory address, or it may be the asterisk character *, indicating that the locations to be used are those immediately following whatever object code came before.

Remarks: *Location* must be an admissible Simian memory location. There may be as many .ORG locations as desired within any one source program. An .ORG directive may be used to set or reset the assembly location counter. If no .ORG directive appears in a program, Simile behaves as if .ORG 20 had been placed at the beginning of the source file. During assembly, Simile generates a .PROG loader directive automatically and places it just ahead of .FINI; the program counter address is that of the last .ORG directive encountered, or 0020 if none was encountered.

Instructions

Simian recognizes instructions belonging to 16 distinct operation code groups, each distinguished by a different bit configuration in the four least significant bits of the instruction word. Some 70 of the most common instructions possible within this repertoire have mnemonic abbreviations that Simile recognizes, such as ADD, SUB, and LD.

Not all possible Simian operations are known to Simile; indeed many conceivable Simian instructions do not even have any mnemonic names. Such instructions are not often used. If they are needed, they can always be included in a Simile input file as hexadecimal values, preceded by a .DATA * directive and followed by .LOAD *.

```
                    ADD
```

Action: Adds *source* operand to *destination*.

Syntax: ADD.*x destination, source*

x may be one of the characters L, S, or B. *destination* and *source* may be register direct, register indirect, or absolute addresses. Additionally, *source* may be immediately addressed.

Flags: VCNZ flags reflect the resulting destination operand; L is reset.

Binary: ADD   *ddddd sssss ll* 0000   *xxx*0

AND

Action: Forms the logical product of the *source* operand with the *destination* and deposits the result in the latter.

Syntax: AND.*x destination, source*
x may be one of the characters L, S, or B. *destination* and *source* may be register direct, register indirect, or absolute addresses. Additionally, *source* may be immediately addressed.

Flags: Z flag reflects operation result, VCNL are not affected.

Binary: AND   *ddddd sssss ll* 0100   *xxx*4

BR

Action: Branches unconditionally, by adding *offset* to the program counter.

Syntax: BR *offset*
where *offset* is a 16-bit signed hexadecimal integer or a symbolic label referring to an address not more than $2^{15} - 1$ bytes removed. Any hexadecimal number beginning with a letter must have a sign or zero prefixed, with no space preceding the letter.

Flags: Flags are not affected by BR operations.

Binary: BR   11111 11111 00 1100   ffcc

B-

Action: Branches conditionally, by adding *offset* to the program counter.

Syntax: B*xx offset*

where *offset* is a 16-bit signed hexadecimal integer or a symbolic label referring to an address not more than $2^{15} - 1$ bytes removed. Any hexadecimal number beginning with a letter must have a sign or zero prefixed, with no space preceding the letter. The suffix *xx* denotes the branching condition, and may take on the following values:

-Z	zero	-NZ	nonzero
-N	negative (signed)	-NN	nonnegative (signed)
-L	less (unsigned)	-NL	not less (unsigned)
-C	carry set	-NC	carry not set
-V	overflow set	-NV	overflow not set

The suffixes are directly attached to the character B, so that BZ signifies *branch on zero*, BNV signifies *branch if no overflow*, and so on.

Flags: Flags are not affected by branching operations.

Binary:			
	BV	01111 11111 00 1100	7fcc
	BC	10111 11111 00 1100	bfcc
	BN	11011 11111 00 1100	dfcc
	BL	11101 11111 00 1100	efcc
	BZ	11110 11111 00 1100	f7cc
	BNV	01111 01111 00 1100	7bcc
	BNC	10111 10111 00 1100	bdcc
	BNN	11011 11011 00 1100	decc
	BNL	11101 11101 00 1100	ef4c
	BNZ	11110 11110 00 1100	f78c

CALL

Action: Branches to subroutine by pushing program counter on the stack, adding *offset* to the program counter, and decrementing the stack pointer 4.

Syntax: CALL *offset*

where *offset* is a 16-bit signed hexadecimal integer or a symbolic label referring to an address not more than $2^{15} - 1$ bytes removed. Any hexadecimal number beginning with a letter must have a sign or zero prefixed, with no space preceding the letter.

Flags: Flags are not affected by CALL.

Binary: CALL   11111 11111 10 1100   ffec

CALL-

Action: Branches conditionally to a subroutine by pushing program counter on the stack, adding *offset* to the program counter, and decrementing the stack pointer 4.

Syntax: CALL*xx offset*

where *offset* is a 16-bit signed hexadecimal integer or a symbolic label referring to an address not more than $2^{15} - 1$ bytes removed. Any hexadecimal number beginning with a letter must have a sign or zero prefixed, with no space preceding the letter. The suffix *xx* denotes the branching condition, and may take on the following values:

-Z	zero	-NZ	nonzero
-N	negative (signed)	-NN	nonnegative (signed)
-L	less (unsigned)	-NL	not less (unsigned)
-C	carry set	-NC	carry not set
-V	overflow set	-NV	overflow not set

The suffixes are directly attached to the characters CALL, so that CALLZ signifies *branch on zero*, CALLNV signifies *branch if no overflow*, and so on.

Flags: Flags are not affected by branching operations.

Binary:

CALLV	01111 11111 10 1100	7fec
CALLC	10111 11111 10 1100	bfec
CALLN	11011 11111 10 1100	dfec
CALLL	11101 11111 10 1100	efec
CALLZ	11110 11111 10 1100	f7ec
CALLNV	01111 01111 10 1100	7bec
CALLNC	10111 10111 10 1100	bdec
CALLNN	11011 11011 10 1100	deec
CALLNL	11101 11101 10 1100	ef6c
CALLNZ	11110 11110 10 1100	f7ac

CMP

Action: Compares, i.e., apparently subtracts *source* operand from *destination* and discards arithmetic result.

Syntax: CMP.*x destination, source*

x may be one of the characters L, S, or B. *destination* and *source* may be register direct, register indirect, or absolute addresses. Additionally, *source* may be immediately addressed.

Flags: V and C are identical to what would be obtained on performing bitwise complementation, incrementation and addition (subtraction done in steps). N, L and Z reflect the outcome of the comparison.

Binary: CMP   *ddddd sssss ll* 0010   *xxx*2

```
┌─────────────────────────┐
│                         │
│                         │
│          HALT           │
│                         │
│                         │
└─────────────────────────┘
```

Action: Halts the processor.

Syntax: HALT

Flags: Unaltered, but usually irrelevant, since flags cannot be examined once the processor is halted.

Binary: HALT   11111 11111 11 1111   ffff

```
┌─────────────────────────┐
│                         │
│                         │
│          INC            │
│                         │
│                         │
└─────────────────────────┘
```

Action: Increments *destination* operand by the integer specified by *source*.

Syntax: INC.*x destination, source*
x may be one of the characters L, S, or B. *destination* may be register direct, register indirect, or absolutely addressed. *source* must be an integer in the range −16 to −1 inclusive or +1 to +16 inclusive. It may not have zero value.

Flags: VCNZ flags reflect the resulting destination operand; L is reset.

Binary: INC   *ddddd sssss ll* 1010   *xxx*a

```
┌─────────────────────────┐
│                         │
│                         │
│          JM             │
│                         │
│                         │
└─────────────────────────┘
```

Action: Branches unconditionally, replacing the program counter content by *address*.

Syntax: JM *address*
where *address* is the 32-bit hexadecimal address to which control is to be transferred, or a symbolic label referring to an address. Any hexadecimal number beginning with a letter must have a sign or zero prefixed, with no space preceding the letter.

Flags: Flags are not affected by JM operations.

Binary: JM   11111 11111 01 1100   ffdc

```
┌─────────────────────────┐
│                         │
│           JS            │
│                         │
└─────────────────────────┘
```

Action: Branches unconditionally to a subroutine beginning at *address*. The program counter content is placed on the stack, the stack pointer is decremented 4, and the *address* is placed in the program counter.

Syntax: JS *address*

where *address* is the 32-bit hexadecimal address to which control is to be transferred, or a symbolic label referring to an address. Any hexadecimal number beginning with a letter must have a sign or zero prefixed, with no space preceding the letter.

Flags: Flags are not affected by JS operations.

Binary: JS   11111 11111 11 1100   fffc

```
┌─────────────────────────┐
│                         │
│           J-            │
│                         │
└─────────────────────────┘
```

Action: Branches conditionally, replacing the program counter content by *address*.

Syntax: J*xx* *address*

where *address* is the 32-bit address to which control is to be transferred if the branching condition is met. It may be a register indirect or absolute address. The suffix *xx* denotes the branching condition, and may take on the following values:

-Z	zero	-NZ	nonzero
-N	negative (signed)	-NN	nonnegative (signed)
-L	less (unsigned)	-NL	not less (unsigned)
-C	carry set	-NC	carry not set
-V	overflow set	-NV	overflow not set

The suffixes are directly affixed to the character J, so that JZ signifies *branch on zero*, JNV signifies *branch if no overflow*, and so on.

Flags: Flags are not affected by branching operations.

Binary:	JV	01111 11111 01 1100	7fdc
	JC	10111 11111 01 1100	bfdc
	JN	11011 11111 01 1100	dfdc
	JL	11101 11111 01 1100	efdc
	JZ	11110 11111 01 1100	f7dc
	JNV	01111 01111 01 1100	7bdc

JNC	10111 10111 01 1100	bddc
JNN	11011 11011 01 1100	dedc
JNL	11101 11101 01 1100	ef5c
JNZ	11110 11110 01 1100	f79c

```
JS-
```

Action: Branches conditionally to a subroutine beginning at *address*. The program counter content is placed on the stack, the stack pointer is decremented 4, and the *address* is placed in the program counter.

Syntax: JS*xx address*
where *address* is the 32-bit address to which control is to be transferred. Any hexadecimal number beginning with a letter must have a sign or zero prefixed, with no space preceding the letter. The suffix *xx* denotes the branching condition, and may take on the following values:

-Z	zero	-NZ	nonzero
-N	negative (signed)	-NN	nonnegative (signed)
-L	less (unsigned)	-NL	not less (unsigned)
-C	carry set	-NC	carry not set
-V	overflow set	-NV	overflow not set

The suffixes are directly attached to the characters JS, so that JSZ signifies *jump to subroutine on zero*, JSNV signifies *jump to subroutine if no overflow*, and so on.

Flags: Flags are not affected by jumps to subroutines.

Binary:

JSV	01111 11111 11 1100	7ffc
JSC	10111 11111 11 1100	bffc
JSN	11011 11111 11 1100	dffc
JSL	11101 11111 11 1100	effc
JSZ	11110 11111 11 1100	f7fc
JSNV	01111 01111 11 1100	7bfc
JSNC	10111 10111 11 1100	bdfc
JSNN	11011 11011 11 1100	defc
JSNL	11101 11101 11 1100	ef7c
JSNZ	11110 11110 11 1100	f7bc

```
LD
```

Action: Loads a copy of the *source* operand into *destination*.

Syntax: LD.*x destination, source*
x may be one of the characters L, S, or B. *destination* and *source* may be register direct, register indirect, or absolute addresses. Additionally, *source* may be immediately addressed.

Flags: Flags are not affected by LD operations.

Binary: LD   *ddddd sssss ll* 0011   *xxx*3

```
┌──────────────────────┐
│                      │
│         NOP          │
│                      │
└──────────────────────┘
```

Action: No operation; processor marks time.

Syntax: NOP

Flags: Flags are not affected by NOP.

Binary: NOP   00000 00000 00 1011   000b

```
┌──────────────────────┐
│                      │
│         NOT          │
│                      │
└──────────────────────┘
```

Action: Bitwise complements *destination* operand.

Syntax: NOT.*x destination*
x may be one of the characters L, S, or B. *destination* may be register direct, register indirect, or absolutely addressed.

Flags: The Z flag reflects the outcome of the operation; all other flags are unaffected.

Binary: NOT   *ddddd sssss ll* 1001   *xxx*9

```
┌──────────────────────┐
│                      │
│          OR          │
│                      │
└──────────────────────┘
```

Action: Forms the logical sum of the *source* operand with the *destination* and deposits the result in the latter.

Syntax: OR.*x destination, source*
x may be one of the characters L, S, or B. *destination* and *source* may be register direct, register indirect, or absolute addresses. Additionally, *source* may be immediately addressed.

Flags: The Z flag reflects the outcome of the operation; all other flags are unaffected.

Binary: OR   *ddddd sssss ll* 0101   *xxx*5

```
┌─────────────────────────────┐
│                             │
│            POP              │
│                             │
│                             │
└─────────────────────────────┘
```

Action: Removes an operand of the specified length from the stack and places it in *destination*; increments the stack pointer by the operand length in bytes.

Syntax: POP.*x destination*
x may be one of the characters L, S, or B. *destination* may be register direct, register indirect, or absolutely addressed.

Flags: Flags are not affected by POP operations.

Binary: POP   *xxxxx* 01001 *ll* 1101   *xxx*d

```
┌─────────────────────────────┐
│                             │
│           PUSH              │
│                             │
│                             │
└─────────────────────────────┘
```

Action: Places *source* operand on the stack and decrements the stack pointer by the operand length in bytes.

Syntax: PUSH.*x source*
x may be one of the characters L, S, or B. *source* may be register direct, register indirect, absolutely, or immediately addressed.

Flags: Flags are not affected by PUSH operations.

Binary: PUSH   01001 *xxxxx ll* 1110   4*xx*e

```
┌─────────────────────────────┐
│                             │
│           REST              │
│                             │
│                             │
└─────────────────────────────┘
```

Action: Pops one byte off stack and writes it into the least significant byte of the processor status register. (Restores previously saved processor status byte from stack.) Increments stack pointer 1.

Syntax: REST

Flags: Flags are not affected by REST.

Binary: REST   00010 01001 00 1111   124f

```
┌─────────────────────────┐
│                         │
│          RET            │
│                         │
└─────────────────────────┘
```

Action: Returns from subroutine by moving the return address from the top of the stack into the program counter, then incrementing the stack pointer 4.

Syntax: RET

Flags: Flags are not affected by RET operations.

Binary: RET   00000 01001 11 1111   027f

```
┌─────────────────────────┐
│                         │
│          ROL            │
│                         │
└─────────────────────────┘
```

Action: Rotates *destination* operand to the left the number of bits specified by *source*.

Syntax: ROL.*x destination, source*
x may be one of the characters L, S, or B. *destination* may be register direct, register indirect, or absolutely addressed. *source* must be an integer in the range −16 to −1 inclusive or +1 to +16 inclusive. It may not have zero value.

Flags: The Z flag reflects the outcome of the operation; all other flags are unaffected.

Binary: ROL   *ddddd sssss ll* 0110   *xxx*6

```
┌─────────────────────────┐
│                         │
│          SAVE           │
│                         │
└─────────────────────────┘
```

Action: Fetches least significant byte of the processor status register and pushes it byte on the stack. (Saves processor status byte on stack.) Decrements stack pointer 1.

Syntax: SAVE

Flags: Flags are not affected by SAVE.

Binary: SAVE   01001 00010 00 1111   488f

```
┌─────────────────────────┐
│                         │
│          SHL            │
│                         │
└─────────────────────────┘
```

Action: Shifts *destination* operand to the left the number of bits specified by *source*. Bits shifted out of the operand are discarded. Positions vacated at the right (*source* positive) or left (*source* negative) are filled in with zeros.

Syntax: SHL.*x destination, source*
x may be one of the characters L, S, or B. *destination* may be register direct, register indirect, or absolutely addressed. *source* must be an integer in the range −16 to −1 inclusive or +1 to +16 inclusive. It may not have zero value.

Flags: The C flag is given the value of the last bit shifted out of the *destination*. The Z flag reflects the final result in *destination*. N, V and L are unaffected.

Binary: SHL   *ddddd sssss ll* 1000   *xxx*8

```
┌─────────────────────────┐
│                         │
│         SHLA            │
│                         │
└─────────────────────────┘
```

Action: Shifts *destination* operand to the left the number of bits specified by *source*, preserving sign. Bits shifted out of the operand are discarded. Positions vacated at the right (*source* positive) are filled in with zeros, positions vacated at the left (*source* negative) are filled in with copies of the original high-order bit.

Syntax: SHLA.*x destination, source*
x may be one of the characters L, S, or B. *destination* may be register direct, register indirect, or absolutely addressed. *source* must be an integer in the range −16 to −1 inclusive or +1 to +16 inclusive. It may not have zero value.

Flags: The C flag is given the value of the last bit shifted out of the *destination*. The Z flag reflects the final result in *destination*. N, V and L are unaffected.

Binary: SHLA   *ddddd sssss ll* 0111   *xxx*7

```
┌─────────────────────────┐
│                         │
│          SUB            │
│                         │
└─────────────────────────┘
```

Action: Subtracts *source* operand from *destination*.

Syntax: SUB.*x destination, source*
x may be one of the characters L, S, or B. *destination* and *source* may be register direct, register indirect, or absolute addresses. Additionally, *source* may be immediately addressed.

Flags: VCNZ flags reflect the resulting destination operand; L is reset.

Binary: SUB   *ddddd sssss ll* 0001   *xxx*1

APPENDIX 4

The ASCII character set

This Appendix describes the ASCII (American Standard for Computer Information Interchange) character set, including the standard names of the characters and their hexadecimal and octal representations.

An ASCII character is defined as a string of seven bits that represents a printable character or a non-printable control function. For example, 110 1000 represents the printable character *h*, while 000 1000 represents the *backspace* function. For ease in reading, the binary digits are often written in groups of four, with each group given its natural hexadecimal representation. Thus 110 1000 is normally written as 68, the groups 110 and 1000 having been interpreted as the hexadecimal numbers 6 and 8, respectively. Octal or decimal representations, in which 1 101 000 appears as 150 (or 104_{10}), are also used. Table A4.1 gives the complete set of characters, including their octal (*Oct*) and hexadecimal (*Hex*) representations as well as their conventional character (*Chr*) names.

The ASCII characters that correspond to letters and numerals are called by their natural names. Of the remaining 66 (out of 128) characters, about half are not printable in the sense that they do not correspond to any prescribed pattern of ink on paper. The first 32 characters (hexadecimal 00 to 1F) and the last entry in the table (hexadecimal 7F) are nonprinting control functions, the remainder are printable special characters, including punctuation marks. The nonprinting characters are frequently called *control* characters, because they are formed by pressing a key while the CONTROL key is held down. For example, the backspace character (hexadecimal 08) is called *backspace* (*bs*) or *control-H*. In writing, the control characters are frequently indicated by the corresponding printable character, prefixed by a caret, e.g., ^H for *control-H*. Names of all the control characters are shown in Table A4.2. There is one nonprinting character which is not also a control character: 7F (octal 177), referred to as *delete*.

The names of punctuation marks and other special characters are defined in the ASCII standard. They are sometimes referred to informally by alternative names not recognized by the standards documents. Table A4.3 gives the names prescribed by the standard, and also some of the common informal alternatives.

Table A4.1. The ASCII character set

Oct	Hex	Chr	Oct	Hex	Chr	Oct	Hex	Chr	Oct	Hex	Chr
000	00	*nul*	040	20		100	40	@	140	60	`
001	01	*soh*	041	21	!	101	41	A	141	61	a
002	02	*stx*	042	22	"	102	42	B	142	62	b
003	03	*etx*	043	23	#	103	43	C	143	63	c
004	04	*eot*	044	24	$	104	44	D	144	64	d
005	05	*enq*	045	25	%	105	45	E	145	65	e
006	06	*ack*	046	26	&	106	46	F	146	66	f
007	07	*bel*	047	27	'	107	47	G	147	67	g
010	08	*bs*	050	28	(	110	48	H	150	68	h
011	09	*ht*	051	29	)	111	49	I	151	69	i
012	0A	*nl*	052	2A	*	112	4A	J	152	6A	j
013	0B	*vt*	053	2B	+	113	4B	K	153	6B	k
014	0C	*np*	054	2C	,	114	4C	L	154	6C	l
015	0D	*cr*	055	2D	-	115	4D	M	155	6D	m
016	0E	*so*	056	2E	.	116	4E	N	156	6E	n
017	0F	*si*	057	2F	/	117	4F	O	157	6F	o
020	10	*dle*	060	30	0	120	50	P	160	70	p
021	11	*dcl*	061	31	1	121	51	Q	161	71	q
022	12	*dc2*	062	32	2	122	52	R	162	72	r
023	13	*dc3*	063	33	3	123	53	S	163	73	s
024	14	*dc4*	064	34	4	124	54	T	164	74	t
025	15	*nak*	065	35	5	125	55	U	165	75	u
026	16	*syn*	066	36	6	126	56	V	166	76	v
027	17	*etb*	067	37	7	127	57	W	167	77	w
030	18	*can*	070	38	8	130	58	X	170	78	x
031	19	*em*	071	39	9	131	59	Y	171	79	y
032	1A	*sub*	072	3A	:	132	5A	Z	172	7A	z
033	1B	*esc*	073	3B	;	133	5B	[	173	7B	{
034	1C	*fs*	074	3C	<	134	5C	\	174	7C	|
035	1D	*gs*	075	3D	=	135	5D	]	175	7D	}
036	1E	*rs*	076	3E	>	136	5E	^	176	7E	~
037	1F	*us*	077	3F	?	137	5F	_	177	7F	*del*

Table A4.2. Names of control characters

Chr	Abbr	Name	Chr	Abbr	Name
^@	*nul*	null	^P	*dle*	data link escape
^A	*soh*	start of heading	^Q	*dcl*	device control 1
^B	*stx*	start of text	^R	*dc2*	device control 2
^C	*etx*	end of text	^S	*dc3*	device control 3
^D	*eot*	end of transmission	^T	*dc4*	device control 4
^E	*enq*	enquiry	^U	*nak*	negative acknowledge
^F	*ack*	acknowledge	^V	*syn*	synchronous idle
^G	*bel*	bell	^W	*etb*	end transmission block
^H	*bs*	backspace	^X	*can*	cancel
^I	*ht*	horizontal tabulation	^Y	*em*	end of medium
^J	*lf*	line feed	^Z	*sub*	substitute
^K	*vt*	vertical tabulation	^[	*esc*	escape
^L	*ff*	form feed	^\	*fs*	file separator
^M	*cr*	carriage return	^]	*gs*	group separator
^N	*so*	shift out	^^	*rs*	record separator
^O	*si*	shift in	^_	*us*	unit separator

Table A4.3. Special characters in the ASCII set

Hex	Mark	Name	Alternative or common names
20		blank	space
21	!	exclamation mark	
22	"	quotation mark	double quote
23	#	number sign	pound sign
24	$	dollar sign	currency symbol
25	%	percent sign	
26	&	ampersand	
27	'	apostrophe	single quote, solidus, acute
28	(	opening parenthesis	left parenthesis
29	)	closing parenthesis	right parenthesis
2A	*	asterisk	star
2B	+	plus	
2C	,	comma	
2D	-	hyphen	minus
2E	.	period	decimal point, dot
2F	/	slant	slash, oblique stroke, virgule
3A	:	colon	
3B	;	semicolon	
3C	<	less than	left-arrow, left angle bracket
3D	=	equal sign	
3E	>	greater than	right-arrow, right angle bracket
3F	?	question mark	
40	@	commercial at	at
5B	[	opening bracket	left [square] bracket
5C	\	reverse slant	backslash, reverse slash
5D	]	closing bracket	right [square] bracket
5E	^	circumflex	caret, up-arrow
5F	_	underscore	
60	`	grave	back quote
7B	{	opening brace	opening (or left) curly bracket
7C	|	vertical line	logical or, vertical rule
7D	}	closing brace	closing (or right) curly bracket
7E	~	tilde	

Index